A Companion to the
ILIAD

A Companion to the

ILIAD

Based on the Translation by Richmond Lattimore

Malcolm M. Willcock

The University of Chicago Press

Chicago and London

Malcolm M. Willcock is Professor of Classics at the
University of Lancaster, England.

THE UNIVERSITY OF CHICAGO PRESS, Chicago 60637
The University of Chicago Press, Ltd., London

© 1976 by The University of Chicago
All rights reserved. Published 1976
Printed in the United States of America
80 79 78 77 76   987654321

Library of Congress Cataloging in Publication Data
Willcock, Malcolm M
  A companion to the Iliad.

  Bibliography: p.
  Includes index.
  1. Homerus. Ilias.   I. Homerus. Ilias.
II. Title
PA4037.W734   883'.01   75-20894
ISBN 0-226-89854-7

Contents

List of Figures   vi
Preface   vii

Book One   3
Book Two   17
Book Three   39
Book Four   45
Book Five   54
Book Six   66
Book Seven   76
Book Eight   85
Book Nine   94
Book Ten   113
Book Eleven   123
Book Twelve   137

Book Thirteen   144
Book Fourteen   157
Book Fifteen   165
Book Sixteen   176
Book Seventeen   192
Book Eighteen   201
Book Nineteen   215
Book Twenty   222
Book Twenty-One   233
Book Twenty-Two   240
Book Twenty-Three   249
Book Twenty-Four   266

Appendix A: Transmission of the Text of the *Iliad* and Com-
mentaries on It   277
Appendix B: Methods of Fighting in the *Iliad*   279
Appendix C: Mythology and the Gods   281
Appendix D: The "*Aithiopis* Theory"   285

Bibliography   289
Index   291

CONTENTS

LIST OF FIGURES

MAP 1. NORTHERN AND CENTRAL GREECE   25
MAP 2. THE PELOPONNESE   29
MAP 3. ASIA MINOR AND THE ISLANDS   36

CHART 1. RELATIVE POSITIONS OF THE GREEK CONTINGENTS AT
    TROY   116–17
CHART 2. THE SHIELD OF ACHILLEUS   210

Preface

The reader of Homer's *Iliad* in Greek has a choice of commentaries to help him understand the text. Readers in translation, whose numbers must be a hundred or even a thousand times as large, have no such assistance. It is to fill that gap that the present book has been written. It is primarily intended for those reading the *Iliad* for the first time, although more advanced students also may, it is hoped, find interest and elucidation in it.

For separate notes it was always evident that a precise point of reference, and therefore a particular translation, had to be chosen. The only known predecessor is *A Companion to the Iliad* by W. Leaf (Macmillan, 1892), which was based on the prose translation by Andrew Lang, Walter Leaf, and Ernest Myers. Through an admirable combination of qualities, including readability, dignity, and simplicity, Richmond Lattimore's translation is the outstanding one for the present age, even more so than "Lang, Leaf, and Myers" was for the end of the nineteenth century. Consequently, and with the kind encouragement of the author, the present commentary uses his text. It may, of course, be employed with other translations, but less easily, for the precise wording of the references will be different, and the line numbers may slightly vary.

The reader in translation is in some ways in a better position to appreciate the whole *Iliad* than the reader in Greek, in that he can read more easily, more quickly, and without concern for linguistic problems. The notes here are directed mostly toward the explanation of words, expressions, and allusions in the text; but they also include summaries of books and sections, and assistance toward the appreciation of Homer's broader composition, by drawing attention to the implications of the narrative and the very effective characterization of the major heroes. The traditional "Homeric Question"—the question of the genesis and authorship of this huge epic, disputed by generations of enthusiastic scholars—is not forgotten.

I have not felt it desirable to repeat the information about Homer, his story, characters, and historical background, that is given in Lattimore's Introduction to his translation (pp. 11–55). Rather, I have supplemented it by four appendixes on special topics, which will be found on pp. 277–87. There is also an Index, referring to discussions in the notes and supplementing the Glossary of Proper Names in Lattimore.

Some of the notes have already appeared in my *Commentary on Homer's Iliad, Books I–VI*, published by Messrs. Macmillan, and are repeated here with the publishers' permission; I am also indebted to the same publishers, and to Dr. Stubbings, for permission to reproduce the maps on pp. 25, 29, and 36 from *A Companion to Homer*, edited by A. J. B. Wace and F. H. Stubbings.

August, 1975   M. M. WILLCOCK

A Companion to the
ILIAD

BOOK ONE

The Greek commander, Agamemnon, is forced by the arguments of Achilleus at a public assembly to agree to return his captive, Chryseis, to her father, a local priest. This leads to a violent quarrel, during which Agamemnon uses his superior rank to inform Achilleus that he will replace Chryseis with Achilleus' own captive, Briseis. Achilleus publicly withdraws from the army and asks his goddess mother, Thetis, to persuade Zeus to help the Trojans. After an interlude, in which Odysseus sees to the formal return of Chryseis to her father, Zeus undertakes to do as Thetis asks; there is then a bad-tempered scene on Olympos between him and his wife, Hera, which is settled by the efforts of Hephaistos.

It is evident from the way the poet moves straight into his story after the briefest of introductions that the general tale of the war against Troy was familiar to his audience, as were the characters. The *Iliad* plot is treated as an episode in the long story of that war.

The composition of Book 1 is simple and natural; it falls into three sections:

1–430   The quarrel itself, its causes and its immediate consequences.

430–492   An interlude showing the passage of time, and allowing the return of the girl Chryseis to her home.

493–611   A balancing scene among the gods.

1. The **goddess** is the Muse, the personification of the poet's inspiration. The oral poet did not consciously compose his verses. They came into his mind unbidden; and he believed, or affected to believe, that the Muse had told him what to say. She is asked to

3

sing, because this heroic verse was not spoken but was intoned to a musical accompaniment. (What was a reality for Homer became a convention for later poets: "I sing of arms and the man" [Virgil]; "Sing, heavenly Muse" [Milton].)

And the subject that the Muse is to sing of, the subject of the *Iliad*, is—we should note—**the anger of Achilleus.** In other words, the plot of the *Iliad* is human and psychological; we are not going to hear a simple chronicle of the events of the Trojan War but the causes and consequences of a quarrel between the Greek leaders.

2. The Greeks in the *Iliad* are called indiscriminately by three names: **Achaians,** Argives, and Danaans (Lattimore 19).

3. Hades: the god of the underworld.

4–5. It is a common threat in the *Iliad* that one will give the enemy's body to the dogs and birds to eat, not allowing his friends to bury him. In practice, however, no corpses are specifically said to be eaten by these scavengers; and in Book 7 the two sides will make a truce for the burial of the dead.

The will of Zeus is a key phrase, meaning, in effect, the plot of the *Iliad.* His "will" is to fulfill the promise he makes to Thetis in the scene starting in line 498. See also 15.61–77 n.

7. Atreus' son. Atreus was the father of the two brothers, Agamemnon and Menelaos; but when *one* person is described as Atreus' son, it will naturally be the elder of the two, the commander-in-chief of the army, Agamemnon. Such referring to people by their father's name (their *patronymic*) is a common feature of the *Iliad.*

Lines 1–7 are all that there is of introduction to the *Iliad.* The poet now proceeds straight to the quarrel and its cause. We may notice that, in these introductory lines, the city of Troy has not even been mentioned; it is worth repeating that the theme of the poem is the anger of Achilleus, and the disastrous effects it had for the Achaians.

9–10. Apollo is the most important divine supporter of the Trojans. He is the archer god, "he who strikes from afar" (15, 21), the god of disease and healing. The **pestilence** (plague) which he sends is further described in 50–52.

13. his daughter. The daughter's name (Chryseis) is given in 111; the details of her story, in 366–69.

14. The **ribbons** were the loose ends of a band of wool (with religious significance) attached to the top of the staff which the priest carried in virtue of his sacred office. He is here simultaneously a suppliant and a priest and so is doubly to be respected. It is quite possible that the ribbons were literally those of Apollo, i.e., that they were normally part of the adornment of his statue in the temple and had been brought by Chryses to confirm his status in relation to the god.

17. Greaves were shin guards, worn particularly as a protection against low-flying stones or arrows.

strong-greaved is an example of the Homeric "stock epithet"—a descriptive adjective which has a general application to its noun but no special significance for the present circumstances. Thus we find *hollow* ships in 26–27 and the *murmuring* sea in 34.

18. The Homeric gods live on **Olympos**, the towering mountain in northeast Greece.

19. Priam's city: Troy.

30. The name **Argos** is used rather casually in the poem. Sometimes it indicates the famous city of Argos (home, in fact, of Diomedes); sometimes, as presumably here, the northeast Peloponnese; sometimes the whole Peloponnese; and sometimes Greece (just as "Argives" is used as a general term for Greeks [2 n.]).

31. It is cruel and insensitive of Agamemnon to speak in these terms to the girl's father. Already here at the beginning the poet has given a little touch toward the delineation of the king's character.

going up and down by the loom: i.e., weaving, a major task of the women in the house. The phrase shows that an upright loom is envisaged, as in the simile of 23.760–63.

37–38. Chryse (home, of course, of Chryses) and **Killa** are towns near Troy; **Tenedos** is an island off the coast.

39. The title **Smintheus** is of considerable interest. It means "mouse god," from a word for mouse which survived in the Cretan dialect in historical times. It is generally believed that this unique name for Apollo derives from a time when he was worshiped in animal form, as Hera was, in the form of a cow, and Athene, of an owl (551 n.). The mouse was perhaps associated with bubonic plague (which is carried by rats), so that the title Smintheus may be particularly appropriate to the present appeal by Chryses. (At 1 Samuel 6:4–5, the Philistines are instructed to make golden images of mice to help remove a plague.)

This line begins a common prayer formula: "If I have ever pleased you in the past, help me now."

40. rich thigh pieces. The practice at sacrifices was to wrap the thigh bones of the animal in folds of fat and then burn these, as symbolic of the whole animal, as an offering to the god. The more nutritious parts were eaten by the worshipers.

42. The **arrows** of the god indicate the plague (9–10 n.).

Danaans (cf. 2 n.) is an ancient tribal name whose origins are totally lost. It is no doubt connected with the mythological figures Danaos and his daughters, the Danaïds, and with Danaë, the mother of Perseus. As to whether the name is to be identified with the Danuna, found in a list of peoples of the sea who attacked Egypt in about 1172 B.C., opinion is divided (PAGE 22).

54. Achilleus takes the initiative and so exposes himself to the possibility of a clash with Agamemnon.

55. Hera, wife of the supreme god, Zeus, is, with Athene, the most constant divine supporter of the Greeks and inveterate enemy of the Trojans.

65. for the sake of: i.e., "for the lack of," "for the nonfulfillment of." A **hecatomb** is a large sacrifice of animals to a god.

71. Ilion: Troy. Kalchas had been the prophet of the Greek army from the beginning (2.300), and had apparently directed the course of the fleet when they came to Troy nine years before.

84. of the swift feet: another example of the stock epithet (17 n.). Achilleus' agility has no relevance to the present situation.

91. claims. This word perhaps gives a wrong impression in English. This line is not an attack on Agamemnon. He *is* **the greatest of all the Achaians,** i.e., the most powerful and kingly, and Achilleus does not dispute this. All the same, Achilleus' promise of support for Kalchas is hardly conciliatory to Agamemnon, who was obviously referred to in 78–79.

111. Chryseis is more a description than a name, as it merely means "Chryses' daughter." Later romances corrupted it eventually to Cressida (cf. note on Troilos, 24.257); but that is all long after Homer.

113. The overt comparison of a slave girl with his wife portrays the same insensitivity in Agamemnon as he showed in his words to Chryses (31 n.).

118. The real reason for the quarrel is that the king is not big enough for his position. He needs recognition and so takes the view that it is improper that he alone should be without a share of this particular lot of booty. Achilleus' reply is perfectly reasonable, apart from the personal remarks in the first line.

125. what we took from the cities by storm. The Achaians, while besieging Troy, had made a number of expeditions against nearby towns. Achilleus claims in 9.328–29 to have personally led the attack on twenty-three.

138. Aias, when mentioned without further identification, is normally the greater Aias, the son of Telamon. He and Odysseus are named here as the two most important leaders of the Achaians, apart from Agamemnon and Achilleus himself.

It is simply assumed that each chief has a female captive from the booty of the captured city.

145. Idomeneus, another of the chief leaders, had the powerful Kretan contingent under his command.

146. The sneer in the second half of the line is an answer to Achilleus' "greediest for gain of all men" in 122.

149–71. Achilleus, who seems hardly to have heard the second half of what Agamemnon said, is now very angry. This speech shows a combination of rhetoric and intense feeling which is reserved to Achilleus in the *Iliad*; one may compare his tremendous outburst in reply to Odysseus in the Embassy scene, in 9.308–429, and his speech to his mother at 18.98–126.

155. Phthia (in Thessaly, in northern Greece) is the home of Achilleus; the Myrmidons (180) are his troops.

159. The purpose of the expedition was to recover Helen, the wife of Menelaos, stolen from him by Paris. Agamemnon, the great king of Mykenai, took action to support his brother; the other Greeks are present out of deference to Agamemnon.

163. when the Achaians sack some ... **citadel.** See 125 n.

184. Briseis, like Chryseis (111), is merely a descriptive name, for she is the daughter of Briseus (392). Achilleus had captured her after killing her husband and brothers when the town of Lyrnessos was taken (2.690, 19.291–96); it was on this same expedition that he took Hypoplakian Thebe (2.691), made numerous captives, including Chryseis (1.366), and killed the father and brothers of Hektor's wife Andromache (6.416–24). (On the similarities between the fates of Briseis and Andromache and on other obscurities about Briseis in the *Iliad*, consult REINHARDT 50–57.)

188. Peleus' son: Achilleus (1). For the use of the father's name on its own like this, see 7 n.

194. Athene descended. Athene comes down from the sky to stop Achilleus from attacking Agamemnon. Visible only to him, she takes him by the hair. It is not easy for us (because we are unbelievers) to understand or accept the activities of the gods in the *Iliad.* They act as independent agents but nevertheless preserve a specific power, each in relation to his or her own separate function. The function of Athene is to be the pro-Greek goddess of organized, disciplined warfare. She normally acts through heroes who are natural winners—Odysseus, Diomedes, Achilleus. Here she instigates, and in some sense represents, the self-control of Achilleus.

201. The phrase **winged words** does not imply anything special in what is said. It is part of an ancient formula, based on the simple fact that words pass through the air from the mouth of the speaker to the ear of the hearer.

202. The **aegis** is a supernatural weapon of Zeus. It is normally defensive and may be thought of as a shield; but it can be used offensively, because, when shaken in the face of the enemy, it strikes terror into their hearts.

The words **once more** do not mean that Athene has come down in this way previously. What Achilleus means is that here is another reason for annoyance: "Have you come here, too?"

206. grey-eyed. See 551 n.

207. but will you obey me? Notice how Homer preserves the human dignity of his characters. They are not pawns in the hands of these powerful gods. Athene can advise, but she does not compel. The decision and the responsibility remain with Achilleus.

211. The words **and it will be that way** mean that what Achilleus says in his abuse of Agamemnon will in practice come to pass.

213. In other words, Achilleus will in due course get material compensation for the present loss of his "gift of honor" (Briseis).

224. Atreides: the commonest form of the patronymic, meaning "son of Atreus" (7).

234. sceptre. We learn elsewhere in the *Iliad* (23.568) that a speaker in the assembly held a scepter handed to him by one of the heralds.

242. man-slaughtering Hektor. The reference to Hektor is a kind of foreshadowing of later events, for he is to be the major threat to the Achaians in the *Iliad*.

247–48. Nestor now intervenes in the quarrel. He is the oldest by far of the Achaian leaders and thus a figure to whom respect is due. He is portrayed as clearheaded and a good adviser, if a little given to reminiscing about his youth. He is one of Homer's favorite characters.

Nestor is king of **Pylos,** a city on the west coast of the Peloponnese, in an area unimportant in later Greece but one of the two or three strongest kingdoms in Mycenaean times (11.681 n.). He is represented (250–52) as having lived through two generations and now being king in the third; i.e., he was in his sixties or seventies.

255. Priam, the patriarchal king of Troy, had fifty sons and numerous sons-in-law (6.244).

259–74. Nestor produces a mythological example, or *paradeigma*, to increase the persuasiveness of his words—a device used several times in the *Iliad*, notably in the example of Niobe in Achilleus' speech to Priam in 24.601–19. It is characteristic of such "examples" that they are constructed according to the principle of "ring composition," which can best be explained here by a schematic summary:

a	259	Accept my advice.
b	260–61	I once associated with better men than you, and they listened to me.
c	261–71	This is the story.

9

b′	271–73	They were better than you, and they listened to me.
a′	274	So you should accept my advice.

Ring composition probably originated as a mnemonic method for the oral bard. It is very common indeed in speeches in the *Iliad*; for other examples, see the Index.

The central myth is from the war between the Lapiths and the centaurs, familiar perhaps from the Parthenon sculptures, now in the British Museum. The centaurs were half-human creatures (the **beast men** of 267) who lived around Mount Pelion in Thessaly; the Lapiths were a human tribe. The war is referred to again in 2.742–44.

It is not at all probable that before Homer there was a story of Nestor going all the way north from Pylos to assist the Lapiths. As in other, similar, cases, it appears that our poet was willing to *invent* mythology when he needed it. The Lapith/centaur war was part of the legends; Nestor's involvement in it is an invention for the purpose of the present speech.

263–64. These are names of Lapiths; **Peirithoös** was their king.

265. Theseus was in legend the friend and comrade of Peirithoös; he was also the traditional hero of Athens. It is a strange fact that this is the only mention of him in the *Iliad*; and this line is so poorly attested (missing from the best manuscripts and not referred to in the ancient scholia) that it is generally believed to be a post-Homeric addition to the text.

275–76. Nestor appeals to Agamemnon; **277–81**, to Achilleus; **282–84**, to Agamemnon again. Nestor is doing his best.

280. the mother who bore you immortal. See 351 n.

307. Patroklos is Achilleus' second-in-command, charioteer, and close friend. As his death in Book 16 is a direct result of Achilleus' refusal to fight, and the major factor in Achilleus' personal tragedy, the poet takes care to introduce him to us at this early stage.

311. Odysseus, the most capable of the Greeks for any job that needs to be done properly, is the natural choice to see that Chryseis is duly returned to her father.

crafty is a translation of one of Odysseus' regular epithets, but the Greek word is more complimentary; "clever" would be better.

314. The army engages in a ritual purification after the plague.

342. makes sacrifice is a mistranslation; the word means "storms," "rages."

351. Achilleus' mother is Thetis, a sea goddess or Nereid, daughter of Nereus, the "old man of the sea" (358). The marriage of Peleus and Thetis was the most glorious in Greek mythology, with the gods themselves present as wedding guests (24.60–63). But the couple had only one child, Achilleus, who was fated to die young (352); and Thetis was no longer living with her now aged husband but had returned to the sea.

353. Zeus is god of the sky and the weather—one reason why the home of the gods is on Mount Olympos.

366. Thebe. This is not the important Greek city of Thebes but the so-called Hypoplakian Thebe, near Troy, home of Hektor's wife Andromache, whose father, **Eëtion,** had been king (cf. 184 n.). **Chryseis** had apparently been taken among the captives there rather than from her own home town of Chryse.

371–75 = 12–16; 376–79 = 22–25. This repetition of lines is a natural feature of oral poetry. The forms of expression are more or less fixed by the meter; and when the same thing is to be said again, it is automatically said in the same words.

371. bronze-armoured. Although iron was in common use in Homer's own day, the epic tradition is very consistent in keeping bronze as the metal for armor and weapons, as it had been in the Mycenaean Age.

396–406. This story of a revolt on Olympos, which Thetis helped to prevent by bringing Briareus/Aigaion to defend Zeus, is not attested anywhere else. Every consideration makes it probable that we have here the free invention of the poet, not an allusion to preexisting myth. Homer requires a reason for Zeus to be under an obligation to Thetis and therefore creates one, in the same way he invented Nestor's assistance to the Lapiths (259–74).

The introductory statement, **many times in my father's halls I have heard you making claims,** is used in the same way at 21.475, where the verisimilitude of the alleged recollection is no greater than here.

11

398. Kronos' son: Zeus.

400. Hera, Poseidon, Pallas Athene. Those who assume that Achilleus is quoting an existing myth have great difficulty in explaining why these three gods in particular should have opposed Zeus. If we accept that the whole story is a Homeric invention, the reason becomes obvious: these three gods are the helpers of the Greeks in the *Iliad;* they would therefore do their best to oppose Thetis' request that Zeus should assist the Trojans (408). By a sort of mirror effect, they take the role of the opposition in the invented myth.

402. creature of the hundred hands. Kottos, Briareus, and Gyas, each with a hundred arms and fifty heads, were a distinct group of monstrous creatures from the early dawn of the world. Hesiod tells how they helped Zeus and the Olympian gods in the war against the Titans (*Theogony* 617–735). Briareus' role here, supporting Zeus, may be an echo of that other story.

403–4. On four occasions in the *Iliad* different names are quoted from the languages of gods and men. They are

1.403	(a giant)	Briareus/Aigaion
2.813	(a hill)	burial mound of Myrina/Hill of the Thicket
14.291	(a bird)	*chalkis/kymindis*
20.74	(the river)	Xanthos/Skamandros

(Gods' names first). The accepted explanation is that the gods' language is the poetic vocabulary transmitted from the past, while the language of men is the common and everyday terminology known to the poet.

The Homeric text gives the second name as Aigaion, which might indeed means **Aigaios' son,** as Lattimore translates it; cf. "Kronion" in the next line. The name seems likely to be that of a sea divinity connected with the Aegean Sea, but no certain information about this person can be obtained from ancient sources. Homer's identification of him with the hundred-handed **Briareus** is unexplained and adds to the impression that these lines are sheer invention.

Similarly, if there are any facts behind the statement that

Aigaion (or Aigaios' son) was stronger than his father, they are not available to us.

405. it refers to his strength. **Kronion** ("son of Kronos") has the suffix -ion, which has the same effect as the suffix -ides in Atreides (224).

407. The attitude of a suppliant was to clasp the **knees** of the person appealed to with one hand and reach for his chin with the other; cf. 500–501.

408. We should not fail to notice that Achilleus is now asking Zeus to help the Trojans, his enemies, to kill the Greeks; his personal honor means more to him than the lives of his friends.

423–24. The absence of the gods at a feast given by the Aithiopians makes a pause in the story, during which Chryseis may be returned to her father. And the interval of eleven days before Thetis can fulfill her errand has the effect of isolating the action of the *Iliad* from the continuum of the Trojan War, especially as there is exactly the same interval at the end of the epic; for such is the length of the truce which Achilleus agrees to with Priam so that the Trojans may mourn and bury Hektor (see 24.31 n.).

The **Aithiopians** are a god-loving people far to the southeast, **at the Ocean,** because the Homeric view of the world was of a flat disk around which ran a river called **Ocean.**

426. bronze-founded. The house of Zeus had a floor of bronze.

436. Ships were moored facing out to sea. The **anchors** were heavy **stones** thrown out at the prow, while the **stern** was tied to the shore by **cables.**

449. barley. Grains of barley were sprinkled between the horns of the sacrificial victim.

451–56. Chryses calls off the curse with a prayer very similar to the one with which he invoked it (36–42).

458–66. These lines contain a complete description of the procedure at a sacrifice. After a prayer, and the scattering of the grains of barley (449 n.), they pulled back the animal's head to expose the neck, cut the throat, and skinned the carcass. They then cut out the thigh bones, covered them with a layer of fat above and below, and laid on top of them pieces of flesh, to symbolize the offering of the whole animal (cf. 40 n.); these were burnt while

13

libations of wine were poured to the god. They then lightly roasted the entrails (the **vitals**: heart, liver, lungs, kidney, stomach), and ate these as a first course. Finally, they cut up the rest of the meat, put it on spits, and roasted it. The whole procedure is described again, in almost exactly the same words, at 2.421–29.

470. It was rare in the ancient world to drink wine neat. It was usually diluted with water, and this was the purpose of the **mixing bowl**.

471. Before the company drank its wine, a small amount was put into each man's cup and was poured out by him on the ground as a libation to the god.

488–92. These lines show the passing of time (the twelve days until the gods should return from the Aithiopians) and indicate that the fighting was going on, but without Achilleus.

493. after this day means from the time when Thetis told her son that the gods would return in twelve days; in other words, it refers back to 425.

500–501. For the attitude of a suppliant, see 407 n.

518–19. Zeus in the *Iliad* is a strange amalgam of

a) The supreme god, without whose will nothing important happens in the world below (5)
b) The sky and weather god (420, 528–30)
c) The father of a large family, who has difficulty exerting his authority, especially over his wife

Thetis' request makes him worried about domestic harmony.

528–30. The imagery of these famous lines seems to be taken from the thundercloud. The dark brows represent the underside of the storm; the flowing hair, the "anvil" of cirrus which commonly spreads from the top of a storm cloud; and the shaking of Olympos, the effect of the thunder.

551. Stock epithets of Hera and Athene, respectively, appear to mean **ox-eyed** and "owl-eyed." It is generally believed that they date from a time when these goddesses were worshiped in animal form or at least with animal heads (like the Egyptian gods). The adjective for Athene may by the time of Homer have come to signify no more than "grey-eyed," the owl having been forgotten, and it is so translated by Lattimore (e.g., 206). Compare the note on Apollo Smintheus (39).

14

562–67. As on other occasions when Zeus faces opposition, he becomes a bully and threatens physical violence.

570. Uranian means no more than "heavenly."

591. The ejection of gods from Olympos by Zeus is a repeated motif. In 15.22–24, several gods are said to have been thrown out on an occasion in the past; and in 19.130–31, we hear how he threw out Ate, the goddess of delusion. Hephaistos refers again to his own fall in 18.395.

591–94. It is instructive for one's appreciation of both poets to see how Milton adapted these lines in *Paradise Lost*. Claiming that the story of the fall of Hephaistos was an inaccurate folk memory of the fall of a rebellious angel, he goes on as follows:

> How he fell
> From Heaven, they fabl'd, thrown by angry Jove
> Sheer o're the chrystal Battlements: from Morn
> To Noon he fell, from Noon to dewy Eve,
> A Summers day; and with the setting Sun
> Dropt from the Zenith like a falling Star,
> On Lemnos th' Aegaean Ile.
>   (*Paradise Lost*, 1.740–46)

The poetic beauty of Milton's lines is already there in Homer, but with greater simplicity.

The island of **Lemnos** (593), in the Aegean Sea, was sacred to Hephaistos, originally, no doubt, because of a volcano on the island (Hephaistos' Roman counterpart was Vulcan). The inhabitants were called **Sintians.**

598. The gods drink **nectar** as men drink wine; they therefore use a mixing bowl (470).

599–600. This is the origin of the expression "Homeric laughter." Hephaistos was lame and clumsy (smith gods are regularly lame); the sight of him taking round the nectar, instead of the usual attractive wine-bearers, drove the simple-minded and carefree gods to laughter and so relieved the tension (570), as no doubt Hephaistos intended.

603–4. The singing of the **Muses**, accompanied by **Apollo** on the lyre, was the usual entertainment on celestial occasions.

605–11. Notice the ending of the book. There have been disease, death, and bitter quarreling among the men down below, and for a moment it looked as though the dispute might disturb the easy tenor of life among the gods. But they soon realize that it is not worth troubling themselves "for the sake of mortals" (574); and after a pleasant evening they go quietly home to bed.

BOOK TWO

Book 2 falls into two parts—the "testing" of the army and the catalogues of the troops. In more detail, they contain:

Lines 1–454: Zeus sends a dream which tells Agamemnon he can finish the war by attacking this day. In an ill-considered stratagem, Agamemnon tests the morale of the army by suggesting that they take to the ships and leave. The suggestion is accepted with alacrity, and it is only through the strenuous efforts of Odysseus that they are brought back to the place of meeting. A dissenter called Thersites is humiliated; powerful speeches are made by Odysseus and Nestor; the army gets ready and moves out to battle.

Lines 455–877: Now comes the Catalogue of Ships, a geographically ordered list of the contingents of the Greek army, with the names of their leaders. The Catalogue fits fairly well with the rest of the *Iliad* but clearly had its origin elsewhere, for in fact it describes the assembly of the fleet before it set sail for Troy and has been superficially modified for its present place. It is followed by a much shorter Trojan catalogue, also geographically set out, detailing the leaders of the Trojans and their far-flung allies. The two catalogues act in part as lists of characters for the *Iliad*.

2. sleep came not upon Zeus. The slight inconsistency with the last line of Book 1 is not serious. Rather, it is a natural and effective way to start the new book. The same device is used at the beginning of Book 10.

20. Dreams are usually said to stand at the head of the sleeper.

46. The **sceptre** showed the authority of the king. This one is further described in 101–8 of this book; it is hereditary in Agamemnon's family (**of his fathers**) and was made by the god Hephaistos (**immortal forever**).

53. Agamemnon decides to hold a meeting of the council prior to the general assembly of the army.

60–70 repeat 23–33; **65–69** appear now for the third time (since 28–32 repeated 11–15). Such repetition is natural in oral poetry.

60. breaker: tamer. For the older generation's connections with horses, see 336.

73–74. I will make trial of them ... and tell them to flee. Agamemnon produces his proposal to test the morale of the army by suggesting flight, as if this is the normal method (**since it is the right way**). In practice, it is only too likely to lead to the result which happens here—a rush for the ships; and when that occurs, the members of the council do not do what Agamemnon asks in 75. There is some confusion here, and it is made worse by the fact that twice elsewhere in the *Iliad* (9.26–28 and 14.74–81) Agamemnon proposes in earnest what he here proposes merely as a test of the troops; so it seems that this weak generalship is in a way thematic of him and assists in his characterization.

However much the proposal is to be criticized, as both foolish in itself and illogical after the promise sent by the dream, it nevertheless leads to a vivid and exciting narrative.

80–83. Nestor has natural good sense and suspects the dream, but he is unquestioningly loyal to the supreme king.

87–90. Like the swarms of clustering bees. The first full simile in the *Iliad*, and the first of many in this book.

101–8. The history of Agamemnon's **sceptre**, with a genealogy of his family.

103. Argeïphontes: an ancient title of Hermes, interpreted by the Greeks as meaning "killer of Argos" (a giant set by jealous Hera to watch over Io in the legend); but the word is very ancient, and its original meaning may not now be recoverable.

104–8. The family tree represented here is

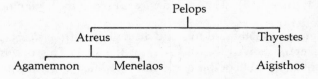

Thyestes apparently held the kingship after Atreus and then left it at his death to his nephew Agamemnon. Of the family feud between Atreus and Thyestes and between their children, Agamemnon and Aigisthos, Homer in the *Iliad* says nothing.

108. lord of many islands and over all Argos. This description of Agamemnon's realm is not consistent (however we interpret **all Argos**—cf. 1.30 n.) with the very restricted kingdom ascribed to him in 569–80. JACHMANN 93–98 argues that the idea of a general overlordship of Agamemnon is a poetic exaggeration, brought out especially in such statements as this.

116. Such is the way it will be pleasing to Zeus. Better, "I suppose this must be pleasing to Zeus."

117. crests: the circle of towers and walls on the acropolis of a city.

124. The throats of the sacrificial victims were **cut** at the pledging of a truce; the verb is thus used in a transferred way.

145. Ikaria: an island near Samos, by the eastern shore of the Aegean Sea, where Ikaros fell, it was said, from the sky.

155. beyond fate. A man's fate was established at his birth. Homer sometimes speaks as if it would be theoretically possible to frustrate it, but in practice this does not happen—the gods, if necessary, stepping in to restore the balance. So here the Greeks might have gone home, contrary to what was fated for them and for Troy, had not Hera taken action.

157. Atrytone: an ancient and obscure title of Athene (cf. Argeïphontes, 103), supposed to mean "the unwearied one."

160–61. Helen of Argos. She is often so described, although her origin and home were in Sparta. "Argos" must here mean the whole Peloponnese (1.30 n.).

169. Odysseus is the obvious person for the task Athene has in mind, and indeed he is the special favorite of the goddess for the qualities he shows here: coolness of mind and speed of thought and action.

201–2. better than you. The social situation is a simple one. The leaders are, because of their birth, the best at both fighting and counsel; the lower orders are inferior at both.

205. It is not clear why **Kronos**, father of Zeus, should have the stock epithet **devious-devising,** unless it was on account of his practice of swallowing his children.

211. The assembly is now in place again.

212. Thersites is the only common man who takes any part in the *Iliad* and the only man described as ugly. All the other figures are kings and leaders; even the minor characters who are named in order to die in the fighting seem to be of the aristocratic class. Thersites, although later sources give him an aristocratic pedigree, represents the ordinary people; he appears only here in the *Iliad*. Homer's attitude toward him, and the attitude of Homer's audience, is shown by the tendentious description. There may be an echo of new political strivings in Homer's own day, with the old aristocracy becoming suspect to the people and discontent beginning to find a voice.

220. Achilleus hated him. Successors of Homer took up the suggestion here and devised a later history for Thersites, in which he met his death at Achilleus' hands for mocking him after he had killed the queen of the Amazons, Penthesileia.

225–42. Thersites' arguments are like a parody of those of Achilleus in Book 1.

260. Telemachos' father. Odysseus is the only character in the *Iliad* who refers to himself in this oblique way, in relation to his son growing up at home (here and at 4.354). Strong family attachment is one of the facets of his many-sided character, as may be seen in the *Odyssey*.

270. Sorry though the men were. They were upset because their morale was low, because of the plague and the quarrel between their leaders, perhaps also because they were not being allowed to depart for home. They were not at all upset at the treatment of Thersites.

278. Odysseus speaks first, then Nestor—the two best counselors of the Achaians. It is not clear why Odysseus should have the title **sacker of cities,** apart from the sack of Troy, which of course has not happened yet.

279. and beside him grey-eyed Athene. It is difficult for our rational minds to accept the actions of the gods in the way more primitive people saw them. When a leader rose to speak in the assembly, a herald stood beside him, giving him the scepter, which was the outward sign that he had authority to speak. When Odysseus rose, there was a general and profound silence; the audience, after the tumult of the rush for the ships and the disturbance caused by Thersites' insubordination, was hushed and expectant. And therefore, according to the poet, it was no ordinary herald, but Athene in the guise of a herald, who stood by Odysseus' side. Compare the similar situation explained in the note on 791.

303. yesterday. In other words, "it seems just like yesterday."

Aulis was the town in Boiotia where the Greek fleet assembled to sail for Troy.

319. Everything that happens, particularly if there is no obvious explanation, may be ascribed to Zeus.

336. Gerenian horseman is a stock title of **Nestor**. The first word is unexplained; the second seems to ascribe him to the older generation, several of whom are given the title "horseman," meaning "charioteer" (cf. 9.432).

Nestor, building on the good effect of Odysseus' speech, takes a much tougher line.

356. Helen's longing to escape and her lamentations. This line, repeated in 590, assumes that Helen was carried off against her will. That is not always the impression given, but doubtless it is how it would seem to the Greeks.

362. in order by tribes, by clans. Nestor speaks of the battle order of the army. This acts as a lead-in to the Catalogue of Ships, which is to come.

389. hiding the man's shape: a reference to a certain type of shield, the body shield found in the early Mycenaean period (7.219).

405–7. Nestor, Idomeneus, the two Aiantes, Diomedes, and Odysseus. A useful list of the chief leaders. Achilleus would of course be added if he were available.

421–32. The description of the sacrifice is an exact repetition of 1.458–69, except that 425–26 replace two similar lines in the passage in Book 1.

447–49. More about the **aegis** (1.202 n.): it has a fringe of golden tassels.

455–83. In the buildup toward the long and detailed list of the

Greek contingents, the poet brings in a succession of no less than five major similes, not to mention other incidental comparisons, to describe the Greek army as it gets ready for battle. The similes describe (a) the Greek armor as shining like fire; (b) the noise as like that of flocks of birds; (c) the numbers as like flies; (d) the leaders as like goatherds; (e) Agamemnon as like a great bull in a herd.

It is generally noticeable in the *Iliad* that accumulation or expansion denotes importance. So here the unprecedented number of similes strengthens the feeling that something very important is coming.

461. The word **Asian** was still limited to a small area of the coast of Asia Minor. The river Kaÿstros came to the sea by the later town of Ephesos. This area was not Greek in the world of the *Iliad*.

478–79. For the method of description, compare Hamlet on his father:

> Hyperion's curls; the front of Jove himself;
> An eye like Mars, to threaten and command;
> A station like the herald Mercury
> New lighted on a heaven-kissing hill.
> (*Hamlet*, 3.4.56–59)

484–93. After the similes comes a conventional appeal to the **Muses** (cf. 1.1) to direct the poet's words. Such an invocation always enhances the importance of what is to follow.

493. From the point of view of the *Iliad*, where all are on land, there is no particular reason for describing the leaders as **lords of the ships**; see note on 494–759.

494–877. The remainder of Book 2 consists of:

494–759   The Catalogue of Ships (the list of the Greek contingents).
760–85   Some comments on it.
786–815   A connecting passage to introduce the Trojans.
816–77   The catalogue of the Trojans and their allies.

THE CATALOGUE OF SHIPS (LINES 494–759)

This long list—of 29 contingents, 44 leaders, 175 named towns or other localities, 1,186 ships, and, according to a plausible calculation (510 n.), about 100,000 men—was not created for its present place in Book 2 of the *Iliad*. The evidence for this is threefold:

(a) Contingents that are important here have no special part to play in the rest of the *Iliad*; in particular, the Boiotians head the list in the Catalogue and are given the largest number of named leaders and towns, but their significance in the *Iliad* itself is not great.

(b) The imperfect tenses throughout ("were leaders of," etc.) and the insistence on the number of *ships* (cf. 493) would better suit the beginning of the war, even the assembling of the whole expedition at Aulis, than the situation found in the *Iliad*.

(c) In three cases the poet has inserted lines to assimilate the Catalogue to the *Iliad* situation. This was necessary because three of the original leaders are not appearing on the field of battle this day, and some explanation seemed called for. The three (all from northern Greece) are Achilleus (refusing to fight), Protesilaos (dead), and Philoktetes (sick).

These considerations compel the belief that a separately existing Catalogue has been inserted into the *Iliad*, with a few modifications which we can easily see and perhaps others which we cannot.

If this is so, where did the Catalogue come from? There is evidence associating "catalogue poetry" with Boiotia and the school of Hesiod. Our Catalogue of Ships begins with the Boiotian contingent and puts more significance upon it than could be justified by the Boiotians' part in the *Iliad* or in any other version of the Trojan War known to us. An origin connected with the Boiotian school of poetry may therefore be suspected.

But what about the geographical information in the Catalogue? Is it fact or fiction? All shades of opinion are held, ranging from those who argue that the Catalogue is a poor invention, interpolated into the *Iliad* by a late and decadent poet, to those who see it as the miraculously preserved record of a historical expeditionary force. While the latter is certainly an overstatement, it is perhaps nearer to the truth. Because of the general conformity with our other knowledge of the Mycenaean world (most of which comes from the findings of archeology), and because of a number of descriptive epithets for towns whose very existence—not to mention importance—had been forgotten in the classical period, we may accept that the Catalogue contains (preserved down the centuries, presumably in verse) invaluable evidence about Greece in the late Mycenaean period, before the arrival of the Dorians.

BIBLIOGRAPHY

Allen, T. W. *The Homeric Catalogue of Ships* (1921).
HOPE SIMPSON AND LAZENBY.
PAGE 118–77.
Thomas, Helen, and Stubbings, F. H. "Lands and Peoples in Homer." In WACE/STUBBINGS 283–310.

The Catalogue describes the Greek world in five major areas:

1. Greece north of the Isthmus of Corinth (494–558).
2. The Peloponnese (559–624).
3. The western islands and western Greece (625–44).
4. The southeastern islands (645–80).
5. Northern Greece (681–759).

If one looks at a large map of the whole area, one sees that this is a spiral, clockwise description of Greece by groups of contingents, with the southeastern islands (Krete, etc.) inserted out of order. It is of much interest that the other islands of the Aegean and the cities on the coast of Asia Minor (both of considerable importance in historical times) are not mentioned at all. All this adds to the impression that the Catalogue describes the state of the Greek world at a particular time in history.

GREECE NORTH OF THE ISTHMUS

Boiotia (Lines 494–510)

As explained in the introductory note to the Catalogue, there is no reason inherent in the *Iliad* why the Boiotian contingent should have the honor of being named first (why not Mykenai?) or why it should have more leaders and come from more named towns than any other contingent. Interesting, however, and producing a strong impression of historical verisimilitude, is the fact that neither Thebes nor Orchomenos finds a place in the list of Boiotian cities.

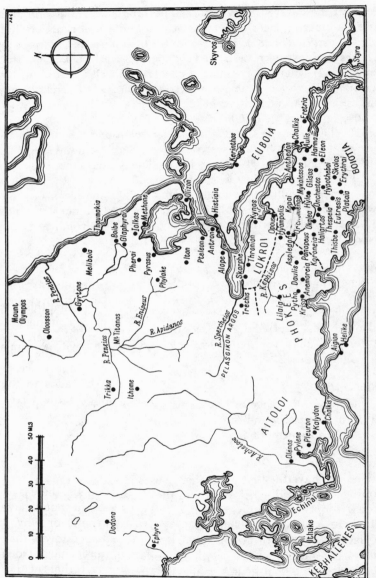

MAP 1. NORTHERN AND CENTRAL GREECE

And yet these were the two most important cities in later Boiotia and had been places of great wealth and significance in the Mycenaean Age (9.381). The reasons for their absence here are that Thebes had just been destroyed by the Epigonoi (4.406), so that only "lower Thebes," meaning a cluster of dwellings around the foot of the acropolis, can be referred to (505), while Orchomenos has an independent contingent (511).

504. For **Glisa,** read *Glisas.*

510. Twice in the Catalogue Homer mentions the number of men carried by each ship of a contingent; here the number is 120; the other figure (line 719) is 50. It was Thucydides who suggested (1.10.4) that Homer may be giving us the largest and the smallest complements and that we might therefore take the mean of these two numbers (85) and multiply it by the total number of ships (1,186) to find the strength of the whole force. The result is a little over 100,000.

Minyan Orchomenos (Lines 511–16)

The Minyans are a shadowy people whose half-forgotten exploits date from an earlier age. They are associated with seafaring (although Orchomenos was far from the coast, being on the inland lake, Kopais) and had connections both with Iolkos and the Argonauts' quest for the Golden Fleece (712) and with Nestor's Pylos (NILSSON 127–50).

Phokis (Lines 517–26)

The important place in Phokis was Delphi (here called **Pytho,** 519), the sanctuary and oracle of Apollo.

521. Read An*emoreia.*

Lokris (Lines 527–35)

Here we have the first major hero, Aias the son of Oïleus. The Lokrians are described elsewhere in the *Iliad* (13.713–18) as light-armed troops, using bows and slings; this may fit the description of Aias here as **armoured in linen** (529), i.e., with a thick linen jerkin in place of the usual bronze breastplate. However, in practice in the *Iliad,* Aias takes his place with the other leading Greeks, and nothing suggests that he is less heavily armed than they are.

The statement (530) that he surpassed all others with the

throwing spear is consistent with the assertion of 14.520–22 that this Aias was the most successful of all the Greeks in the pursuit of a fleeing enemy.

Euboia (Lines 536–45)

Euboia is the long island opposite Lokris. Chalkis and Eretria were important cities in the age of colonization (eighth century B.C.).

Athens (Lines 546–56)

We approach this contingent with interest because of the later importance of Athens, which was also a significant Mycenaean citadel. Moreover, the *Iliad* was probably edited in Athens in the sixth century, so that one might expect some patriotic enhancement of the city's prestige. In practice, however, the entry is unimpressive; no other localities in Attica are mentioned except Athens itself; and the leader is the obscure Menestheus, not a son or sons of Theseus, as in the epic Cycle and later Athenian poetry (cf. 1.265 n.).

547. **Erechtheus,** mythical king of Athens, was worshiped with Athene on the acropolis. He is described here as having been spontaneously generated from a ploughed field—an instance, no doubt, of the frequent claim of the Athenians to be the only original, autochthonous, inhabitants of Greece.

553. Skill at marshaling the troops is a useful, if rather unheroic, quality (the mention of Nestor helps).

Salamis (Lines 557–58)

Lines 557–58 raise many questions. Aias could not, of course, help coming from the tiny island of Salamis and so having a very small number of ships. But two lines are far too meager for such a great hero; they do not even give him his usual title, "son of Telamon," to distinguish him from the other Aias (527). Moreover, it was frequently alleged in the ancient world that line 558 was deliberately invented by an Athenian (Solon or Peisistratos) and inserted into the *Iliad* to support Athens' dispute in the sixth century with its neighbor, Megara, over possession of Salamis. If this story is true, line 558 may have displaced a longer description of Aias, or he may even not have appeared in the original Catalogue.

558. This statement is inconsistent with the evidence of the *Iliad;* in 8.224 (=11.7) Aias is described as holding one of the two positions of most honor and danger, the extreme ends of the Greek line.

2. THE PELOPONNESE

Argos (Lines 559–68)

A surprising fact about the geographical area described in this section is that it not only cuts the king of Mykenai off from his natural access to the Aegean Sea but also removes from his domain the city Argos and the massive fortress Tiryns in the Argive plain. Agamemnon is left with an apparently much less useful kingdom to the north and west of Mykenai, while Diomedes controls the east and south.

The three leaders of the Argos contingent are all of the Epigonoi (see 4.405–10 n.), i.e., they are sons of three of the Seven against Thebes (of Tydeus, Kapaneus, and Mekisteus).

561. For **Eïonai,** read *Eïones.*

Mykenai (Lines 569–80)

On the division between Agamemnon's kingdom and Diomedes', see the preceding section, on Argos. Agamemnon is not, in fact, wholly cut off from the Aegean Sea, because Korinth had harbors on both sides of the Isthmus; but his domain is surprisingly limited. It has been suggested with some probability that the Catalogue here describes the situation at the end of the Mycenaean Age, when the king of Mykenai had been shorn of some of his power.

Sparta (Lines 581–90)
590 = 356.

Pylos (Lines 591–602)

For the recent conclusive identification of Pylos, see 11.681 n. It was evidently the second most important city of the Mycenaean Peloponnese (as is shown by the number of ships).

595. The story of **Thamyris,** a singer (i.e., poet), exemplifies a common theme. A mortal gets above himself and challenges the gods; the result is always disastrous. Compare Lykourgos in 6.130–40, Bellerophontes in 6.200–202, and Niobe in 24.602–9.

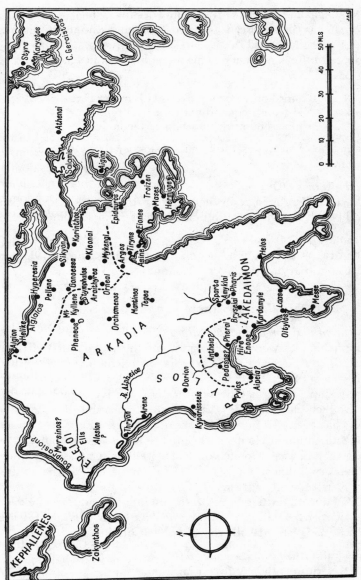

MAP 2. THE PELOPONNESE

596. Oichalia was in the north, in Thessaly (730).

599. It has always been assumed (though without any strong reason) that the word translated **maimed** means "blind" here. Compare Milton's reference to his own blindness in *Paradise Lost*, 3.33–35:

> Those other two equal'd with me in Fate,
> So were I equal'd with them in renown,
> Blind Thamyris and blind Maeonides,

referring (in "Maeonides") to the ancient story that Homer himself was blind.

Arkadia (*Lines 603–14*)

612–14. There is logic in the assertion that the Arkadians, an inland people, would have to borrow ships from someone else.

Elis (*Lines 615–24*)

The area is Elis, but the people are called **Epeians** (619). For **Kteatos** and **Eurytos** (621)—the Moliones—see 11.708 n.

3. THE WESTERN ISLANDS AND WESTERN GREECE

Doulichion and the Echinades (*Lines 625–30*)

The Echinades were small islands off the estuary of the river Acheloös, by the coast of Akarnania. Doulichion, however, has not been identified. A great difficulty is that Meges has a contingent of forty ships, whereas Odysseus has only twelve, which suggests that Doulichion should be a large area. Discussion of its whereabouts has been tied in with the more significant argument about the identification of Homer's Ithaka. The latest view is that Ithaka is Ithaka and that Doulichion may well be Leukas, the long promontory—almost an island—off the cost of Akarnania (so HOPE SIMPSON AND LAZENBY 101).

629. Phyleus, in a quarrel with his father, had emigrated to Doulichion from Elis. In 13.691 and 15.519, Meges' troops are called Epeians (see 619 above), from their origin.

Ithaka and Other Islands (*Lines 631–37*)

632. Neriton is the mountain on Ithaka.

634. Samos is the large island later called Kephallenia. "Men of

Kephallenia" (631) is a general name for Odysseus' troops (cf. 4.330).

635. The mainland possessions of Odysseus are thought to have been on the coast of Elis rather than north of the Gulf of Corinth.

Aitolia (Lines 638-44)

The poet feels that he should explain why the obscure Thoas is leader rather than a member of the famous heroic family of Aitolia, Oineus and his sons, Tydeus and Meleagros. Tydeus had moved to Argos, where his son Diomedes is now king.

4. THE SOUTHEASTERN ISLANDS

This group of contingents raises a particular question. The Dorian Invasion was known to the Greeks as "the return of the children of Herakles." In general, the archaizing of the heroic tradition was strong enough to prevent any mention of, or allusion to, Dorians; but there seem to be indications of them here, in the southeast: (a) Tlepolemos (653) was a son of Herakles, and Pheidippos and Antiphos (678) grandsons; (b) there is a reference to a threefold tribal division (a typical Dorian feature) at Rhodes in 655 and 668; (c) the one actual mention of Dorians in either the *Iliad* or the *Odyssey* comes at *Od.* 19.177, where they are among a list of the different peoples to be found in Krete.

It is not easy to draw historical conclusions from this evidence, because of course the date of the Catalogue's information must remain uncertain, and any theory of the Dorians' occupying the southeastern islands before they reached the mainland of Greece is not supported by the findings of archeology; but we are left with the feeling that here, if anywhere in the *Iliad*, we are in touch with the Dorians.

Krete (Lines 645-52)

The history of Krete in the period 1450-1200 B.C. is much in dispute at the present time. One difficulty is to bring together the literary and the archeological evidence. According to orthodox archeological opinion, Knossos was destroyed about 1400 B.C., and Krete as a whole was reduced to insignificance during the whole of the following period. In the *Iliad*, on the other hand, Idomeneus is ruler of a powerful kingdom, which sends to Troy 80 ships, a number exceeded only by Mykenai and Pylos.

The towns in 646–48 are all from a strip in the center of the island. Reference to 100 cities (649) may be a recollection of earlier days.

646. For **Gortyna** read *Gortys*.

Rhodes (Lines 653–70)

Rhodes was an Achaian colony before it was Dorian, and the three cities, Lindos, Ialysos, and Kameiros, were already there in Mycenaean times. The small number of ships, however, suits a new foundation, as described in the text here.

659. Several cities were called **Ephyra;** this one was (we are told) in Thesprotia, in northwestern Greece.

661–66. fugitive. The killing of a relation is commonly put forward in the myths as a reason for tribal movement, blood guilt compelling the killer to leave home.

Syme, a Small Island North of Rhodes (Lines 671–75)

Kos and Other Islands (Lines 676–80)

677. Eurypylos' city. This King Eurypylos, grandfather of Thessalos (679), should not be confused with the leader of the contingent described in 734–37, or with the other Eurypylos, the son of Telephos, who came to defend Troy after the end of the *Iliad* and was killed by Neoptolemos (*Od.* 11.520).

5. NORTHERN GREECE

Nine baronies, the geographical limits of which are not clear, take the place of what in post-Homeric and classical times was Dorian Thessaly. The uncertain state of affairs in this area seems to suit the situation toward the end of the Mycenaean Age, with peoples on the move and pressure from the north.

In this part of the Catalogue are the three evident additions designed to adapt the document to the *Iliad* situation. They are lines 686–93, 699–709 (in line 710, the Greek text has "him," not "Podarkes"), and 721–28.

Pelasgian Argos (Lines 681–94)

This area was, as it were, the matrix of Greece. For the tribes paused in Thessaly on their way further south; and we find here names related to limited areas which were later to have much wider significance. So Argos, Achaia, and (preeminent in the end) Hellas.

691–92. Mynes was king of **Lyrnessos** (19.296). The king of **Thebe** was Andromache's father, Eëtion.

Phylake and Other Places (Lines 695–710)
698–702. Protesilaos had been the first Greek casualty.

Pherai, Iolkos (Lines 711–15)
Iolkos was famous in its own cycle of legend, that of the Argonauts. It is strange that such an important area should contribute only eleven ships.

Methone and Other Places (Lines 716–28)
Philoktetes was brought by the Greeks to Troy from Lemnos soon after the end of the *Iliad* story. They had received a prophecy that Troy could not be taken without the bow and arrows of Herakles, which were in his possession. He killed Paris.

Trikke and Other Places (Lines 729–33)
731–32. Asklepios, the great healer, was son of Apollo.

Ormenion (Ormenios) and Other Places (Lines 734–37)

Argissa and Other Places (Lines 738–47)
740. these: the Lapiths. Compare Nestor's tale in 1.263–72.
743–44. hairy beast men. The centaurs lived on Mount Pelion, the **Aithikes** in the mountains to the west of Thessaly.

Dodona and Other Places (Lines 748–55)
The place names here are even more difficult to identify than usual, apart from Dodona, famous for its oracle of Zeus, which was far to the west, in the later Epiros. Achilleus prays to Zeus of Dodona in 16.233.
755. The strongest oath which the gods could swear was by the river **Styx,** the river of the underworld (15.37).

Magnesia (Lines 756–59)
The river Peneios, whose upper waters are referred to in 753, flows to the sea through the Vale of Tempe; Mount Pelion is some way to the south. Perhaps these two are supposed to be the limits of Prothoös' kingdom.

760. These then were the leaders. The Catalogue of Ships names forty-four Achaian leaders, of whom ten are killed in the course of the *Iliad*, three by Hektor.

763. Eumelos was actually son of Admetos, and grandson of Pheres. He competes with these horses in the chariot race at the funeral games for Patroklos in Book 23.

766. Apollo had served Admetos as a herdsman. **Pereia** may be a variant spelling of Pherai (711).

777. covered, to protect them from the dust.

782–83. Typhoeus was the last of the opponents of Zeus, a monstrous creature, not human in shape like the giants or Titans. He was cast down beneath the surface of the earth by the thunderbolts of Zeus, and his stirring there, on his hard bed of stone, served to explain local earth tremors and volcanic activity. When there was a thunderstorm in the mountains, people would say that Zeus was "lashing the earth" in anger against Typhoeus.

The **land of the Arimoi** was identified as Kilikia, on the south coast of Asia Minor. Pindar, in his *First Pythian*, has Typhoeus born in Kilikia but suppressed by Zeus under volcanic Mount Etna in Sicily.

786. Now to the Trojans came Iris. A switch of view prepares the way for the Trojan catalogue.

791. Iris is not only imitating the voice of Polites, but she looks like him as well (795). It is, as often, a little difficult for our rational minds to see what this means. Polites had, after all, been detailed to watch for the Greek advance. Who was it, then, who came to the Trojan assembly? Iris or Polites? The answer is that Polites indeed came running from his lookout post on Aisyetes' tomb. His message was of the utmost importance, and suddenly there was new fire and life in the Trojan assembly. In this enhanced vividness the Greeks saw the presence of a god; and what god but Iris, the divine messenger? So Iris was there, in the shape of Polites. Compare 279 n.

813–14. For a different terminology in the languages of men and gods see 1.403–4 n.

BOOK TWO

THE TROJAN CATALOGUE (LINES 816–77)

The Trojan catalogue is far shorter than the Greek Catalogue of Ships, and the geographical and other information contained in it is briefer and more factual. The method of presentation is geographical also, but on a different scheme from the Greek catalogue. Here, after (1) a list of contingents from Troy itself and the surrounding countryside (816–43), the remaining peoples are treated as on four lines radiating outward from Troy. These are: (2) the European allies (844–50); (3) those to the east, along the south shore of the Black Sea (851–57); (4) those inland into Asia Minor (858–63); and (5) those to the south, along the west coast of Asia Minor (864–77). Apparently by convention, the poet tells us when we have reached the limit of one particular direction line from Troy by using a word meaning "far away" for the remotest group in each case.

The Trojan catalogue has less claim to a pre-Iliadic existence than the Achaian. All the same, it contains valuable information about the demography of Asia Minor and Thrace before the Ionian migration. It is striking that important Greek cities like Smyrna and Ephesos are not mentioned at all, that Miletos is named only as the home of barbarous-speaking Karians, and that the islands of the Aegean, such as Chios and Samos, are disregarded.

1. TROY AND THE TROAD

Troy Itself (Lines 816–18)

Dardanians (Lines 819–23)

The leaders are still Trojans, **Aineias** representing the younger branch of the royal family, and **Antenor** being the chief "commoner" of Troy.

"Trojans" from under Mount Ida (Lines 824–27)

The home of **Pandaros** is elsewhere called Lykia (5.105, 173), but this must be a Trojan "Lykia," up in the north, for the true Lykians lived far away, at the southwest corner of Asia Minor (876–77). The statement in 827 that Apollo himself gave Pandaros his bow means nothing more than that Pandaros was an exceptionally good shot (see 4.106–11).

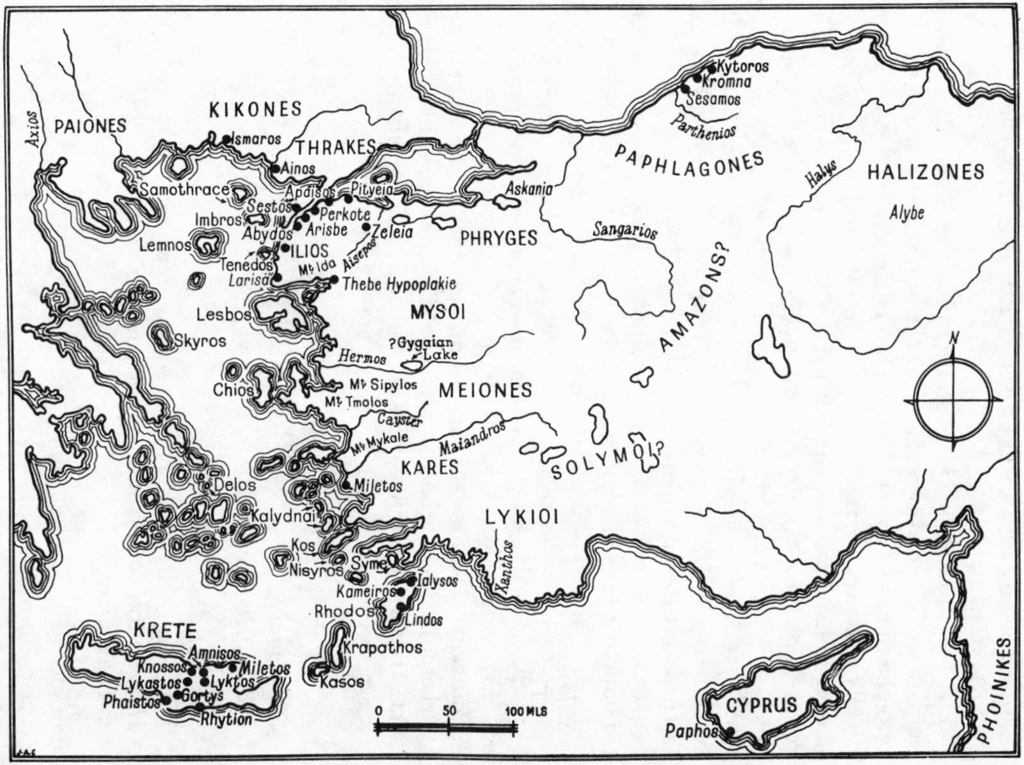

MAP 3. ASIA MINOR AND THE ISLANDS

BOOK TWO

Adresteia and Other Places East of Troy (Lines 828–34)
   834. The two sons of Merops are in fact killed in 11.329–34.

Cities on the Shores of the Hellespont (Lines 835–39)

"Pelasgians" from Larissa (Larisa), South of Troy (Lines 840–43)
   The name "Pelasgian" relates to a very early people, found all over the area; cf. Pelasgian Argos, 681.

2. THE EUROPEAN ALLIES
(FROM THRACE OVER TOWARD MACEDONIA)

Thracians (Lines 844–45)
   845. held within merely means that the Hellespont was their boundary.

Kikones (Lines 846–47)
   The Kikones were famous as the victims of Odysseus' first adventure (*Od.* 9.39 ff.).

Paionians (Lines 848–50)
   Later in the *Iliad*, Asteropaios is treated as leader of this people (cf. 21.140–43 n.); **Pyraichmes,** however, is not forgotten (16.287).

3. ALLIES FROM THE SOUTH SHORE OF THE BLACK SEA

Paphlagones (Lines 851–55)
   851. The leader's name should be Pylaimenes.
   852. The **Enetoi** may well be remote ancestors of the Venetians (Livy 1.1).

Halizones (Lines 856–57)
   The remote and obscure names are reminiscent of the river Halys and of the Chalybes, famous as metalworkers.

4. ALLIES FROM NORTH-CENTRAL ASIA MINOR

Mysians (Lines 858–61)
   860. Ennomos' death is not in fact mentioned in the river battle in Book 21; nor is Nastes' (874). Very many were killed there by Achilleus.

Phrygians (Lines 862–63)

5. ALLIES FROM THE WEST COAST OF ASIA MINOR

Maionians (Lines 864–66)

Karians (Lines 867–75)

Lykians (Lines 876–77)

Sarpedon and **Glaukos** are the most important, and the most sympathetically treated, of the allies.

The Trojan catalogue names twenty-seven leaders, of whom seventeen are killed in the course of the *Iliad*, four falling to Aias and three each to Achilleus and Diomedes. This heavy casualty rate suggests that the Trojan catalogue was composed for the *Iliad*, although of course the geographical information which it contains comes from an earlier period, before the Ionian Migration.

BOOK THREE

Book 3 contains two alternating themes, (a) the single combat between Paris and Menelaos and (b) the people within the city of Troy. We are first introduced to Paris (Alexandros), the unworthy cause of the war; and then, in a pause before the duel starts, we see Helen on the walls of Troy, speaking to old King Priam and identifying for him the leaders of the Achaians, who are of course well known to her. The duel itself, which follows, is technically undecided, because Aphrodite spirits Paris away before Menelaos can kill him. The book ends in Troy again, with the scene of Aphrodite summoning Helen back from the wall to the bed of Paris.

Neither the single combat between the two most interested parties (the alternative husbands of Helen) nor the scene in which Helen on the wall identifies the Greek leaders for Priam has any logical place in the tenth year of the war. Both would be better at the beginning, when the Greeks first arrived. This is true also of the catalogues in Book 2 and of Agamemnon's review of the army in Book 4. It seems that the poet wishes to make his poem a true *Iliad*—a story of Troy—as well as a description of the consequences of the wrath of Achilleus. So for several books now we hardly hear of Achilleus, and Zeus does not even begin to fulfill his promise to Thetis until Book 8.

1–9. A moralizing contrast between the disorganized Trojans and the well-disciplined Greeks.

6. **Pygmaian men.** The story of the war between the cranes and the pygmies is a folktale reflecting some knowledge of a diminutive African people. It probably arose from the sight of cranes flying south in formation, uttering loud cries.

15. As the two armies come together, we expect a general engagement; instead, Paris (Alexandros) steps forward from the Trojan ranks, and Menelaos immediately faces him from the Greeks. This is typical of Homeric fighting; the massed armies are present but are ignored. The fighting described in the *Iliad* consists mainly of clashes between individual leaders, who step out of the ranks as champions.

17. the hide of a leopard. Paris' equipment is abnormal and is obviously intended to have a characterizing effect. Later (330–38) he puts on the regular armor of the Homeric hero.

33. As a man who has come on a snake. This is the fourth powerful simile taken from nature in these first thirty-five lines; they make a colorful beginning to the book.

38. Hektor's natural reaction to Paris is that of a stronger elder brother: dislike.

54. The **favours of Aphrodite** are his attractiveness and charm.

57. you had worn a mantle of flying stones: you would have been stoned to death.

59. you have scolded me rightly. It is part of the character of Paris that he shows an acceptance of his own faults which disarms criticism.

70. Paris not only carried off Helen but took a number of her (and Menelaos') **possessions** with her.

73. For the verb **cut**, see 2.124 n.

103. two lambs. A white one for the Olympian god, a black one for the earth deity.

119. two. The translation reflects an error in the text of the Greek edition. Talthybios was sent to get one lamb, not two (104).

THE TEICHOSKOPIA, OR VIEW FROM THE WALL
(LINES 121–244)

The Teichoskopia, or View from the Wall, in which Helen identifies the Greek heroes for Priam and others, fills the time between the heralds' departure for Troy and their arrival there to summon Priam. It is a wonderful scene, in which we discover more about the personalities, and even about the appearance, of the

Greek leaders, and meet, for the first time, Helen, the cause of the war.

121–23. Iris. For the messenger goddess in the likeness of a human, cf. 2.791.

125–28. There is something very convincing in the picture of the beautiful Helen placidly composing pictorial representations of the battles being fought on her behalf.

working into it (126) implies the weaving of figures into the pattern of the fabric (LORIMER 397).

144. This line presents an ancient problem. Aithra (**Aithre**), **Pittheus' daughter,** was a figure of Athenian mythology, being the wife of their king, Aigeus, and mother of the famous Theseus. The appearance of this aged queen at Troy as the handmaid of Helen seems to call for explanation. This was forthcoming in the story, known as early as the epic Cycle, that when Helen was carried off by Theseus and Peirithoös, some time before she married Menelaos, her brothers Kastor and Polydeukes rescued her and, while doing so, carried off in reprisal Theseus' mother Aithra, who thus became a slave of Helen. The rescue of Aithra by her grandsons was a well-known incident in post-Homeric descriptions of the Fall of Troy.

It seems likely that Homer or a predecessor, choosing at random from the epic stock a name for the handmaid of Helen, chanced to hit on "Aithra, daughter of Pittheus"; the explanatory legend then arose through attempts of poets and mythologists to integrate this awkward detail into the total picture.

There was speculation in ancient times that **Klymene** was a relation of Peirithoös, as Aithra of Theseus. **Of the ox eyes** is a stock epithet of Hera (1.551), but is occasionally used of other women.

146–48. The counselors of the Trojans. **Panthoös** is father of Poulydamas, who plays a large part later in the *Iliad* (11.57–60 n.). **Thymoites** is not otherwise known. The three in 147 are brothers of Priam, according to 20.238. For **Antenor,** see 2.819–23 n. **Oukalegon** means "not caring," a very strange name, which caught the fancy of Virgil (*proximus ardet Ucalegon*, "Ucalegon's house next door was on fire," *Aeneid* 2.311–12).

151. clear, as cicadas. The comparison is suggested by the soft, dry voices of the old men as they talk; the Greeks thought highly of the sound of cicadas.

154–60. The poet has often been praised for this passage, in that, instead of attempting to describe Helen's beauty, he shows the reaction it produces in the old men of Troy.

164. I am not blaming you. For the attitude that human beings are not to blame, because their mistakes are sent to them by the gods, compare Agamemnon's excuses in 19.86–90.

166. The true Teichoskopia now begins. A selection of the Greek leaders are identified and to some extent physically described— Agamemnon, Odysseus, Aias, Idomeneus.

175. my grown child. Helen's daughter was Hermione, who later married Orestes.

184–89. Phrygian men ... Amazon women. The battle between the Phrygians and the Amazons by the banks of the river **Sangarios**, at which Priam says he was present, has been tentatively identified with disturbances caused by the invading tribes at the time of the breakup of the Hittite Empire in the twelfth century. If so, this is one of the memories of the Mycenaean period which have survived into the *Iliad*. The Amazons are mentioned again in 6.186, as a people whom Bellerophontes was required to fight in Asia Minor.

193–94. A splendid portrait of **Odysseus,** giving the impression of having been taken from life. This is no tall, handsome, godlike hero.

204–24. The speech of **Antenor.** The embassy of Odysseus and Menelaos to recover Helen is mentioned also at 11.140. That they stayed with Antenor led eventually to the legend that he had private relations with the Greeks and was spared when the city was taken. The description of Odysseus' oratory in 216–23 looks once again like a portrait taken from life; he is evidently no ordinary speaker. The comparison of his words to the falling snow is of slow inevitability and cumulative effect.

236–44. A pathetic end to the scene. Helen does not know that her two famous brothers, **Kastor** and **Polydeukes,** are dead.

In 243, the adjective applied to the earth should be "life-giving" rather than **teeming.** The nineteenth-century critic Ruskin praised the poet for his sensitivity in giving the earth the epithet "life-giving" at the moment when it is being described as the covering of the dead. Present-day scholars are more likely to consider it a stock epithet (see 1.17 n.), with no particular meaning for this passage.

273–74. Passing the hairs from the heads of the sacrificial animals to all the princes has the effect of involving them symbolically in the solemn occasion.

276. Ida: a mountain south of Troy. Zeus, as weather god, is regularly associated with mountaintops.

277. Helios: the sun god.

278–79. vengeance on dead men. This shows the beginning of a belief in divine retribution for wrongdoing; it is still limited to perjury, however, because in that offense the credit of the gods is directly involved. By the time of the *Odyssey*, the gods are said to show their disapproval of the wicked deeds of men (*Od.* 14.83–84). But in the *Iliad* (with the exception of a passing comment in a simile at 16.386–88) the gods please themselves, taking sides in human disputes irrespective of the merits of the case.

you who under the earth. The parallel passage in 19.259–60 identifies these as the Furies.

330–38. This is one of four full-scale descriptions of the arming of a hero in the *Iliad*. The others are of Agamemnon in 11.17–44, of Patroklos in 16.131–44, and of Achilleus in 19.369–91. The description follows the same order each time (greaves, breastplate, sword, shield, helmet, spear[s]), and differs only by the insertion of special details (such as 333 here) or by ornamental expansion for greater effect. The basic phrases are clearly traditional.

The order is the natural one. Both sword and shield are supported by straps over the shoulder, so they naturally have to be put on before the helmet and after the breastplate.

333. Lykaon is killed by Achilleus in 21.116.

334. The **nails of silver** were rivets, with silver-plated heads, for attaching the handle of a sword to the blade. Examples of such rivets were found in the shaft graves at Mykenai (LORIMER 273).

340–80. The duel between Menelaos and Paris. Menelaos is clearly superior in every respect. Paris, however, has Aphrodite on his side.

362. the horn of his helmet. It appears that there were one or more projections (horns) at the front of the helmet.

389–420. A strangely disturbing scene between Aphrodite and Helen. Aphrodite is simultaneously the internal sexual motivation in Helen and a powerful external goddess. Helen tries to resist this force, but she is too weak.

426–36. Helen . . . spoke to her lord in derision. Here too Homer shows his knowledge of human behavior. Helen acts very like a wife. Upset because Paris did so badly in the fight, she shows this by sarcasm and criticism.

441. Paris is shameless. What about the truce and the agreement between the two sides? He cares nothing for all that.

443–45. the first time. Paris refers to his seduction of Helen and their first intercourse—not in Sparta, but after they had left there. **Kranae** merely means "rocky"; no island of that name is known, and it may simply be an adjective, not a proper noun.

461. The **Achaians**, naturally, **applauded;** the Trojan reaction is not stated.

BOOK FOUR

Book 4, like Book 3, contains one major scene—Agamemnon's review of the army—that is suited rather to the beginning of the war than to the tenth year but is nevertheless of value in increasing our recognition of the different Greek leaders.

The book begins (1–222) with the treacherous breaking of the truce by Pandaros—necessary for the continuation of the war, and adding a new reason for the inevitable destruction of Troy. Then comes Agamemnon's review (223–421), culminating in the scene with Diomedes, who is intentionally highlighted here because of his domination of the battle in the next two books. Then follows the first description of fighting (422–544)—introduced by a number of similes, to show the importance of the occasion. It is a general, bloody struggle, giving a somber background to the brighter and more heroic achievements of Book 5.

1–72. A scene on Olympos, showing the gods planning to continue the war. They are quite ruthless and amoral, bargaining with one another about the destruction of cities, as if it is all a game.

2. Hebe: goddess of youth and handmaid to the gods.

8. who stands by her people: a possible translation of an old cult title of Athene, Alalkomeneïs, of disputed meaning.

51–52. Argos, Sparta, Mykenai. There has been speculation that the reference to possible destruction of these three major cities may allude to the Dorian Invasion, which put an end to the Mycenaean Age in the period after the Trojan War. This is not, however, necessary; Hera's words are meaningful enough in themselves.

59–60. As the daughter of **Kronos,** Hera was the sister, as well as the wife, of Zeus (14.295–96).

75–77. a star: i.e., a shooting star. For another of Athene's descents in visible form, see 17.547–52, where she comes down in a rainbow.

88–91. The entry in the Trojan catalogue contains several details which are repeated here:

> They who lived in Zeleia below the foot of Mount Ida,
> men of wealth, who drank the dark water of Aisepos,
> Trojans: of these the leader was the shining son of Lykaon,
> Pandaros, with the bow that was actual gift of Apollo.
>
> (2.824–27)

93–103. Athene persuades Pandaros to break the truce. This does not, however, in any way lessen Pandaros' own responsibility for his treachery; indeed (104), he is a fool to be persuaded. Then Athene moves swiftly to the side of Menelaos, to see that the arrow does not do him any serious harm; in the following book, inevitably, Pandaros is one of the first to fall, and it is Athene who directs the spear of Diomedes so that it makes a most painful and unpleasant wound (5.290). The gods are ruthless.

101. Apollo's title *Lykēgenēs* (101) is here translated **light-born,** a derivation connecting the first part of the word with Latin *lux,* "light." Alternative theories connect it either with wolves or with the place Lykia. Apollo may have been in origin a wolf god (perhaps as god of shepherds). On the other hand, he had definite connections with Lykia, and Pandaros himself is, surprisingly, said to come from Lykia in 5.105, 173; note also the name of his father, Lykaon.

106–11. The facts stated here—that Pandaros provided himself with the goat horns and got a human craftsman to make the bow for him—have seemed to some to clash with the statement in 2.827 (quoted at 88–91, above) that Apollo himself gave Pandaros his bow. The two are not inconsistent, for the gift of a god may well be different (less material) than human gifts. To say that Apollo gave him his bow means no more than that he was a successful archer. Compare Paris' words in 3.65, in allusion to "the favours of Aphrodite": "Never to be cast away are the gifts of the gods."

The bow is the short "recurved" bow, not the long bow of early English history (see F. H. Stubbings in WACE/STUBBINGS 519). The whole of this passage is fully discussed by LORIMER 290–95. She shows that the information about the goat horns and the making of the bow in 106–11 is more poetic than realistic; but the shot itself is accurately described in 122–25.

In line 109 the horns are described as being of **sixteen palms' length**. A "palm" is the breadth of four fingers—about three inches. The length of each horn is therefore four feet, which is evident exaggeration, since it would make too large a bow.

118. for **bitter arrows,** see 217–18 n.

122. grooves: on the side of the arrow, for the archer to hold with his fingers as he draws the bow.

123. This is the only mention of **iron** for weapons in the *Iliad*, apart from the unique club of Areïthoös in 7.141; elsewhere, bronze is the metal in use.

128. Athene is stage-managing the scene (93–103 n.). **Spoiler** is her title as a fighting goddess, i.e., "She Who Brings in the Spoils."

133. corselet: breastplate; of leather in early times, later of metal. The metal one would be tied together at the side, as it consisted of a front and a back plate; the leather one would be tied, perhaps with an overlap, in the middle. The description of Menelaos' defensive armor, penetrated by the arrow, is not clear (indeed it is described by LORIMER 205 as chaotic); but Menelaos was surely hit in the stomach, not the side. Accordingly, a leather corselet, like a leather jerkin, is more probable here than a metal breastplate.

137. guard: a sort of metal kilt, defending the lower part of the body.

153–54. Agamemnon's affectionate concern for his younger brother is one of the more amiable features of his character.

163–165. Hektor repeats these key lines in 6.447–49. Both attacker and defender know that Troy is doomed.

171. thirsty. The plain of Argos was regularly described by adjectives meaning "dry."

172. If Menelaos dies, the Greeks will have less reason to stay, as they are there ostensibly to restore his wife to him.

193. For **Machaon,** see 2.729–33.

197. Trojan or Lykian. The Lykians (the troops of Sarpedon and

Glaukos, 2.876–77) are the most important of the allies of Troy and may therefore stand for the allies in general. There is, however, the odd fact that Pandaros, who actually shot the arrow, is said in 5.105 and 173 to come from "Lykia," although his people are "Trojans" and live under Mount Ida (2.824–26). There may be a confusion in the epic tradition here; certainly in this line—and even more in the repeated "Trojans, Lykians and Dardanians who fight at close quarters" (8.173, etc.)—Lykians closely connected with Troy would be more natural than the remotest of the allies.

212. he is probably Machaon, not Menelaos.

217–18. the bitter arrow. The description of the doctor sucking blood from the wound led Gilbert Murray to the view that behind the Homeric poems lay a tradition of the use of poison on arrowheads (never alluded to in the *Iliad*, although it is in the *Odyssey*), evidenced also in such epithets for arrows as **bitter** (cf. 118, etc.). Murray considered this an example of the expurgation of certain more barbarous practices from the world of the Homeric poems (*The Rise of the Greek Epic*, 4th ed., pp. 129–30).

219. Cheiron, the wise centaur, lived on Mount Pelion and taught the most eminent of the heroic youth of Greece—Asklepios, Iason, and Achilleus (11.831).

THE EPIPOLESIS, OR REVIEW OF THE ARMY BY AGAMEMNON (LINES 223–421)

The Epipolesis, or Review, of Agamemnon is a set piece distinguishing Book 4, as the Teichoskopia did Book 3. It reinforces the characterization of a number of Greek leaders, so that we feel we know them better. Agamemnon, with the responsibility of a general before the battle, distributes praise and blame. He praises those (Idomeneus, the Aiantes, Nestor) who are actively preparing to fight and blames those (Menestheus, Odysseus, Diomedes) who appear to be holding back.

242. arrow-fighters: a word of abuse (Diomedes calls Paris "you archer" in 11.385), because archers keep safely out of the thick of the battle.

253. champions: the front rank (cf. 3.15 n.).

259–63. Agamemnon means that at council meetings (**the gleam-**

ing wine of the princes) most members do not have an automatic refill, but Idomeneus' glass is always topped up.

273. The two heroes called **Aias** are leaders, respectively, of the troops from Salamis and of the Lokrians. Although they share the same name, their contingents are quite different; and indeed the Lokrians are described (13.713–18) as light-armed troops, not wearing the bronze armor of the rest of the Greeks. Here the picture is different. The troops seem to be massed together, and the Aiantes are treated as a pair, as they also are in Book 13. It is not unlikely that the very ancient figure of Aias has, through differentiation in local legends, inspired a double for himself and that the pair of Aiantes really goes back thus to a single person. (An alternative theory has it that "Aiantes" originally meant, not the two heroes named Aias, but Telamonian Aias and his brother Teukros; so PAGE 235–38; R. Merkelbach, *Glotta* 38 [1959–60]: 268–70.)

301–9. The traditional descriptions of fighting that lie behind the *Iliad* have in general forgotten how **chariots** were used in battle. In the *Iliad*, the leaders are driven to and round the battlefield in chariots but only rarely fight from them. When a fight is imminent, they usually leap down to the ground from the chariot, which the driver then keeps at hand in case of need (cf. 226–30). Nestor's tactical advice here, for chariot fighting in formation, may show a more accurate memory of how they were used in practice in the Mycenaean Age. As he says (308), this is how earlier generations won their battles. The only parallel for massed chariot fighting in the *Iliad*, interestingly enough, is in Nestor's own story of the battle between the men of Pylos and the Epeians in 11.736–48.

319. Nestor later (7.136–56) gives a long description of this combat with **Ereuthalion.**

322. By **riders** he means those on chariots.

327. For **Menestheus,** see 2.546–56. It is interesting that he should be standing next to Odysseus, who has qualities which the later Greeks would ascribe to the Athenians. These two are not, however, associated elsewhere in the *Iliad.*

330. The **Kephallenians** are Odysseus' people (2.631).

Homer says that the troops had not yet heard that the fighting was starting again. Odysseus, however, should have known, for he was one of the marshals (3.314) of the single combat between Paris and Menelaos, and it was Pandaros' infringement of this combat that was causing the fighting to be renewed. There is here, as elsewhere, a slight ambiguity about the behavior of Odysseus, whose prudence is dwelt on lovingly by the poet. In the other, more simple, heroes, such as Agamemnon, Achilleus, and Aias, Odysseus' cleverness inspired suspicion and some dislike (339).

339. profit ... treachery. Agamemnon would not speak to any other of the leaders like this.

349. looking at him darkly. Odysseus, intelligent and self-restrained though he is, cannot let Agamemnon's remarks go unanswered. He shares with the rest the heroic sense of honor.

353. A sneering remark, suggesting that Agamemnon himself may not be up with the front-line troops when the time comes.

354. father of Telemachos. Cf. 2.260 n.

361. ideas of kindness: i.e., thoughts that are favorable to Agamemnon and the Greeks.

365–400. Diomedes, although now leading the troops from Argos, was the son of **Tydeus** of Aitolia (399). Tydeus and **Kapaneus** (father of Diomedes' friend **Sthenelos**) had been two of the seven southern Greek heroes who had spearheaded the attack on Thebes in the generation before the Trojan War. We have here, in Agamemnon's speech, references to the preliminaries of that war of the Seven against Thebes, which was the main event in the Theban (as opposed to the Trojan) cycle of legends.

Polyneikes (377), son of Oidipous, had a claim to be king of Thebes but was kept out by his brother **Eteokles** (386). The two expatriates, Polyneikes and Tydeus, married daughters of Adrastos, king of Argos, and collected an army from the Peloponnese with which to attack Thebes. The Thebans are called **Kadmeians** (385) after Kadmos, their founder.

Agamemnon's speech (370–400) takes the form of a mythological example aimed at goading Diomedes to try harder. It is composed in the common ring form (cf. 1.259–74 n.):

a	370–71	Why are you skulking, son of Tydeus?
b	372–75	Tydeus used not to skulk.
c	376–98	A story about him.
b'	399	Such was Tydeus.
a'	400	His son is inferior to him.

376–81. An attempt to explain why Mykenai, the leading city of Greece, had nothing to do with the expedition of the Seven against Thebes. The real explanation, of course, is that these were distinct cycles of legend.

383. Asopos: a river south of Thebes.

389. to try their strength with him: i.e., in athletic competitions.

390. such might did Pallas Athene give him. Athene supports those who have the positive qualities to win success. Thus she is the divine helper of Tydeus, Diomedes, Odysseus, and Achilleus.

395. The names **Autophonos** and **Polyphontes** mean, respectively, "Murderer" and "Mass Killer." This is immediate invention, of an almost comic kind. One may compare the smith Harmonides ("Son of Fitter") in 5.59, and the seer Polyidos ("Much-seeing") in 13.663.

401. Unlike Odysseus, **Diomedes** accepts the king's rebuke without answering back and reproves his friend Sthenelos for doing so. Diomedes has the qualities of the ideal junior commander; he is respectful to authority, clearheaded, immensely capable, and controlled. All the same, he does not forget this insult (see 9.34).

405–10. we are better men than our fathers. Sthenelos refers to the expedition of the Sons of the Seven, the Epigonoi, who took and destroyed Thebes (cf. 2.505) where their fathers had failed. Sthenelos and Diomedes were, of course, two of the Epigonoi; another was Euryalos, son of Mekisteus, the third of the leaders of the men of Argos (2.565). We know next to nothing of the incidents of that second expedition.

420–21. A magnificent description of Diomedes. We are being prepared for his exploits in Book 5.

422–56. Still preliminary to the battle, with several similes to add to the anticipation of the hearers.

439. Ares, the god of war, who supports the Trojans, is of non-Greek (Thracian) origin; **Athene** is the more rational goddess of Greek warfare. The allegorical figures of the next line motivate both sides.

457–544. A concentrated description of indeterminate and bloody fighting makes a background for the long *aristeia* of

Diomedes in Books 5 and 6 (for the term *aristeia*, see the introductory note to Book 5). Homer shows the even fight, with no advantage to either side, by precisely alternate killing of Trojans and Greeks. Seven die in all, numbers 1, 3, 5, and 7 being Trojans; 2, 4, and 6, Greeks. No fewer than three of the seventy-one leaders of contingents in the two catalogues of Book 2 are among those killed in this short encounter (Elephenor, Diores, Peiros).

457. Antilochos, son of Nestor, is an eager young man, suitable as the first victor.

463. Elephenor: leader of the Euboians (2.540).

467. Agenor: son of Antenor (21.545 n).

473–89. The killing of **Simoeisios** by **Aias.** This is a good example of the poet's creative imagination. The young man, born by the bank of the river, had been called after it (his father's name, Anthemion, means "flowery," a common epithet of river banks). When he dies (482), he falls like a poplar tree which lies "by the banks of a river" (487). There is a mutual interaction between the simile and details of Simoeisios' personal history.

like some black poplar (482). STRASBURGER 38–39 points out the realism of the effect of certain wounds as described in the *Iliad.* Those who fall like a tree (and there are many), i.e., stiff and unconscious, have received a blow in the top half of the body—the head or chest. So also Echepolos (462), who had been hit in the head, fell "as a tower falls."

500. He had kept horses over there in Abydos, perhaps a stud farm belonging to King Priam.

508. Pergamos: the citadel of Troy.

515. The title **Tritogeneia,** referring to Athene, is of uncertain meaning. Modern scholars connect it with marine names (Triton, Amphitrite) and think it may mean "sea-born." This would entail a story of the goddess' origin different from the one in which she is born from the head of Zeus (5.875 n.).

517. Diores: leader of the men of Elis (2.622).

520. Peiros: leader of the Thracians (cf. 2.844, where he is called Peiroös).

527. Thoas: leader of the Aitolians (2.638).

539. "Would" rather than **could** gives a more accurate sense.

BOOK FOUR

This **man** is wholly hypothetical, an imaginary observer present in the midst of the battle and protected by Athene.

BOOK FIVE

Book 5 is the first full book of fighting, and a long one at that. There is, however, none of the tedium which some may find in Books 13–15, because it is a record of positive success, dominated by the brilliant figure of Diomedes. This is his *aristeia* (i.e., the period when a single warrior dominates the battlefield, as Agamemnon also does in the first part of Book 11, and Achilleus in Book 20). He even wounds two gods—an achievement which would send a thrill of fear through the mind of a believer of old.

The following summarizes the action of the book:

1–83	General Greek successes.
84–165	Diomedes' minor victories.
166–453	Diomedes kills Pandaros and wounds Aineias and Aphrodite.
454–710	General fighting. The Trojans attack. Encounter of Sarpedon and Tlepolemos.
711–909	The goddesses intervene. With Athene's help, Diomedes wounds Ares himself.

Diomedes is in a sense a substitute for Achilleus. It is difficult to see how both could be in action together. By the time Achilleus returns in the final books, Diomedes has been wounded and is off the scene. As his personal antecedents are with the Theban, rather than the Trojan, cycle of legends (see 4.365–400 n.), many have thought that he and Sthenelos may have been late additions to the tale of Troy.

5. Sirius, the brightest star in the sky, rises in late summer. As the Greeks considered the ocean to run round the edge of a flat,

disklike earth, most of the stars, as well as the sun and moon, rise from the ocean and set into it.

29. the anger in all of them was stirred. Rather, "the spirits of all were dismayed." The death of Phegeus leads to a Trojan rout (see Appendix B, p. 280).

37–83. Before we return to Diomedes, the individual successes of six Greek leaders are recorded. They are Agamemnon, Idomeneus, Menelaos, Meriones (Idomeneus' second-in-command), Meges (2.627), and Eurypylos (2.736). By this catalogue, the poet shows the superiority of the Greeks. Their enemies are turning to flight, as is indicated by the fact that one is in his chariot (39), another is mounting his (45), and five are hit in the back (40, 56, 66, 73, 80). Compare 7.15 n., where it is shown that a similar short catalogue indicates a rout of the Greeks.

43. It is a little disconcerting to find a man called **Phaistos** being killed by Idomeneus, for Phaistos was the second city of Krete, and Idomeneus was king in the first city, Knossos. One wonders if there is any story behind this. Most probably, however, this is merely a chance association of names on the part of the poet, who has to choose a large number of minor figures, who appear once only, as victims of the greater heroes.

51, 61. Artemis herself taught Skamandrios to hunt, and Phereklos was an excellent smith because **above all others Pallas Athene had loved him.** Exceptional skill at anything was attributed to divine favor, and in Homer's language this is personalized, as if the gods were agents, like humans. Compare the statement in 2.827 that Apollo himself gave Pandaros his bow.

59. Harmonides means "Son of Fitter," a good name for a smith. Compare the names of the would-be assassins in 4.395.

60. The **smith** is Harmonides; **who** refers back to Phereklos.

65–67. It is characteristic of **Meriones** that he is responsible for some of the most unpleasant wounds in the *Iliad* (Friedrich 52). Perhaps this is a way for Homer to give a separate identity to a hero of the second rank. Other examples may be found in Book 13, at 568 and 651 (the latter a repetition of the present wound, though caused by a different weapon).

The description seems to be of surprising anatomical accuracy.

According to a note by A. R. Thompson in *Proceedings of the Royal Society of Medicine* 45 (1952): 765, "The weapon would enter through the middle of the right buttock and pass through the great sacro-sciatic notch, enter the pelvis, pass through the base of the bladder and come out under the pubic arch."

95. It was **Pandaros** who broke the truce in Book 4 by shooting Menelaos.

105. Here and in 173 Pandaros is said to come from **Lykia.** This must be different from the Lykia in the south of Asia Minor from which the allies led by Sarpedon and Glaukos came, for Pandaros' home was at the foot of Mount Ida, near Troy, and his people are called "Trojans" in 200 and 211, as well as in the catalogue (2.826).

107. drew back . . . to his chariot. Diomedes has been fighting on foot. **Sthenelos,** his friend, second-in-command, and charioteer, would have the task of keeping the chariot as close as possible, as a safeguard against some such eventuality as this.

112. The arrow was so far in that it was better for Sthenelos to pull it right through than back against the barbs.

115. For Atrytone (Athene), see 2.157.

116–17. if ever before. . . . A common form of prayer (cf. 1.39).

144–65. Diomedes kills in succession four pairs of opponents, all except the first pair being brothers. The reason for their being in *pairs* is clearly that he was catching them in their chariots (160), and the chariots were manned by two: one to hold the reins and one to fight. In the same way, Agamemnon kills three pairs of Trojans at the beginning of his *aristeia* in Book 11 (11.92–147).

148. Polyidos ("Much-seeing") is a good name for the son of a seer; in 13.663 this same name is given to another seer.

150, 158. Homer understands and can express the human tragedies caused by the war to the old people left at home. In Virgil's *Aeneid* this aspect of war outweighs all others.

166. This is our first meeting with the famous **Aineias,** apart from the entry in the Trojan catalogue (2.819–21). He is second only to Hektor among the Trojan fighters and has the advantage of a goddess mother; but he is from the minor branch of the Trojan royal family (20.215–40) and stays in the background.

186. his shoulders. The god mantles his own shoulders in mist, i.e., stands there invisible.

190. Aïdoneus: a longer form of the name Hades, god of the underworld.

192. The thought in Pandaros' mind is that, since his archery has been unsuccessful, he should change his style and fight at close quarters from a chariot like the rest. Unfortunately he has left his chariots at home. The personality of Pandaros emerges from all his words and actions as that of a foolish, blustering, and self-justifying man.

194. blankets: to keep off the dust (2.777).

200. there presumably means "in the chariot."

218. there will be no time for changing: there will be no lessening of the menace offered by Diomedes until Aineias and Pandaros go and face him.

227. while I dismount. This is the normal practice of the chariot troops: the driver keeps the chariot at hand, while the fighter dismounts to fight. On the present occasion, however, Pandaros stays on the chariot and attacks Diomedes from there.

236. The word translated **single-foot,** a common epithet of horses in the *Iliad,* alludes to the fact that a horse does not have a cloven hoof.

265–66. Ganymedes, son of Tros, was carried off to Olympos for his beauty, to act as wine-bearer to Zeus. The genealogy of the Trojan royal family is given at 20.215–40.

289. to glut.... An obscure formulaic phrase for death in battle; it is found also at 20.78 and 22.267.

290. Athene directed the spear. She had persuaded Pandaros to shoot Menelaos in the first place and had then moved smartly over to protect Menelaos from the shot; now she supervises the punishment of Pandaros.

The unusual wound is described in 291–93. Although the description gives an impression of accuracy and clarity, it is difficult to understand. Pandaros is on a higher level than Diomedes, because he is still on the chariot; but the spear, after hitting him on the bridge of the nose, passses through his mouth and comes out under his chin. The only intelligible explanation, offered already (among others) by the ancient scholia, is that

Pandaros ducked to avoid the spear. VAN DER VALK 2:139 thinks that the poet may have been distracted by a moral purpose: he wishes to have Pandaros' tongue cut because he is guilty of perjury, having shared responsibility for the truce oaths with the other leaders (3.274).

330. the lady of Kypros: Aphrodite.

333. Enyo: a goddess of war, associated with Ares, who is sometimes called by the evidently related name Enyalios.

353. Iris acts as agent of the gods, as heralds do for the kings down below. Usually it is a question of taking messages, but here she assists Aphrodite from the field and acts as her charioteer back to Olympos.

371. Dione is a feminine form of the name "Zeus"; she was an ancient wife of his, particularly connected with his worship at Dodona. She appears here as mother of Aphrodite.

374. This seems to be a playful and rather sly dig at Aphrodite, whose misdemeanors tend to take place in private.

375. A good example of a stock epithet (1.17). Aphrodite is *not* **sweetly laughing** at this moment.

382–415. Dione's speech is an example of the use of mythological examples for consolation. Three parallels give a cumulative effect. The plan of the speech is:

a	382	You must endure your pain.
b	383–84	Many of the gods have endured pain for similar reasons.
c	385–402	Three examples.
d	403–15	Comments on the foolhardiness of mortals who cause such pain to gods.

It is interesting that the three examples given (of Ares, Hera, and Hades being hurt by mortals) are to all intents and purposes unique to this passage. It makes one suspect that they were invented, or at least modified, by the poet for the purpose of this speech.

385–91. Otos and **Ephialtes** were young giants, who never grew to adulthood but nevertheless shook the gods on Olympos. Here they are said to have shut Ares up in a bronze jar (better than **cauldron**). This seems to be a fairytale motif (compare djinns shut up in bottles), as is the theme of the stepmother who thwarts the children (389). **Hermes** too is thematically the right person to "steal Ares away," for he was patron of thieves and no mean exponent of their art himself.

That a god could actually have perished (388) is carrying anthropomorphism rather far; contrast 402.

392–404. son of Amphitryon: Herakles. The woundings of Hera and Hades by arrows from Herakles may have taken place on the same occasion. At 11.689–90 Nestor tells of an attack on Pylos by Herakles, and a scholion there says that "three gods supported Neleus (Nestor's father, the king of Pylos)—Poseidon, Hera, and Hades, and two supported Herakles—Athene and Zeus." Other authorities also mention a fight between Herakles and Hades at Pylos (Pindar, *Ninth Olympian* 33; Apollodorus, *Bibl.* 2.7.3; Pausanias 6.25.2).

It is possible, however, that in the case of the fight with Hades, "Pylos" did not originally mean the city of Neleus at all but simply "the gate," i.e., the gate of hell (in Greek, *pulē* = "gate"). The idea that Herakles fought death himself appears in the tale of Alkestis (in Euripides' play) and in one of the labors—the bringing-up of the dog Kerberos from the underworld (8.367–68). There is probably deep confusion here (see Nilsson 203).

Paiëon (401) is the god of healing, later identified with Apollo.

406–15. poor fool. Dione makes an essentially Greek point: a person who fights against the gods does not live to a peaceful old age. The reference to Diomedes' mourning wife is an evident threat; but although various stories were told of Diomedes' experiences after he returned home, none of them conforms to the picture in Dione's words here. We must take her to be describing what *can* happen to those who attack the gods, not what *will* happen to Diomedes.

408. Compare Gray's *Elegy*, "No children run to lisp their sire's return / Or climb his knees the envied kiss to share."

412. Aigialeia: Diomedes' wife; daughter of Adrastos, king of Argos. As Tydeus also married a daughter of Adrastos (4.365–400 n.), Diomedes married his aunt.

422. The reference is, of course, to Aphrodite's encouragement of Helen to go with Paris. Behind the hatred of the Trojans by Hera and Athene lies their resentment at the Judgment of Paris, when he had chosen Aphrodite as the most beautiful of the three goddesses, and she, in turn, had promised him the most beautiful woman in the world as his wife. This Judgment of Paris is specifically mentioned in the *Iliad* only once (24.28–30), but it is implicit in other situations, such as this.

432. We now return to the situation as it was in 346.

436–42. three times. A threefold attack is a repeated theme, used exactly like this in 16.702–9, when Patroklos attacks the walls of Troy and is pushed back by the same defender, Apollo.

447. Leto: the divine mother of Apollo and Artemis.

453. guard-skins: probably smaller and lighter shields, with a fringe of tassels hanging down from them.

460. Not so much **alighted on** as "sat on."

462. Akamas. See 2.844.

471–92. Sarpedon's speech to Hektor.

471. in abuse. It is a repeated theme for Sarpedon or Glaukos, representing the allies, to speak harshly to Hektor, claiming that the Trojans leave all the fighting to them; cf. 16.537–40.

480. This line has a powerful double effect: (*a*) It produces a personal sympathy for Sarpedon in the reader, which will be increased by his great words and deeds in Book 12 and his death in Book 16; (*b*) by the mention of his wife and son, it prepares the way for the scene of farewell between Hektor and his wife and baby son at the end of Book 6. This foreshadowing of the fate of a major character by what is said of a minor character is one of the special features of the *Iliad*'s narrative technique. This particular effect is repeated at 688 below.

481. The point is a general one; Sarpedon has great possessions, which his absence makes vulnerable.

490–92. Awkwardly expressed. Hektor should (*a*) be placatory to the allies, (*b*) be steadfast in the fighting, and (*c*) by these actions escape the sort of personal criticism that Sarpedon is at this moment directing at him.

499. threshing floors are sacred. Demeter, goddess of the corn, herself separates the wheat from the chaff. Winnowing is done on a windy day, for the wheat is thrown into the air, and the chaff, which is lighter, is blown away by the wind. The point of the simile is merely the dustiness of the Greek army (502).

510. as he saw that Pallas Athene: not the reason in fact given by Apollo when he spoke to Ares in 455–59.

542. Diokles of Pherai (here **Phere,** 543) appears also in the *Odyssey*, giving hospitality to Telemachos at the half-way stage of. his journey across the Peloponnese, from Nestor at Pylos to Menelaos at Sparta (*Od.* 3.488 and 15.186). Such consistency between the two epics suggests a fixing of detail in the epic tradition, so that even a minor figure like Diokles appears to be a historical reality.

565. Antilochos, young son of Nestor, is an effective fighter among the younger heroes. This passage adds to our knowledge of the characters. We learn that Menelaos is no match for Aineias and that therefore his kindheartedness (561) has made him foolhardy; we learn also that the other Greeks kept something of a watch on Menelaos in the battle, no doubt because they liked him, but also because they could not afford to lose him (4.172).

So Menelaos' life is saved by Antilochos. This should be remembered when we read of the clash between these two at the end of the chariot race in the funeral games in Book 23, when Menelaos accuses Antilochos of cheating in the race (23.566–613 n.).

576. Pylaimenes. See 2.851.

580. Antilochos' alertness pays off, and he gets the horses (588–89). He has the same success in 13.396–401.

586–87. The Greek text suggests, more clearly than Lattimore's here, that the body of Mydon stood upright on its head for some time until the horses trampled it down. This has been much discussed, and medical writers have spoken of the rare effects of rigidity through shock which may accompany violent death. Even if this is so, however, the picture of the body standing on its head is fantastic and unrealistic (FRIEDRICH 13–16).

612. Amphios, son of Selagos, who lived in Paisos, is not to be confused with Amphios, son of Merops, one of whose towns was Apaisos (2.828–31). It is probably another example of chance association of names in the poet's mind (cf. 43 n.).

BOOK FIVE

628–98. Interest is added to this fight between **Tlepolemos** and **Sarpedon** by the provenance of the two opponents. Tlepolemos was the leader of a newly founded Achaian colony on the island of Rhodes (2.653–70); Sarpedon was king of the Lykians, on the mainland opposite Rhodes. Hostility between the two was natural in their homeland; and many have thought that their fight here at Troy is the result of a transfer by the *Iliad* poet from some other poem.

Speeches of intimidation (lines 633–54) before beginning the fight are common.

631. the own son and the son's son. Sarpedon was son of Zeus (6.199); Tlepolemos, as son of Herakles, was Zeus's grandson.

640. on a time. Herakles had attacked and destroyed Troy long before Agamemnon's army came. Laomedon, king of Troy, had promised Herakles the famous horses (265–67) as a reward if he saved his daughter, Hesione, from the sea monster (cf. 20.145). But when Herakles fulfilled his side of the bargain, Laomedon refused the reward.

656. in a single moment. The mutual hatred between these two seems to be shown by the fact that they throw simultaneously, disdaining self-defense. Usually the fighters take turns.

684–88. A speech to Hektor balances Sarpedon's earlier speech (472–92). Sarpedon's attitude is different now, but he still takes the opportunity to mention his wife and baby son at home (480 n.). Hektor no more replies here than he did there.

702. Ares went with the Trojans. It is worth noticing the implications of divine activity in this passage. Even a modern writer could say, "The god of war was on the side of the Trojans," but Homeric poetry takes that sort of metaphorical statement and actualizes it, so that an anthropomorphic Ares accompanies the Trojan attack. The poet can then say (703–4), "Whom first and whom last did *Hektor and Ares* slay?" and even (842) show Ares in process of personally stripping the armor from a Greek victim.

722–32. The light-weight chariot was taken to pieces for storing. These lines describe its assembly. As this is a chariot of the gods, it has metal, often precious metal, where earthly chariots would use wood or leather, and has a larger number of spokes in its wheels and of handrails on the car. The **felly** (724) is the rim of the wheel; the **running-rim** (725) is like a tire.

738–42. aegis. Homer attempts to describe the terrible aegis (cf. 1.202). It is not at all clear how we are to envisage Terror, Hatred, etc., as represented on the aegis, if this is in fact what the poet means. The Gorgon's head (741), however, was a common design for the center of a shield; compare the shield of Agamemnon in 11.36–37 and the note there.

The **Gorgon** was Medousa, whose face turned people to stone. Perseus killed her, cut off her head, used it for vengeance on his persecutor Polydektes, and then gave it to his protectress Athene, to be placed on her shield.

743–44. For the **horns** on the helmet, see 3.362. The **sheets** were metal disks attached to the front of the helmet for greater protection. As to the meaning of **wrought with the fighting men of a hundred cities,** it escapes understanding, unless this was some kind of pictorial design on the helmet.

749–51. The gates of heaven are formed by the clouds (called **the dense darkness** here) and the guardians of the gates are the **Hours,** the goddesses of the seasons. This makes some sense meteorologically.

760. Kypris: Aphrodite (cf. 330).

777. ambrosia: not explicitly said to be the food of the gods in the *Iliad*, although it is implied in 19.347–48; this line shows that it is thought of as a plant. It is used as a supernatural cleansing and preserving agent in 14.171, 16.670, and 19.39.

778. There is comedy here in the description of the delicate little steps taken by the goddesses.

785. This is the only mention of **Stentor** in Homer; from it the power of his voice has become proverbial.

789. The **Dardanian gates** must be the same as the Skaian gates, the main gateway of Troy.

795. the wound that Pandaros made. This is the wound Diomedes received in 98. The strap of the hand-grip shield would go over the right shoulder.

800–813. Athene's speech, which is closely parallel to that of Agamemnon to Diomedes in 4.370–400, uses a mythological example (Diomedes' father, Tydeus) to encourage him to fight harder. This speech, too, is in the familiar ring form. LOHMANN 14 divides it as follows:

a	800	Tydeus fathered a son unlike himself.
b	801	Tydeus was small, but a fighter.
c	802	Even when I *forbade* him to fight....
d	803–8	The story.
c′	809–10	I *urge* you to fight.
b′	811–12	But you are either tired or afraid.
a′	813	You cannot be Tydeus' son.

801. It is interesting that Tydeus should be described as **small**. Pindar even makes Herakles a small man in the *Fourth Isthmian* 57. Odysseus (3.193–94) is not so much small as stocky.

803–8. went by himself. For more information about this embassy of Tydeus, see 4.382–98. He challenged the young Thebans (807) to athletic contests; this would not be clear from this version alone.

805. invited suggests what is not in the Greek; she says she *told* him to relax and not annoy the Thebans.

818. orders. Diomedes is referring to her words in 129–32.

831–34. Victory in war favors now one side, now the other. Turn that into anthropomorphic terms, and Ares becomes shifty, false, unreliable.

841. For **single-foot**, see 236 n.

842. Ares, as god of war, has a hand in death in battle; here the situation is actualized. Compare 702 n.

845. the helm of Death: the "cap of darkness" which makes the wearer invisible—a folktale feature.

851. Ares is on foot: Diomedes and Athene are in the chariot. So it is over *their* horses, not **his**, that Ares lunged.

864–65. The phenomenon is not clear. Most suitable as an image of the departure of Ares would be a whirlwind or tornado, which may indeed be associated with the conditions here described.

875. you brought forth this ... **daughter.** Presumably here and in 880 the poet is alluding to the legend that Athene was born from the head of Zeus, so that he was her sole parent.

885–87. Ares' alternatives are a little confused. As he is immortal, he cannot die (cf. 388).

893. I am broken by her arguments. A closer translation would be, "only with difficulty do I overcome her in argument."

894. Hera was Ares' own mother, and yet she had instigated this painful experience for him.

898. The word translated **gods of the bright sky** is the same as that translated "Uranian gods" in 373 and really means "sons of Heaven (Ouranos)." In this case, however, it makes better sense to refer the allusion to the true sons of Ouranos, the Titans, who, with their king, Kronos, are living in banishment in Tartaros, far below the earth (8.13, 478–81).

899. Paiëon. See 401.

908 = 4.8.

BOOK SIX

Greek successes continue in Book 6. Helenos, the Trojan seer, persuades Hektor to return to Troy while the rest hold back the Greeks, so that he may ask the women of the city to make special prayers to Athene for help. While Hektor is on his way, Diomedes and Glaukos meet in the battle, discover that they are old family friends, and exchange armor. Hektor, in separate and balanced episodes, sees the three women of Troy—his mother, Hekabe; Helen, the cause of the war (at home with her husband, Paris); and finally his wife, Andromache. This scene, with the baby frightened by his father's helmet, adds a new dimension to the epic. The plight of the women and children in the city is sympathetically brought to our attention, and Hektor's death is clearly foreshadowed. At the end, Paris catches up to Hektor as he is leaving the city, and the two brothers sally forth together.

4. **Xanthos** = Skamandros (20.74).

5–36. Here we have a catalogue of Greek successes, like that at the beginning of Book 5, and with the same purpose: to show the natural Greek superiority. No fewer than ten Greek leaders have personal triumphs in these lines, three at some length—Aias, Diomedes, and Euryalos (the third Argive leader, 2.565), and then seven very briefly—Polypoites (the Lapith, 2.740), Odysseus, Teukros (half-brother of Aias), Antilochos, Agamemnon, Leïtos (Boiotian leader, 2.494), and Eurypylos (2.736). Diomedes kills a pair in a chariot, and Euryalos two pairs—an indication, as always, that the Trojans are running away.

8. **Akamas:** see 5.462.

12–19. Diomedes' victory gives the poet the opportunity for a pathetic reference to the home life of his victim before the war. Kalesios, the charioteer, has a name with means "Inviter," suitable to the servant of such a hospitable man.

22–23. Abarbare and **Boukolion** are names that suggest they have some story behind them, but they are never heard of elsewhere. Assuming that Laomedon is the famous king, Boukolion was Priam's illegitimate elder brother.

37–65. Menelaos is about to take Adrestos prisoner but is stopped from doing so by his elder brother, Agamemnon. Thus we see more of the characters of these two: Menelaos kindly and a little weak (cf. 5.565), and Agamemnon very concerned with his brother's quarrel, and with an insensitiveness perhaps inevitable in one bearing the responsibilities of commander-in-chief. Adrestos bears a famous name, that of Adrastos, king of Argos (5.412), with the Ionic *e* for *a*. He is not further identified, either by patronymic or place of origin.

66. Nestor is the natural choice for tactical advice.

86. but you, Hektor, go back to the city. It may be, and has been, objected that this is no time for Hektor to leave the army, and another messenger could have been sent. The aim of the poet is of course to get him back to Troy, for the sake of the scene with Andromache.

88. temple of Athene. The Trojans worship the same gods as the Greeks. A special function of Athene was as tutelary goddess of cities (see 305). It is therefore not surprising that there should be a temple of Athene on the acropolis of Troy, even though she is so pro-Greek in the *Iliad*.

91. the great house: Priam's palace, not the temple.

113–15. Some difficulty has been caused by Hektor's words here, in that they differ from Helenos' instructions in 86–97 (which are what Hektor in fact follows in Troy). The differences are not important. Public statements are for public consumption; Hektor merely generalizes what he intends to do, and he chooses words that will not alarm the troops.

117. If the shield hit both **neck** and **ankles,** it was probably the old Mycenaean body shield, not the round shield of normal use (see

7.219 n.). Hektor will have slung it round his back by its strap as he went.

119–236. The famous scene of chivalry between **Glaukos** and **Diomedes**, two opponents in the battle who find that they have family ties of friendship.

127–43. The statement of respect for the gods contains a mythological example, and the whole is composed in the now familiar ring form. LOHMANN 12 convincingly gives this example no fewer than nine parts:

a	127	Threat of death.
b	128	But if you are one of the gods...
c	129	I will not fight with a god.
d	130–31	Lykourgos, who did so, did not live long.
e	132–39	The story of Lykourgos.
d'	139–40	He did not live long, because the gods hated him.
c'	141	So I would not fight with a god.
b'	142	But if you are a man...
a'	143	Threat of death.

Nothing could be more exact.

Lykourgos was a king of Thrace, who tried to drive the new Bacchic religion out of his country, as Pentheus did from Thebes (see Euripides' *Bacchae*). That he chased the "nurses" of Dionysos down from the mountain, striking them with an ox goad, and that Dionysos himself took refuge with Thetis in the sea, is a strange and primitive tale, which seems to display a familiarity with some of the stories connected with the cult of Dionysos (see W. K. C. Guthrie, *The Greeks and Their Gods*, pp. 161–62).

The nurses (**fosterers**) of Dionysos (132) were the nymphs of the sacred mountain, Nysa; they looked after the baby Dionysos (*Homeric Hymn* 26.3).

The **wands** (134) are the *thyrsoi* of Dionysiac worship. The **ox-goad** must be connected with the bull/god identification in that religion.

146. As is the generation of leaves... A famous statement of the brevity and insignificance of human life.

150–211. Glaukos, having pointed out the unimportance of family trees, proceeds nevertheless to recount his own genealogy at length. This gives the impression of nervousness, as if he is not too keen to bring the conversation to an end. Aineias behaves in a very similar manner in Book 20, when, unlucky enough to meet Achilleus in battle, he recounts his family history in an apparently nervous way. The present line appears there as 20.213.

Several cities were called Ephrya (**Ephyre**, 152; cf. 2.659); this one is Korinth. The description **in the corner of Argos** seems odd to us, for Korinth lies in the key position on the road which connects the Peloponnese with northern Greece.

Sisyphos (153) was one of the great sinners whose eternal punishment is described in the *Odyssey*, Book 11. His actual offense is obscure, but his reputation in legend is that of the craftiest of men (as here). **Aiolos** (154) was the ancestor of the Aiolian race.

The family tree is as follows:

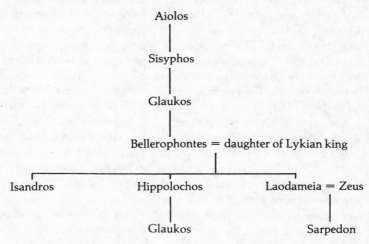

Aiolos
|
Sisyphos
|
Glaukos
|
Bellerophontes = daughter of Lykian king
|
Isandros — Hippolochos — Laodameia = Zeus
| |
Glaukos   Sarpedon

156–205. Glaukos now tells the story of **Bellerophontes** (later known as Bellerophon). It has been noticed that the tale is told in an *allusive* way, with many details and explanations not supplied, as if this is based on a longer version known to the poet. The same impression is given elsewhere in the *Iliad* where a mythological story outside the scope of the Trojan War is told, notably in the tale of Meleagros in Book 9. Points about which the poet leaves us in ignorance are: the name of the king of Lykia (173); the name of his daughter, whom Bellerophontes married (192); the divine parentage of the Chimaira (180); and the cause of the gods' hatred of Bellerophontes (200) and of Artemis' anger against his daughter (205). Moreover the winged horse, Pegasos, is not mentioned in this version, whether through intentional omission or not (181 n.).

157–59. Bellerophontes in Korinth was a vassal of **Proitos** of Argos. (In the Catalogue of Ships, Korinth was subject to the king of Mykenai.)

160–66. The attempt by a queen on the virtue of a handsome young man, followed by a false accusation to her husband when she is refused, is a common folktale motif (Potiphar's wife and Joseph; Phaidra and Hippolytos; Hippolyte, wife of Akastos, and Peleus).

168–69. symbols,... inscribed in a folding tablet. This is the only reference to writing in Homer. The recent decipherment of the Linear B tablets from Knossos and Pylos encourages us to believe that here, in the Bellerophontes story, we have an authentic memory from the Mycenaean Age. The poet was no doubt himself aware of the art of alphabetical writing, which the Greeks borrowed from the Phoenicians in the eighth century; but it would have been too much of an anachronism to describe such an innovation in heroic verse. The vague reference here (**murderous symbols**) reflects rather a dim memory, preserved in the poetic tradition, of the Mycenaean syllabic script.

172. There was a river **Xanthos** in Lykia as well as at Troy.

174. Nine days. It was normal practice to entertain and feed the guest before you asked him questions (as can be seen on various occasions in the *Odyssey*). Nine days seems somewhat exaggerated, but this is a royal court, and an important guest.

179–95. Further folktale motifs appear. The young prince is set three impossible tasks; and when he has successfully completed them, he is rewarded with the hand of the princess and half the kingdom. In the middle of all this the poet has added a more heroic theme, the ambush set to kill the hero, which he himself slays instead (a theme used also for Tydeus at 4.391–98).

181. The **Chimaira** is the only composite creature in Homer, unless one counts the centaurs, who are not actually described. It is worth noting that the animal is not Greek but is from the East, where such things were commoner. The rather fuller description in Hesiod (*Theogony* 319–24), followed by representations in ancient art, shows an animal with three heads—a lion's in front, a snake's for a tail, and a goat's growing from the middle of its back.

Homer does not mention the winged horse, Pegasos, which in other versions gave Bellerophontes an advantage in his fight with this monster.

184. The **Solymoi** were, according to Herodotus (1.173), the original inhabitants of the country, displaced by the Lykians when they came.

186. The third task was to fight the **Amazons**, female warriors. They are mentioned also at 3.184–89, where see note.

191. stock of the god. According to the genealogy we have been given (155), Bellerophontes was the son of a human father, Glaukos. Elsewhere, however, in the myths, his father is said to have been Poseidon.

200–202. The description of the later fate of Bellerophontes evidently interrupts the history of his three children. There is no better place for these lines, however. It seems that they are an insertion by somebody, whether the poet or another, who, not wishing to omit the final fate of the hero, chose an awkward moment for it rather than none at all (cf. the intrusive lines about the final fate of Niobe, 24.614–17).

It is not explained why he was **hated by all the immortals.** Fortunately Pindar (in the *Thirteenth Olympian* and the *Seventh Isthmian*) gives us sufficient information. Bellerophontes fell into the pattern of Lykourgos (130–40) and others (cf. Thamyris, 2.594–600; Niobe, 24.602–9) who, through forgetfulness of their own insignificance as mortals, entered into competition with the gods. In a fine allegorical image, like that of Ikaros flying too high and too near the sun, Bellerophontes is said to have tried to fly Pegasos to heaven; he was unseated by Zeus and wandered about alone and mad.

The Aleian plain was in Kilikia, in the south of Asia Minor.

BOOK SIX

205. Artemis killed the daughter. Artemis is regularly the goddess responsible for the sudden death of women. Why she was angry is not stated; perhaps it was because of Laodameia's presumption in having been loved by Zeus.

208. to be always among the bravest . . . : a fine statement of the competitive heroic code. The line recurs in 11.783, as alleged instruction to Achilleus from his father.

215. guest friend. In those far-distant days of separate communities, in which a stranger might be in considerable danger, some security was provided by a system of family friendship, or "guest friendship." The tie of having been entertained in somebody's house, and of having exchanged gifts, was remembered into the following generations, and even the actual gifts exchanged were remembered, as here.

216. Oineus was Diomedes' grandfather, king of Aitolia. Tydeus (222) had been killed in the expedition of the Seven against Thebes (4.365–400).

234–36. gold for bronze. Modern critics have found it disconcerting that the chivalrous meeting between Glaukos and Diomedes should end with the intrusion of such materialistic considerations. But in fact the Homeric heroes *are* materialists and prize the accumulation of property both for its own sake and for the honor and status it brings (compare Phoinix' final argument to Achilleus in 9.602–5). Thus to get far the better of the exchange of armor is a form of success for Diomedes. The phrase **Zeus stole away the wits** implies delusion, infatuation, "Ate" (see 8.236–37 n.).

237–529. Hektor's visit to Troy. There is a balance in this composition among the three scenes which it contains. Hektor meets in turn the three women of Troy: his mother, Hekabe, in 251–85; Helen (and Paris) in 313–68; and Andromache in 394–502. Each of the women, in her own way, tries to get Hektor to relax (258–62, 354–58, 431–34), and to each he replies as befits their relationship.

244. Fifty is the traditional number of the sons of Priam, an Eastern king. Not all of them, of course, are the children of Hekabe (24.495–97). Twenty-two of Priam's sons and two of his sons-in-law are named in the *Iliad*.

72

252. Laodike was one of Priam's married daughters (3.124) and so lived in one of the chambers mentioned in 247–50.

284–85. Hektor heartily dislikes Paris. Hekabe, who is Paris' mother too, does not reply to this.

289. Sidon: the chief town of the Phoenicians.

298. Antenor's wife, **Theano,** priestess of Athene, is daughter of Kisseus, king of Thrace. Later mythology made Hekabe also a daughter of Kisseus and so sister of Theano; but in the *Iliad* Hekabe's father is called Dymas (16.718).

317. It is clear from this that neither Paris nor Hektor lived in the palace of Priam, where there were fifty rooms (244) for the fifty sons. They had built themselves separate houses nearby.

319. eleven-cubit-long spear. Eleven cubits is about sixteen feet. This is a possible length for a thrusting spear but too long for a throwing spear (see LORIMER 261).

321. The self-centered Paris is moodily handling his armor. He has been in his own room ever since he was spirited away by Aphrodite after losing the single combat with Menelaos in Book 3.

333. scolded me rightly, not beyond measure. Cf. 3.59 n.

342. Hektor has had enough of Paris.

344. Helen is fairly free with self-criticism (cf. 3.180).

350. No doubt partly a reaction to Hektor himself.

382–87. The style here is typical of popular poetry. *Question:* Is it A, or B? *Answer:* No, it is not A, nor is it B, but it is C. Similarly, Athene and Diomedes in 5.810–21. (See KAKRIDIS 108–9.)

393. So Hektor was not going up on to the wall or tower to find Andromache but was proceeding straight out to the plain, after failing to find her at home. She left her place on the wall and came running to meet him.

397. Plakos was a spur of Mount Ida, south of Troy. So these Kilikians are far away from Kilikia, in the very south of Asia Minor. Compare Pandaros' Lykians (5.105).

414. Achilleus had commanded expeditions against towns near Troy. For this one, against Thebe, in which Chryseis was also taken captive, see 1.366.

419–20. The activity of mountain **nymphs** comes as something of a surprise in such a realistic story. WILAMOWITZ 313 deduced that the poet is describing a topographical feature known in the poet's own day as the Grave of Eëtion, a mound with elm trees round it.

427–28. Compare 205 n. Andromache's mother would naturally go back to her own father when her married home ceased to exist. It would be her **father** who paid the ransom.

433. The **fig tree** is mentioned also in 11.167 and 22.145.

435. to storm it. We hear no more of such an attack on the city by the Greeks. Probably the whole idea is a momentary invention by the poet, to give Andromache an excuse for asking Hektor to stay near the city.

441. shame is a sensitivity to what *other people* will say. The characters in the *Iliad* are much less concerned with what is objectively right or wrong than with their standing in the eyes of others, i.e., with their honor. (See E. R. Dodds, *The Greeks and the Irrational*, pp. 17–18.)

447–49. Said also by Agamemnon in 4.163–65.

456. Argos here is perhaps just Greece, not (as often) the Peloponnese. Of the two springs, **Hypereia** was in Thessaly (2.734), while **Messeis** was either also in Thessaly (so Strabo 432) or at Therapnai, near Sparta (Pausanias 3.20.1).

501. Hektor's household mourns him while he is still alive; and the reader gets the impression that this is the last farewell between Hektor and Andromache. In fact it is not so, for Hektor returns to Troy at 7.310, and there is a truce at the end of Book 7. From the beginning of Book 8, however, Hektor does not again return to Troy.

503–29. The poet does not choose to end the book on the note of family sorrow. With a strong contrast, we turn to the excited and selfish figure of Paris, who has done as he was asked, and summoned up the energy to return to the battle.

506–11. The simile of the high-spirited horse galloping into the fields is used in exactly the same words for the return of Hektor in 15.263–68. This is a good example of the effect of formulaic composition. It is incorrect to assume that one of the passages is an imitation of the other; the poet has simply used the same material on two occasions.

518–19. Paris thinks only of himself and tries by this unnecessary self-criticism to improve his brother's opinion of him. Hektor in reply speaks more kindly, realizing that Paris has been hurt by his criticisms in 326 ff. This is all very human.

BOOK SEVEN

In Book 7, after Hektor and Paris sally forth together from the city, the first day of fighting, which began in Book 2, comes to an end with a challenge issued by Hektor to fight any Greek, and his consequent duel with Aias. The book ends with a truce for the burial of the dead, during which the Greeks take the opportunity to build a fortification round their camp.

4-5. Events which cannot easily be explained, such as natural phenomena (a storm, or, as here, a change in wind direction) are automatically ascribed to a god.

8. We learn more of this **Areïthoös**, "the club-man," in 138–46, below. There is a chronological difficulty about his having a **son** at Troy (see 148 n.).

9. Arne: a town in Boiotia (2.507).

15. The phrase **as he leapt up behind his fast horses** implies that the Greeks in their turn have started to fly. Homer intends to give the impression of Trojan success by this indication, as by the three victories in lines 8–16, all from the same side.

22. The **oak tree** was a feature of the plain, near the Skaian gates of Troy (6.237).

31. you refers to Athene and Hera, the two goddesses who favor the Greeks.

34. Worker from afar: see 1.9–10 n.

44. Helenos, Hektor's brother, has prophetic powers.

52-53. it is not your destiny yet to die. There are those who have thought that this private information detracts from the courageousness of Hektor's challenge, but they reckon without the uncertainty that is inevitably attached to such communications.

59. Gods may take the shape of birds; e.g., in 14.290 and several times in the *Odyssey*.

70. The **oaths** are those made in Book 3, at the beginning of the fighting on this day, in preparation for the duel of Paris and Menelaos. They have come to nothing because (*a*) Paris was saved from imminent death by Aphrodite and (*b*) Pandaros treacherously broke the truce by shooting Menelaos (beginning of Book 4).

86. the broad passage of Helle: the Hellespont.

94. at long last Menelaos. Menelaos feels a responsibility, as it is on his behalf that the war is being fought. However, he is as much aware as the others that he is one of the weaker fighters and thus no match for Hektor. This explains the asperity of his remarks.

106. The Greek leaders protect Menelaos (cf. 5.565), as their reason for being at Troy would disappear if they lost him. Agamemnon's concern is more personal, being that of an elder brother (4.154).

113–14. Although Hektor is a wildly attacking fighter, to whom even Diomedes may give way (5.605), this assertion looks more like an invention to suit Agamemnon's present speech than a statement of fact.

123–60. Nestor, as on other occasions (cf. 1.254–84) supports a speech of advice with a reminiscence of his own heroic achievements in youth. It looks very much as if, against a background of saga material (the legend of Areïthoös, the club-man), Nestor's own exploit is ad hoc invention to suit the purpose of the present speech.

125–28. Peleus, father of Achilleus, was king of the Myrmidons; the title **horseman** is given to heroes of the older generation. The occasion of this alleged conversation was the visit of Nestor and Odysseus, when they were recruiting the army for Troy (11.768–69).

129–60. The mythological example is, as often, in ring form— here in seven parts, as there is a story within a story:

a	129–31	All of you are afraid of Hektor.
b	132–35	I wish I were young again.
c	136–37	Ereuthalion, the champion of our opponents once, had the armor of Areïthoös.
d	138–47	Story of the death of Areïthoös.

c'	148–56	Ereuthalion now had his armor, and challenged us to fight. I killed him.
b'	156–58	I wish I were young again.
a'	159–60	All of you are afraid of Hektor.

131. and the life breath: better, *"that* the life breath..."; this would be Peleus' prayer if he heard of the present disgrace.

134–35. The location of the rivers **Keladon** and **Iardanos,** as of the town **Pheia,** is uncertain. Presumably they were somewhere on the frontier between the territories of Pylos and Arkadia.

142. This **Lykourgos** is not the king of Thrace mentioned in 6.130 but an Arkadian king (Pausanias 8.4.10).

146. the armour Ares had given him. The statement that Ares himself had given Areïthoös his armor need not be taken as literally true. It is a more or less figurative way of saying that Areïthoös was a great warrior. Compare the statement in 2.827 that Apollo had given Pandaros his bow.

148. It all seems very long ago. Lykourgos killed Areïthoös and then, when he grew old, gave his armor to his squire Ereuthalion. Nestor killed Ereuthalion in his first youth (153) and is now old. At the lowest computation it must be fifty years since the death of Areïthoös, and it could be much more. Thus fifty is the minimum age for Menesthios, his son, who was killed in line 8. The explanation of course is that Homer does not care too much about such details.

162–68. A catalogue of the chief fighters of the Greeks in the absence of Achilleus.

179–80. We may notice the popular "ranking order" of the leading Greeks in the absence of Achilleus, and particularly that Agamemnon, who has weaknesses as a commander-in-chief, is nevertheless considered one of the three best fighters. In the course of the *Iliad*, all three—Aias, Diomedes, and Agamemnon—are shown to be at least a match for Hektor (see 11.360 n.).

195–99. These five lines were considered spurious by all three of the Alexandrian scholars who dealt with the text of Homer: Zenodotus, Aristophanes of Byzantium, and Aristarchus. Their reason seems merely subjective, based on the apparent inconsistency in Aias' words. There is no reason why we should follow them. Aias first asks the Achaians to pray silently to Zeus, for fear that they may seem to the Trojans to be afraid of the outcome. He then changes his mind, in a perfectly natural way, and claims that he does not care what the Trojans think.

211. wall: i.e., defense.

219. carrying like a wall his shield. This formula is used three times in the *Iliad* (at 11.485 and 17.128 as well as here), always of Aias. The reference is to much older armor, and indeed an older style of fighting, than that described in the *Iliad*. Early Mycenaean representations (mostly on objects found in the shaft graves at Mykenai) show a huge body shield, shaped like a half-cylinder or figure-of-eight, which protected, by itself, the whole body of the fighter. With this equipment no breastplate or other defensive armor (except perhaps a helmet) would be worn. The warrior in effect carried a wall around with him and fought from behind it. What is of particular interest is that the evidence suggests that the body shield went out of use some *two hundred years before even the supposed date of the Trojan War.* Somehow the memory of it survived in this phrase, associated only with the Telamonian Aias. This suggests (*a*) the tenacity of the formulaic phraseology and (*b*) that Aias was not originally connected with the Trojan War but was a hero of a previous age.

The body shield seems to be alluded to on three other occasions in the *Iliad*. In 6.117, Hektor's shield, slung round his back, hit his neck and ankles as he walked; in a scene in Book 8 (267–334), Teukros, the archer, operates from behind the protection of Aias' shield; and in 15.645 the unfortunate Periphetes trips on the lower rim of his shield, "which reached to his feet."

In spite of this accumulation of evidence, it is clear that the poet was not describing something he knew. In the coming duel, Aias' shield is given a central knob or boss (267), which implies an ordinary round shield.

220. Such a famous shield seems to the poet to need the name of a particular craftsman. **Tychios** is evidently, however, an invented name, for it just means "Maker"; cf. the smith Harmonides ("Son of Fitter") in 5.59.

251. Throughout the duel Aias outdoes Hektor at every stage. There is not the least doubt who is the superior fighter.

274. The **heralds,** who have been acting as umpires, bring the duel to an end before Hektor is seriously hurt. It is better that this chivalrous episode should end in politeness, like the Glaukos/ Diomedes meeting in Book 6.

277. It is the Trojan herald, **Idaios,** who proposes that they stop fighting. This is in accordance with Homer's Greek patriotism.

299–305. glorious presents. It is normal in the heroic world to exchange gifts on an occasion like this. They will serve to keep alive the memory of it in time to come.

322. the chine's portion. The continuous piece of meat from the backbone, the chine, was always considered the portion of honor at a feast.

323–482. From here to the end of the book, what has been a clear and simple narrative becomes at some points imprecise and obscure. Apart from some awkwardnesses of expression, three major problems have been much discussed:

1. In 334–35 a unique proposal is made for the preservation of the ashes of the dead, and their eventual transportation back to Greece.
2. No very satisfactory reason is given for the building of a defensive wall round the Greek camp at this time in the tenth year of the war (337–43).
3. The poet is untypically careless about the passage of time, in that a truce is made of uncertain duration, and the normally explicit sequence of days and nights is short-circuited in 432–33.

These difficulties are discussed in the notes on the relevant lines.

325. Nestor is typically the counselor, the natural one to suggest any new action. Compare 9.53, 96; 10.204.

334–35. carry the bones back to a man's children. The pathetic preservation of the ashes of the dead in urns, so that they can eventually be taken back to their own homes and families, is mentioned nowhere else in the *Iliad,* not even in the description, later in this book, of the carrying-out of these proposals of Nestor (430–41). Patroklos' bones are collected, it is true, from his funeral pyre in 23.252; but that is so that they can be kept for later burial with the bones of Achilleus after his death, not for transport home. Moreover, as the funeral pyre is to be a common one (336), it would not be possible to distinguish each man's bones.

In view of these facts, Aristarchus condemned these lines, and he has been followed in this by many modern critics. The extreme position is taken by Page, who sees here one of the latest, if not the very latest, of the post-Homeric additions to the *Iliad*, containing in fact an allusion to a specifically Athenian practice, instituted probably in the year 464 B.C., of bringing home for burial the ashes of those killed on campaigns abroad (PAGE 323, following an article by F. Jacoby).

That the lines are illogical cannot be denied. The argument that they were composed under the influence of an Athenian custom instituted in the fifth century, however, raises more problems than it solves. To require a historical precedent is to deny any exercise of the poet's imagination. It is of course possible that they are a post-Homeric addition to the text; but, if so, we merely ascribe to the interpolator the inconsistency and lack of logic which we hesitate to ascribe to Homer.

336–38. The idea is to pile earth on the pyre to make a mound and use that as the starting point for a line of defensive fortifications around the camp. It is awkwardly expressed.

Nestor gives no reason for building the wall at the present time, except that he has mentioned the loss of many men in today's battle (328), and he foresees Trojan attacks (343). Critics have been worried by the logic of this, on the grounds that the time to build a defensive wall was on first landing, at the beginning of the war, and that in any case there is no evident reason for building one now, as the fighting in Books 4–7 has been almost wholly favorable to the Greeks. More plausible reasons which Nestor might have adduced are war weariness on the part of the Greeks (shown in their reaction in Book 2 to Agamemnon's tentative suggestion that they should return home) and the great disadvantage that has come on them with the withdrawal of Achilleus from the fighting. Achilleus himself says, in 9.352–54, that, so long as he was in action, the Trojans would not leave their city.

In reality, however, these rational arguments are not the way to answer a poetic quesiton. The wall is going to play a large part in

Book 12; the poet is preparing us for that battle by describing its construction here. And, in answer to the argument that Books 4–7 have shown an unbroken sequence of Greek successes, that is merely Homer's patriotic manner; the Trojans have had their successes too, and the army, at least, is not optimistic about the next day's prospects (479–81).

It is at first sight disturbing that Thucydides (1.11.1) speaks of a wall having been built at the beginning of the war and thus seems to ignore the building of one at this point in the *Iliad*. As with the return of the ashes, however, it introduces far greater problems to deduce from that that all mentions of the building of the wall in this and later books are interpolations in the *Iliad* dating from a time after Thucydides (as PAGE 315–22 does); and in fact, if one pays close attention to the *Iliad*, one may find that the wall referred to by Thucydides is mentioned in 13.683 and 14.32.

339. There are several **gates;** see 12.175 n.

347. Antenor, the leading Trojan outside Priam's royal family, was perhaps less committed to the war (3.204–24 n.).

352. true pledges. He refers to the oaths taken in Book 3, before the duel between Menelaos and Paris, then broken by Pandaros' treachery (cf. 70 n.).

375–78. So *both* sides wish to arrange a truce for the collection and cremation of their dead. Idaios' visit to the Greek camp in the morning saves the Greeks the trouble of sending the same message to the Trojans.

382. When Idaios arrives, he finds the Greeks already in assembly.

390. I wish that he had perished. It is hardly the herald's place to make this comment.

402. The phrase **terms of death** involves the same metaphor as "the threads of victory" in 102; it seems to be taken from ropes and rope ends.

409. there is no sparing time: "there is no grudging," "one should not hold back."

421. the sun of a new day. This is still the same morning. Idaios' visit to the Greek camp has taken place very early.

433. But when the dawn. This must be a new day, the second of the truce. The poet has not expressed it clearly; he is usually most explicit about the coming of night and the dawn of a new day.

435–40 = 336–41, with necessary modifications caused by the change of tenses.

441. The **stakes** are at surface level, on the inside edge of the ditch (cf. 12.55 n.).

442–63. A short scene among the gods. Poseidon is annoyed because he fears this new Greek wall will put in the shade the wall built for the Trojans by himself and Apollo (452). The scene has a double function: to enhance the magnificence of the new fortifications and to explain why there is no wall remaining there now (see 461–63 n.).

452. Apollo and Poseidon had built the great wall of the city of Troy for King Laomedon, the father of Priam. The story of the building of those old city walls by the gods fits well with the archeological evidence of massive defenses for Troy VI, more powerful than those of Troy VIIa (the Troy of Priam and the Trojan War) (PAGE 59–72). The work of Apollo and Poseidon is further described in 21.441–57.

461–63. The destruction of the wall after the Greeks left is described in greater detail in 12.13–33. The poet seems chiefly concerned to account for its absence from view in his own day.

467–69. Lemnos: a large island near Troy. Its king, **Euneos,** seems to be a war profiteer, trading with the Greek camp and buying and selling prisoners of war. Apart from these lines, he appears in 21.41 and 23.746.

It comes as something of a surprise to discover that Euneos' connections are with the Argonautic story, a quite separate cycle of legends, not otherwise alluded to in the *Iliad.* **Jason** and the Argonauts, on their way to the Black Sea, stayed for a time on the island of Lemnos, which was occupied only by women, all the men having been killed. Jason himself was the guest of the queen of the island, **Hypsipyle.** The appearance of a son from that liaison in the context of the Trojan War gives a strange impression of historical reality.

472. thence: i.e., from the ships mentioned in 467—not, of course, from the special gift cargo of the sons of Atreus.

479. them refers either to Greeks and Trojans alike or to the Greeks alone—probably the latter.

480–81. They spilled the wine on the ground. For the practice of making libations, see 1.471 n.

BOOK EIGHT

Book 7 ended in an atmosphere of foreboding, with ominous thunder during the night. Now, in Book 8, Zeus is about to fulfill the promise he made to Thetis in Book 1, that he would grant victory to the Trojans until Agamemnon and the Greeks compensated Achilleus for the dishonor done to him.

Book 8 involves a complete day's fighting, with a great deal of divine activity, Zeus arranging for the Trojans to be victorious, and the pro-Greek goddesses attempting to thwart him. The effect, however, is confused, because the poet has a patriotic bias and tends to indicate that, other things being equal, the Greeks are still more than a match for their opponents, even in the absence of Achilleus. Thus the reader receives an impression of Greek rather than Trojan success and is therefore a little surprised by Hektor's optimism in his speech to the army in 497–541 and by the pessimism of the Greeks in Books 9 and 10. We should pay due attention to the picture of Trojan victory in 212–16 and 343–49.

In outline, the book runs as follows:

1–52	Zeus forbids the gods to take part.
53–65	The battle begins.
66–98	Zeus-supported Trojan success.
99–129	Diomedes restores Greek superiority.
130–97	Zeus-supported Trojan success.
198–211	Hera tries unsuccessfully to intervene.
212–52	The Greeks under severe pressure.
253–334	Teukros restores Greek superiority.
335–49	Zeus-supported Trojan success.
350–484	Hera tries unsuccessfully to intervene.
485–88	Night falls.
489–565	The Trojans elated by victory.

From this intricate and repetitive sequence one can see why Book 8 received its ancient name, "The Unfinished Battle." The day ends too soon, at least for the Trojans.

5–27. Zeus intends to sway the battle and forbids the other gods to intervene. This prohibition is in force for much of the rest of the *Iliad*, although it is disobeyed from time to time by certain gods. At the beginning of Book 20 Zeus rescinds it and allows a free-for-all.

10–16. For Zeus's becoming angry and threatening physical violence, cf. 1.562–67 n.

13. Tartaros is not Hades but an abyss far below, where the enemies of Zeus, in particular Kronos and the Titans, were immured; cf. 478–81.

15. The **gates of iron** and the **doorstone** of bronze are an indication of the difficulty any prisoner would have in getting out of Tartaros.

19–27. The picture of the proposed tug-of-war is not quite clear. The rope is to be stretched from the sky to the earth, and Zeus is to pull from above, and the gods from below. So far, so good. But in 24–26 he says that he would be able to pull up the gods and the land and sea as well and that *then* he would tie the rope round a peak of Olympos and leave everything hanging in mid-air. This suggests a greater dissociation of Olympos from the earth than we find easy to understand; but the passage is not to be taken seriously.

39. Zeus's reply is that of a fond father to a strong-willed daughter. It is repeated, in more tragic circumstances, at 22.183–84.

47–48. Gargaron: the central peak of Mount Ida.

69–70. The **scales** of Zeus, mentioned metaphorically in 16.658 and 19.223, are actually operated here and in 22.209–12, where the fates of Hektor and Achilleus are weighed just before the final stage of their single combat (8.69–70 = 22.209–10). The **two fateful portions of death** which are put in the scales would seem at first sight to suit the individuals of Book 22 better than the two opposing armies, which is the case here; but the metaphorical allusions to the scales of Zeus in Books 16 and 19 refer to the defeat of an army.

The weighing of human fates in the scales is not a process of decision by Zeus; it is rather a symbolic representation of what is fated to happen.

75. stroke and **flash**: thunder and lightning.

78–100. This incident, which takes place as the Achaians turn to fly, is an excellent example of the poet's method of character-drawing by typical behavior. In twenty lines we are reminded of the archery of Paris, the good sense of Nestor, the speed of Hektor, the uncomplicated bravery of Diomedes, and the prudence of Odysseus.

The scene is important for another reason. One of the famous stories of the Trojan War told of the filial devotion of Antilochos, the young son of Nestor. This took place in the period shortly after the end of the *Iliad*. Nestor was, as here, cut off at the front of the battle, his horse shot by an arrow from Paris; Memnon (not Hektor) was approaching to kill the old man, but young Antilochos rescued his father at the cost of his own life (Pindar, *Sixth Pythian* 28–42). Most critics have considered that the *Iliad* version is secondary, a Homeric reflection of the more famous and significant episode (see Appendix D).

80. only ... Nestor stayed. Nestor is one of Homer's favorite characters, and there is a touch of comedy in the description here. All the greatest kings turned to flight; Nestor alone stayed, that guardian (**watcher**) of the Achaians—not that he wished to, but his horse had been shot.

87. The term **trace-harness** shows—what was not previously stated—that the horse shot by Paris was not one of the pair harnessed to the yoke of the chariot but rather a trace horse at the side. The practice of having this third horse occurs in the *Iliad* only here and in Book 16 (152–54 and 467–75, where also it is the trace horse which is hit). The purpose is obscure. Dionysius of Halicarnassus alleges (7.73) that such a horse was used in chariots at Rome in his own day, following the ancient but disused Greek practice. It is difficult to see how an additional horse could pull straight, or be of any use in battle, even if it might conceivably be helpful at the turning points on a race course. (See Delebecque 98–102.)

97. gave no attention represents in English an ambiguity that is also there in the Greek. Odysseus, like Nestor, is one of Homer's favorites, and he dwells lovingly on his intelligence, general ability, and power of survival. Obviously, in dealing with a hero, it would be improper to impute cowardice; let us say that Odysseus was suffering from a temporary deafness.

106. The **Trojan horses** are those that Diomedes took from Aineias in Book 5. Their breed was the finest in the world (5.265–72).

113–14. Sthenelos, a hero in his own right, acts as charioteer to his friend Diomedes; **Eurymedon**, the charioteer of Nestor, is of less significance. He recurs once (11.619).

119. but struck the charioteer. It becomes clear that it was a dangerous task to be charioteer to a rash fighter like Hektor. He loses two drivers in this book (Eniopeus here and Archeptolemos in 312); and their deaths foreshadow that of Kebriones, the replacement for Archeptolemos, which takes place in the fight between Hektor and Patroklos at the end of Book 16.

130. The danger is that Diomedes' attack was likely to reverse the effect of Zeus's decision to help the Trojans.

131. they means the Trojans; "in Ilion" would be clearer than **against Ilion.**

162. pride of place: i.e., at feasts.

169–70. Three times he tried . . . , and three times. The number three is typical in this sort of situation, of a man trying to assert himself against the will of heaven or the restrictions of fate. Compare 16.702–9 n.

183. The translation **the very Argives** is unnecessary; better, "them, the Argives."

185. It is extraordinary that Hektor should address *four* horses, seeing that the four-horse chariot is unknown in Homeric fighting (one is mentioned in 11.698, but in connection with a chariot race at some games). And, in any case, the verbs in 186 and 191 are in the *dual* number, showing that two horses only are addressed. Many editors therefore, following Aristarchus, mark the line as spurious. On the other hand, it cannot simply be removed; 186 would be an abrupt opening to the speech, not in Homer's manner (cf. 19.400). This is one of several difficulties in Hektor's speech. The names are typical names for horses.

188–90. These lines have caused much concern, especially the giving of wine to horses. Lattimore does his best in the translation to make the sense acceptable; but in fact what Hektor says is "She put before you the sweet-hearted wheat, and mixed wine for you to drink when *you* might wish, before she did these things for me, her husband."

It is certainly odd, but we should remember that these are a hero's horses. And, if such mundane support is necessary, both Columella (*De re rustica* 6.30.1) and DELEBECQUE 59 provide evidence that wine is in fact given to horses that need special care.

192–95. The famous golden **shield of Nestor** and the god-made **corselet** (breastplate) **of Diomedes** are never mentioned except in these lines. It is highly probable that they arise from the momentary invention of the poet and do not reflect previous legends about these two heroes. In the case of Diomedes' breastplate, Hephaistos, the divine smith, is of course the obvious god to have made it, just as he makes the armor for Achilleus in Book 18.

The **cross-rods** in line 193 are either supports or handgrips on the inside of the shield.

198–211. **Hera** tries, unsuccessfully, to persuade **the great god Poseidon** to intervene to help the Greeks. This short scene prepares the way for Hera's later, more successful, persuasion of Athene (350–80) and also for the situation in Books 13 and 14, where Poseidon and Hera do cooperate in assisting the Greeks.

Helike and **Aigai** (203) were famous centers of the worship of Poseidon; both were in Achaia on the north coast of the Peloponnese (in the kingdom of Agamemnon in the Catalogue, where the former is named, 2.575).

213. The **ditch** and the **wall** are those built on Nestor's advice in 7.436–41.

222–26. There is characterization here. **Aias** and **Achilleus**, the bravest of the heroes, take the positions of danger at the extreme **ends** of the line, while **Odysseus**, the man of practical intelligence, is at the center (the **midmost**) of things. (The lines recur at 11.5–9. For a diagram of the whole Greek line, see 10.113 n.)

230. For **Lemnos**, cf. 7.467–69 n.

236–37. Better: "Father Zeus, did you ever previously delude a mighty king with such a delusion as this?" The Homeric concept of

Ate ("delusion") is of an infatuation which temporarily destroys a person's judgment, so that he behaves as he would not normally behave. It is commonly said to be sent by Zeus. The Ate of Agamemnon lay in his treatment of Achilleus in Book 1; its consequences are now apparent to him (cf. 19.86–89).

238. I.e., I did not pass by *any* altar of yours.

240. For fat and thighs, see 1.40 n.

250. Zeus of the Voices means the oracular god, the god of omens.

266. Teukros the archer, half-brother of Telamonian Aias, is named as ninth because his *aristeia* is about to take place. Odysseus would normally come at this position in the list (cf. 7.168, 10.231). It is probably intentional, and due to Homer's amused observation of his character, that Odysseus, who paid no attention to Diomedes' shout in 97 but swept on back to the ships, is missing from the roll call now.

267–68. For the great body shield of Aias, see 7.219 n.

299. mad dog. Hektor is considered dangerous by the Greeks because he is so wild and rash in the fighting; Diomedes calls him "this fierce man" in 96.

311. Apollo faltered his arrow. Apollo, as the guardian of Troy, protects Hektor.

312. Archeptolemos: cf. 119 n.

318. Kebriones plays an important part toward the end of Book 16, being the last (named) victim of Patroklos before Patroklos himself is killed. Hektor's enlisting of him as his charioteer here in Book 8 prepares for that later scene.

324. shoulder. This is the *left* shoulder. The archer stands sideways and shoots in line with his own body. The Greek bow was not the long bow of early English usage but the smaller bow with double curve (cf. "curved" in 266, 4.106–11 n.). And this bow was pulled to the chin. As Teukros draws, he is pulling the bowstring past his left shoulder, and Hektor, standing a little to his right, throws a stone which breaks both bowstring and collarbone. Consequently, his left wrist goes numb, and he drops the bow.

328. The sinew might be the muscle of the arm but is more probably the bowstring (cf. 15.463–65, a near repetition of the present situation).

348. The Gorgon's head was a frightening mask with staring eyes; it appears as the central decoration on the aegis of Zeus at 5.741 and on Agamemnon's shield at 11.36.

350–51. Hera and Athene are always on the lookout to support the Greeks. Their plan here is of course in direct disobedience to Zeus's orders in 7–16, above.

362–69. The references to **Herakles** in the *Iliad* are quite numerous, and together they give a connected picture of his activity (see NILSSON 197–204). They can be divided into three groups:

1. The tale of his birth in Thebes (14.323–24, 19.96–133), of his subservience to King Eurystheus of Mykenai (8.362–69, 15.639–40), and the labors he had to perform. The only labor (of the later canon of twelve) referred to in the *Iliad* is the one mentioned here, the bringing-up of the dog Kerberos from the underworld. In much of this there is allusion also to the animosity of the goddess Hera against him, and one passage, which may be Homer's own invention, speaks of his eventual death through "the anger of Hera" (18.117–19).

2. The tale of his attack on Troy because of the fraud of Priam's father, Laomedon (5.640–42, 20.145–48, 14.250–56, 15.26–30, the last two referring to Hera's machinations against the hero on his return journey).

3. The tale of his attack on Pylos (5.392–404, 11.689).

367. Hades of the Gates alludes to the gate of hell, which allows no way out (cf. Tartaros in 15, above). The Styx (369) is the river of Hades.

371. who kissed his knees. . . . This was in 1.500–501. Thetis had taken the normal suppliant's position, which was (1.407 n.) to clasp the knees with one hand and reach for the chin with the other. Athene suggests that Thetis went one stage further and kissed Zeus's knees.

379. dogs and birds. Cf. 1.4–5 n.

384–96. The description echoes that of 5.733–52.

398. Iris, the divine messenger, is always at hand for Zeus. One of the differences noticed between the *Iliad* and the *Odyssey* is that in the latter the divine messenger is Hermes, not Iris.

455–56. once hit in your car. What he says is rather, "Once hit by the lightning stroke, you could never have come back in your car to Olympos"; it is a small point, but the text as translated contradicts 402–5.

463–68 = 32–37, with small variations; 465 has also occurred at 354. This sort of repetition is an obvious feature of oral poetry. It may be noticed, as a characteristic observation of human behavior, that Zeus in his reply is less sympathetic to the feelings of his wife than he was to those of his daughter in 39–40.

476. This is the first mention of **Patroklos** since Book 1.

478–81. I care not. Zeus means, of course, that he doesn't mind how far she goes; but there is also a threat, because **Tartaros** (more precisely localized in line 16, above) is the prison of Kronos and the Titans, children of Ouranos, the previous dynasty to rule the world, which Zeus had overthrown. **Iapetos,** father of Prometheus, was one of the Titans (by some connected with Japheth, son of Noah); **Kronos** was Zeus's own father.

485. The end of the day.

488. thrice-supplicated: much prayed for.

494. eleven-cubit-long spear: see 6.319 n.

505. In other words, Hektor has decided that they will stay out on the plain through the night, to be ready to attack again first thing in the morning.

519. The walls are **god-founded** because first built by Poseidon and Apollo (7.452).

524–25. In other words, he has given his instructions for this night and will give new instructions in the morning.

538–40. Oh, if I only could be ... **immortal** ... Even to consider such a possibility shows dangerous presumption in a human being. Hektor often displays this sort of lack of judgment.

548 and 550–52. These lines are not found in any manuscript of the *Iliad*. They are quoted from "Homer," but not specifically from the *Iliad*, in the pseudo-Platonic dialogue the *Second Alcibiades*, p. 149. An early editor added them to the text; his successors at the present day mostly remove them. The lines are not in themselves objectionable, but the passage may gain in brevity without them, quite apart from the uncertainty of their attestation.

553–65. The end of the book is justly famous. With an uplifting simplicity the Trojan campfires are compared to the stars in a clear night sky, while at the end the horses stand by their chariots and wait for the dawn.

555–59. There is a complication in this beautiful simile, for 557–58 also appear in a simile at 16.299–300. The Alexandrian critics consequently wished to excise these two lines here. In fact, line 557 is unexceptionable, as the outlines of the hills are clear and visible on a moonlit and starlit night. Line 558, however, is far more suitable in Book 16, where the simile is not of a clear night but of the dispersing of thick clouds over a mountain. Then sudden shafts of clear light do come down between the clouds to the ground (which is what line 558 means); there is no such special phenomenon on a clear night. On the other hand, the fact that the line is less suitable here does not mean that it is a post-Homeric addition. It is a recognized feature of formulaic composition that familiar phrases are supplied to the poet's mind by the general context, leading sometimes to just such minor carelessness in detail.

BOOK NINE

Book 9, in many ways the finest in the *Iliad*, is a self-contained whole, devoted to the Greek Embassy to Achilleus in the night following their defeat in Book 8. The Greeks send three envoys—Odysseus, Phoinix, and Aias—and the main part of the book consists of the speeches of each of these three and the reply of Achilleus to each. Before the Embassy proper come the preliminaries and the arrangements for it, the proposal itself being typically made by Nestor; and after it we are shown the reaction of the Greek leaders to the news that it has failed. Balance is provided at the beginning and end by a pair of strong speeches by Diomedes.

There has been much discussion of the place of the Embassy in the *Iliad*. Analytical critics have been drawn, by seemingly inescapable arguments, to detect two separate stages of interpolation. First, because certain passages in later books fail to mention that the Greeks have already offered compensation to Achilleus (see notes on 11.608 and 16.49–86), it is argued that there existed at one stage an *Iliad* without an Embassy, i.e., that Book 9 as a whole is a later addition. Second, within the Embassy as it stands, the position of Phoinix is questionable. He has never been mentioned before; his presence in Agamemnon's shelter (168) is unexplained; and when the Embassy sets out for Achilleus, a series of verbs in the dual number (182–98) seems to leave Phoinix out of account. From this it is argued that at one stage the Embassy contained only Odysseus and Aias, Phoinix being a subsequent addition (see PAGE 297–315).

The opposing view would be that most of the difficulties found here, as elsewhere, are directly attributable to the conditions of oral composition; that the extraordinary quality, of Achilleus' speeches particularly, deserves attribution to Homer as much as any other part of the *Iliad*; and that even the very difficult dual forms of the verb in lines 182 ff., and the apparently inorganic nature of Phoinix' presence, may simply reflect stages in Homer's creative work. The greatest and most authoritative of the analysts described Phoinix' speech as "the jewel in the crown" of this fine book (WILAMOWITZ 65).

Features that are perhaps most memorable are:

1. Achilleus' questioning of the heroic code within which he himself has his being (314–63, 400–420).
2. The powerful rhetoric of his words throughout his speech, but especially in 336–43 and 374–92.
3. The way he modifies his position in his three speeches (359–61, 618–19, and 650–53).
4. The brilliant telling of the paradigmatic story of Meleagros in Phoinix' speech (529–605).

5. The mention of **north** and **west** winds blowing from Thrace locates the poet on the west coast of Asia Minor, not on the mainland of Greece.

13–14. Agamemnon ... shedding tears. The picture of Agamemnon weeping before the army may strike us as not very heroic and is perhaps intended to give exactly that impression. In his favor, however, it should be said that he is overcome, not by personal fear, but by the loss of prestige which he is suffering in the defeat of the Greeks.

23–25 = 2.116–18.

26–28. let us run away with our ships. This is typical strategy for Agamemnon. In 2.139–41 he proposed flight as a psychological maneuver intended to strengthen the morale of the army. Here, and at 14.74–81, he is in earnest. His proposals never work.

31. Diomedes speaks up also in a similar situation at the end of the book (696). He is a young man, but by no means lacking in self-confidence.

34. I ... whose valour you slighted. In 4.370–400 Agamemnon publicly reproved Diomedes for apparently avoiding the front line. Diomedes there showed great restraint and refused to answer back to his commander-in-chief. From what he says here, however, he was more sensitive to the criticism than he seemed.

63–64. Proverbial lines about the outlawing of a man who causes civil strife. They are only marginally relevant to the present situation.

67. by the ditch. The guards are to go to the space outside the wall, but on the near side of the ditch (87).

71. For our, read "your." Agamemnon has his own official stock of wine (7.470–71).

81–84. The leaders of the guard. **Thrasymedes** plays a part in the later books of the *Iliad*, although a lesser one than his brother Antilochos; **Askalaphos** and **Ialmenos** are leaders of the contingent from Orchomenos (2.512); **Meriones** is the most often named of the heroes of the second rank; **Aphareus** and **Deïpyros** are mentioned only here and in Book 13, where both are killed (as also is Askalaphos); **Lykomedes** reappears several times (see 17.345 n.).

96–105. Nestor, like an experienced orator, speaks hesitantly at the beginning of his speech. He knows that he is going to propose something which may not seem easy to Agamemnon and also that he is going to blame Agamemnon for past mistakes. Therefore he begins in a complimentary way and takes his time before coming to the point.

108–9. urged you strongly not to. See 1.275.

121–56. The magnificence of the reparation offered to Achilleus by Agamemnon is a measure of Achilleus' honor. Achilleus has been insulted; but if he accepts compensation such as this, his status will be higher than before the insult.

122. unfired: not yet used.

128–30. whom he captured. Achilleus tells us later (328–29) that he has led twenty-three expeditions against smaller towns in the vicinity of Troy. The attack on **Lesbos,** the large island some way south of Troy, must have been one of them. Agamemnon's habit of choosing the best of the booty for himself (130) is one of the things Achilleus complains of (332–33).

145. Chrysothemis and Laodike and Iphianassa. The names of the three daughters strike us as surprising in view of the stories of the children of Agamemnon as we meet them in the Attic tragedians. Elektra is not mentioned here; and if "Iphianassa" is a variant of "Iphigeneia," then Homer appears to be ignorant of the sacrifice of Iphigeneia before the Greeks sailed for Troy. The *Odyssey* knows of the vengeance of Orestes (named here in 142) for his father, but it, too, is silent about both Elektra and Iphigeneia. Later poets tried to introduce consistency by assuming Laodike to be another name for Elektra and treating Iphigeneia and Iphianassa as separate daughters. The whole is a good lesson for us that the "facts" of mythology were not fixed.

It has been pointed out that the names of the three daughters in this line reflect aspects of the majesty of the great king (they might be translated "Divine Right," "Justice over the People," and "Dominion"), which is not true of the names Elektra or Iphigeneia. It would be dangerous, however, to draw conclusions about relative antiquity from this observation.

146. bride-price. The usual practice in heroic times is for the suitor to give gifts to the father of the bride.

149. seven citadels. The seven cities which Agamemnon here undertakes to give to Achilleus have occasioned some surprise. They are not in Agamemnon's own kingdom, based on Mykenai in the northeast Peloponnese (2.569–75), but in Messenia, in the center of the south coast. If they belong to anyone, they should belong to Nestor at Pylos; and they are described at 153 by a phrase that is used for a Pylian city at 11.711. It is not clear how Agamemnon could dispose of cities that were not under his direct control.

Two explanations (among several) may be mentioned. According to one, the phrase "at the bottom of sandy Pylos" (153) need not mean that the cities were actually subject to Pylos but merely that they were on its frontiers. In that case, they might have constituted a small separate Mycenaean kingdom, whose chief city would no doubt be Pherai (151; cf. 5.543). This would make it easier for the poet to let Agamemnon dispose of them. (So R. Hope Simpson in *Annual of the British School at Athens* 61 [1966]: 113–31.)

Alternatively, the whole problem may be due to a romantic attempt to elevate the sovereignty of the great king of Mykenai by giving him rights over the territory of his subordinates. JACHMANN

93–98 finds this sort of exaggeration at several points, especially where Agamemnon is described (2.108) as "lord of many islands and over all Argos," a phrase which certainly does not accord with his restricted kingdom in the Catalogue of Ships.

168. Phoinix, a family retainer of Achilleus, tells his past history later in the book. He has not appeared previously. He is named first by Nestor; but there is no explanation of his presence in the council, and the dual forms of the Greek verbs in 182 ff. disregard him (see 182 n.). The phrase **be their leader** is not consistent with what actually happens, and in 192 that function seems to be ascribed to Odysseus; perhaps it merely means "let him go first."

169. Aias is chosen as the bravest of the other Greeks and, for that reason, the closest to Achilleus. In later mythology he was Achilleus' first cousin (Telamon and Peleus were brothers); but this relationship is not alluded to in the *Iliad*. **Odysseus** is the practical, intelligent, man, an obvious choice for any task that requires careful handling. The addition of two heralds adds formality and a religious sanction to the embassy.

171. The instruction to **keep words of good omen** is not for the envoys but for the whole company. There should be silence for the religious ceremony—the prayers and the libation (176).

180–81. Peleion = Achilleus, son of Peleus. Nestor reckons that Odysseus is the most likely to persuade him.

182. So these two walked. The Greek language possessed a dual number in addition to singular and plural. The verb here is in the dual (the word **two** itself does not appear in the Greek), as are seven more words referring to the envoys (up to line 198). This is the most difficult problem in the whole *Iliad* for those who believe in the single authorship of one poet ("Homer"). Nestor has just clearly named five men to go on the embassy to Achilleus: Phoinix first, Aias, Odysseus, Odios, and Eurybates. The two heralds we may reasonably discard; they presumably kept a respectful distance. But three ambassadors, each of whom fulfills his appointment by making a formal speech to Achilleus later in the book and receives his own reply from him, cannot properly be described in the dual number.

This difficulty has been used in recent years as one of the chief arguments in the question of single or multiple authorship of the

Iliad. Many scholars (e.g., LEAF 1:371 and PAGE 297–304, among those writing in English) have claimed that the figure of Phoinix has been added to a preexisting Embassy, in which only Odysseus and Aias appeared, and that the duals of 182–98 have been (with extraordinary carelessness) left unchanged by the interpolator. Support is found for this theory in the basic improbability (168 n.) of Phoinix' presence in the council meeting, in that he was not an important leader and in any case was at this time one of Achilleus' noncombatant Myrmidons. On the other hand, to obtain the supposed previous state of the Embassy, we should have to remove all references to Phoinix, as well as his speech and Achilleus' reply. And this cannot be done by simple excision of lines. For example, if 168 goes, there is no sense in "after him" in 169. Moreover, if it *were* possible to remove Phoinix completely, the balance of the Embassy would be seriously upset. The short comments of Aias are reasonable when two have spoken before him, but they would seem very flat if Odysseus and he were the only delegates.

There is no getting away from the problem of the duals, however, and there is of course no doubt that they refer to Odysseus and Aias. The traditional explanation is that Phoinix went on ahead or simply showed the others the way (cf. 168 n.), being of lower status; this, however, should not be pressed too far, for Phoinix' speech to Achilleus is the longest and the most human and sympathetic of the three. A similar line of argument holds that Phoinix is not an *ordinary* member of the Embassy. He has a special relationship with Achilleus; and, though he has been asked to speak on behalf of the Greeks, he can hardly represent them formally. In the event, he does not return to the council with the others but stays on in Achilleus' hut. So the situation we may simply have to accept is this: that Phoinix was first named by Nestor and is later present and speaks in Achilleus' quarters; but the walk together along the shore of the sea, and the formal welcome by Achilleus when they arrive, are limited to the two great heroes who are the official representatives of the Greeks.

Alternatively, if we feel convinced by the evidence that Phoinix is an interloper, we should consider the possibility that we are here looking into Homer's workshop. If the poet was used to the theme of an Embassy of two, much handled over many years, and then for his monumental composition of the *Iliad* wished to add Phoinix as a third—because of the speech which Phoinix is to give—perhaps we *should* find exactly the awkwardnesses noted in 168 and in the duals here.

183. holder and shaker of the earth. These are titles of the god Poseidon, beside whose element they are walking.

184. Aiakides. Aiakos was the grandfather of Achilleus, being father of Peleus.

188. Eëtion's city. Eëtion was Andromache's father and king of the town of Thebe, near Troy (6.414–16).

189. singing of men's fame. Achilleus is relaxing by singing the glories of previous heroes, songs which may be the precursors of Homer's epic poetry. When he comes to the end of his song, his friend Patroklos will take over.

197. and greatly I need you. The words may also, and perhaps more probably, mean "so you have great need of me."

209. Automedon is third in the Myrmidon chain of command. He acts as charioteer to Patroklos in Book 16 and has his own *aristeia* in 17.426–542.

218. Achilleus wishes to be in a position to watch Odysseus.

220. firstlings: parts of the meat thrown into the fire as a burnt offering.

223. This is a typically brilliant touch of characterization. We observe instantaneously the ponderous Aias, the unassertive Phoinix, and Odysseus quick off the mark and sure of what he wants to achieve. Odysseus is probably Homer's favorite character. For other examples of minute observation, cf. 180 and 620–22.

THE SIX SPEECHES OF THE EMBASSY SCENE
(LINES 225–655)

The order and length of the six speeches of the Embassy scene—one from each of the delegates and Achilleus' reply to each—are as follows:

225–306	Odysseus	308–429	Achilleus' reply
434–605	Phoinix	607–19	Achilleus' reply
624–42	Aias	644–55	Achilleus' reply

Thus the first three are the longest, being of 82, 122, and 172 lines, respectively.

ODYSSEUS' SPEECH (LINES 225–306)

Odysseus makes it his own chief aim to transmit clearly the offer of compensation which Agamemnon made at the council meeting.

225. The second half of this line is, alternatively, "*we* have no lack of good things to feast on"; this makes better sense and provides a suitable and relevant beginning for Odysseus' speech.

252–53. Odysseus went round Greece with Nestor recruiting the heroes for the war. His presence in Phthia is mentioned by Nestor in 11.766; and cf. 7.127 for the same occasion. The words ascribed to Peleus in 254–58 are ad hoc invention for the purpose of the present situation ("avoid quarreling"!), as are the words ascribed (in 11.785–88) to Patroklos' father Menoitios on the same occasion.

264–99 repeat 122–57, with only the minimal changes necessary because of the change of persons. This repetition of a block of lines is typical of oral poetry; the messenger presents his message exactly as he received it (cf., e.g., 2.28–32).

304. you might kill Hektor. Odysseus tries to appeal to Achilleus' ambition and desire for honor.

ACHILLEUS' REPLY TO ODYSSEUS (LINES 308–429)

Achilleus' reply to Odysseus is the most powerful speech in the *Iliad*. Achilleus has been a simple hero, embodying the perfection of the qualities of the heroic age. In other words, he has lived for "honor"—for his standing in the eyes of other people. His aim (and achievement) has been to surpass all others. Now, in the bitterness of the public insult he has received from Agamemnon, he questions the whole basis of his life; he questions whether honor is indeed more valuable than life, whether heroic achievements, with all their attendant risk and strain, are worthwhile, when he, after all he has done, can be treated like this.

312–13. that man, who hides one thing ... and speaks another. There is something of a dig at Odysseus here. The other heroes were suspicious of Odysseus' cleverness, though they appreciated his value to the army. One may compare Agamemnon's violent address to him in the Review at 4.339. Similarly, in the *Odyssey*, there is some ambivalence in Alkinoös' comment, at 11.363–64, on Odysseus' highly colored account of his adventures: "Odysseus, when we look at you, we do not have any thought in our minds that you are a liar and a deceiver."

316–22. A succession of more or less proverbial comments on the uselessness of heroic effort.

327. women. The wives of the defeated enemy are a major part of the booty. The Trojans are often described as fighting to defend their wives and little children.

328–29. Achilleus has been engaged on expeditions against the cities around Troy during the long years in which the Greeks have been besieging Troy and the Trojans have not come out to fight (352–53). Here he claims to have made twenty-three successful attacks. It was on one of them that the girls Chryseis and Briseis were taken, causing the quarrel in Book 1.

336. Achilleus calls Briseis **the bride of my heart** in preparation for the brilliant argument of 337–43. She is not really a bride; but he wishes to compare Agamemnon's forcible appropriation of her with Paris' carrying-off of Helen.

349–50. wall and **ditch.** He refers to the Greek defenses built in 7.436–41.

363. Phthia, in south Thessaly, was Achilleus' home.

374–400. We may admire the vigor of Achilleus' refusal: **I will join with him in no counsel . . . ; I hate his gifts . . . ; nor will I marry his daughter.**

378. light as the strip of a splinter: of no value or account.

381–84. Orchomenos and **Thebes** were the two great cities of Boiotia in the Mycenaean Age. The first line ends, in the Greek, at "Thebes." When it was first composed (not necessarily or even probably by Homer), it referred without question to the two Greek cities. Then, early in this line's history, the next three lines were added, beginning "of Egypt" and thus transferring the reference to the old capital of Egypt, far up the Nile. If Homer himself made the modification, it might be because the *Iliad* is very conscious of the recent destruction of Boiotian Thebes by the Epigonoi (2.505, 4.406). That city might therefore not seem a suitable example of wealth for Achilleus to choose.

Just as the wealth of Orchomenos and Thebes relates to Mycenaean times, so also the allusion to the wealth of Egyptian Thebes is probably Mycenaean in origin; LORIMER 97 argues that the time when Egyptian Thebes was known to the Greeks as a great and fabulously wealthy city could hardly be later than the first quarter of the fourteenth century B.C. Evidently we are in the presence here of formulaic material embodying remote memories of glory and wealth.

It has been interestingly suggested that the description of the vast number of horses and chariots which could issue from each of the **hundred gates** of the city (383–84) may be due ultimately to a misunderstanding of the hieroglyphic inscriptions still visible on the walls of the great temple there (LORIMER 98).

395. Hellas, which eventually became the name for the whole of Greece, has still in Homer the limited connotation of a part of Thessaly (2.683).

400–409. The heroic code led men to treat their lives as of less significance than their honor. As Sarpedon says at 12.322–28, seeing that death will come anyway, sooner or later, a hero fights bravely and either wins glory himself or gives it to another. Achilleus now, at the climax of his speech, raises the question whether any marks of honor (i.e., possessions) are worth risking one's life for. He is questioning the whole basis of the heroic code.

404–5. Pytho: the old name for Delphi. The oracle of Apollo was the cause of the rich offerings accumulated there.

410–16. two sorts of destiny. This is the famous choice of Achilleus. As he had a goddess for a mother, he had the misfortune to know his fate, and he knew that it might go one of two ways: either short life and fame at Troy, or long life and obscurity in Phthia.

Although these lines have always been thought very significant for the character of Achilleus in the *Iliad*, they are probably a momentary invention for the present passage. Achilleus' fateful choice is never referred to again, and in 16.50–51 he explicitly denies that he has had any warning from his mother.

422. since such is the privilege: i.e., to receive reports and make plans.

426–29. Achilleus' turning to Phoinix shows artistry on Homer's part; it gives Phoinix his cue to speak, as it were.

432. It is noticeable that skill in driving chariots (**horseman**) is associated particularly with those who did their fighting in the previous generation, such as Nestor (52), Phoinix (here), Peleus (438), and Oineus (581). Chariots are hardly used in the *Iliad* fighting.

PHOINIX' SPEECH (LINES 434–605)

Phoinix' speech does not have the same intensity as that of Achilleus, but its content is even richer. In conformity with the character of an old man (and, in this, similar to several speeches by Nestor), Phoinix introduces reminiscence and digression, but by no means irrelevantly or without purpose. There are three such digressions in his speech:

447–95   Phoinix' personal history
502–12   The Parable of the "Prayers"
527–99   The mythological example of Meleagros

447. It is not easy to get the geography of this tale clear. **Hellas** is described in 2.683 as being part of Achilleus' kingdom (cf. 395), whereas here Phoinix says that he left Hellas and took refuge with Peleus. The problem is not made easier by the statement in 10.267 that the house of Amyntor, son of Ormenos (father of Phoinix, 448), was at Eleon, which was in Boiotia. Either there is a complicated history behind all this, of which we hear disjointed hints, or Homer is not particularly concerned about geographical accuracy. The story here can be understood if we assume that "Hellas" refers to a larger area of Thessaly than the part of it which was in Peleus' domains, or that Peleus' kingdom is being thought of as strictly Phthia (which seems to be the implication of 478–79).

448. Amyntor, son of Ormenos, appears once again, in 10.267, where it is said that it was from his house that Autolykos stole the boar's-tusk helmet.

450–52. Phoinix' trouble was due to an extreme case of stress within the family, as was that of Meleagros (see later in the speech). It is a strange and disturbing story and perhaps, as told here, is an abbreviation of some other version; for example, it is not clear why large numbers of relations should have come to prevent Phoinix from leaving home, as is told at some length in 464–73. (Rhys Carpenter, in *Folk Tale, Fiction, and Saga in the Homeric Epics* [1946], pp. 170–72, suggests that the explanation may be found in a tale told by Herodotus of the human sacrifice of the eldest son of the house of Athamas at Alos in southern Thessaly [Herodot. 7.197].)

454–57. The **furies** of the underworld (Erinyes) punish those who have treated parents badly; Hades (**Zeus of the underworld**) and **Persephone** are the gods down there. These spirits and divinities of vengeance come in again, in the opposite order, in Meleagros' story (569–72).

455–56. I . . . **on my knees:** better, "he . . . on his knees." Amyntor was thinking of himself as a potential grandfather.

458–61. These lines are not in any manuscript of the *Iliad*. They are quoted by Plutarch, who confidently says that Aristarchus cut them out because of the impropriety of line 458. They were restored to the text by a modern editor.

464–73. It is not clear why the kinsmen should take such precautions to prevent Phoinix from leaving home. Perhaps it is simply that the clan lived closely together and closed its ranks to keep in an errant member.

468. The **flame of Hephaistos** means no more than fire, Hephaistos being the god of fire.

474–79. There is an air of excitement and adventure about the story, as if it had been told in more detail on another occasion.

The Parable of the Prayers (Lines 502–12)

The so-called Parable of the Prayers is an allegory, like something from Bunyan's *Pilgrim's Progress*, and has no parallel on anything like the same scale in the *Iliad*. To understand what is being said, it is important to realize the exact connotation of the words translated as **Prayers** and **Ruin**. "Ruin" is Ate (8.236–37 n.), a sort of madness that is considered external to a human being; i.e., it comes upon him from outside himself and makes him act as he would not normally act, causing offense or injury to others. Agamemnon has admitted in 115–16 that he was under the influence of Ate when he dishonored Achilleus in Book 1. "Prayers," although the usual term in English, is nearly meaningless; the word means "requests for forgiveness," i.e., apologies.

503. It is not easy for an offender to say that he is sorry; his handicaps are symbolically transferred to the Prayers.

508–12. In other words, if A wrongs B but later apologizes, then it is up to B to accept the apology; if he refuses, then this is arrogant of him, and he may find that he makes some disastrous mistake himself. This is of course exactly what happens to Achilleus. His refusal of Agamemnon's offer of compensation in this book leads directly to his irrational decision (in Book 16) to send his closest friend, Patroklos, out on his own and so to his death.

M. Noé (in *Phoinix, Ilias und Homer* [1940], p. 32) points out that the religious thought here, that Zeus may punish those who do not accept apologies when offered, is almost exactly the same as that in the Lord's Prayer: "Forgive us our trespasses, as we forgive them that trespass against us"; and it is especially like the further comment in Matthew 6:14–15, "For if ye forgive men their trespasses, your heavenly father will also forgive you; but if ye forgive not men their trespasses, neither will your Father forgive your trespasses."

514. This is rather awkwardly expressed; **lordly though they be** refers to **others**. A proper attitude of respect to the Prayers leads to a change of mind in other people, even heroes.

524–26. This is a general statement, leading to the particular example of the Meleagros story.

The Story of Meleagros (Lines 529–99)

The story of Meleagros is a mythological example (or *paradeigma*) introduced to increase the persuasiveness of Phoinix' argument. The broad idea is, "You should accept the gifts that are offered and return to the fighting, because that great hero, Meleagros, when in a situation surprisingly similar to yours, would certainly have done better to have accepted the offered gifts." What is particularly interesting is that the details of the Meleagros story seem to have been altered to make it closer to the present and future situation of Achilleus. The similarity in the *paradeigma* has to a large extent been invented by Homer for the purpose of the argument. See 550–99 n.

This part of Phoinix' speech falls into two rather different sections:

529–49. The background story, of the war among the peoples of Aitolia, and its cause, the hunt for the Kalydonian boar. This section, although apparently compressed, is a clear account of the legend.

550–99. Meleagros' situation (with a digression on his wife's past history), and the successive attempts to persuade him to return to the fighting. It is in this second section that the invention of the *Iliad* poet seems to have been exercised.

529–49. The "saga" background of the myth. The passage has the common ring form, in five parts:

a   529–32   The Kouretes and the Aitolians were at war.
b   532–33   Artemis had sent an "evil" against Oineus.
c   534–37   He had failed to make her the proper sacrifice.
b′   538–46   So she sent the wild boar; it did great damage, but was eventually killed.
a′   547–49   A quarrel arose over the spoils, and the Kouretes and the Aitolians went to war.

So, line 549 at the end returns to the statement of line 529 at the beginning.

529. Aitolians here means strictly the people of Kalydon, where Meleagros' father, Oineus, was king. The **Kouretes** were a neighboring people, living in Pleuron (not named here). Both cities are in Aitolia in the wider sense (see 2.639–40).

543–44. The assembly of heroes to hunt the Kalydonian boar would offer the same opportunities for heroic adventures as the assembly of the Argonauts or, indeed, the expeditions against

Thebes or Troy. There can be little doubt that the story had been the subject of heroic poetry.

548. They quarreled about who was to have the honor of keeping the spoils.

550–99. The mythological example (*paradeigma*) of Meleagros. The parallel with Achilleus' situation is suspiciously close. Meleagros *withdrew from the fighting* because of *anger* against his mother Althaia, who had prayed for his death because he had killed her brother. There was *increasing danger to his people*, and successive *delegations came with offers of gifts* to ask Melagros to *give up his anger and intervene. He refused them until, at the end, when the danger was most imminent, the one who was closest to him* (his wife Kleopatra) *managed to persuade him.* He saved the city but did not get the gifts.

It will be seen that the parallels include not only the present situation of Achilleus but his later actions as well. Meleagros' wife, Kleopatra, takes the part of Patroklos (556 n.).

Almost all the details here are inconsistent with the story of Meleagros as it is known elsewhere. The usual story is a folktale reflecting family tensions, the wife's divided loyalty between her old and her new family, and involving "sympathetic magic." Althaia had in a box a half-burned piece of wood which represented her son's life. When he killed her brother, or brothers, in the fighting after the hunt for the boar, her ties to her own family overcame her mother love, and she threw the brand onto the fire. At that moment, still in the fighting, Meleagros collapsed. This is told most vividly by Bacchylides (5.94–154). There is no place in it for the anger and withdrawal from battle, the delegations, and the eventual decision to return. These details come from Achilleus' situation in the *Iliad*; his circumstances have been intruded into the story of Meleagros.

(For the evidence of Homer's cavalier attitude to mythology, here and elsewhere in the *Iliad*, cf. M. M. Willcock, "Mythological Paradeigma in the *Iliad*," *Classical Quarterly* 58 [1964]: 141–54.)

550–52. These lines reflect the situation at Troy. Indeed, Achilleus said exactly this in 352–53,

and yet when I was fighting among the Achaians
Hektor would not drive his attack beyond the wall's shelter.

Here, however, they raise a difficulty. Outside whose wall were the
Kouretes unable to hold their ground? Does 552 mean that they were
previously unable to sustain their position outside the walls of
Kalydon (as 530–31 would suggest)? Or that, when Meleagros had
been in action, it was the Aitolians who were on the attack and the
city of Pleuron that was besieged? It is likely that the usual story
had Meleagros driving the Kouretes within the walls of their own
city (so, at least, Bacchylides 5.150) and that Homer has introduced
(invented) the attack on Kalydon in order to get the parallel with
the present situation of the Greeks. In consequence, he now has
two cities successively besieged—a strangely mobile war in Aitolia;
but he is thinking of the city of Troy and the Greek camp.

555. Meleagros' **wrath** is explained in 566.

556. Scholars have noticed that **Kleopatra,** who plays in the
Meleagros story the part played by Patroklos in the *Iliad* story, has
a name which simply reverses the constituent parts of *Patro-klos*,
and they have argued that one of the two names is an invention
based on the other. This is important: if accepted, either it indicates
that the *Iliad* plot itself is modeled on a preexisting "Meleagris"
(now lost) and that the character Patroklos is Homer's own
invention; or it means that this detail too (the name of Meleagros'
wife) is a most casual and light-hearted invention by Homer. Some
support for the latter opinion is given by the fact that Kleopatra
had another name, Alkyone (562).

557–64. A digression on the past history of Meleagros' wife's
family, especially her mother, Marpessa. This short biography—of
a heroine loved by both a hero and a god—is reminiscent of the
Catalogues of Women in Hesiodic poetry and of the pageant of
queens and princesses in *Odyssey* 11.235–327. The details are most
allusive and obscure, and everything about the passage leads one to
suppose that these lines have been inserted here from some other
version. The digression is in ring form, 565–66 repeating the
position of 555–56.

558. **Idas** and his twin brother Lynkeus were Messenian heroes;

they were in the usual lists for both the Kalydonian boar hunt and the Argonautic expedition.

567. her brother. Meleagros killed his uncle (in other versions, his uncles) in the fight for the spoils of the boar.

569–72. Compare 454–57 n.

571–72. Erinys is the fury of the underworld; that she heard the prayer of Althaia implies that Meleagros will die; that, however, is not part of Phoinix' tale.

574–86. Various delegations come, in an "ascending scale of affection," to ask Meleagros to give up his anger. This is a folktale motif, as KAKRIDIS 19–23 has amply shown, and this fact is enough to explain Althaia's presence among the suppliants (584). The order is: priests—father—sisters and mother—comrades—wife. Kakridis also convincingly points out that Homer has placed the comrades of the warrior as high in the scale as he could—higher than their proper position—for the reason that it is Achilleus' own friends who are appealing to him at this moment. Once again the circumstances at Troy are affecting the details of the story of Meleagros.

598–605. Phoinix' closing argument seems materialistic. Meleagros saved his city but did not get the promised gifts; Achilleus should come while the gifts are still on offer. But, of course, what is in question is only partly the material value of the compensation; more important is the honorific effect of public reparations, which would give added status to the recipient.

ACHILLEUS' REPLY TO PHOINIX (LINES 607–19)

Illogically, in view of his stated decision to leave, Achilleus says (608–10) that his god-given superiority will remain in the Greek camp so long as he lives.

616. Be king equally with me. The meaning of this line, which Phoinix will do well not to take literally, is, "ask for anything you want, provided you are on my side."

618–19. we shall decide tomorrow ... whether to go back home. We notice that Achilleus no long says (as he did in 356–63 and 428) that he will sail home tomorrow; now he says that they will *decide* in the morning. In his reply to Aias (650–53) he will stop threatening to return home altogether.

AIAS' SPEECH (LINES 624–42)

Aias says that Achilleus is being unreasonable (632–36). Even a man whose brother or son has been killed accepts compensation—**the blood price.** This relatively new social custom is alluded to also at 18.497–500 (in the Shield of Achilleus). A killer, whether the killing was intentional or accidental, was guilty of the blood of the dead man, and this used to oblige the relatives to avenge the death and kill in their turn, thus leading to an unending vendetta unless the murderer fled the country, which he frequently did (see, e.g., 2.664). A relaxation of this otherwise insoluble problem was eventually achieved by the acceptance of "blood money" by the relatives of the dead. Honor was then satisfied, and the killer could continue to live in the community.

638. The straightforward soldier Aias takes a simple mathematical view of the matter.

640. Respect your own house. He means the responsibility of a host to his guests; cf. 204.

ACHILLEUS' REPLY TO AIAS (LINES 644–55)

This is Achilleus' second modification of his position (650–55; compare 618–19 n.). It is this statement that he recalls at the beginning of Book 16 (61–63) as a reason for not helping the Greeks himself at that point but, instead, sending out his friend, Patroklos.

664–68. Both Achilleus and Patroklos sleep with women taken captive on Achilleus' expeditions (328–29 n.). The expedition to **Lesbos** was referred to by Agamemnon in 129; **Skyros** causes more difficulty. It is fairly remote from Troy; and it was at Skyros that Achilleus was said (though not by Homer) to have been hidden to try to avoid the summons to the Trojan War; and there, too, his son, Neoptolemos, was now growing up (19.326–27). To solve the difficulty, ancient commentators invented another Skyros, a small town near Troy. **Enyeus** (668) is unknown.

682–87. he himself has threatened. Odysseus reports Achilleus' first threat (in the answer that he himself received), to leave the following morning, and says nothing about the important changes of mind in Achilleus' replies to Phoinix and Aias. This is obviously the clearest way to show the failure of the embassy. Note, however, that Diomedes (702) does not believe that Achilleus will fulfill his threat.

693–96. Compare 29–31. Repetition of situations and lines is typical of oral poetry, and, as a result of the repetition, certain situations become thematic. For example, it becomes characteristic, and to be expected, of Diomedes that he is the one who, albeit modestly, first breaks the silence after an awkward pause, when nobody else feels like speaking (cf. also 10.218–19). Another result is that the speeches of the independent-minded Diomedes provide a structural balance at the beginning and end of Book 9.

BOOK TEN

Book 10, usually called the Doloneia, has a unique position in the *Iliad*, in that it is a complete incident in itself and could be removed from the epic without leaving any trace. The wonderful horses captured by Diomedes are never referred to again, not even in the chariot race at the funeral games in Book 23.

A note in the scholia, repeated by Eustathius, runs as follows: "The ancient critics say that this rhapsody was a separate composition by Homer, and not included by him in the *Iliad*, but added to the epic by Peisistratos." This statement is connected with the occasional assertion in late antiquity that the text of Homer was established at Athens under the tyrant Peisistratos in the sixth century, when arrangements were made for its recitation in full at the Panathenaic festival (Lattimore 13, n. 2).

The whole question of the "Peisistratean recension," as it is called, is a difficult one; and the origin of the above quotation may be no more than somebody's guess, based on the inorganic position of the Doloneia in the *Iliad*, as explained above. But the assertion does accord with the views of many modern critics, who, arguing that Book 10 was not part of the original plan of the *Iliad*, distinguish it from the rest on the grounds of both language and style. They naturally differ from the scholiasts on the question of authorship, as the opinion that it is a later addition is now assumed to mean that it is post-Homeric.

The linguistic argument is that there is an unusual number of "late" forms in this book; in fact, it is commonly said that the language of it is closer to the *Odyssey* than to the *Iliad*. Unusual forms can certainly be pointed out; and many of them look like pseudo-archaisms, as if a later poet, not of the oral tradition, is trying his hand. This sort of linguistic evidence, however, can be only comparative, as "late" forms are found in every part of the *Iliad*. A. Shewan (see bibliography at the end of this note) actually denies that there is any greater concentration of them in Book 10 than in Book 1.

Perhaps stronger are the arguments from style, which have been put forward most forcibly in recent years by F. Klingner and W. Jens. What these scholars stress as typical of the poet of the Doloneia is a mannered love of antithesis and contrast (cf. 323 n.), which sometimes causes him to say something illogical or unmotivated in its own place merely to prepare for the balance to come (e.g., it can be argued that 208–10 are not sensible in themselves and have no purpose except as the first part of an artistic equation with 309–12); not very different from this feature is a predilection for surprise turns in the story, so that the expressed hopes and fears of almost everyone (except Diomedes and Odysseus) are contradicted by the event. It may be thought that these are strong arguments, if inevitably somewhat subjective, and that the Doloneia does have a different *flavor* from the rest of the *Iliad*.

All the same, even those who argue for later inclusion may no longer believe that this is a totally separate poem which has somehow got attached; they must admit that it has been tailored to its present place in the *Iliad*, because, while it itself has no effect on the later story, it nevertheless assumes at many points the situation of the Greek army in the night following the defeat of Book 8. This is supported by the convincing arguments of B. Fenik, who, in comparing the play *Rhesus* (ascribed to Euripides) with Book 10, shows that the tragedy gives evidence of a version of the story of Rhesos independent of the *Iliad* and that the differences in Book 10 are caused by adaptation to the *Iliad* situation.

Less convincingly, some have argued that it is unacceptable to have a second event in the night between the battles of Books 8 and 11, in addition to the Embassy to Achilleus. To this it may be replied that it suits the pro-Greek feelings of Homer, and is in any case psychologically desirable, that something should happen to raise the Greeks' morale, because otherwise the eager and successful fighting at the beginning of Book 11 would come in strangely after the depression at the end of Book 8, followed by the gloomy failure of the Embassy in Book 9.

After considering all these arguments, we may find ourselves in a position not far removed from that quoted from the scholia and Eustathius. We may accept that the Doloneia is separable from the *Iliad* and surmise that it existed as an independent, and no doubt popular, item in the poet's repertoire. Such independence could explain the differences of language and style. But this does not preclude the view that the book's insertion here, and any modifications that were necessary for that purpose, were the work of the *Iliad* poet himself.

BIBLIOGRAPHY

Shewan, A. *The Lay of Dolon.* 1911.
Klingner, F. "Über die Dolonie." *Hermes* 75 (1940): 337–68.
Jens, W. "Die Dolonie und ihr Dichter." *Studium Generale* 8 (1955): 616–25.
Fenik, B. *Iliad X and the Rhesus.* 1964.

1. The beginning of Book 10 is closely tied to the end of Book 9 by a technique which was used also to connect Book 2 to Book 1.

12. The campfires were vividly described in 8.553–63.

38. spy. With considerable artistry the poet makes Menelaos raise the idea of sending out a spy here, at the beginning, so as to prepare the minds of the audience for what is to come.

50. It is assumed that for success one needs the help of a god; and for the highest achievements it helps to have a divine parent, as Achilleus has in his mother, Thetis.

56. sacred duty of the guards: merely a periphrasis for "the guards." They had been sent out on Nestor's suggestion in 9.80–88, to take up a position between the Greek wall and the ditch outside it. Seven commanders were there named, including Thrasymedes, Nestor's son, and Meriones.

65. "Wait here" does not make much sense. In fact, although Agamemnon has not expressed it clearly, the council meeting is to be combined with an inspection of the guard outside the wall. Menelaos, who is to summon Aias and Idomeneus and go with them outside the gate of the camp (126), has now asked whether he is to stay with them there or return to his brother. "Wait *there*," replies Agamemnon.

68. naming him with the name of his father. The polite form of address with the name of the father is in fact used by Agamemnon addressing Nestor in 87 and by Nestor addressing Odysseus in 144 and Diomedes in 159.

69–71. Agamemnon is very much aware of his superiority in rank. Normally he would send subordinates to do this sort of work; but the position is critical.

110. Aias the swift-footed. This is Aias, son of Oïleus, who was a fast runner (i.e., an attacking fighter, 14.520–22). The great Telamonian Aias was less mobile.

The **son of Phyleus** is Meges (2.625–30).

113. It is now clear why Menelaos was sent by Agamemnon to get Telamonian Aias and Idomeneus (54). These two must be located at the end of the line, in the other direction from those named in 109–10.

CUILLANDRE 28–34 has deduced the positions of the more important contingents in the Greek line from the evidence here and elsewhere in the *Iliad* (especially 13.681–93). His results are shown in Chart 1. Odysseus occupies the exact center (cf. 8.223). The relative positions of the contingents to the right of the center, between Diomedes and Achilleus, are less certain than some of the others. The Boiotians and the northern Greek troops originally led by Philoktetes but now led by Medon would also be found there (13.685–93).

The presentation on the chart, where the contingents are shown as forming a single line, cannot be exactly right, because some of the ships were drawn further up the beach than others, so that there was depth in the Greek line (see 14.31–36). According to 13.681, the ships of Aias, son of Oïleus, and those of Protesilaos had been pulled furthest inland.

CHART 1. RELATIVE POSITIONS OF GREEK CONTINGENTS AT TROY

Extreme Left					*Center*	
Aias, son of Telamon	Idomeneus	Menelaos	Agamemnon	Nestor	Odysseus	Eurypylos
Salaminians	Kretans	Spartans	Mykenaians	Pylians	Ithakans	Northern Greeks

120–25. Agamemnon feels defensive on behalf of his younger brother; cf. 237–39.

137–79. Here we have an artistic contrast between the two heroic figures, Odysseus and Diomedes, who are to play the largest part in this book. These two complement each other, Odysseus being the man of sense and foresight, Diomedes the perfectly efficient soldier. So Odysseus is found sleeping prudently in his hut; Diomedes is asleep on the ground outside his hut, his armor and his companions around him. Odysseus wastes no words, takes in the situation, and complies; Diomedes, on the other hand, answers Nestor with complete composure and good humor.

194. The guards were on the Greek side of the ditch; the members of the council now go through, onto the actual battlefield, to hold their meeting.

196. Compare 57–58.

212–17. glory . . . and an excellent gift. As may be seen from the compensation offered to Achilleus in Book 9, honor is seen by these heroes in material terms. A public collection and presentation of gifts would add status to anybody.

217. Better, "he (the volunteer on this occasion) will always be invited to feasts and festivals" (cf. 8.162).

218–19. Compare 9.693–96 n.

229. Nestor's son: Thrasymedes; being young, he is particularly eager to go. Odysseus (231) typically comes at the end of a list of volunteers (7.168).

237–40. For Agamemnon's care for his younger brother, cf. 120–25. Menelaos is not a first-rate fighter.

245. To say that **Pallas Athene loves** Odysseus means that he is a successful man. He is both prudent and decisive; and the goddess of

					Extreme Right
Diomedes	Aias, son of Oïleus	Meges	Menestheus	(Protesilaos) Podarkes	Achilleus
Argives	Lokrians	Islanders	Athenians	Northern Greeks	Myrmidons

Greek success therefore helps him, as indeed she helps Diomedes and Achilleus and used to help Diomedes' father, Tydeus.

255, 260. **Thrasymedes** and **Meriones** are naturally fully armed, since they are in command of the guard. They therefore lend equipment to Diomedes and Odysseus, who came to the meeting more or less unarmed. The point of the unusual helmets is that they should not reflect light during the night.

261–65. **helmet ... of leather.** This is the celebrated boar's-tusk helmet. The **felt** (265) was the material in the middle; it was held by a network of straps on the inside, and it allowed the attachment of small plates of boar's tusk on the outside.

The description was not understood until W. Reichel, at the end of the last century, associated it with small pieces of boar's tusk, with holes in them for attachment to something, found in a number of sites of Mycenaean Greece, and also with a couple of ivory representations of the head of a man wearing a helmet, one of them from the shaft graves at Mykenai. It is now accepted that this is the oldest kind of helmet found on the Greek mainland, a kind that went out of use before the end of the Mycenaean Age. It is virtually certain that nobody can have seen an actual example of it in Homer's day and that the detailed description here had been preserved in the poetic tradition. Notice that it is not only described in these lines as an object of evident interest but that it has a pedigree of famous owners. (LORIMER 212–14; NILSSON *HM* 138.)

266–70. The pedigree of the helmet. It belonged first to Amyntor, son of Ormenos (father of Phoinix, according to 9.448); it was then stolen by the famous thief Autolykos (maternal grandfather of Odysseus; *Od.* 19.395) and was given by him to Amphidamas, who lived on the island of Kythera, south of Sparta, who in turn gave it to a Kretan, Molos, the father of Meriones. This shows how an object of value might travel in the Mycenaean world, particularly through the system of "guest friendship" (see 6.215 n.). This helmet had moved from Greece north of the Isthmus to the southern coast of the Peloponnese and then to Krete.

Eleon (267) was a town in Boiotia, mentioned in the Catalogue (2.500). In Book 9, however, Phoinix says that his father lived in Hellas, which was part of Thessaly (9.447); and in any case Amyntor's father, Ormenos, ought to be connected with the town

Ormenion in Thessaly (2.734). It is not possible for us now to tell whether we are receiving echoes of long-forgotten legends or whether Homer is taking names out of a hat.

Skandeia (268) was the port of the island of Kythera.

285–90. The story of Tydeus' embassy to Thebes before the main Argive army arrived is told more fully at 4.382–98 and is also mentioned at 5.803–8. The **grim deeds** which Tydeus did on the way back refer to his killing all except one of an ambush laid for him by the **Kadmeians** (Thebans). The **Asopos** is a river in southern Boiotia.

294. drench her horns in gold. Gold leaf was put on the horns of a sacrificial ox to make the offering more magnificent. There is a description in *Odyssey* 3.432–38.

299. The scene changes. Hektor also wishes to send out a scout.

316. evil: better "poor" or "mean."

317. a single son among five sisters. It is not fanciful to see this as information about personality rather than biography. Dolon evidently lacks self-criticism and thinks himself more important than he is; perhaps he has been "spoiled" by his five sisters.

321. The **sceptre,** normally held by the speaker in formal assembly, is apparently available on this occasion also.

323. Observe the impudence of Dolon. It would be contrary to all propriety that such an insignificant person should drive the chariot and horses of Achilleus. Hektor, in offering this reward (305–6), had not thought the matter out specifically. It is part of the artistry of the book that Dolon and Hektor are now speaking about getting the best horses and chariot of the Greeks, whereas the result of the night's events will be that Diomedes and Odysseus get the best horses in the Trojan camp.

351–53. range: the *width* of the area of a field that a team can plough in one day, given a standard length of furrow. Lines 352–53 then explain that mules achieve more than oxen.

382–457. There is something coldly efficient about this interrogation. Odysseus appears sympathetic; "don't worry about death," he says; and later (400) he even smiles at Dolon. It is Diomedes who does the killing (455).

402. Aiakides: Achilleus, *grandson* of Aiakos.

413. Dolon does not seem to realize how dangerous the information is which he is so willing to give in the hope of saving his own life. He is petrified by fear.

415. the barrow of godlike Ilos. The tomb of Ilos was a feature of the plain (11.166). Ilos, grandfather of Priam (20.232), was the king who had founded Ilion (Troy).

418. The **watchfires** of the Trojans are those of 8.554. The point of these lines is that the Trojans themselves are keeping a watch, but their allies are not.

428–31. The nine nations named here fit quite well with the eleven allied peoples whose contingents are described in the Trojan catalogue in 2.840–77. Those from central and western Asia Minor (Pelasgians, Mysians, Phrygians, Maionians, Karians, Lykians) tally exactly; it is only among the more remote allies that the list here is defective. The catalogue has Thracians and Kikonians as well as Paionians from the European side, and also Paphlagones and Halizones from along the Black Sea; in their place, this passage adds Leleges and Kaukonians, who do not appear in Book 2, although both are named later in the *Iliad* (Leleges, 20.96; Kaukonians, 20.329).

432. Dolon's question is disingenuous. He can hardly think that Odysseus is asking for this information from idle curiosity.

435. Rhesos. In the tragedy *Rhesus*, ascribed to Euripides, the only extant Greek tragedy whose plot is taken from the story of the *Iliad*, Rhesos the Thracian king is the son of the river Strymon. The fact that Eïon was the name of a town at the mouth of the Strymon (Thucydides 1.98) may have something to do with the name of Rhesos' father as given here.

454. chin. For the attitude of supplication, see 1.407 n.

464. By **once again** he means "further," "in addition to the success we have already had."

479–502. Odysseus and Diomedes act as a team. Odysseus offers his companion the choice, to get the horses or to kill the men. Diomedes chooses the latter, and Odysseus shows his cool intelligence by dragging the corpses out of the way, so that their retreat may not be impeded.

496–97. These two lines, while undoubtedly effective and memorable, are strangely impressionistic. We are left uncertain whether Rhesos was breathing heavily because he was having a nightmare or because he was dying and also whether in fact he had a dream at all or whether it is merely a figure of speech. (Dreams are also said elsewhere to stand by the dreamer's head.)

Diomedes was a *grandson* of Oineus; cf. Aiakides (402 n.).

507. Athene performs her common function of being, simultaneously, both an external goddess and the good judgment of the human warrior; cf. 1.194.

513. mounted behind the horses. It is generally accepted that Diomedes and Odysseus ride on horseback out of the Trojan camp, leaving the magnificently ornamented chariot (438, 501) among the dead Thracians. The formulaic language, however, has no phrases for horse-riding, a practice referred to only in the present exceptional circumstances and in a simile at 15.679–84. Consequently, here and in 529 Homer uses the normal phrase for mounting the chariot (copied in this by Lattimore's translation).

Some modern scholars (e.g., Shewan, Bayfield) have supposed that Diomedes did, after all, take the chariot (which he was considering doing in 505) and that they attached the horses to it without Homer's saying so. This is contrary to the impression received by the great majority of readers and opposed by both the ancient scholia and the author of the tragedy *Rhesus* (*Rhesus* 783). Moreover, the repeated phrase **whipped them with his bow** in 500 and 513–14 would be meaningless if they now had the chariot itself with the "glittering whip" (501) inside it.

The whole picture is confused by the limitations of the formulaic language. In real life, moreover, if the two horses were galloping along tied together (499), the chance of a successful ride for the two heroes would be slight; the only mitigation of this difficulty that the ancient commentators were able to suggest is that this pair of horses was well used to being in harness together. (For the problems of the whole passage, consult DELEBECQUE 78–80. A. Morard, in "Note sur le chant X de l'Iliade," *Bull. de l'Association Guillaume Budé* 22 [1963]: 385–403, looks at the description from the viewpoint of an expert in horsemanship.)

531. since this was the way he desired it: an attempt by Lattimore to give sense to the line. In 11.520 the same expression refers to the wish of the horses, not the rider; here, however, that is inappropriate, as these are not Greek horses. Many scholars have considered 531 an interpolation, and it is in fact omitted in the best manuscripts.

561. thirteenth: i.e., not counting the king.

564. So it appears that the council members had waited out in no-man's-land for their return.

570. ship. This is probably Odysseus' ship, not Diomedes'. Odysseus is the careful man, and it is he who will see to it that the dedication to Athene is properly carried out.

576. It is a little surprising to find **bathtubs** in the Greek camp. The word is found only here, but the warming of water for washing is mentioned more than once (18.346, 23.40).

BOOK ELEVEN

Book 11 is essential to the plot of the *Iliad* for two reasons. First, it contains the wounding of the major Greek heroes, Agamemnon, Diomedes, and Odysseus, which facilitates the Trojan victory; and second, the scene at the end between Patroklos and Nestor begins the sequence which leads to the tragedy of Book 16 and Achilleus' eventual return to the battle. Before the wounding of the Greek heroes, Agamemnon is compensated for the rather poor showing he has had up to now (see 9.9–28, 10.3–16) by being given an *aristeia* as glorious as that of Diomedes in Book 5. We are reminded that the Greek army counted him as one of their three best fighters in the absence of Achilleus (7.179–80).

The structure of the book is as follows:

1–66	Preparations for battle.
67–283	*Aristeia* of Agamemnon.
284–594	Hektor and the Trojans attack. Diomedes and Odysseus are wounded. Telamonian Aias covers the Greek retreat.
595–847	Patroklos and Nestor.

1. Dawn. The goddess of the dawn was thought to live in the East (naturally), with her human husband Tithonos. This is clearly a formulaic line for the start of a new day.

4. portent. Homer does not tell us what shape this portent took. No satisfactory concrete explanation has been offered, and perhaps none should be sought. The activity of this goddess is presumably not on the visual plane.

17–44. One of the four full-scale descriptions of the arming of a hero in the *Iliad* (cf. 3.330–38 n.). It is the longest of the four and contains the most ornamentation, because Agamemnon, the great king of Mykenai, is the most magnificent of the four warriors.

20. Kinyras was a legendary king of Kypros (Cyprus) and priest of Aphrodite.

24–28. A description of Agamemnon's very special corselet, or breastplate. It had colored strips of different metals. The numbers of **circles** are most easily explained by the assumption that the breastplate was in two parts, a front and a back, and that on each half, inlaid in the bronze, were twenty-one bands (whether vertical or horizontal) arranged as follows (C = "cobalt"—in Greek *kyanos*, more commonly described as blue enamel; G = gold; T = tin): G T C T G T C T G T C T G T C T G T C T G. If this is correct, it would appear that Homer has a reasonably clear idea of what he is describing and so has probably seen something like it—an impression given also by the description of the Shield of Achilleus in Book 18. On the front, superimposed on the stripes, three snakes curved up on each side of the wearer's neck.

All the same, it is not a clear picture. LORIMER 208 thinks that this may be a scale corselet of Near Eastern origin (note that it was sent from Kypros), made of rows of overlapping metal plates. F. H. Stubbings (in WACE/STUBBINGS 509) draws attention to the Mycenaean Linear B ideogram for *thorex* (breastplate), which seems to have horizontal bands running across it. On the other hand, the snakes twisting up to the wearer's neck have no parallels in the Mycenaean remains, and the closest objects of comparison for them are from the "orientalizing" art of the eighth century (NILSSON *HM* 125). .

27. the son of Kronos. Zeus, being the weather god, is responsible for **clouds** and **rainbows**.

29. nails: rivets, for attaching the blade to the handle.

32–35. The shield. The epithet **man-enclosing** suggests the Mycenaean body shield (7.219); but, if so, the origin of the word has been forgotten, because the poet proceeds to describe an evidently round shield. The **ten circles** of line 33 would be concentric between the rim and the center. This is how a convex leather shield, made of oxhide, would appear (but exaggerated, because it would not have ten layers), with the full depth at the center and one thickness only at the rim; thus the metal facing of Agamemnon's shield imitates the effect of a leather shield.

The twenty **knobs** of line 34 are ornamental studs; the one of line 35 is the central boss.

36–37. The decoration on the shield. The face of the **Gorgon,** a frightening mask, was a common motif on shields in archaic art, although all known examples date after the middle of the seventh century, considerably after the time of the composition of the *Iliad.* The Gorgon's head was in the center of the shield, and around it were "Fear" and "Terror." How they were pictured is left to our imagination. The aegis worn by Athene in 5.738–42 is similar; it had Hatred, Battle Strength, and Onslaught, as well as a Gorgon's head, on it, and Terror "all about it."

41. two-horned, four-sheeted. See 5.743–44 n.

47–55. After the description of the arming of Agamemnon, the poet wishes to present the Greek army sallying forth to battle. This is followed (56–66) by a description of the advance of the Trojans. It all adds to the effect of significant buildup for the fighting to come.

47–52. The meaning is difficult to follow. Most probably what the poet intends is as follows: The Greek leaders (who, as we know, use their chariots primarily as transport) dismounted at the ditch and crossed on foot. They then formed up *on the other side of the ditch* (51) much more quickly than their charioteers could get the chariots into position behind them. **Horseman** in lines 51 and 52 is a collective term, meaning the mass of charioteers with their chariots. It appears from 12.118–19 that the Greeks had left a causeway at one point when they were digging their ditch, so that their chariots could get across into the plain. (So ALBRACHT 1:15–16; 2:5.)

57–60. Hektor, Poulydamas, Aineias, Polybos, Agenor, and Akamas. These Trojan leaders (except for Polybos, who is named only here) play their part in the attack on the wall in Book 12, but except for Hektor himself they do not recur in Book 11. Pouly-damas (really Polydamas, but the first syllable has been lengthened for metrical reasons) is in a sense Hektor's double, whose main function in the *Iliad* is to give Hektor good but unheroic advice.

72. The phrase **held their heads on a line** is not perfectly clear, but evidently the meaning is that the fighting is hand to hand, and neither line will give way.

75. Zeus had forbidden the other gods to take part (8.7–16).

86. Not **supper**, because this day's fighting goes on until Book 18, and midday comes at 16.777. This is, rather, the time when the woodcutter, who has been working since dawn, rests and has his meal; i.e., it is mid-morning.

92–147. Agamemnon establishes his supremacy on the battlefield by killing successively three pairs of Trojans—pairs because they are in chariots, while he is on foot. In the same way, Diomedes at the beginning of his *aristeia* in Book 5 killed in quick succession four pairs of Trojans, including, as here, two sons of Priam (5.144–65).

101. Antiphos has already appeared in 4.489.

103. The bastard ... was charioteer. The illegitimate son has lower status and so acts as charioteer to his brother.

105. knees: foothills.

139–41. This delegation of Menelaos and Odysseus to Troy at the time of the Greek arrival, to demand the return of Helen, is mentioned by Antenor (who had acted as their host) in 3.205–24. Agamemnon's memory of the affair may be ad hoc invention, to justify his coming brutality; line 141 differs from what Homer himself said at line 125.

163. Zeus's removal of Hektor from the fighting is either the same event as that told at greater length in 185–210, or it is a preliminary act followed up by the other. If the former, then parallels can be found in the *Iliad* for a brief statement like this, followed a little later by an expanded version (cf. 15.416 n.). Line 198, however, suggests that Hektor is already out of the fighting when Iris comes to him with the message from Zeus.

166–67, 170. The tomb, or **barrow**, of Ilos, the **fig tree,** and the **oak tree** near the Skaian gates are all features of the plain. For the first, see 10.415.*

218–20. An address to the **Muses** is a way of enhancing the importance of what is to follow and so of drawing attention to a critical moment in the story (cf. 2.484–93 n.).

221–63. Agamemnon kills one of a pair of brothers and is then wounded by the other, whom he immediately kills. This sequence is repeated exactly in 426–49 for the wounding of Odysseus.

221. Iphidamas: a fourth son of Antenor, for three were mentioned in 59–60; Koön, in 248, is a fifth.

223. Antenor's wife, **Theano,** was daughter of Kisseus, king of Thrace.

226. We cannot help noticing that Kisseus' daughter would therefore be Amphidamas' aunt. The motif however is not so much genealogical as thematic: the old king, wishing to associate the young prince with himself in the government of the country, gives him his daughter's hand in marriage (so the king of Lykia and Bellerophontes in 6.192). The poet may not specifically have noticed that in this case the young prince is the old king's grandson.

229. Perkote: on the Hellespont (2.835).

243. For gifts from the suitor to the father of the bride, cf. 9.146.

270. The **spirits of childbirth,** called Eileithuiai, are "Hera's daughters" (271) because Hera was goddess of marriage.

299–300. Who then was the first, and who the last that he slaughtered...? The rhetorical question has the same effect as the appeal to the Muses in 218–20: to enhance what is to come. Here Hektor's successful attack is shown by a list of names of enemies killed; none of them is known from elsewhere.

312. Odysseus cried out to ... Diomedes. This is a similar, but contrasting, situation to the one at 8.92, where Diomedes called out to Odysseus; and the response here is also in contrast to the one there. These two heroes were of course in action together in the night expedition of Book 10.

329. It is highly unusual that the names of the two sons of Merops are not given. We know them, however, because these are important men—Adrestos and Amphios, leaders of one of the local contingents in the Trojan catalogue in Book 2; indeed, the four lines 329–32 here are identical with 2.831–34. Of several suggested explanations for the omission of their names, perhaps the most attractive is that the poet's spotlight is not on them but on their father and his unhappy fortune in knowing what was to happen and being unable to prevent it (so STRASBURGER 26).

353. three-ply. Helmets apparently could be made of three layers of bronze, or two of bronze and a leather lining; **hollow-eyed** refers to the eyeholes in the visor of the helmet.

The statement that Apollo gave Hektor his helmet need not be taken literally. Apollo was the god defending Troy and so, of course, defending Hektor (cf. 363); Hektor's most frequent epithet is "of the glancing helm" (315), and here his helmet has saved him. Put these facts together, and you may say that the god "gave" Hektor his helmet. Compare 7.146, where it is said that Ares gave Areïthoös his armor.

357. following his spear's cast. After throwing his spear, a warrior would apparently dash forward and recover it.

360. Hektor is shown here to be no match for Diomedes. It is reasonable to suppose, from Zeus's interference in 186 ff., that he was inferior to Agamemnon as well; and in the single combat in Book 7 he had the worst of it against Aias. If we add the incomparable Achilleus, it is clear that the best fighter on the Trojan side would not have ranked higher than fifth among the Greeks. This shows Homer's nationalistic leanings.

368. The **son of Paion** is Agastrophos, wounded in 338.

371–72. For the tomb of **Ilos,** see 10.415 n.

377. It is somehow thematic that Paris should shoot Diomedes in the **foot,** for Diomedes has been a substitute for Achilleus in the first part of the *Iliad,* and Paris later shot Achilleus, fatally, in the heel. The wound seems to be typical also for the brave Diomedes; this arrow goes clean through his foot, as the arrow of Pandaros in 5.100 went clean through his shoulder.

389–90. witless child, woman, useless man, no fighter. The fighter at close quarters scorns the archer, who keeps out of the thick of the battle.

404–10. A famous speech. Odysseus, always a rational man, calmly deliberates on his dangerous situation and comes up with the true heroic response. There may well be compensation here for the seeming overprudence of his behavior at 8.97. The poet is concerned among other things to glorify the major Greek heroes. In 441–45 we should notice the courage and superiority of Odysseus; although cut off from his friends, and now wounded, he frightens Sokos by sheer force of personality.

422. Ennomos: not the Mysian leader of 2.858, who is still alive in 17.218 and, in any case, is said to have been killed by Achilleus in the river (2.860).

445. "Famous for his horses" is a stock epithet of **Hades** (cf. 5.654).

453–54. the tearing birds. This is the third reference in this vivid book of fighting to the ghastly work of vultures (see 162, 395).

463. Menelaos is lightweight as a fighter but a sympathetic and conscientious man. It is characteristic that he should be the one to hear Odysseus' shout and try to do something about it. He calls for Aias to help again in 17.119.

474–81. A long simile, with two points of contact with the battle scene, as sometimes happens in Homer, so that the parallel is of a moving action, not just a static picture.

The final detail—**the lion eats it**—suits the situation in the simile but hardly the real circumstances, unless we are to read into it the later traditional antipathy between Aias and Odysseus (see 23.700–739 n.).

485. For Aias' shield **like a wall,** see 7.219 n.

498. Such indications of position as are found in the *Iliad* are consistent with the view that **the left of the battle** always means the left from the Greek point of view (CUILLANDRE 99).

499. It comes as something of a surprise both that Hektor is in full action on the Trojan right (he was last seen in 360, withdrawing from Diomedes) and that the fighting there is described as the hottest (**more than elsewhere**); indeed, the second point is contradicted by Kebriones in 529. What happens is that the poet, even in his detail, concentrates on the scene he is immediately describing. Here he stresses the violence of the fighting on the wing, incidentally enhancing the heroic stature of Hektor; in 528–30, needing to bring Hektor across to the center, to restore the position upset by Aias' attack, he makes Kebriones use the obvious argument.

506. For **Machaon,** surgeon in the Greek army, see 2.729–33.

521. Kebriones became Hektor's charioteer in 8.318, after two previous charioteers had been killed. The poet keeps him in our minds in Books 11 and 12, to prepare us for his important role toward the end of Book 16.

542. Following this line in many editions of the text is the line "for Zeus felt disapproval when he fought a better man," which is not in any manuscript but is quoted from this context by Aristotle and Plutarch. It was added to the text by early editors and is printed but marked as spurious by most recent ones. Compare 8.548, 550–52; 9.458–61. The effect of the total removal of the line, however, is that all the line numbers from here to the end of the book are one less than those in the regular editions.

543–73. Glorification of Aias, the perfect rear-guard fighter. Homer achieves this by two similes, strikingly juxtaposed, of a lion and a donkey, followed by a general description of Aias' defensive technique.

544. swung the shield behind him. The maneuver was to slide the great shield around to the wearer's back by its strap, to protect the warrior as he retreated. It is not so easy to see how this would work in practice, as he presumably would not simply turn his back on the enemy and walk away.

561. This is a joke; they manage to drive him out when he no longer wants to stay.

580. Eurypylos is Alexandros' third victim, of the five Greek heroes who are wounded in this book (see 369, 505). We remember also that it is Paris/Alexandros who will shoot and kill Achilleus himself after the end of the *Iliad* (22.359). Many have felt that Hektor's special place in the *Iliad* story has obscured the probable fact that Paris/Alexandros had more significance in the traditional saga of the Trojan War. Hektor kills no significant Greek except Patroklos.

592. Better, "leaning their shields against *their* shoulders," although it is not clear exactly what that means. It suggests serried ranks.

595. From here to the end of the book the scene changes to the Greek camp and to a meeting between Patroklos and Nestor. This final third of Book 11—a long book—is significant for the development of the plot of the *Iliad* (see the introductory note to this book, above). Homer has prepared for it by introducing two similar incidents into the fighting—Alexandros' wounding of first Machaon and then Eurypylos. The first incident motivates Nestor's withdrawal from the battlefield and so makes the coming scene possible; the latter provides a friend in need, to delay the return of Patroklos to Achilleus (805–47).

600. Fighting is Achilleus' life, and he misses it; so he goes up onto the stern of his ship to watch at a distance. Homer gives him a very natural motive for sending Patroklos to Nestor.

608. now I think the Achaians will come to my knees ... This line has caused extreme and unnecessary difficulty. A common comment is that it ignores the Embassy to Achilleus in Book 9, which in fact took place only the previous evening. From this the conclusion has been drawn that Book 9 itself was a late addition to the *Iliad*, not known to the author of this line. It seems, on the contrary, perfectly human for Achilleus, who is still angry, to exclaim, on seeing the Achaians defeated, "Now they will have to come and beg me to return," caring nothing for the fact that they have already come once for that purpose. (Compare 16.49–86 n.).

631–34. The **cup** of Nestor is the third description in the *Iliad* of an artifact which could have been made only in the Mycenaean Age (to be added to Aias' tower shield in 7.219 and the boar's-tusk helmet of 10.261–65). Added interest has been given to Nestor's description by the gold cup found by Schliemann in the fourth shaft grave at Mykenai. This cup, now in the National Museum at Athens, is considerably smaller than the one Homer describes, but it has doves on its handles and two supports at the side, which used to be identified with the pair of **bases** mentioned in 634. Modern opinion, however, has gone against this latter view and believes that Nestor's cup had some sort of double bottom.

635–36. Another man with great effort. There is humor in this. It is a sort of heroic compliment, like Achilleus' being the only person able to wield his own great spear (16.141–42) or, in the *Odyssey*, Odysseus' having a bow which none but he could bend.

638–39. This mixture of **wine, grated cheese,** and **barley,** unkindly described by Leaf 1:508 as a sort of stimulating porridge, is made also by the witch Kirke for Odysseus' companions in Book 10 of the *Odyssey* (234–35), but with honey added as a fourth ingredient. Honey is available here, too (630).

NESTOR'S SPEECH TO PATROKLOS (LINES 655–802)

We cannot fail to notice that in response to Patroklos' insistence that he is in a hurry and must not keep Achilleus waiting, Nestor replies with a speech of nearly 150 lines, including a long reminiscence of his youth, during which time natural politeness and respect for the old keep Patroklos standing there. Nestor is one of Homer's favorite characters. He has the old man's tendency to digress and reminisce about the past, but there is always some point to it. Here he is softening up Patroklos, as it were, in preparation for an important and definite suggestion at the end of his speech.

The speech falls into three parts:

655–68   The present critical situation.

669–760   An example of heroic behavior taken from Nestor's own achievements in youth.

761–802   A reminder of Patroklos' own responsibilities and a suggestion of what he might do to help.

661. This line is not in the best manuscripts. If genuine here (it is found in the same context at 16.27), it was perhaps condemned by an Alexandrian scholar, probably Aristarchus, on the grounds that, as Eurypylos was wounded after Nestor left the field, the old king ought not to show knowledge of it. This would be typical of the pedantic criteria of the Alexandrians.

Nestor's Reminiscence (Lines 669–760)

This is the longest of the four major digressions in Nestor's speeches in the *Iliad*. The others are 1.260–73, where Nestor went to help the Lapiths against the centaurs; 7.132–58, where Nestor killed a huge opponent in single combat; and 23.629–45, where Nestor was once an all-conquering athlete.

The reminiscence here is about a war between the people of Pylos and their northern neighbors from Elis. A common view has been that it is an excerpt from some other poem about the legends of Pylos, with Nestor as hero, inserted here in the *Iliad*. There is no doubt that the events are described with much accuracy and corroborative detail (see the sequence as set out later in this note and in 706 n.). Moreover, they describe a local situation which can have existed only in the remote past, for none of the place names in the story was securely identifiable in the classical period. It seems likely that what we have here is a real relic of a tradition about long-ago border raids, a tradition the descendants of the Pylians carried with them when they left Greece and migrated across the Aegean Sea; this tradition would later have been modified by Ionian poets and finally adapted to the *Iliad* by Homer as a typical reminiscence of Nestor. However, it is not at all necessary that it should always have been associated with Nestor's name or that there was an epic version of Nestor's exploits (a "Nestoris"), used as a quarry by Homer.

The tale is not told chronologically but in a natural storyteller's way, as follows:

670   *The essential fact:* There was a battle between the Pylians and the people of Elis.

671–87   *The immediate occasion:* It resulted from a cattle raid led by Nestor.

688–706   *The remoter cause:* Pylos had been weakened by Herakles and had thereafter suffered from depredations by their hostile Epeian (= Elean) neighbors.

706–12   In reprisal for the cattle raid, the Epeians attacked the Pylian border town of Thryoessa.

713–32   The Pylians came to its defense.

733–60   The Pylians won a great and glorious victory.

For a fuller discussion of this tale, consult F. Bölte, "Ein pylisches Epos," *Rheinisches Museum* 83 (1934): 319–47.

681. Neleian: i.e., belonging to Neleus, Nestor's father.

There has been much dispute in this century as to the location of Nestor's Pylos. Two sites have had their supporters, Kakovatos in Triphylia, halfway down the west coast of the Peloponnese, and Ano Englianos, a little inland of the Pylos in Messenia, much further south, which was famous for the Athenian exploit in Book 4 of Thucydides. Recent excavations by Carl Blegen have been decisive for the latter, as the site at Ano Englianos has disclosed a Mycenaean palace of great magnificence. On the other hand, a Pylos so far south, well over a hundred miles from the border with Elis, does not suit the details of Nestor's tale. The captured cattle could not possibly have been driven down to Messenian Pylos so as to arrive there in the night following the raid—which is the most natural interpretation of line 682. Kakovatos is some twenty miles from the Elean frontier, so that, allowing for moderate exaggeration, its position would better suit Nestor's tale. We should remember, however, that we may be trying to harmonize two different things: the archeological evidence, reflecting real historical situations, and heroic actions set in a now legendary world by a poet living some hundreds of years later.

689. Herakles' campaign against Pylos is apparently referred to in 5.392–402, where Dione consoles her wounded daughter, Aphrodite, by relating other occasions when mortals wounded gods. Whether there is any historical fact behind it is difficult to discern; some would like to see a connection with the Dorian Invasion (called by the Greeks "the return of the children of Herakles") and the breakup of the Mycenaean Age. For the alternative explanation—that there is confusion here and that "Pylos" in the story of Herakles originally denoted "the gate of the underworld," see 5.392–404 n.

698. four horses. This is the one certain allusion in the *Iliad* to a four-horse chariot (Hektor addresses four horses by name in 8.185, but there are serious difficulties about that passage), and it is to be noticed that our context is of racing, not of war. On hearing of a four-horse chariot on its way to Elis to compete for a prize in the games, we naturally think of the Olympian games, held at Olympia on the Alpheios River (711) in Elis every fourth year throughout classical times and traditionally founded (or refounded) in 776 B.C. On the other hand, the only games mentioned in Homer are funeral games; and Nestor's tale in 23.631 of funeral games at Bouprasion in Elis suggests a tradition of games in that area, but no necessary allusion to Olympia.

A **tripod** was a regular prize at games (23.264, 702); for its use, see 18.373 n.

700. Augeias was a king of Elis; the cleansing of his stables was one of the labors of Herakles. His grandson was one of the leaders of the Greek contingent from Elis (2.624).

706. The tale has a carefully worked-out time sequence:

Day 1. Nestor's successful armed raid (671–80).
     Night: Captured beasts are driven into Pylos (681–82).
Day 2. Division of the spoils at Pylos (684–705).
Day 3. Epeians attack Thryoessa (706–12).
     Night: Athene brings the news to Pylos, where the
     people are immediately ready to fight (713–16).
Day 4. They take up a position on the river Minyeïos (721–23);
     from there they march to the Alpheios, arriving in the
     afternoon (724–25).
Day 5. They attack the Epeians (734–35).

708. The **two Moliones**—also called the sons of Aktor, although
their real father was Poseidon (750)—were Kteatos and Eurytos,
famous twins. Their respective sons are two of the leaders of
the contingent from Elis (2.621). Mythological tradition made
them Siamese twins (23.638–42 n.).

710. **Thryoessa,** at the ford of the Alpheios, which was the
boundary between Pylos and Elis, is called Thryon in the
Catalogue (2.592).

721. **Minyeïos.** The river preserves the name of the Minyans, a
shadowy people particularly associated with Orchomenos, in
northern Greece (2.511). There was some connection with Pylos;
we are told that Nestor's mother, Chloris, came from Minyan
Orchomenos (*Od.* 11.284), and Neleus himself was said to have
migrated from northern Greece to the Peloponnese. (See NILSSON
127–50.)

739–40. **Agamede,** by her name and her specialized knowledge,
can hardly fail to remind us of the witch Medea; but it is difficult to
find a connection.

747. fifty chariots. One suspects some exaggeration in Nestor's
memory due to the passage of time. The **two** in each chariot were of
course the driver and the fighter.

755–57. Bouprasion, the Olenian rock, and **the hill of Alesios**
are all named in the entry for Elis in the Catalogue of Ships
(2.615–17). The latter two places might well be near the river
Alpheios in southern Elis, but Bouprasion seems to have been the
plain of northwest Elis (HOPE SIMPSON AND LAZENBY 97–99). If so,
the description of the pursuit has been exaggerated.

764–88. Nestor recalls to Patroklos the time before the beginning of the Trojan War, when he and Odysseus went round Greece to collect the Achaian army (cf. 9.252–53 n.). Patroklos was living with Peleus in Phthia, having had to leave his own home of Opous when he had the misfortune to kill another child in a game (23.85–88). On this occasion it appears that Menoitios, Patroklos' father, was there too; Homer needs this to be so, for the alleged advice that Nestor is going to quote. So Nestor and Odysseus came upon the four of them, two fathers and two sons.

783. be always best in battle and pre-eminent beyond all others. A statement of the competitive heroic code, eminently suitable for Achilleus. The line is found also at 6.208, as paternal instruction to the Lykian Glaukos.

786. elder. Patroklos is older than Achilleus—rather to our surprise, in view of the protectiveness of the younger hero.

793–94. if . . . his honoured mother has told him something. This looks very like an allusion to Achilleus' statement in his speech to the Embassy that he has been told by his mother that he has a choice of two fates: a short and glorious life or a long and inglorious one (9.410–16). On the other hand, when the question is actually put to him, Achilleus says no (16.50–51).

803. Patroklos says nothing. This shows that he is strongly affected by Nestor's words. Also he needs to get away.

831. For Cheiron, see 4.219 n.

840. We may notice the sympathetic and gentle nature of Patroklos. The poet is simultaneously preparing for the tragedy of his death in Book 16 and getting him out of the way during the intervening books of fighting.

BOOK TWELVE

In Book 12, the Greeks, having temporarily lost three of their major heroes, are on the defensive, and the Trojans attack the wall (whose building, at the end of Book 7, prepared for the set-piece description here). Book 12 is a complete action in itself, for it ends with the breakthrough when Hektor smashes open the gate of the main entrance to the Greek camp with a massive stone at line 459; there is now nothing between the Trojans and the Greek ships except a demoralized mass of men.

Homer has a clear picture of what he is describing and expressly divides the Trojan army into five divisions at the start (86–104) so that he can give the effect of pressure at different points along the wall, a near breakthrough elsewhere causing a weakening of the defense in the center, so that success eventually falls there. The actual sequence is:

118–94	Asios (Division 3) attacks the side gate.
195–289	Hektor (Division 1) attacks the center.
290–429	Sarpedon (Division 5) presses home an attack so hard that defenders have to be moved from facing Hektor in order to hold the line.
430–71	Hektor breaks through.

Memorable in this book are numerous similes and the noble speech of the sympathetic Sarpedon in 310–28.

6–9. The repeated statement that the wall was built without due reverence to the gods leads into a long explanation in 10–33 of how it was obliterated by "natural causes" after the end of the war. Divine annoyance had already appeared immediately after the wall was built (7.443–63). As usual in this early period, the gods object

137

because of an infringement of their own status, not in support of a general moral principle. So, here and in Book 7, it is Poseidon and Apollo who take action, because they were the gods who had once built the massive city walls of Troy for Laomedon, Priam's father, and they are jealous that the new Greek wall will diminish the fame of their efforts. The whole passage seems to be an attempt to explain why the wall was not there in Homer's own day.

12. the wall stood firm. Not quite true, because the wall is breached at 12.398, and later Apollo is said to flatten a whole section of it, like a child knocking down a sand castle (15.361); but it is enough that in general the wall stood for the duration of the war.

19–22. all the rivers. The first five rivers are named only here in the *Iliad*. **Aisepos** occurs elsewhere, in connection with Pandaros' Lykians, through whose land it flowed; **Skamandros** and **Simoeis** come in frequently. Surprisingly, seven of the eight names listed here appear in a different order in a list of twenty-five selected rivers in Hesiod's *Theogony* 338–45. There has been some dispute about the priority in this case between the *Iliad* and Hesiod. Considering how insignificant these rivers are, except to the northwest corner of Asia Minor, we may reasonably assume that Hesiod took them from Trojan War poetry—though not necessarily, of course, from the *Iliad*.

30. passage of Helle: the Hellespont.

46. it is his own courage that kills him. These words seem to be a clear foreshadowing, within the simile, of Hektor's death. We should be careful, however, because the same thing is said in another simile at line 150 of this book, and there it foreshadows nothing.

50–51. the . . . horses balked at the edge. DELEBECQUE 77 points out that the description of the horses hesitating at the ditch, afraid to cross, is intelligible only if there is an underlying confusion between riding and chariot-driving. It is patently obvious that horses could not pull a chariot across a ditch, although without a chariot they might jump it. On the other hand, there is no example of the heroes riding on horseback in the *Iliad*, except in the special circumstances of the return from the night expedition in Book 10.

55. The surface of the floor means the ground on the Greek side of the ditch, where they had driven in stakes to make an additional obstacle (7.441).

59. the dismounted were strong in their effort. What Homer seems to mean is that the soldiers on foot were instantly intending to cross.

60. For **Poulydamas,** see 11.57–60 n.

65. to get down: probably means to dismount from the chariot in order to fight (the normal procedure).

77 and **84–85.** These lines appeared at 11.47–49, in another order, in a description of the Greek army sallying forth for battle in the morning. They suit the present attack better. Such repetition of the same lines in similar circumstances is a typical feature of oral poetry.

87–104. five well-ordered battalions. The Trojan army is divided into five divisions for its assault on the wall. It is pretty clear that this is not traditional material but is invented for the present scene by the poet of the *Iliad*.

It is surprising—at least if we make the natural assumption that the ordinary troops will follow their own leaders—that the first three divisions are all led by Trojans, the fourth by their neighbors, the Dardanians, and one sole division by allies. This does not accord with statements elsewhere which suggest that the allies are more numerous than the Trojans (e.g., 2.123–33).

Three leaders are given for each division: (1) Hektor, Poulydamas, Kebriones; (2) Paris, Alkathoös, Agenor; (3) Helenos, Deïphobos, Asios; (4) Aineias, Archelochos, Akamas; (5) Sarpedon, Glaukos, Asteropaios.

Of these, half are killed in the second half of the *Iliad*; perhaps only those who had some place in later legends, and therefore must survive, do so. Hektor and Asteropaios are killed by Achilleus; Kebriones and Sarpedon by Patroklos; Alkathoös and Asios by Idomeneus; Archelochos by Aias. An Akamas is killed by Meriones in 16.342; but he is not identified as this son of Antenor and may be someone else of the same name.

91. Homer wishes to keep **Kebriones** before us, in preparation for the climax of Book 16. See notes on 8.119 and 318.

93. Agenor is the best known of the sons of Antenor. Two of his brothers join Aineias in the fourth division (99). Three other brothers were named in Book 11 (at 59, 221, 248).

94–97. Helenos and **Deïphobos** are well-known sons of Priam. **Asios** comes into prominence immediately (110) and again at his death in Book 13. The lines describing him occur also in the Trojan catalogue (96–97 = 2.838–39).

98–100. Aineias, Archelochos, Akamas. These three are the leaders of the Dardanians in the Trojan catalogue (2.819–23).

101–2. Glaukos and **Sarpedon** lead the Lykians; **Asteropaios** is a leader of the Paionians, from the land over toward Macedonia. He is not named in their contingent in the catalogue (2.848–50), but he introduces himself to Achilleus as their leader at 21.155.

110. The behavior of **Asios** has been seen as a sort of foreshadowing of the fate of Hektor. Here we have a man who refuses to accept the good advice of Poulydamas, and his death follows. Hektor refuses to accept Poulydamas' advice later in this book (231–50) and in 18.249–313, and his mistaken self-confidence leads to his death.

117. through the spear of Idomeneus. The fight between Asios and Idomeneus comes at 13.384–93. **Deukalion** was son of Minos, the legendary king of Krete.

118. to the left of the ships. It appears that there was a side entrance to the Greek camp. As it is used by the chariots, it must have been approached by a break in the ditch for them to get through (cf. 11.47–52 n.).

128. Lapithai. Although the Thessalian tribe of Lapiths is named only here and in 181, we hear of their war against the centaurs at 1.262–72, and the two heroes in action here (Polypoites and Leonteus) lead the relevant contingent in the Catalogue of Ships (2.738–47).

137. these: now refers to the Trojan attackers.

139–40. Asios and all five of his companions are killed in the ensuing fighting, **Iamenos** and **Orestes** in 193–94, the others in Book 13. **Adamas** is probably the son of Asios himself, not of some other man of the same name (see 17.583 n.).

141–42. This sentence describes the activity of Polypoites and Leonteus when the Trojan attack was in prospect. When it came near, the two Greeks moved forward out of the gate.

148. tearing slantwise. The position of a boar's tusks is such that it uses them for a sideways slash, not a straight attack.

151. grinding scream. A new point of comparison is introduced at the end of the simile. Originally the comparison with two wild boars was based on the violent forward rush of the two defenders; now there is a secondary point, of the sound made by the boars compared with the sound of missiles striking armor.

175. at the various gates. This line expressly states that there were several gates in the Greek wall. We hear of two—the one on the Greek left, attacked by Asios (118), and the one, probably in the center, broken in by Hektor at the end of this book.

195. The poet now turns to the first division of the Trojans, under Hektor, who are attacking the main gate of the camp (in the center, as may be deduced from 13.312). The method of description follows a general principle pointed out by T. Zielinski (in *Die Behandlung gleichzeitiger Ereignisse im antiken Epos, Philologus Supplementband* 8 [1899–1901]: 405–49)—namely, that the poet is compelled by his conventions to describe simultaneous events as successive. Thus we find that Hektor's troops have been waiting because of a portent. In fact, they could not, from the poet's point of view, start fighting until Asios had stopped. Compare 15.157–220 n.

235–36. counsels of ... Zeus. Hektor refers to Zeus's message to him in 11.192–94 (= 207–9).

237–38. trust in birds. In spite of Hektor's faith in Zeus, and the high patriotism of 243, this scorn for omens is hardly sensible and borders on blindness and delusion (cf. 13.823 n.). Scorn for the "birds flying overhead" is used by Sophokles in *Oedipus the King* 965–66 to show the unjustified (and, in the event, fatal) self-confidence of Oidipous and Iokasta; the suitor Eurymachos shows the same delusion in *Od.* 2.181–82.

240. to the left: toward the west and the sunset. The Trojans are facing north, the Greek camp being on the south shore of the Hellespont.

278–86. This long simile seems to be an expansion of the shorter snowstorm simile of 157–58. Both describe the same thing, the constant hail of stones.

286. The word translated **rain** must mean "snowstorm" here.

290. Homer now switches to the attack made by the Trojan fifth division, the allies under Sarpedon. They press so hard against the stretch of the wall opposite them that the greater Aias and his brother Teukros have to leave their position opposite Hektor and come to defend this danger spot. The effect is to weaken the defense against Hektor, who breaks through. This is an accurate and perceptive description of how a real battle might go.

310–28. This famous speech of Sarpedon to his friend Glaukos is a clear statement of the principle of *noblesse oblige.* The king is under an obligation to his people to fight bravely because they believe in him. Sarpedon goes further and rationalizes the heroic willingness to win honor even at the risk of one's life. "If it were possible to live for ever," he says, "I should not think these risks worthwhile; but seeing that death will come one way or another, we may as well try for glory."

331. Menestheus shivered. Menestheus, leader of the Athenians, is not a very impressive figure in the *Iliad.*

336. In 8.334 **Teukros** left the field, wounded by Hektor. It looks as if the statement that he has only just arrived is a reference to that wound of yesterday.

366. Lykomedes, one of the younger heroes, had been among the leaders of the night guard sent out in 9.80–84.

372. There has been some discussion of why Teukros had to have somebody to carry his bow for him. Perhaps it is no more than an added touch of distinction.

384. For **four-sheeted,** see 5.743–44 n.; but the word is obscure.

397. Observe how Sarpedon, who made the speech about courage and duty (310–28), is pulling at the battlements with both hands, only a few feet away from the defenders.

421–23. The simile is of a dispute between two farmers about the boundaries of their individual strips in the "common field" of a village (see W. Ridgeway, "The Homeric Land System," *Journal of Hellenic Studies* 6 [1885]: 320–23).

426. guard-skins: see 5.453 n.

433–35. The second simile taken from contemporary life by the poet is a comparison of the exact balance of the battle with the scales in which a poor working woman weighs out wool for her daily task of spinning. The additional information about the woman, how she needs to provide for her children, is of course irrelevant to the purpose of the comparison; it shows however the poet's sympathy for human troubles. This naturally struck a chord in the sensitive mind of Virgil, who added still more detail to the picture in *Aeneid* 8.408–13.

445–50. An expansion of the stock lines 5.302–4.

463. like sudden night. There are two parallels to this striking likeness. In 1.47, Apollo, bringing the plague, comes "like night" to the Greek ships; in *Odyssey* 11.606, Herakles stalks through the ghosts "like dark night," with his bow ready to shoot.

BOOK THIRTEEN

Books 13 and 14 mark a major "retardation" of the plot. Hektor has broken through the Greek wall, and the Trojans are all set to attack the ships. Now, however, the Greeks rally, hold their position, and eventually drive the Trojans back. Only in Book 15 is the Trojan advance resumed. The poet describes these events on the divine plane as well as the human. The Greek rally is explained by the fact that Zeus (who is responsible for everything) temporarily takes his eyes off the battle in Book 13, and is otherwise distracted in Book 14, so that a Greek sympathizer, the sea god, Poseidon, takes the opportunity to encourage and assist his side. He does this incognito in Book 13 but openly in Book 14, when Zeus is asleep.

The long Book 13 is divided as follows:

1–239	Poseidon encourages the Achaians to make a stand.
240–329	Idomeneus and Meriones meet behind the lines.
330–515	*Aristeia* of Idomeneus on the left of the battle.
516–672	Fierce and evenly balanced fighting continues on the left.
673–837	Confrontation of Hektor and Aias in the center.

4–6. The **Thracians** were nomads, living in the plains on the European side of the Hellespont; the **Mysians** are not the allies of Troy from central Asia Minor (2.858) but a northern tribe, the "Moesi" of the Romans. The **Hippomolgoi** (Hippemolgoi would be a better spelling) means "mare-milkers," as is explained at the beginning of line 6 (cf. Herodotus 4.2, where it is reported how the Scythians used to milk mares). The **Abioi** are described as the **most righteous of all men**, partly because the Greeks had a view of the simple justice of the uncultivated people of the far north ("Hyper-

144

boreans" to later poets), and partly from the sound of the name, which might mean "not using violence."

7–9. he had no idea. Zeus had expressly forbidden the other gods to interfere in the battle (8.7–16). He saw no risk of disobedience.

10–38. The epiphany of Poseidon. This justly famous passage marks the start of the second half of the *Iliad*. Poseidon, brother of Zeus and nearly equal in power, was watching the battle from the top of the mountain on the island of Samothrace (12–13). The peak of Samothrace is so high that, although the island of Imbros (33) lies directly between, it is visible from all parts of the Trojan plain. This strongly suggests that whoever first imagined Poseidon watching from there knew the area personally.

Poseidon went first to his own sanctuary of Aigai—whether this was the famous Aigai on the north coast of the Peloponnese, sacred indeed to Poseidon (8.203), or some other place of the same name in the area of the *Aegean* Sea. He goes there to arm himself and get his chariot, so that he may move to battle like a human hero. The image of the god of the sea driving his chariot over the waves, dolphins and other sea creatures gamboling around him, has been much imitated in painting and sculpture.

Tenedos and Imbros (33) are lower islands than Samothrace and nearer the coast.

45. Poseidon appears first in the form of Kalchas, the seer of the Greek army (1.69). His encouragement of the Greeks is directed at:

a) the two heroes Aias (47–58), where he assumes the form of Kalchas;
b) certain minor leaders (95–124), in the same form;
c) Idomeneus (219–38), in the form of Thoas, leader of the Aitolians.

53. berserk. Hektor, not the equal of the major Greeks in skill, is frightening because of his wild and dangerous fighting (8.299).

54, 58. Poseidon's references to Zeus in connection with Hektor draw attention to the opposition between the two great gods at this point.

62. burst into winged flight. It is a little uncertain whether Poseidon took bird shape for his departure, as gods sometimes do, or whether he merely departed at great speed, compared by the poet to a hawk. The minor Aias' words at 70–72 suggest the latter.

91–93. A list of minor heroes. **Teukros** is half-brother of the Telamonian Aias; **Leïtos** and **Peneleos** are two of the five leaders of the Boiotains (2.494); **Thoas** alone is a major hero, leader of the Aitolians; **Deïpyros** was one of the leaders of the guard (9.83; he is killed later in this book, at 576); **Meriones** and **Antilochos** both play a large part in the fighting here, as they do in the whole *Iliad*.

137–42. The simile of the stone rolling down the hillside has two points of contact with Hektor's attack: the unstoppable momentum of his initial onrush, and the fact that he comes to a stop when the Greeks put up a firm resistance. This double point of contact is a notable feature of the more developed Homeric similes.

156–68. The first encounter—that between Deïphobos and Meriones—has a structural significance in the book. The fight comes to nothing here, for Meriones breaks his spear (leading him to go back behind the lines to get another, where he meets Idomeneus, his superior officer, and returns to the battle with him); it is resumed at 528.

Deïphobos and Meriones are apparently at this stage in the center of the battle, somewhere near Hektor, who is certainly there (312–15). Later they reappear on the Greek left.

Lines 157–58 describe the cautious advance of a skilled fighter with a large shield; contrast 371.

169–205. Homer sets the scene for the book by a brief description of fierce fighting in the center, where Hektor and Aias are the protagonists.

185. Amphimachos is an important person, a leader of the contingent from Elis (2.620); his father was one of the twin Moliones, sons of Poseidon (206), although their putative father was Aktor (see 11.749–50).

195. Stichios is mentioned again in 691.

202–5. hewed away his head. Aias son of Oïleus is a mean and brutal man. The greater Telamonian Aias would not treat a dead enemy in this way.

206. grandson: see 185 n.

210. Idomeneus is singled out by the poet for an *aristeia* in this book. He has, throughout, been one of the leading Greeks; and now that three of the best are wounded, it gives an opportunity to those who, as fighters, are below the top level. Idomeneus is an older man, already going grey (361). His kingdom of Krete is evidently of great importance in the Achaian realm, for it produced the third-largest contingent—of eighty ships (2.652), equal to Diomedes' Argos, and fewer only than Mykenai itself and Nestor's Pylos.

Homer gives Idomeneus a plausible excuse for not being engaged in fighting at the present moment (210–14); in fact, he is not even wearing his armor.

216. Thoas: see 92. For his home (217–18), cf. 2.638–44.

246–97. This long conversation between **Idomeneus** and **Meriones** has been much criticized, particularly in recent years, as repetitive and ineffective—with the suggestion that it is a late addition to the *Iliad*, i.e., not by Homer. It is better to see in it humor on the poet's part. He is amused by the reactions of these two friends, unexpectedly meeting some way behind the front line. Each is uncomfortably aware of what the other may be thinking; and so each, without explicit accusation or apology, defensively protests his personal courage.

The nervous defensiveness shown here is closely paralleled in Aineias' long and repetitive speech when he is unlucky enough to meet Achilleus in 20.200–258. There, too, modern critics, by taking too serious a view of the passage, have found much fault with it.

256. Meriones came back to get another spear from his own collection (168). He now apparently changes his mind and asks Idomeneus if he can borrow one of his. In 268 he says (surprisingly) that his quarters are not near those of Idomeneus. We may, however, remember 4.253–54, where it is said that Idomeneus commands the front troops of the Kretans, Meriones the rear.

290. It almost seems that Idomeneus lingers over the description of these unpleasant wounds, as if he is enjoying the discomfiture of his lieutenant.

298–303. Meriones and Idomeneus are compared to Ares, god of war, entering battle with his son and agent, Terror. The situation is not quite clear. What is probably intended is that the Ephyroi and the Phlegyes (tribes of Thessaly) are at war; Ares goes to help one side or the other side—not, of course, both.

307. Deukalides is an abbreviated form of the patronymic for "son of Deukalion." This Deukalion was a son of Minos, the legendary king of Krete (451).

308–9. Meriones asks Idomeneus whether they should enter the battle on the right, in the center, or on the left. The center is occupied by the main attack of Hektor, resisted by the two Aiantes and others. Homer intentionally sends Idomeneus to the left, so that he can have his own *aristeia* without interfering with those other heroes. On the left he will encounter, among others, Asios, who attacked a gate on the Greek left in 12.118. In practice, no fighting is ever said to take place "on the right." It is just possible that this is because Achilleus' ships are at the extreme right (see chart, pp. 116–17), and the Trojans would be more hesitant about attacking in that area (so CUILLANDRE 57).

325. There are two kinds of fighting for the Homeric warrior: **close combat,** in which the necessary qualities are physical strength, mental endurance, and good weapon drill; and more open fighting, when one army is pursuing and the other being pursued, when speed of foot is the first requirement (see Appendix B). Aias is a huge man, outstanding in the first kind of fighting but not mobile enough for the second.

345–60. The poet pauses to summarize the situation on the divine plane.

358–60. a crossing cable. A difficult metaphor. It seems that the battle is compared to a rope tying the two armies together and pulled tight by the great gods Poseidon and Zeus.

361–515. The *aristeia* of **Idomeneus.** He kills three important warriors: Othryoneus, suitor for Priam's daughter Kassandra; Asios, son of Hyrtakos, familiar to us from 12.108–74; and Alkathoös, brother-in-law of Aineias. This major hero now gets involved; the battle is evened up; and, exhausted by his efforts, Idomeneus withdraws.

371. with high stride. Othryoneus is overconfident. His promise to Priam shows that this is characteristic of him; the weakness makes him incautious. It is something of a moral tale.

373–82. vaunting. The boast over a fallen foe is a regular feature in the fighting; cf. 446. It is assumed that Idomeneus knows the personal history of Othryoneus.

we would give you the loveliest of Atreides' daughters (378). Compare Agamemnon's offer to Achilleus, 9.141–48. Idomeneus is, of course, being sarcastic.

384. Asios shared with Helenos and Deïphobos the command of the third division of the Trojan army in the attack on the wall in Book 12. He alone disregarded the advice of Poulydamas to leave their chariots at the ditch and attack on foot (see 12.110 n.). Homer seems concerned to remind us of this dangerous self-confidence, for he mentions the horses of Asios in 385 and 392.

The brilliant and terrible lines describing the death of Asios in 389–93 are repeated word for word at the death of Sarpedon, killed by Patroklos in 16.482–86. This is a good example of the sort of repetition inherent in formulaic composition: a sequence is available to the poet, and he uses it when he thinks best. The lines were not first composed for either of these two occasions.

396. Antilochos is an alert young man. He killed a charioteer in the same circumstances in 5.580 and there, too, got away with the chariot and horses.

402. Deïphobos reappears (see 156–68 n.), wishing to avenge his fellow commander, Asios.

421–23. These lines were used for the removal of the wounded Teukros from the battle scene in 8.332–34, Mekisteus and Alastor there too being the stretcher-bearers. There seems something slightly wrong here, because 412 and 416 certainly suggest that Hypsenor is dead, and dead men do not groan.

Mekisteus, son of Echios. In 15.339 a Mekisteus *and* an Echios are killed, suggesting that the poet was subconsciously affected by a connection between these two names; cf. 792.

427–28. Aisyetes. In 2.793, the "burial mound of ancient Aisyetes" is a feature of the plain. **Alkathoös**, like Asios, was one of the divisional commanders in the Trojan attack in Book 12. He had shared the second division with Paris and Agenor (12.93).

443. This is an imaginative variation on the more ordinary description of the shaft of a spear still quivering after it has struck the ground (e.g., 16.611–13). Commentators have been skeptical whether the beating of the heart could transfer much motion to the other end of a spear stuck into it.

444. Ares: i.e., war. Not the personified god, who is perforce keeping out of the battle (521–25).

450. The translation is not quite accurate. **Krete** was not the mother (although it is common enough for the local nymph, having the same name as the place, to be the mother of the local hero), for Minos' mother was Europa (14.321). Better, "Zeus first got Minos, who cared for his people in Krete."

459. For **Aineias,** see 5.166 n. The motif of anger as a reason for staying out of the battle will remind us of Achilleus and Meleagros (9.555). Achilleus himself alludes to Aineias' unsatisfactory position in relation to Priam and his family when he speaks to him in 20.178–83.

478. Askalaphos, Aphareus, Deïpyros: three figures named in a catalogue of leaders merely to enhance the effect of their death in the next hundred lines. Askalaphos, son of Ares himself, is one of the leaders from Orchomenos (2.512); he, Aphareus, and Deïpyros (the last-named already mentioned in 92, above) were all among the leaders of the guard in 9.81–84.

484–85. were we two of the same age. Idomeneus reminds us of the point made in 361—that he is no longer young—and thus prepares us for his withdrawal.

488. sloped their shields. See 11.592 n.

496. about Alkathoös. As often, the thick of the battle is around the corpse of a fallen leader. Each side wants to get possession of it, the one to strip off the armor, the other to prevent that from happening; cf. 194.

506. Oinomaos was a follower of Asios, named in 12.140. Although the poet does not say so, presumably Idomeneus aimed at Aineias, missed, and hit Oinomaos.

512–13. dash in after his spear. For the need to retrieve the spear, cf. 11.357; see also 531, below.

514–15. Defending himself by sheer technique, Idomeneus withdraws from the fighting.

516–672. The fighting continues on the left, evenly matched now that Idomeneus has departed. On the one side are Aineias, Deïphobos, Helenos, and Paris; on the other, Meriones, Antilochos, and Menelaos. The evenness of the struggle is shown by the fact that four warriors are killed on each side; each of the Trojans has a success, as does each of the Greeks—Meriones scoring two. In addition, Deïphobos and Helenos are both wounded and forced to retire (by Meriones and Menelaos, respectively). Thus the Greeks have rather the better of it.

517. fixed hatred. Homer does not mean a long-standing feud but rather that Deiphobos has been the opposing leader to Idomeneus in much of the present battle and has had to suffer the loss of friends, such as Asios, and the taunts of his victorious opponent (446–49).

521–25. These lines remind us that the gods are supposedly restrained from taking part in the battle; they also make a link with 15.110–12, where Ares does hear of his son's death.

541. For **Aphareus,** see 478 n.

545. Thoon: a follower of Asios, named in 12.140.

546. This **vein which runs up the back till it reaches the neck** has caused some discussion. Some modern scholars have considered it imaginary. Others have identified it with the aorta, or the vena cava. There is no reason why Homer's generation should not have been acquainted with the main blood vessels of the body, from observation on the battlefield. Neither of these vessels, however, runs near enough to the surface to be "shorn away entire" by an attack with the spear from behind.

554–55. Poseidon guarded the son of Nestor. Poseidon had close connections with Pylos; he was father of Neleus and so great-grandfather of Antilochos.

The poet keeps Poseidon's presence in view, so that we do not forget. He appeared momentarily also in Idomeneus' *aristeia*, at 434.

560. Adamas, son of Asios, is the third of those named in 12.140 to be killed within seventy lines.

568. For unpleasant wounds characteristically caused by **Meriones,** see 5.65–67 n. He does it again in 651.

576. For **Deïpyros,** see 478 n. In the sequence that follows here, **Helenos** is put out of action in much the same way as his brother Deïphobos was, sixty lines before.

588–90. beans. In the ancient world, beans were dried and were then separated from their pods by beating. What was left was then tossed up into the air by the winnower with a shovel. The chaff would fall short, while the beans would carry further. A wind would not be necessary but would assist the separation. (Columella, *De re rustica* 2.10.12–14.)

600. in a sling the henchman held. The expression is obscure. It probably means, "which his (i.e., Agenor's) squire held in his hands."

612. A battle **axe** is mentioned only here and at 15.711.

617. both eyes dropped, bloody, and lay in the dust. Homer's descriptions of wounds are usually realistic (see note on 651–52) or nearly so (e.g., 546), but occasionally they are impossible or grotesque. This (repeated in 16.741) is an example of the last. The eyes cannot in fact drop out of the head.

620–39. Menelaos' speech is full of hatred and bitterness, combined with a rather weak resentment that the Trojans are fighting so successfully. He is, of course, the chief victim of the Trojans' offense against the laws of hospitality and so finds it difficult to understand why Zeus, god of hospitality, does not destroy them.

651–52. See note on 568. Strangely enough, Meriones kills a man in 5.66–67 in the same way as this, though on that occasion with a spear. For a medical description of the wound, see 5.65–67 n.

It is to be noticed that Harpalion, with this painful wound, does not fall "like a tree" (4.482 n.; cf. 178, 389, 437) but crumples up **like a worm.**

658. his father ... walked beside them. The poet has forgotten that the father of Harpalion, Pylaimenes, king of the Paphlagonians, was killed by Menelaos in 5.578. This used to be considered a serious inconsistency in the story of the *Iliad*. Nowadays we are more likely to say that Homer, concentrating on the pathos (a father's bereavement), inadvertently slips up. With so many names of men killed, it is surprising that errors of this sort are so few.

659. The **man-price** was compensation which the relatives of a killed man might accept in civil life and so avoid a continuing blood feud (see 9.632–36 n.). This convention is, of course, inapplicable in war.

661. guest friend: see 6.215 n.

663. Euchenor is the only man from Korinth in the *Iliad*. It was always a wealthy city, with a key position at the Isthmus, which divides the Peloponnese from northern Greece. Compare "Korinth the luxurious" in 2.570.

669. price: the penalty he would have to pay to avoid military service (cf. 23.296–99).

673–837. The scene switches from the left to the center, where Aias faces Hektor.

681. Hektor presses straight on through the Greek line, from the central gate where he broke through, to the ships of "Aias and Protesilaos." It is easy to see why **Protesilaos** is mentioned here: he had been the first Greek to leap ashore and had been killed instantly (2.702); it is therefore logical that his ship should be the one pulled furthest up the beach. And it is his ship which is later actually set on fire by the Trojans (15.704, 16.122).

As to **Aias**, this must be the lesser (Oïlean) Aias, the leader of the Lokrians, and not his greater Telamonian namesake. This is so because (*a*) we learn from 8.224–26 (= 11.7–9) that the greater Aias had taken one of the two positions at the end of the line; (*b*) the encampment of Aias son of Oïleus seems to be near that of Odysseus in 10.110, and Odysseus' ship was in the exact center (8.223); and (*c*) the Lokrians are particularly described as defending in this area in line 686, as indeed are the troops whom Protesilaos used to lead (called here Phthians and now led by Podarkes [693]).

The line-up of the Greek army is given in a chart on pp. 116–17. See also 10.113 n. Hektor, having broken through in the center, seems now to be attacking toward the right.

683. This low **wall** is not the same as that breached by the Trojans in Book 12. More probably, here and at 14.32 Homer refers to a defense work built after the initial landing, years before. This first wall is presumably the one referred to by Thucydides in a famous passage (1.11.1), where he says of the Greek expedition,

"But when they arrived and were victorious in a battle—[and] this [victory] must have happened, because otherwise they would not have been able to build the defenses of their camp . . ."

684. the Trojans and their horses. The Trojans are supposed to have left their chariots and horses at the ditch, according to Poulydamas' advice in 12.75–78. Either Homer has forgotten this, or we must assume that they have had them brought up, after breaking through the wall. Similarly, Hektor is in a chariot in line 749. And the Trojans are certainly attacking with horses in 15.385.

685–722. A small catalogue of the Greek tribes defending in this area serves to add geographical interest and no doubt to stimulate local patriotism in Homer's audience. Five tribes are named in 685–86, and then they are all repeated, mostly with the names of their leaders, in the following lines.

The **Boiotians** have least mention, only their name itself being repeated later (700). The **Ionians,** with their trailing tunics, turn out to be the Athenians. This is the only occurrence of this famous division of the Greek race (Ionian) in Homer, just as there is only one mention of Dorians (*Od.* 19.177). The description **with trailing tunics** is a sort of tribal epithet, certainly not relevant to their dress in battle. Of the Athenians named in 691, **Stichios** (cf. also 195) is killed in Book 15.

Next in the expanded list come the **Epeians** (691–92). The name means properly the people of Elis in the northwest Peloponnese. In the Catalogue of Ships, however, **Meges** does not lead that contingent but rather a contingent from the unidentified Doulichion and the western islands (2.625–30). This may not be a real inconsistency, however, because 2.629 alludes to the fact that Meges' family was really from Elis and had left its home one generation before to live in the neighboring islands.

The **Phthians** are led by Medon and Podarkes (693). This, too, is a little odd. In the Catalogue of Ships the land later called Thessaly is divided into nine baronies, with uncertain land borders. Two of the nine contingents are now led, respectively, by Medon and Podarkes, each, as it happens, substituting for an original leader who is no longer present (Philoktetes and Protesilaos; see 2.727 and 704). Phthia, however, is normally the name of a part of

Achilleus' domain (2.683), and his troops, the Myrmidons, are of course not fighting at this time. There appears to be geographical uncertainty (or perhaps imprecise use of tribal names) in the still-unsettled northern area (cf. 9.447 n.).

Medon (694–97) is half-brother of Aias son of Oïleus, but lived away from his natural home (presumably Lokris) because of blood guilt—a common explanation of emigration. That he should live in Phylake raises yet another small difficulty, because Phylake, according to the Catalogue, is now in Podarkes' realm, not in that of Medon (2.695).

Podarkes (698) was Protesilaos' brother.

701–22. A memorable simile describes the hard work of fighting performed by the two Aiantes—unlike in build as in nature but acting as a tried partnership in the battle. It is followed by the only real description of light-armed troops in the *Iliad*. The Lokrians, who came from a poor and mountainous area, no doubt were always more likely to produce guerilla troops than fully armed hoplites. Here they operate behind the front line, with slings and arrows. Their leader, Aias, fights in armor at the front, like the other leaders; but in 2.529 even he was given the epithet "armoured in linen," i.e., with a linen jerkin instead of a breastplate—which suggests a more lightly armed man.

For the shield of the greater Aias (710), see 7.219 n.

726–47. This is the third of Poulydamas' four tactical speeches in the *Iliad* (see 18.243–314 n.). Here Hektor accepts his advice but later forgets the caution enjoined, at least implicitly, in 743–47.

745. yesterday: the defeat of the Achaians in Book 8.

754. The comparison of Hektor, on the move, with a **snowy mountain** has seemed overbold to some. Without doubt, the point is his height and great physique, so that all look up to him. Giants are likened to mountains in the *Odyssey* (9.191, 10.113).

759–60. The list, repeated with an addition in 770–72, gives a kind of summary of the main Trojan losses in this book.

769. Evil Paris ... Not unusual words for Hektor to use in addressing his disliked younger brother (cf. 3.39). Paris accepts it calmly.

155

776. it would be better. "I am likely" is a closer translation.

790–92. Another short catalogue. The Trojans have rallied their forces. Most of these names are new.

Askanios (792) is the (eponymous) leader of the Phrygians from Askania (2.862); his brother **Morys** was not mentioned in the catalogue. According to the *Iliad* story, 793–94 are incorrect, for several days have elapsed since the catalogue. As in the case of Pylaimenes (658 n.), the explanation for the slip is probably that the poet is using a stock theme involving the pathos of war: the fact that these men had arrived at the front only yesterday.

In 14.513–14, Meriones will kill Morys *and* Hippotion, a phenomenon like the one explained in 421–23 n. (the case of Mekisteus and Echios).

795–99. Another powerful double-sided simile (cf. 137–42 n.). The Trojan champions attack with the violence of a sudden squall; it causes huge lines of waves in the sea, and these are like the serried ranks of the advancing Trojan troops.

809. Throughout these middle books of the *Iliad*, Homer keeps before us the confrontation of Hektor and Telamonian Aias. They met at the beginning of this book (189–94) and will clash again in both Books 14 and 15.

823. the bird sign. Hektor habitually disregards omens (cf. 12.237–38 n.). He is also characteristically wrong about what is going to happen. The wish expressed in 825–27 (like that of 8.538–40) is a dangerous one for a human who is not even the son of a goddess.

inarticulate ox is not how Hektor addressed Aias in 7.288, when he had been having the worst of their single combat.

BOOK FOURTEEN

Book 14, which continues the "retardation" begun in Book 13, shows Zeus further distracted from the battle, so that his plan for the defeat of the Greeks is thwarted. With Poseidon's help, the Greeks drive the Trojans back. The book falls neatly into three parts:

1–152   A meeting between Nestor and the three major heroes wounded in Book 11—Agamemnon, Diomedes, and Odysseus.
153–351   The seduction of Zeus by his wife Hera.
352–522   Victory for the Greeks.

1–8. We are back to the situation at 11.623–42, where Nestor had brought the wounded Machaon out of the battle and was giving him refreshment and conversation in his hut, waited on by his servant, Hekamede. The **outcry** of line 1 is the shout of both armies at the end of Book 13. The phrase **though he was drinking** disturbed the serious-minded ancient commentators (those Alexandrians whose views are recorded in the scholia); it is not suitable that Homer should suggest that this distinguished old man was fond of his wine! In fact, Homer is fond of Nestor and slightly amused by him. See the exaggerated compliment, also connected with drinking, in 11.635–36. The simile in lines 16–19, below, may also be ironically exaggerated.

9–10. It is not clear why the heroes should so casually take each other's shields. Nestor's own shield was described in most improbable terms by Hektor in 8.192 (as all of gold); but that seemed to be momentary invention, and hardly a reason for Thrasymedes to have borrowed it now. Strangely enough, Thrasymedes for his part lent Diomedes a shield for the night expedition (10.257).

27–29. They were all wounded in Book 11: Agamemnon at 253, Diomedes at 377, Odysseus at 437.

32. had built their defences. This probably refers to a wall built at the time of first landing (see 13.683), not the wall built in Book 7 and breached in Book 12. Homer is imagining how the huge Greek fleet could be drawn up on a fairly small beach. The two capes (36), of Sigeion and Rhoiteion, are in fact about five miles apart, according to LEAF 2:67.

44–47. that word. See 8.180–83, Hektor's shout to the Trojans, and 8.526–34, Hektor's speech to the Trojan assembly.

49–51. For the suggestion of disaffection in the army, see 13.109, 19.85, and the implications of Thersites' speech in 2.225–42.

74–81. This is the third time Agamemnon has proposed that they give up the war and go home. The first was the unsuccessful test of the morale of the army in 2.139–41; the second, in 9.26–28, was—like the present one—in earnest, and Diomedes showed himself as firm in reaction then as Odysseus is now. It all adds to the portrait of Agamemnon as a less than ideal commander.

83–102. Odysseus is very firm. He shows a much better understanding of the psychology of the troops than Agamemnon—who gives way to him at once, as he did in a previous clash with Odysseus in 4.350–63.

110–12. Diomedes is young (9.57–58) but high-spirited and ambitious. He is not one to hold back in a critical situation.

113–25. The genealogy may seem ill-timed to us, but tastes have changed. **Oineus** (117) was the father of both **Tydeus**, Diomedes' father, and Meleagros (9.543). Tydeus left his home in Aitolia and went to live in Argos, where he married a daughter of the king, Adrastos (**Adrestos** in Homer's Ionic dialect). He died in the expedition of the Seven against Thebes (cf. 4.370–400).

136. in the likeness of an old man. Poseidon appeared first (in Book 13) as Kalchas, then as Thoas, and now as a nameless old man. His divinity, however, becomes clear in line 148.

147–50. a huge cry. This is incautious, if Poseidon still wishes to escape the notice of Zeus. The danger that Zeus will turn his eyes back to the Trojan plain (see 13.3) is a satisfactory immediate cause for Hera's action, which now follows.

BOOK FOURTEEN

THE DECEPTION OF ZEUS (LINES 153–351)

"The Deception of Zeus" is the name this striking and attractive episode bore in antiquity. Hera, realizing that her husband must be thoroughly distracted from the battle, decides to use her feminine charms to this purpose. It is a particular case of Homer's regular use of the gods to lighten the grim reality of the battlefield and even to provide some comic diversion. Here there is evident comic intention in lines 158, 296 (see note), and 315–28. There is also a great deal of charm; and the end (346–51)—particularly beautiful in its description of nature in springtime sending forth its new flowers and grass, in symbolic sympathy with the amorous god—has given some scholars the idea that behind this light-hearted tale lies a spring ritual connected with the reawakening of fertility and the rebirth of nature.

166–86. Hera prepares herself. It is, as REINHARDT 291 points out, an arming scene parallel to those of the human warriors about to enter battle (3.330–38 n.) or that of her brother, Poseidon, in 13.23–27.

188. Hera needs the help of **Aphrodite** in a metaphorical sense: she wishes to inspire in Zeus the feelings which Aphrodite represents. As is common in the *Iliad*, this figurative or metaphorical situation is represented as a real relationship between two humanized figures. Hera has to be careful how she puts her request, because Aphrodite, in the story, supports the Trojans, not the Greeks.

197–210. **Then with false lying purpose.** Hera invents a plausible reason for needing the charms Aphrodite has at her disposal. **Rheia** was wife of Kronos and thus mother of Hera. **Kronos** ruled the world until Zeus overthrew him and banished him and his supporters, the Titans, to Tartaros, "as far below Hades as the earth is below the sky" (8.16; cf. 279, below). Hera says that Okeanos and his wife Tethys, the ancient gods of the sea, looked after her during that great disturbance (compare Thetis' protection of Dionysos in 6.136 and of Hephaistos in 18.398); they are now mutually disenchanted, and she wishes to bring them together again.

That the gods have risen from **Okeanos** (201; cf. 246) does not

159

accord with mythological genealogies, which make them sons of Heaven (Ouranos); but that the sea is the origin of all life is no surprising concept to us.

215. This **zone** is not a belt (as in 181) but a band or strap. On it are depicted the powers which it controls, exactly parallel to the figures on the aegis of Zeus (5.739–40).

225–30. Hera travels from Olympos toward Troy the way a human would go, minimizing the sea-crossings. She first goes north, past **Pieria** in Thessaly and **Emathia** (Macedonia); then from **Athos,** at the point of the peninsula of Chalkidike, she crosses the sea to the island of **Lemnos.**

230. Thoas, king of Lemnos, is different from the Aitolian leader of that name. He was the father of Hypsipyle (7.469).

231. Sleep, the brother of Death. A natural image. The two act together in 16.682, carrying the body of Sarpedon away to his home. Why Sleep is located on Lemnos has not been explained.

233–35. if ever before ... The common prayer formula (cf. 1.39) comes rather strangely from the queen of the gods.

249–61. Before now, it was a favour to you. Sleep recalls a past occasion when he suffered because of something very like what he is being asked to do now. It has to do with the old legend, alluded to several times in the *Iliad,* of an earlier attack on Troy by Herakles. More information about this particular incident is given at 15.18–30.

Night (259), the mother of Sleep, according to the Hesiodic *Theogony,* was herself a most ancient deity, daughter of Chaos.

Once again, in this conversation between Hera and Sleep, we can see Homer treating figurative or metaphorical situations as literal and real (see 188 n.). Sleep is a person who has to be bribed to assist Hera's plan.

Some scholars have thought that these lines disclose that an episode very like the Deception of Zeus took place in a poem about Herakles which preceded the *Iliad* and was in this respect its model. The alternative explanation is more probable: that Homer has invented the Herakles incident for the sake of the present conversation of Sleep with Hera (cf. Meleagros' situation in 9.550–99).

267. Here there seems to be an indefinite number of **Graces;** later there were just three.

271–74. The oath by the **Styx** is the mightiest oath for the gods (cf. 15.37–38). The Titans (279) seem here to represent the gods of the underworld, whose particular function was to punish breakers of oaths (see 3.278–79 n.).

281. Imbros is between Lemnos and the Trojan plain. Lekton (284) was a promontory at the foot of Mount Ida.

286–91. Sleep takes cover. As to the **aether** in 288, later writers (and indeed Homer; e.g., 13.837) used this term for the pure higher sky (the stratosphere), as distinct from the air near the earth, which was subject to mist and cloud. This would entail a gargantuan pine tree. More probably here, as LEAF 2:87 suggests, all that is meant is that the tree rises above the hillside mist into clear air.

For the different languages of gods and men (291), see note on 1.403–4. The bird **chalkis/kymindis** has not been identified.

296. their dear parents knew nothing of it. This suggests a human situation. The difference in the case of Zeus and Hera was that they were brother and sister (18.356); so they had the same parents.

301–6. Hera repeats what she said to Aphrodite. The excuse now has the additional advantage that it is suggestive, encouraging the thoughts that are already in Zeus's mind. The submissiveness of 309–11 is also a wifely ploy. These observations were already made by the ancient scholiasts.

317–28. The list of previous loves has seemed out of place or comic to most interpreters. Zeus had become associated with many local nymphs and goddesses as a result of the fact that he, the great sky god, was brought down by the Indo-European Greek people into an area where a mother goddess was worshiped, under different names in different places, and often with a local consort. To avoid a total clash of religions, Zeus often took over the role of the consort, with the consequence that he seems in the legends a most Casanova-like figure.

There is no reason to doubt the authenticity of the passage. The expression of 315–16 and 328 is parallel to that of Paris when he speaks to Helen in much the same circumstances in 3.442 and 446. That there is humor in it, from this sophisticated poet, is evident.

For **Peirithoös** (317–18) cf. 1.263. **Ixion** was punished in mythology for attempting to rape Hera; according to the indication here, he was only trying to get his own back.

Akrisios (319) was the Argive king who shut his daughter **Danaë**

in a tower to discourage lovers. Zeus descended "in a shower of gold."

Phoinix (321) is the eponymous ancestor of the Phoenicians, who are sometimes confused with the Kretans in the early myths. **Minos** (322) of Krete and **Rhadamanthys** (322) were brothers, kings and lawgivers in this world and the next (*Od.* 4.564, 11.569).

Semele (323), daughter of Kadmos, and **Alkmene** (323) wife of Amphitryon, were both Thebans.

The child of **Demeter** (326) was Persephone; the offspring of **Leto** (327) were the great gods Apollo and Artemis.

332–36. The possibility of being seen, and the shame that she would then feel, have a parallel in the ribald tale of Ares and Aphrodite, sung in Scheria in the *Odyssey*, Book 8 (see especially 8.361–66).

344. Helios: the sun.

346–51. young, fresh grass. See the last part of the note, above, on 153–351.

352–522. Poseidon is now in a position to help the Greeks openly, since Zeus is asleep. The rest of the book falls into four parts:

352–401	Poseidon encourages the Greeks to attack.
402–39	Aias knocks out Hektor.
440–507	An even battle rages for a time, but the Greek pressure is the greater.
508–22	The Trojans in full flight.

354–55. Sleep went on the run. Hera did not specifically tell him to do this (see 15.41–43).

371–83. Poseidon recommends an exchange of armor, the better fighters taking the better equipment, the worse the worse. The proposal in 371–73 is clarified in 376–77; and in the following lines the three wounded leaders organize the general exchange. The whole idea seems a little impractical for an army that is already engaging the enemy. The Alexandrian scholars cut out 376–77, and LEAF 2:92 and WILAMOWITZ 234 thought they should have added 382. If that were done, 371–73 might just mean, "let us each get our own best equipment," not "let us institute a major exchange." There is some logic in this; but it is safer to leave the lines as they are. The author of an epic poem is not limited to ideas that would be practical in everyday life.

392. the sea washed up to the ships. Apparently his own element is demonstrating its solidarity with Poseidon.

394–401. Three powerful comparisons (from sea, fire, and wind) greatly enhance the significance of the renewed battle.

403–20. Both hits (403, 412) are carefully and clearly described. The *crossing* of the **two straps** in 404 implies that Aias was wearing the Mycenaean body shield. The sword strap would naturally go over the right shoulder, and so would that of a hand-grip shield (see 5.795 n.); but the strap of the great body shield would hang over the left (LORIMER 182). Here we must assume that Aias has slung the shield round his back (cf. 11.544).

425–26. Agenor (son of Antenor) is fairly commonly mentioned. **Sarpedon** and **Glaukos** were last heard of in Book 12, when Sarpedon first breached the wall, and Glaukos was wounded (12.387). Glaukos is still unable to take part in the fighting in 16.508. Homer may have momentarily forgotten this.

433–34. the crossing place of the … river. The ford of the Skamandros (**Xanthos**) has not been mentioned previously. In fact, there has been no suggestion that the river had to be crossed on the way from Troy to the Greek camp. Rather, it is at the side of the battlefield (11.499). These lines are repeated at 21.1–2 and 24.692–93. At no place, however, is it explicitly stated that they crossed the river; so perhaps no inconsistency is involved. The ford would be a feature of the river, a stopping place on the journey from city to camp, to let the horses drink (24.350), but not to be crossed.

440–507. The poet wishes to show a balanced fight before the Trojans break and run. He therefore describes five encounters, each leading to the next. The Greeks win 1, 3, and 5, the Trojans 2 and 4 (a pattern exactly the same as that in 4.457–507, in the first fighting in the *Iliad*). The final description is the most striking, ending with the gruesome sight of the Trojan's head being held up on the point of a spear as a trophy; this puts an end to the Trojan will to fight.

443. Satnios, born by the river Satnioeis, reminds us of Simoeisios, the victim of the other Aias in that scene in Book 4 (474).

450. Prothoënor was one of the five Boiotian leaders (2.495).

454–57. The first of a sequence of taunts, continued in 470 ff., 479 ff., and 501 ff. There is a similar sequence in 13.374, 414, and 446. Notice the grim humor of 457.

463. Archelochos and his brother **Akamas** (476), sons of Antenor, share with Aineias the command of the Dardanians (2.823, 12.100).

479. arrow-fighters: clearly an insulting term, conveying the scorn of the close fighters for those who operate at a distance (11.385).

487. Peneleos was another of the Boiotian leaders (2.494).

491. Hermes was god of flocks and herds, also of wealth. Phorbas' prosperity was an evident sign that Hermes loved him.

499. it is the head, not the eyeball. This gruesome sight ("curious and striking," MAZON 198; "far-fetched and improbable," FRIEDRICH 20) is the climax of the sequence of fighting after Hektor's withdrawal.

508. An appeal to the **Muses** elevates the situation, suggesting that what is about to come is of great significance; cf. 11.218–20, 16.112–13, and (in expanded form) 2.484–93.

511–22. The Trojans are in full flight, and various Greeks get easy victories, particularly the fast runners.

Hyrtios (511) is not the leader ascribed to the Mysians in 2.858.

Phalkes (513) was named in 13.791 and **Morys** in 13.792, where he was described as the son of Hippotion. Subconscious association of the names probably caused Homer to have a **Hippotion** killed here as well.

Periphetes (515) may be a textual corruption for Polyphetes (13.791).

516. Menelaos recalls this killing of **Hyperenor** in 17.24, when he meets Euphorbos, Hyperenor's brother. It appears there that Hyperenor was a son of Panthoös and so also a brother of Poulydamas.

520–22. Aias ... the son of Oïleus is small and quick and thus particularly suited to the chase (in contrast to his namesake, the Telamonian Aias, whose *forte* is hand-to-hand conflict [13.325]). In 2.530 he is also praised for his spear work. He takes part in the foot race in Book 23, whereas the greater Aias takes part in the wrestling, the fight in armor, and the discus throw.

BOOK FIFTEEN

By the end of Book 14, Hektor is *hors de combat* and the Trojans are in flight. Book 15 contains the third stage of the battle which began after the breakthrough in Book 12. Book 15 is long—like Book 13; it is divided as follows:

1–280	Zeus wakes on Ida, and takes steps to reverse the situation.
281–366	The Greeks are driven back into their defenses.
367–405	Interludes of Nestor and Patroklos.
406–591	The battle at the ships.
592–746	Hektor breaks through to the ships.

Scholars have been divided about Book 15. Some consider it a perfect and most perceptive battle description (e.g., P. Cauer, *Grundfragen der Homerkritik*, 3d ed. [1921–23], pp. 500–517), while others find it chaotic, with two or more versions of the same events (e.g., the Greeks desperately fighting from the ships themselves at 387, 416, and 677). What can be stated with certainty is that the individual incidents are very precisely described. See, for example, the Trojan victory of 306–27, the massed attack on ditch and wall at 352–66, and Hektor's breakthrough in 615–52.

Another feature of this book of fighting is the unusually large number of striking similes; see, for example, the three in quick succession in 618–36.

1. For the **ditch** and the **stakes,** see 7.441, 12.52–57.

9. He saw Hektor lying in the plain. This returns us to the situation of 14.439.

18–33. Lines known as "The Punishment of Hera." For the brutality of Zeus, cf. 8.12. The punishment on a previous occasion had been that she hung from her chained hands, two weights

165

(anvils) attached to her feet. This is similar to slave punishments in the ancient world. They were strung up by their hands to a beam and beaten—or just left hanging. The weights from the feet would be a form of torture.

Why they should be **anvils** may be, as LEAF 2:106 suggests, simply that an anvil was the largest mass of movable metal commonly known. Alternatively, we may have here a verbal echo of old stories about the sky and the earth, tales of the gods, in which the word used later for "anvil" in fact meant a thunderbolt (so C. H. Whitman, "Hera's Anvils," *Harvard Studies in Classical Philology* 74 [1970]: 37–42). There is a strange statement in Hesiod's *Theogony* 722–25 that the sky is so far above the earth that it would take an *anvil* nine days and nights to fall from the one to the other and that Tartaros is so far below the earth that an anvil in free fall would take an equally long time (cf. 8.16). Such echoes, however, come from a distant past; to Homer himself, no doubt, when he was imagining this scene, the word meant "anvil," not "thunderbolt."

The **chain** is **golden** simply because gold is the metal of the gods; recall Poseidon's equipment in 13.22–25.

Zeus's casting from the threshold of Olympos any gods he could catch is a repeated theme; cf. the Hephaistos story in 1.591 n.

The occasion of Zeus's previous anger was the same as that referred to by Sleep in 14.250–57, namely, Hera's attack on Herakles as he was sailing back to Greece after his sack of Troy. Some extra details are given here.

35–46. Hera, frightened, takes a great oath that she is not responsible for the actions of Poseidon. She barely avoids perjury; but Poseidon's entry into the battle at the beginning of Book 13 was indeed of his own volition and not suggested by Hera; and she had covered herself in Book 14 by not specifically telling Sleep to go and tell Poseidon that he could operate more openly, now that Zeus was asleep (Sleep divined her intention and took the message without being asked; see 14.354–55 n.). Zeus is probably not deceived, but he smiles quite amiably at her (47) and sends her to get Iris and Apollo for him; he then summarizes what is to happen (63–77).

57. Iris is to have the same errand as in 8.398, where Zeus sent her to tell Hera and Athene to withdraw.

61–77. The program of future events. This is *the will of Zeus* (1.5). He said in 1.547–48 that Hera would be the first to be told of any of his plans that were to be divulged, and here she *is* told.

The **designs of Athene** (71) which will help to capture Troy probably include the Wooden Horse; Athene was said (in later sources) to have advised the craftsman.

In 72–73 Zeus repeats his interdiction against any of the gods interfering in the battle (cf. 8.7–16).

80–82. A unique simile, likening Hera's progress to the speed of thought.

87. Themis is a personification of what is right, of propriety; she was influential in assemblies of gods and men (*Od.* 2.69).

99. one: the indefinite; "anyone." She is not yet alluding to a particular god.

110–12. This is sheer troublemaking by Hera. **Askalaphos,** Ares' son, was killed at 13.518, where our present scene was foreshadowed by the statement (13.521–25) that Ares had not yet heard of his death.

Had Ares intervened to avenge his son, he would have seemed to change sides, for Askalaphos was a Greek, while Ares has so far been favoring the Trojans. However, the gods may well have a son or a priest on either side (Hephaistos shows pity for a Trojan in 5.23); and in any case, Ares is a fickle god, helping now one side, now the other (5.831–34).

117–18. struck by Zeus' thunderbolt. Ares felt he was in danger of this fate also at 5.886.

119. Fear and **Terror** are assistants of Ares (4.440), by an obvious imagery; Terror indeed is his "beloved son" in 13.299.

123. Athene is accustomed to controlling Ares (cf. 5.766).

157–220. Zeus wishes to send both Iris and Apollo on errands— Iris to Poseidon, Apollo to Hektor. The way the poet describes it, Iris is sent first, and it is only when her errand has been completed (219) that Zeus turns to Apollo with "Go now, beloved Phoibos, . . . " This agrees with the general Homeric method of describing simultaneous events as successive (see 12.195 n.). There is an extended parallel in the first five books of the *Odyssey*. In *Odyssey*, Book 1, it is arranged at a council of the gods that two errands will be undertaken: Athene will go to Ithaka to encourage

Telemachos, and Hermes will go to Ogygia to tell Kalypso that she must release Odysseus. The first of these visits occurs immediately, and Telemachos' consequent activities go on for four books; then, at the beginning of Book 5, we find ourselves again at a council of the gods, and Zeus sends Hermes off to Kalypso.

201–4. Iris goes beyond her function as a messenger and gives wise advice. The **Furies** look after proper respect toward members of one's family—from children to parents, normally (9.454); here, from younger brother to older brother.

220. After this Zeus ... spoke to Apollo. See 157–220 n.

225. gods ... who gather to Kronos: the Titans (see 14.197–210 n.).

258. cavalry: meaning, of course, chariots; there is no horse-riding in Homer, except in unusual circumstances (10.513).

263–68. As when some stalled horse. This fine simile was used for the handsome Paris, emerging from the city onto the plain at 6.506–11. Most commentators have considered that it suits Paris better than Hektor, and some have wished to excise it here. On the other hand, as remarked in the note on the passage in Book 6, such repetition is absolutely typical of oral composition, and the simile may be relevant at both places. Bowra 92 thinks that the repetition is conscious and intentional, making a parallel betwen the two brothers.

281–99. Thoas advises the Greeks to make an ordered retreat. The multitude of ordinary troops should withdraw to the ships while the leaders are holding back the Trojans. This passage has been criticized, but it makes good sense. The Greeks are in disorder after their successful pursuit of the Trojans at the end of Book 14; they are out on the plain, and it will be difficult for them to get their army back across the ditch. Thoas' suggestion will allow the escape of those who otherwise would be caught in Hektor's imminent attack (so Albracht 1:42, 2:13).

Thoas, leader of the Aitolians, is a man of authority. Poseidon took on his shape when he addressed Idomeneus in 13.216.

301–2. A small catalogue of those who are leading the rear-guard action. We notice that **Idomeneus** is back; **Teukros** and **Meges** are named because they will be in action shortly (442, 520).

306–27. A clear account of a successful attack. The Trojans join battle in force; the Greek troops opposing them (the rear guard proposed by Thoas) hold firm for a time but then give way and run like stampeding cattle.

For the joint attack of **Hektor** and **Phoibos Apollo** in lines 306–7 compare 5.590–95, where Hektor and Ares attack together.

328–42. The Greeks, now in flight, are easy victims for the Trojans. Only Greeks die here. And the order reflects the relevant importance (valor) of the heroes. Hektor and Aineias each kill two, and their opponents also are the strongest. Then Poulydamas, Polites, and Agenor have one victory each, over less significant opponents. Finally, Paris kills an unknown man, the whole catalogue being rounded off by the description of the wound in this case.

329. **Stichios** is an Athenian (companion of Menestheus, 331); we met him at 13.195. **Arkesilaos,** one of the five Boiotian leaders (2.495), joins his colleague Prothoënor, who was killed at 14.450; Klonios, a third, will be added in 340.

332. For **Medon,** see 13.694–97 (lines identical to 333–36 here). This is an important success for the Trojans, for Medon was the leader of the northern Greek contingent previously led by Philoktetes (2.727). **Iasos** (338) at least has a pedigree.

339. **Mekisteus** carried a wounded man out of the battle in 8.332 and a dead one in 13.421. On those occasions he was called "son of Echios," which no doubt caused an association in Homer's mind, leading to the name of the second victim in this line (cf. Morys and Hippotion in 14.513–14).

340–41. For **Klonios,** see Arkesilaos, above, 329 n. **Deïochos** is unknown.

343–51. While the Trojans pause to collect spoils, the Greeks, in utter confusion, make their way past the ditch, with its stakes on the far side; then, spreading out in all directions after passing that obstacle (345), they reach the defensive wall. Hektor's shout to let the spoils alone is parallel to a shout from Nestor in 6.68–71.

352–66. The Trojans continue their massed attack, with chariots, right through the Greek defenses, with Apollo clearing a way for them, as he promised to do in 260. They come first to the ditch

(355–59), and Apollo pushes in the sides to make a causeway for them to cross over—a causeway perhaps twenty paces wide (358–59, where the translation should be "as *wide* as the force of a spearcast"); they then come to the wall, which Apollo knocks down. (They swarm over it in 381–86.)

The simile in 362–64 is striking—of a child playing with sand castles on the beach. In this, as in the description of the little girl who wants to be carried (16.7–9), we see the breadth of Homer's sympathy and his appreciation of the behavior of children as well as of grown men and women.

370–78. Nestor, who now appears in the story at critical points, like a tragic chorus, prays to Zeus and gets a favorable omen. That the same omen acts as an encouragement to the Trojans (379–80) has worried some commentators. But, as REINHARDT 305 points out, Zeus's intentions are not straightforward. For a Greek resurgence, the Trojans must first reach the ships.

372–75. if ever . . . For the prayer form, cf. 1.39 n.

385–89. The poet has the exotic idea of a fight between chariots and ships. This is not followed through, but the introduction in 388 of the long **pikes**, used for sea fighting, foreshadows Aias' heroic deeds in 677–88. The **heads** in 389 are those of the pikes.

390. We return to **Patroklos**, who, at the end of Book 11, when he was on his way back from Nestor to Achilleus, had stopped to help the wounded Eurypylos. The story is nearing its climax, and Homer needs to set Patroklos in motion now, so that he will return to Achilleus and make his fatal request at the beginning of Book 16.

406–591. General fighting around the ships. The Greeks at this point are fighting desperately, but with some success.

416. It is a question whether this is the same ship as the one that Hektor and Aias dispute in 705—the ship of Protesilaos. If so, the poet seems to have anticipated himself, or some confusion may have entered the story (see introductory note to this book). More probably what we see exemplified here is a rather strange technique of the oral poet: to foreshadow in general terms what he will later treat more specifically. Compare the pikes of 388 and Zeus's withdrawal of Hektor in 11.163.

419–20. Kaletor, Klytios' son. Klytios was one of the aged counselors of Troy, seen on the wall with Priam at 3.147. The genealogy of 20.238 shows that he was Priam's brother, so his son, Kaletor, was Hektor's cousin (422). Sons of the other two counselors in 3.147 appear in the ensuing fighting here, at 525 and 546.

431. Kythera is the large island off the south coast of the Peloponnese. Lykophron is another man who had had to leave home because of blood guilt (cf. Medon, 335).

441. the bow that Apollo gave you. As the scholia say, this does not involve a material gift from Apollo; the phrase means only that Teukros was an outstandingly good archer. Exactly the same thing is said of Pandaros in 2.827.

442–70. The brief action of the archer Teukros here is closely similar to his *aristeia* in 8.266–334. There he killed, among many others, Hektor's charioteer, and his successes came to an end only when Hektor hit him on the shoulder with a stone, which also broke his bowstring.

445–57. This is a good instance of the danger to which the charioteer was exposed in battle. Kleitos was paying attention to his horses, while keeping the chariot as close as he could to his "number one," Poulydamas. When he was killed, Poulydamas' first action was to get a replacement charioteer, as was Hektor's at 8.126 and 318.

462. Telamonian: Teukros was a half-brother of Aias.

484–513. Typical generals' exhortations to the troops. They use the obvious arguments, which we find repeated over and over again in the later Greek and Roman historians. The Trojans are to remember that they are defending their country and their wives and children; the Greeks, that they have nowhere further to retreat to (505). Similar, but briefer, exhortations are found from Aias again in 561–64, from Nestor in 661–66, and, most typically, from Aias a third time in 733–41. Such repetition emphasizes the desperate situation of the Greeks.

515–23. An even struggle is indicated by alternate Trojan and Greek killings.

515. The name **Schedios** seems to involve a mistake. He is **son of**

Perimedes and **lord of the men of Phokis;** but the leader of the Phokians in 2.517 was Schedios son of Iphitos, and *that* Schedios will be killed by Hektor in 17.306. Of course, there could be two Phokian leaders called Schedios, but that is less likely than a minor slip by the poet.

520. Meges' troops are called **Epeians** also at 13.691–92.

525. Lampos was another of the counselors on the wall, brother of Priam; cf. 419–20 n.

528. Phyleides: i.e., Meges. The description of his breastplate in 529–34, including its history, adds significance to the fight and to Meges himself; compare the history of Agamemnon's breastplate in 11.19–23, followed by its description.

531. Ephyra and the river Selleëis. We are told by the scholia and by Strabo 8.338 that there were a town and a river with these names in Elis; when this same line was used at 2.659, however, as the home of Astyocheia, a wife of Herakles, we were told that town and river were in Thesprotia, in northwestern Greece.

539. Yet Dolops stood his ground. It was normal to leap out from the first rank, discharge one's spear, and then get back to safety, as Antilochos does in 585. Dolops fails to complete this sequence and pays the penalty.

546. Hiketaon: see 420, 525. Melanippos, like his cousins, is introduced merely to be killed (576). Perkote, where he used to live, was on the Hellespont (2.835).

568–91. An isolated success for **Antilochos.** Menelaos, apparently unable to achieve the stripping of the armor of Dolops, on which he was engaged at 544–45, is himself on the way back to safety, but he urges Antilochos to make a sally. The relationship between these two—the king of Sparta, whose wife was the cause of the war, and the young and eager son of Nestor—is delicately portrayed by Homer. See 23.566–613 n.

The description of Antilochos' actions in 573–91 is a vivid and exact portrayal of the battle drill of the front fighters (not, of course, of those like Hektor, Diomedes, and Achilleus, who are above such limitations). All the details, as well as the two similes, add to the picture.

592. A new stage of the battle begins; it is accompanied by yet another statement of the intentions of Zeus.

604. without the god: i.e., on his own account. The following lines describe Hektor's grim figure. The "slaver around his mouth" suggests the wild, berserk fighter whom we have met before (cf. "this mad dog" at 8.299).

614. Athene helps Achilleus at the killing of Hektor in Book 22.

615–37. Hektor's final breakthrough repeats the sequence of the Trojan attack in 306–27, in that the Greeks manage to hold him for a time (617, with the following simile of a rock standing against the force of the sea). But then (624) a new simile describes him as like a great wave breaking over a ship, causing terror among the sailors; and when a third simile likens him to a lion which gets in among some cattle, killing one of them and stampeding the others, that is the time when the Greeks flee yet again.

In line 623, **lit about with flame** refers to the shining of his armor. The **foam** of the wave in line 626 may well be connected with the slaver around his mouth (607).

638–52. The killing of **Periphetes of Mykenai.** He is the ox killed by the lion in the simile that immediately precedes these lines. Homer needs a striking victim for Hektor, to match the high tension of the moment. He achieves this (*a*) by associating the man killed with the past saga of Herakles and (*b*) by inventing a particular and unusual accident that leads to his death.

Eurystheus was the king of Mykenai who used to send Herakles on his tasks—the twelve labors. It appears from here that he used an envoy, called Kopreus, to pass on his instructions to the hero. The name Kopreus is formed like many other disyllabic names of the past generation, in -eus (cf. Atreus, Oineus, Neleus, Tydeus); but it also seems to be a pejorative nickname, for *kopros* is the Greek for "dung." There probably lies behind this a history of popular tales in which Herakles was the hero and Eurystheus the villain—his henchman therefore receiving no favorable treatment. Homer, however, has no wish to belittle Hektor's victim, so he adds (641) that he was a far better man than his father.

In 645 Periphetes trips over the edge of his shield, as he tries to retreat, and falls on his back. Such a shield can only be the great Mycenaean body shield (7.219), the same shield as "clashed against the ankles and neck of Hektor" as he departed for the city in 6.117. It is a little difficult to imagine how the unfortunate man fell on his back. Perhaps he had slung the great shield round his back (cf. 11.544), and this caused him to stumble.

Periphetes is the only Mycenaean, apart from Agamemnon himself, who is named in the *Iliad*. He may well be an invention of Homer's, although, as suggested above, his father, Kopreus, seems to have had a history.

656. shelters: their huts, built apparently among and behind the first rank of ships drawn up on the beach.

668–73. Athene removed the **mist** from their eyes so that they could clearly see Hektor attacking. As we have not previously heard of the mist, this surprises us. It seems that this is a common theme (FENIK 53). The thick of the battle becomes embroiled in mist (16.567, 17.269, 368), and this makes it particularly difficult for those caught up in it, as we may see from Aias' famous prayer at 17.645–47. It is better for the Greeks to be able to see Hektor and the Trojans clearly as they attack.

674–78. Aias . . . went in huge strides up and down the decks. A memorable picture of the mighty Aias, striding from deck to deck of the ships (i.e., from one stern platform to the next), keeping the Trojans at a distance with a tremendous pole or **pike twenty-two cubits long** (twice as long as Hektor's spear in 6.319, i.e., thirty-two feet).

679–84. A most unusual simile is used to describe Aias. He is like a trick rider who stands on the backs of four galloping horses tied together and changes his position from back to back—the sort of skill we may see in the circus. The heroes do not normally ride on horseback (258), but Homer knows of such activity from his own day.

705. For **Protesilaos,** see 2.698 and 13.681. As he was first to land, it is not surprising that his ship is the one furthest up the beach, which Hektor attacks and eventually sets on fire.

714. glancing from shoulders gives an erroneous impression. What seems to be intended is that some of the swords fell from the hands of their owners, while others fell, scabbard and all, when the sword-strap over the shoulder was cut or when the shoulders themselves were chopped by axes.

718. give single voice to the clamour of battle: raise the war cry.

721–23. our counsellors' cowardice. Hektor's explanation of his failure to attack the ships in the past disagrees with the frequent statement elsewhere that, so long as Achilleus was fighting, Hektor and the Trojans did not dare to leave the city (5.788–90, 9.352–53, 13.105–6). This is doubtless Homeric invention, and it is in character: Hektor might well look at it this way.

729. According to J. S. Morrison and R. T. Williams, *Greek Oared Ships* (1968), pp. 48–49, the feature translated here as the **seven-foot midship** was a beam running across the boat and projecting on either side of the hull, below and forward of the steersman's seat in the stern. This suits the picture of Aias withdrawing a short distance but continuing to use his pike.

731. beat off . . . : i.e., beat off from the vessels any Trojan who carried fire.

733–41. Aias' exhortation (see 484–513 n.) contains the typical encouragement to invading troops when they are driven back: "We *must* fight; we have nowhere to go for safety."

741. not the mercy of battle: not in softness of fighting.

BOOK SIXTEEN

Book 16 is the turning point of the *Iliad*. In it we see the culmination of the plot that began with the quarrel in Book 1 and continued with the rejection of the Embassy in Book 9 and the defeat of the Greeks and the wounding of their leaders in Book 11.

Achilleus, his mind still clouded by anger, makes the irrational decision to allow his closest friend, Patroklos, to lead the Myrmidons into battle, in order to protect the ships and save the Greek army. Patroklos, after great achievements, is finally killed by Hektor. Mirroring Patroklos' own death, at the end, another sympathetic figure, Sarpedon, is killed halfway through the book, giving Patroklos his greatest victory.

It is these two deaths, and to a lesser extent that of Kebriones in 737, together with the moving epitaph of 775-76, that introduce a tragic tone to the *Iliad*, which will not leave it from now on. For the first time the hearer or reader feels more than momentarily involved in the fate of the defeated.

The book falls into six parts:

1-100	Patroklos and Achilleus.
101-23	Climax of the Trojan attack; Hektor sets fire to the ship.
124-283	Patroklos leads the Myrmidons into battle.
284-418	The Trojans are driven back. *Aristeia* of Patroklos.
419-683	Death of Sarpedon. Fight over his body.
684-867	Patroklos' last fight.

2. Patroklos finally returns. Achilleus had sent him to Nestor in Book 11 to find out the identity of a wounded warrior. After discovering the answer and listening to a long speech from the old king of Pylos, including (790–802) a suggestion for Patroklos himself, which he now proceeds to follow, he had left there to return; but he met the wounded Eurypylos on the way and kindly looked after him (end of Book 11). Only at 15.405 did Patroklos leave Eurypylos and set out on the last stage of his return to Achilleus.

3. wept warm tears. The heroes weep more easily than would a northern warrior; cf. Agamemnon at 9.14–15.

6–19. Achilleus' speech to Patroklos is a delicate combination of gentleness and irony. For the beautiful smile of the little girl who wants her mother to carry her, compare the boy and the sand castle in 15.362–64. From line 12 comes the irony. Achilleus knows perfectly well why Patroklos is weeping but affects to believe that it may be some bad news from home of which he is unaware.

Menoitios and **Peleus** are the respective fathers of Patroklos and Achilleus.

20. the rider. This honorific term is used of Patroklos because he was normally Achilleus' charioteer; it is applied also to Peleus in line 33 (cf. 9.432 n.).

Note how Homer addresses Patroklos in the second person in this line; the reason is no doubt partly the formulaic language of the *Iliad*, but the effect is one of sympathy for the character. It has been noticed that only two heroes are regularly addressed in this way: Patroklos and Menelaos, both kindly and sympathetic men.

33–35. not Peleus and Thetis, but the sea and the rocks. Chiastic presentation, for the sea is feminine and the rocks masculine; and underlying it, perhaps, is the fact that Thetis was a goddess of the sea, while Peleus has his name from the wild mountain, Pelion. These lines were much imitated by later poets of the ancient world.

the rider: see 20 n.

36–45. This is the suggestion put into Patroklos' mind by Nestor in 11.793–802. It was indeed his own death that Patroklos was asking for; but if Achilleus will not go out himself to fight, this is the best hope for the Greeks.

49–86. Achilleus' reply has been the subject of much discussion. The difficulty is that at three points (50–51, 72, and 84–86) he seems to have forgotten what happened in Book 9 during the Embassy scene (cf. 11.608). This has so impressed analytical scholars that they argue as self-evident that the poet of the beginning of Book 16 cannot have known Book 9 and that therefore the Embassy was not yet part of the *Iliad* when Book 16 was composed (PAGE 307–11). This is obviously a very significant conclusion for a theory of the composition and authorship of the *Iliad*. E. Bethe, the German scholar, went so far as to call this "the most violent contradiction in the *Iliad*" (a description which better suits the unhappy duals of 9.182 ff.). Against this it can be argued that Achilleus evidently quotes from his speech to Aias in the Embassy at 61–63; and LOHMANN 274–75 shows that lines 49–63 are composed with a structure closely similar to that reply to Aias in 9.644–55—a strong argument for common authorship. Let us take up the three parts of Achilleus' reply that lie at the basis of this controversy.

In lines 50–51, we find: **there is no word from Zeus my honoured mother has told me.** At first sight this seems starkly contradictory to the unforgettable 9.410–16, where Achilleus told the envoys his mother had told him he had two possible fates: early death if he stayed at Troy, a long life if he returned home. Defenders of the lines argue that Achilleus is not explicitly denying that he has received a warning from his mother but instead is saying that any such warning is not the reason for his refusal to fight. This somewhat strains the Greek, although it is possible. A different explanation is offered in the note on those lines in Book 9, namely, that the story of his mother's warning is a momentary invention for that particular passage in Achilleus' speech and should not be taken to influence the *Iliad* to any wider extent. If this is correct, it also tells us something about Homer's methods of composition.

Second, how, in line 72, can Achilleus say, **if . . . Agamemnon treated me kindly,** when, only the night before, Agamemnon had sent the best of the Achaians to him with an offer of the most magnificent compensation? So runs the analysts' complaint. The acceptable and sufficient answer is that Achilleus is not thinking of compensation, at this point, but of the way Agamemnon treated him.

Third, in lines 84–86, Achilleus does say—in the context of urging Patroklos to return after he has driven the Trojans back, and not to push his success too far—that he wants the Greeks to restore Briseis to him and give him compensatory gifts. The logical critic finds it unbelievable that Achilleus should say this when the offer to do exactly what he is asking for was made the night before. To him it may be replied that Achilleus' present concern is the safety of Patroklos (see 80–96 n.) and that the compensation required is no more than a secondary argument. We can also add, if we wish, that it is characteristic of an angry man, in demanding compensation, to forget that an attempt at offering it has already been made (this is the explanation proposed above, at 11.608).

57. a strong-fenced city: Lyrnessos (see 2.690).

60–61. it was not in my heart to be angry forever. This is an important characterizing point. Achilleus, whose fatal anger is the subject of the *Iliad*, is essentially a mild man; this will be seen later at the reconciliation in Book 19 and especially in the scene with Priam in Book 24.

61–63. until . . . the fighting . . . came up to my own ships. Exactly what he said at 9.650–53, in the speech in reply to Aias, where he modified the more extreme intentions expessed in his previous two replies (see note in Book 9).

70. Achilleus would evidently prefer to go out himself; he enjoys fighting and is hurting himself, as well as Agamemnon, by refusing to do so.

80–96. Achilleus' instructions to Patroklos to drive the enemy from the ships *and then come back* show his anxiety for his friend. The argument that, if Patroklos is too successful, Achilleus' own honor will be diminished is merely a pretext. That his real concern is for Patroklos is shown by lines 89–90 and 96 (also 246–48) and by the strong emotion in the prayer that follows (97–100).

97–100. These lines were considered suspect by the Alexandrian scholars, as suggesting homosexual feeling between Achilleus and Patroklos. This is hypersensitive, as WILAMOWITZ 121 argues. The lines show strong attachment to his friend and hatred for both the Greeks and the Trojans, but hardly eroticism.

We may notice Homer's use of tragic irony in the expressed wish, for events turned out the opposite of what Achilleus hopes for; in fact the rest of the Greeks sacked Troy after he and Patroklos were both dead.

101–23. We return briefly to the scene as it was at the end of

Book 15. Aias is finally driven back, and the Trojans have their greatest success in setting fire to the ship of Protesilaos. The critical situation is marked by the poet, as often, by an invocation of the Muses (112).

114. Notice how it is inevitably **Hektor** who does the great deeds on the Trojan side; they have no one else. It was he who broke the gate in the wall at the end of Book 12; who took hold of the ship of Protesilaos in 15.716; and who now (114–15) drives Aias back. The **ash spear** of this line is presumably the immensely long pike for sea fighting (15.677) with which Aias had been keeping off the attackers (15.730, 742).

131–44. The third of the four arming scenes in the *Iliad* (see 3.330–38 n.). The only expansions of the basic sequence in this case are lines 134 and 140–44. Line 134 is to remind us that Patroklos is donning Achilleus' armor, not his own. Lines 140–44 make it clear that Patroklos is no Achilleus. He may be able to wear his armor, but he cannot use **the Pelian ash spear** that none but Achilleus could wield. This famous weapon, evidently legendary, had been given to Peleus, father of Achilleus, by the centaur Cheiron. According to the scholia, the gift was made at the wedding of Peleus and Thetis (see 18.84–85 n.).

145–47. Automedon (seen before at 9.209) is third in the Myrmidon hierarchy. When Achilleus was fighting, Patroklos, his "number two," would drive the chariot. Now that Patroklos has gone up to first position (that of fighter), Automedon takes the reins. The point of the phrase **stood most staunchly by him** in 147 is the duty of the charioteer to stay close, whatever the danger (cf. 15.445–57 n.).

149–51. Xanthos and Balios. These are immortal horses. **Podarge,** their dam, was a "harpy," or storm wind; she is to be thought of here as of horse shape, for she was grazing in a meadow. That horses could become pregnant by the wind was a view of the ancient world (Virgil, *Georgics* 3.271–79), implying great speed in their offspring.

152–53. In the traces ... he put ... Pedasos. One other trace horse appears in the *Iliad*, in connection with Nestor's chariot at 8.87 (see note). There too it is the trace horse which is killed (as

here at 467–75). No doubt the purpose of the introduction of this
horse is to give the poet the opportunity for a vivid description,
while the chariot may nevertheless still be set right and brought
to safety.

Eëtion's city was Thebe (cf. 9.188).

168–97. To mark the Myrmidons' entry into battle, the poet
introduces a small catalogue of their forces. They are divided into
five divisions, like the Trojans and their allies for their attack at
12.86. The fifty ships of line 168 accord with the Catalogue (2.685);
fifty men per ship is also the number given for another of the
northern Greek contingents in 2.719.

The divisional commanders are mostly new, and the first three,
about whom most information is given, do not recur in the *Iliad*.

174. **Spercheios** was the river of Achilleus' home (see 23.142).
That a girl could become pregnant by a river is not entirely
dissimilar from the belief that horses could become pregnant by
the wind (149–51 n.). A similar story is that of Tyro, with whom
the god Poseidon lay in the guise of the river Enipeus (*Od.*
11.238–53).

181. The title **Argeïphontes** has appeared already at 2.103.
Hermes is also called by a title translated as "the healer" in
line 184, a name found only in the *Iliad*, of uncertain etymology
and meaning.

183. **Artemis** is **clamorous** probably because of the shouts of
hunters. A **golden distaff** might be attributed to any goddess, since
goddesses would perform on Olympos the tasks of women on
earth—here spinning and weaving. But the distaff least suits
Artemis, the virgin huntress; consequently, the ancient explanation
was that "distaff" was being used, by metonymy, for "arrow."

187. **Eileithyia** was the goddess of childbirth.

189. **Aktor** was the name of Patroklos' grandfather (14), but this
is probably some other man. The name is not uncommon.

191. **Phylas:** Polymele's father, the child's grandfather (181).

195. **Peleian Achilleus' henchman:** Patroklos.

196. We are a little surprised to find the aged **Phoinix** (9.168)
leading a division; but, if Nestor could, so could he.

BOOK SIXTEEN

197. Alkimedon acts as charioteer to Automedon after Patroklos' death (17.467).

215–17. This description of massed troops has previously appeared at 13.131–33.

228. sulphur was a purifier and disinfectant; Odysseus used it to fumigate his house after the killing of the suitors (*Od.* 22.481).

233–35. Achilleus' invocation of Zeus is addressed to the Zeus of his homeland in northern Greece, the god of the ancient sanctuary and oracle of **Dodona** (2.750). The description affords obscure evidence about that cult. **Pelasgian** was a very ancient name for a people of the Aegean area—Achilleus' own kingdom being called "Pelasgian Argos" (2.681). The **Selloi** appear to have been a primitive ascetic sect (235).

236–38. These lines were used in 1.453–55 by Chryses when he wished to reverse the curse he had put on the Greeks by the agency of Apollo. They do not suit Achilleus exactly, because he had not done the asking but had sent his mother to do it.

255–56. This is characteristic. Achilleus likes to watch the battle and really regrets not being in it; cf. 11.599–600.

259–65. The **Myrmidons**, previously like wolves (156), are now likened to wasps—both striking similes. In the last line (265) Homer humanizes the wasps (**swarm out to fight for their children**) in a way more characteristic of Virgil, who is particularly sensitive to small creatures.

281. The Trojans, on seeing the leader in Achilleus' armor, at first thought that Achilleus himself (**Peleion**) had come out. No wonder they were thrown into confusion. This was part of the reason for Patroklos to wear Achilleus' armor.

284–418. The first stage of Patroklos' *aristeia*. It falls into three parts: first, Patroklos kills one leading Trojan (284–305), immediately relieving the pressure; then, a long list of Greek leaders each register a kill (306–63); third, Patroklos is brought in again and pursues the Trojans across the plain, killing large numbers of them (364–418). The whole sequence is very similar indeed to the beginning of the *aristeia* of Diomedes in Book 5, where the equivalent sections are 1–29, 29–84, and 85–165.

287. For **Pyraichmes**, see 2.848. By thus killing one of the

leaders, Patroklos drives the Trojans back from the burning ship.
297–300. A striking and beautiful simile. Zeus, the sky god, disperses the clouds from around the top of a mountain, and immediately shafts of bright light come down onto the mountain sides, so that the outlines stand out clearly. This describes the relief that comes to the Greeks when the massed Trojans are driven from the ships.

The simile has in part appeared before, in the vivid lines describing the Trojan watch fires at the end of Book 8. Scholars agree that the common lines (299–300) are more appropriate here, although few would wish to lose them from 8.557–58.

306–51. These lines describe the fight that occurs as the Trojans try to make a stand after being driven from the ship. Nine Greek leaders each kill an opponent—Patroklos himself, Menelaos, Meges, Antilochos and Thrasymedes (the two sons of Nestor), the lesser Aias, Peneleos the Boiotian (14.487), Meriones, and Idomeneus. This list is made up of those who have taken most part in the fighting in Books 13–15, apart from Telamonian Aias, whose absence here is explained in 358–59. The fact that only Greeks win shows that theirs is the victory; and the last Trojan but one, Meriones' victim, is actually trying to climb on to his chariot to get away when he is hit (343).

317–29. Brothers against brothers. The two opponents of Nestor's sons are not Trojans but Lykians, followers of Sarpedon (327). Their names indeed (Atymnios and Maris) sound non-Greek, and so does the name of their father, Amisodaros. His responsibility for the **Chimaira** (for which see 6.179) must reflect some legend.

342. An **Akamas**, son of Antenor, was leader of the Dardanians, along with Aineias and Akamas' brother, Archelochos (killed by Aias in 14.464); see 2.823 and 12.100. It is generally assumed that this victim of Meriones is the same man, but the identification by name alone can hardly be secure. Quintus of Symrna (*The Fall of Troy* 10.168) has Akamas son of Antenor killed by Philoktetes long after the end of the *Iliad*; other evidence quoted in KULLMANN 180, n. 2, adds further doubt.

358–63. Aias is always at Hektor, and Hektor uses his good technique to defend himself, thus holding up the Greek attack so that his comrades can withdraw.

364–65. The simile has been questioned because **a cloud goes deep into the sky** has not seemed to commentators to have much connection with **the noise of their terror** beside the ships. The explanation lies in the field of meteorology. What is described in the simile is the great thundercloud, cumulonimbus. It goes high into the sky and is associated with violent wind and storm (the **hurricane** of 365). The roaring of the wind is a satisfactory point of comparison for the noise of the Trojans.

368. Hektor . . . abandoned the people. Hektor's behavior seems at first sight inconsistent with that described in 363. In fact, however, throughout these books we have the repeated situation of the Trojans (occasionally the Greeks) holding the battle even for a time but then being forced to give way. Here Hektor mounts his chariot to withdraw and is followed by the other chariots (370); the mass of ordinary troops is left behind. The ditch, which was a fairly easy obstacle when they were attacking (15.355–60), is far more difficult now that they are streaming back in panic. The narrow causeway made by Apollo so that the chariots could cross (15.357–59) would be of little use in these circumstances.

There is probably a contrast here with the disciplined retreat of the Greeks, following the advice of Thoas in 15.281–305.

371. The expression is a little awkward. The verb at the beginning (**left**) is to be taken with **their masters' chariots** at the end of the line: "Many fast horses left their masters' chariots, broken short at the joining of the pole."

378. Patroklos has now mounted his own chariot for the pursuit. The poet does not need to tell us each time he mounts or dismounts. At 401 he is on foot; at 427 he is in his chariot.

380. A miraculous leap of the immortal horses. In natural terms, it would have been impossible for them to pull a chariot across a ditch like this. There may be an underlying confusion with horse-riding here, as at 12.50.

384–92. the hurricane. This seems to be the great storm portended by the massive cloud in 364. The attribution to Zeus (in 386–88) of a concern for general morality is unique in the *Iliad*.

397. The **high wall** is the city wall of Troy. The **river** (Skamandros) flows at the side of the battlefield (11.499).

398. Exactly what Poulydamas feared (13.745).

399–418. Patroklos kills freely. None of his victims is known from elsewhere. **Thestor** in 402 is evidently the charioteer of **Pronoös**, killed after his superior, as often. He, **Enops' son**, reminds one of Satnios, Enops' son, killed at 14.447. His death is particularly gruesome.

Erymas in 415 has the same name as the man Idomeneus killed at 345. It would be difficult for Homer to choose different names every time.

419–683. Patroklos' *aristeia* culminates in his fight with **Sarpedon**, king of the Lykians and the most important of Troy's allies. To kill such a man raises Patroklos' status to the highest and makes him a more fitting victim for Apollo and Hektor.

Sarpedon has been carefully presented by the poet so that he is a sympathetic figure for the reader. We have seen him in Books 5 and 12. In the former, where he fought a wild fight against the Rhodian Tlepolemos, he attracted our attention by twice referring to his wife and baby son at home (5.480, 688). In the latter, he made the famous speech to his friend Glaukos on the subject of *noblesse oblige* (12.310–28) and then showed his courage by being the first to break the Greek wall, pulling with both hands at the battlements within close range of the enemy (12.397). He is a sympathetic, brave, and noble man; all the more tragic, then, is his death in the fight that ensues here.

423. this man. Sarpedon still seems to be uncertain who Patroklos is. Compare 5.175, at the same point in Diomedes' *aristeia* in that book.

431–61. A divine comment. Sarpedon is the son of Zeus, and Zeus wonders whether to rescue him from his imminent death. The exchange with Hera should be carefully noted as a statement of the relationship between Zeus and fate. The situation is that Zeus undoubtedly has the power to go against what is fated but in practice does not do so because of Hera's argument that it would upset the balance of the world. Whether this means that "Zeus is *not* subject to fate" (LATTIMORE 54) is debatable.

Zeus is responsible for all that happens in the world, and so he frequently fulfills what is fated. Fate is limited to death and finality—the death of a man or the destruction of Troy. When these are due, they will happen, and Zeus will see to it that they happen (cf. 644–47). When gods rescue their protégés elsewhere (Aphrodite: Paris in Book 3 and Aineias in Book 5; Poseidon: Aineias in Book 20; and Apollo: Hektor in Book 20), we may take it that the humans were not fated to die *then*.

Hera's suggestion in lines 453–57—to let Sarpedon die but receive **due burial**—is carried out in 681–83. That **Sleep** and **Death**, two brothers (682, cf. 14.231), carry the body back to his homeland for burial is probably etiological in origin. If a feature in Lykia was known as the "Grave of Sarpedon," the poet would need to have him transported there if he wished him to die at Troy.

The rain of **blood** (459) appeared before, at 11.54; it is better motivated here.

464. strong henchman: i.e., charioteer.

467–75. The **trace horse** (see 152–53 n.) is, of course, expendable. When it is killed, Automedon reacts as Nestor did in 8.87, cutting the traces to get rid of the encumbrance.

481. The loss of the sympathetic Sarpedon is a shock to the hearer. Patroklos will be next.

482–86. These same lines were used of Asios when he was killed by Idomeneus in 13.389–93. We may note an effect of tree similes: the hero is tall and slim (**towering,** 483).

492. The dying Sarpedon calls to his friend Glaukos. This simultaneously prepares us for the next stage of the battle, the fight for Sarpedon's body, and gives a final impression of a man of feeling.

504. What exactly **came away** with the spear? According to the scholia, **midriff** here means the membrane of the diaphragm below the heart, i.e., what is called the pericardium.

507. once free of their master's chariot. There is uncertainty about the meaning. The Greek words appear to say, "as they were now free of their masters' chariot." But Sarpedon's horses had not become separated from the chariot, although they had lost both masters, Sarpedon and the charioteer, Thrasymelos. The simplest explanation is that this is a casual echo of 371, where the same phrase is used more intelligibly.

510. For the **wound,** see 12.387.

514–16. Glaukos naturally prays to the Lykian god, Apollo;

compare Pandaros in 4.119. It is a true religious thought that the god can hear his worshiper wherever he is.

537–40. This is typical of the way the allies address Hektor. He has to put up with their criticism, for they are volunteers, come to help, and he has no authority over them. Compare the speech of Sarpedon to Hektor in 5.472 and of Glaukos again in 17.142.

558. who first scaled the wall. This occurred at 12.397.

567. Zeus swept ghastly night over the encounter. Compare 15.668 n., where Athene *removed* mist to help the Greeks fight more easily.

569–662. The fight over the body of Sarpedon. It is even for a long time, but eventually (657) the Greeks push the Trojans back.

570–76. The battle begins with the death of a man not heard of before, **Epeigeus,** described as **not the worst of the Myrmidons.** He is killed by Hektor. And we are told of his background: that he had committed homicide of a cousin in his own country, had had to go into exile, and had been accepted as a suppliant by Peleus and Thetis in Phthia. STRASBURGER 30 perceptively suggests that the fate of this man foreshadows that of Patroklos, killed by Hektor at the end of this book—and by no means "the worst of the Myrmidons." For we hear eventually (in 23.84–88, when the ghost of Patroklos appears to Achilleus) that he had had the same history: he too had killed a playmate in his own land, had been received by Peleus in Phthia, and had then been sent to Troy with Achilleus.

This attractive theory is subject to some doubt, however, because exile for manslaughter is a relatively common theme, often used to explain migration of a person or tribe; compare Tlepolemos in 2.662, Medon in 13.696, and Lykophron in 15.432.

577–643. The poet portrays an even struggle by having alternate Greek and Trojan losses (in 577–607) followed first by an indecisive interchange between Aineias and Meriones (608–31) and then by a general description of turmoil. The victors in the first section are those we would expect: Hektor, Patroklos, Glaukos, and Meriones.

604. The comma at the end of this line should be removed. Onetor was priest of **Idaian Zeus,** god of Mount Ida.

614–15. These two lines (= 13.504–5) are missing from almost all the manuscripts and are merely repetitive here. They were presumably added in error at one time, in part of the tradition.

617. a dancer. It has long been assumed that there is an allusion here to Kretan skill in dancing, exemplified in frescoes at Knossos and in the final scene on the Shield of Achilleus, the dancing place made for Ariadne in Krete (18.591).

641–43. flies. The simile occurred in almost the same words at 2.469–71.

644–47. Evidently it is Zeus's function to *fulfill* fate; see 431–61 n.

658. The **balance** (or scales) of Zeus: a figurative means of expressing the way things are turning out; see 8.69, 19.223.

667–83. See 454–57.

670. The immortal **ambrosia** seems to be a preservative for human flesh. Compare the treatment of Patroklos' body in 19.39.

686. The **command of Peleiades** (i.e., of Achilleus, the son of Peleus) was that given at 87–96.

702–9. This is clearly a thematic sequence: "**Three times** he attacked; **three times** the divine defender (characteristically Apollo) pushed him back. When he came in for the fourth time, the god spoke, '**Give way!**' " Essentially the same set of lines was used at 5.436–42, where Diomedes rushed on Apollo, who was rescuing Aineias. And compare Patroklos' final charge in 784–87 (once again meeting Apollo), and Achilleus' in 20.445–47.

To need a god to stop one is evidence of superlative fighting ability.

The **angle of the towering wall** in 702–3 reminds archeologists of the great city walls of Troy VI (see 7.452), sloping at the bottom but vertical above (LORIMER 433).

717. This **Asios**, brother of Hekabe, is of course different from the Asios, son of Hyrtakos, whom we met in Books 12 and 13. For Phrygia and the river Sangarios (719) see Priam's reminiscence in 3.184–87.

723. So might you . . . hold back. Rather, "so might you suffer for holding back from the fighting"; i.e., I would punish you for it.

727. Kebriones now comes into the limelight. He was asked by Hektor to take over the reins of the chariot after two previous charioteers had been killed in Book 8. Since then he has been brought intermittently before our notice. He was one of the divisional leaders in the attack on the wall in Book 12.

729. a deadly confusion. The Greek attack, right up to the city wall, naturally led to some confusion in the ranks.

737. The **charioteer** is killed first, as in 463.

741. his eyes fell out. This is the second time this anatomical impossibility has occurred; the first was at 13.617.

745-50. The almost obligatory "vaunting speech" after the kill. Compare the passages quoted in 14.454–57 n.

753. The simile seems to foretell the end of Patroklos. See, however, 12.150, where a similar thing is said with no such implication.

765-76. A powerful simile and vivid description lead up to the unforgettable epitaph of 775–76. The battle is now for the body of Kebriones, as it was before for Sarpedon and will be, in the next book, for Patroklos.

775-76. The most impressive epitaph in the *Iliad* was surely not created for such a relatively minor figure as Kebriones. This is a formulaic phrase, used in part for Achilleus himself in 18.26 and wholly for him at *Od.* 24.39–40. But it is unlikely that its application to Achilleus was original either; he is not particularly noted for **horsemanship,** although he was of course superior at that, as at all heroic activities (23.275). One suspects that this line and a half was first used to describe one of those old horsemen of the earlier generation (see 9.432 n.). At all events, it probably had a long history before its use here in the *Iliad*.

777-79. middle heaven. Critics have accused Homer of introducing a second noon into this long day of fighting, the first having appeared at 11.84–86. However, it was argued in the note to 11.86 that the time described there (when the woodcutter rests from work and takes his meal) was rather mid-morning; and, since the time described here may be well into the afternoon, there is no necessary inconsistency.

780. beyond their very destiny. This is a striking phrase. Normally things may be said *almost* to have happened contrary to fate—had not Apollo or some other god intervened. To say that something was actually achieved beyond what was destined is to elevate the heroes even higher than usual.

784–85. As the end of Patroklos approaches, the narrative becomes impressionistic, less exact. The sequence (**Three times** ...) is the same as that of his attack on Troy in 702—and once again he comes up against Apollo.

791–821. The death of Patroklos is almost like a ritual killing. First Apollo strikes him in the back, so that he is almost senseless, and knocks his armor off; then an unknown, Euphorbos, wounds him in the back (interestingly enough, just in the place where Apollo had struck him); and finally Hektor moves in and finishes him. The choice of sequence seems strange to us. Why did not the poet let Patroklos meet Hektor in a straight fight, and lose, as he presumably would (in spite of 847–48)? The answer seems to be that, when something of great significance happens in the *Iliad*, the poet automatically attributes it to a god. When Hektor eventually meets Achilleus, once again we might expect a straight description of a heavyweight contest; but, as here, divine intervention makes it easy for Achilleus—unnecessarily, for he would certainly have won without it.

805. his shining body went nerveless. He was paralyzed and unable to move, like Alkathoös in 13.435 and the unnamed charioteer of Asios in 13.394.

808. son of Panthoös. Euphorbos is, then, a brother of Poulydamas. Homer immediately introduces heroic achievements for him, to raise him closer to the level of significance of his action. We have not heard of him before and will hear of him again only when he reaps the natural reward for this present deed at the hands of Menelaos in Book 17.

830–54. The two speeches, of victor and vanquished, are closely similar to those of Achilleus and Hektor in 22.331–36 and 356–66. Indeed, this scene is a foreshadowing of that one. Hektor, so proud here, is the dying man there. In both passages the victor begins by assuming a particular intention or expectation on the part of the vanquished, who in reply forecasts the victor's own death. Then three identical lines describe the death itself (16.855–57 = 22.361–63); and finally the victor in both cases replies to the last words of his opponent.

838–42. he must have said ... Hektor is wrong. This is not at all what Achilleus said to Patroklos. What he said was that Patroklos should return as soon as he had beaten the Trojans back from the ships. It is a recurrent feature of the characterization of Hektor that he makes mistaken assumptions; that is not quite the hybris of the tragic hero, but it is a dangerous state of error. See 13.823; and compare 860–61, below.

849. The son of Leto: Apollo.

857. This pathetic line is repeated once—at the death of Hektor himself.

BOOK SEVENTEEN

Book 17 is wholly devoted to the fight for the body of Patroklos. Two such fights occurred in Book 16 (for the bodies of Sarpedon and Kebriones); typically, its greater length shows the greater importance of the present struggle. Nothing very decisive happens, and commentators in modern times have uniformly found the description unsatisfactory, suggesting either that there have been rhapsodes' additions to the narrative or (MAZON 208) that Homer was tired. We may, however, give him credit for intending the over-all effect of continuous, wearisome struggle for possession.of the corpse. The book may be divided as follows:

1–83	Menelaos and Euphorbos.
84–261	Preliminaries to the battle.
262–425	Dour struggle.
426–542	Episode of the horses of Achilleus. *Aristeia* of Automedon.
543–699	The Trojans exert the greater pressure. The Greeks manage to send a messenger (Antilochos) to tell Achilleus the bad news.
700–761	Slow Greek withdrawal, carrying the body.

FENIK 159–60 has pointed out a repeated pattern in the fighting here. No fewer than four times do we get a speech of rebuke to a Trojan leader which immediately encourages him to take strong action. These speeches are

75–81	Apollo/Mentes to Hektor.
142–68	Glaukos to Hektor.
327–32	Apollo/Periphas to Aineias.
586–90	Apollo/Phainops to Hektor.

Similarly, on the Greek side, a speech from Athene/Phoinix to

Menelaos in 556–59 has the effect of putting new strength into him.

Underlying the basic situation in this book, as many commentators believe, is another image: the famous fight for the body of Achilleus himself after the end of the *Iliad*, when he had been killed "by Apollo and Paris at the Skaian gates" (22.359–60). We hear in the *Odyssey* (5.309–10, 24.41) of that occasion, and elsewhere of how Odysseus held back the Trojans while Aias lifted up the mighty corpse and carried it back—a scene that must have been similar to the one at the end of this book. (For such connections between the *Iliad* and events in the Cyclic *Aithiopis*, see Appendix D.)

1–81. By the inherent assumptions of epic poetry, Euphorbos must die now. He has done a deed above his stature, in taking part in the death of Patroklos (16.806–15). Compare the similar situation of Pandaros at the beginning of Book 5. It is fitting that Menelaos should be the victor, and the avenger of Patroklos, because there is a bond of gentleness between them (see 671), and Menelaos is, after all, the injured party among the Greeks, on behalf of whom the whole war is being fought.

The poet has carefully removed Hektor from the scene, so that this duel can take place. He does this by having Hektor chase after the horses of Achilleus, after killing Patroklos (16.864).

24–27. Hyperenor ... taunted me. It is a little strange that when Menelaos killed Hyperenor at 14.516 the Trojan did not make the insulting remark ascribed to him here. The significant explanation is that this is immediate invention for the purpose of the present speech, to provide evidence of the alleged insolence of the sons of Panthoös.

52. braided locks. The description is evidently of a particularly ornate hair style; finds from excavations have shown thin spirals of gold and silver which are thought to have been used to hold together separate locks of hair.

63–64. The simile describes the two stages of Menelaos' activity against Euphorbos. First he kills him; then he bends over him to strip the armor. So the lion kills and then feeds on his prey.

73–74. The **leader of the Kikones** in 2.846 was Euphemos. **Mentes** could of course be a subordinate commander; but there is an odd similarity to Athene's visiting Telemachos "in the likeness of Mentes, leader of the Taphians" in *Odyssey* 1.105, as if this name is associated with such epiphanies.

76–78. These lines have appeared before, in Odysseus' speech to Dolon at 10.402–4.

83. in its darkness. This means no more than that the heart is dark because it is shut up in the body. Compare 1.103, and 17.499, 573, below.

90–105. The soliloquy of Menelaos is almost a parody of Odysseus' soliloquy at 11.403–10. Later, both Agenor (21.552–70) and Hektor (22.98–130) engage in similar soliloquies when they observe the imminent arrival of Achilleus. Menelaos is the only one who rationalizes an intention not to fight. All the same, his decision is sensible, if unheroic.

91. The **magnificent armour** is probably that worn by Patroklos, not that of Euphorbos, in spite of 60; cf. 113 and 122 n.

116. For **the left of the battle,** see 11.498 n. Aias has normally fought in the center, facing Hektor. But he evidently got detached from Hektor in the latter part of Book 16; he was not there when Patroklos was killed.

122. Hektor has taken his armour. German "analysts" have been much concerned about the arms worn by Patroklos and now taken by Hektor. They see a contradiction between the scene at the end of Book 16, when Apollo struck the armor off Patroklos, to prepare for his death, and the assumption here, in Book 17, that Hektor has stripped the armor from the body, as if it were still wearing it (cf. Zeus's remark at 205). Perhaps we do not need to consider this too rationally. Menelaos, who was bestriding the body (6), withdrew on the approach of Hektor (108); he now (122) naturally assumes that Hektor has the armor. In line 125 the poet states it for a fact. Whether the armor was on the corpse or lying on the ground near it, and how literally we are to take the actions of Apollo in 16.791–805, are more obscure questions.

126–27. to cut his head from his shoulders . . . to give [the body] to the dogs. This seems unlike Hektor, who has shown no such gruesome intentions in the previous fighting. Does it reflect in advance the treatment of his own body at the hands of Achilleus? See 18.177 n.

128. carrying like a wall his shield: cf. 7.219 n.

142. For the allies' habit of rebuking Hektor, see 16.537–40. Untypically, Hektor here replies. The accusation of personal beauty (implying cowardice) is normally directed against Paris (3.39, 13.769).

160–63. The idea of an exchange of bodies is unique, if perfectly reasonable. Glaukos does not know that Sarpedon's body has been transported to Lykia by Sleep and Death (16.682–83).

194–96. that armour immortal. It was not made clear before this that the armor of Achilleus, worn by Patroklos in Book 16, was itself a divine gift, like the armor which will be created to replace it at the end of Book 18. The occasion of the original gift was the marriage of Peleus and Thetis (see 18.84–85 n.).

205. as you should not have done. There is evidently no general impropriety in taking the armor of your dead foe. What Zeus means is that Hektor does not have the stature to wear the immortal armor of Achilleus.

213. companions in arms: the allies, as opposed to the Trojans. The catalogue that immediately follows is mostly of names known to be from the allied contingents, and it is to the allies that Hektor expressly addresses himself in his speech beginning in 220. This seems to be a kind of response to Glaukos' criticisms in 142–68.

216–18. Mesthles is leader of the Maionians (2.864), **Glaukos** of the Lykians. **Thersilochos,** a Paionian, is killed in 21.209. **Medon** and **Deisenor** are not otherwise known.

Hippothoös is leader of the Pelasgians from Larissa (2.840); **Asteropaios** is the *Iliad*'s leader of the Paionians, although he does not appear as such in the Trojan catalogue (2.848). He fights Achilleus in 21.139–204.

Phorkys is leader of the Phrygians (2.862); **Chromios** (in Book 2 called Chromis) and **Ennomos** lead the Mysians (2.858).

250. drink the community's wine. Agamemnon keeps open house for the Greek leaders, the wine being provided as a gift (7.471) or at public cost; cf. 4.259–60, 9.71 n.

256. The surviving major leaders of the Greeks assemble to help fight for the body.

270. The mist adds confusion and danger to the fighting. By it Zeus shows his sorrow for Patroklos. The motif has appeared already (15.668, 16.567), will be reinforced during this battle

(366–69), and will lead Aias to make his famous prayer in 645–47.

274–365. An even fight is shown, as elsewhere, by alternate killings, Greek and Trojan. The victims are leaders or important men:

Aias kills Hippothoös (cf. 217), leader of the Pelasgians.
Hektor kills Schedios, leader of the Phokians.
Aias kills Phorkys (cf. 218), leader of the Phrygians.
Aineias kills Leiokritos, companion of Lykomedes.
Lykomedes kills Apisaon, companion of Asteropaios.

279–80. This is the stock description of Aias as second only to Achilleus.

297. the brain ran ... The ugly description is probably, as FRIEDRICH 46 says, an attempt to go one better than the more straightforward description in 86.

306–7. For **Schedios,** see 2.517. Another Phokian leader called Schedios was killed at 15.515.

325. Aineas' aged father: Anchises. The **thoughts** ... **of kindness** mean that he was a loyal family friend.

327–32. The speech of Apollo is a little unclear. He means, "How could you emulate famous heroes, who have fought to the bitter end to defend a city even when god was against them, when you do not try particularly hard when Zeus is on your side?"

345. Lykomedes is the most significant of the figures in the *Iliad* about whom no real details are given. He appears among the younger leaders at 9.84 and 19.240 and is left by Telamonian Aias at 12.366 to assist the Lokrian Aias to hold the position on the wall. The scholia on 19.240 say he was a Kretan.

377–83. The two sons of Nestor were fighting an easier battle elsewhere (on the left, as usual, 682). The purpose of this brief mention is to prepare for the introduction of **Antilochos** later in the book, as the most suitable person to tell the news to Achilleus, and for Menelaos' errand to find him. Homer takes the opportunity to reinforce our realization of the practical good sense of Nestor.

We last saw Antilochos and Thrasymedes at 16.317–25.

384. daylong. This seems like something of an exaggeration, as it was well into the afternoon at 16.779. But this is no doubt a formulaic expression, used (like those at 366, 412–13, 424) to give a cumulative impression of unremitting fighting.

389–93. The **pulling** at the body from both sides is brutally compared to a primitive method of curing and stretching a hide. The similarity lies in the fact that so many are pulling, but it stays in the same place (FRÄNKEL 59).

408. word from his mother, not known to mortals. Achilleus' private source of information through his goddess mother is a motif which the poet uses when he pleases, sometimes alleging specific knowledge, sometimes denying it; cf. 9.410, 16.51, 18.9.

426–542. The episode of the divine horses of Achilleus mourning for Patroklos, followed by the *aristeia* of their charioteer, Automedon.

443. we: i.e., we gods; for in 23.277–78 Achilleus himself says that they were given to Peleus by Poseidon.

454–55. These lines were in the mouth of Zeus at 11.193–94. They are less appropriate here, for the Trojans do not in fact get through again to the ships; they do not even reach the ditch (see 18.215–31).

459–65. This is a strange episode. Automedon cannot do any damage to the enemy, because he is alone on the chariot and can manage only the horses. It has been suggested (E. R. Dodds, *The Greeks and the Irrational*, p. 4) that this is an example of Ate, Delusion, the temporary leaving of one's senses (cf. 470). Perhaps it is rather a symbolic tribute to Patroklos.

467. Alkimedon was one of the Myrmidon divisional commanders (16.197).

483. sprang down: for that is the method of fighting from chariots (4.301–9 n.).

494. Chromios was mentioned above (218). **Aretos** has not appeared before; his role here is to be killed. Automedon ought to have a success and can obviously not kill Hektor or Aineias.

547–52. There is something slightly odd about the simile. It is intended primarily to describe Athene's descent from heaven to earth. But, as the poet goes on, it appears (551) that Athene actually *comes down* in a rainbow. There is an exact parallel to this at 4.75, where Athene's descent on a similar errand is likened to a falling star, and it is then apparent that the armies actually see a falling star.

In line 549, **when heat perishes** means "when it gets very cold," as in thunderstorm conditions.

570. This is the strangest of the many similes used to describe Menelaos in this book. He was like a mother cow in 4–5, a lion several times, an eagle in 674, and now a **persistent mosquito.** Homer is fond of Menelaos—perhaps less so than of Odysseus and Nestor, but nevertheless fond. Menelaos is trying hard to live up to the heroism demanded of him by circumstances.

575–76. Eëtion's son. The familiar Eëtion was king of Thebe and Hektor's father-in-law. This man **Podes,** however, cannot be *his* son, because (*a*) Andromache says in 6.421 that all her brothers are dead and (*b*) Podes is evidently a home-bred Trojan, a personal friend of Hektor's.

583. As **Phainops, Asios' son,** comes from Abydos, and Abydos is in the realm of Asios, son of Hyrtakos (2.836), we may reasonably assume that these are father and son. This adds some probability to the assumption that Adamas, Asios' son (12.140, 13.560), was serving with his own father and was thus Phainops' brother.

For father and son together in the army, compare Pylaimenes and Harpalion (13.644) and, of course, Nestor and his two sons, Thrasymedes and Antilochos.

593–94. Zeus inspires terror in the Greeks. The **aegis,** which he holds up, probably originated in a view of the dark underside of the stormcloud. This has normally been forgotten, and it is thought of as a sort of divine shield, borrowed, when needed, by Athene and Apollo. Here, however, the description seems to be closer to the origin of the concept.

597. With the flight of the Greeks, we may compare 8.78 ff. The rout is started on this occasion by the unusual wounding of two Greek leaders, Peneleos and Leïtos, both Boiotians (2.494).

605–25. A rather confused description, although it all becomes clear if one accepts the facts as they are given. Idomeneus is regularly *on foot,* and indeed he and Meriones came on foot to this battle in Book 13. It seems now that Meriones' charioteer had brought up his master's chariot; but seeing Idomeneus, the Kretan supreme commander, in danger, he had driven close to him. Idomeneus was still on the ground when he threw a spear at Hektor (605); by the time Hektor replied (609), Idomeneus had mounted Meriones' chariot. The charioteer, Koiranos, paid for this brave act with his life.

Now Meriones, also concerned for Idomeneus, his superior commander, who (we remember) is an older man and thus less agile in combat and retreat (13.361, 510–15), gathers the reins from the ground, hands them to Idomeneus, and tells him to get out quickly. Meriones himself stays in the battle (668); this also is a brave act, to which Homer does not feel it necessary to draw attention.

645–47. Father Zeus, draw free from the mist ... Aias' prayer to Zeus that, if they are to die, they should at least die in the light has been among the most quoted passages of the *Iliad*, usually with a psychological implication not present in Homer. It is the culmination of the various references to a mist over the battlefield (270).

653. Why **Antilochos?** The answer is connected with the continuing story of the war after the end of the *Iliad*. In the section of the legend which was covered in the post-Iliadic *Aithiopis*, Antilochos appeared in a role like that of Patroklos in Homer's poem, being killed by the chief enemy hero (Memnon) and avenged by Achilleus. From this point to the end of the *Iliad*, Homer seems to be preparing for that later event. Antilochos and Achilleus are brought into contact here and in 18.16–34, and then twice in the funeral games of Book 23 (541–56, 785–97). He is a sympathetic and attractive young man, eager to do well; by the end of the *Iliad* a friendship, like that with Patroklos, seems to have been established between him and Achilleus (see Appendix D).

Antilochos also has a particular relationship with Menelaos (see 23.566–613 n.), which makes it suitable that Menelaos should be the one to contact him here.

666. Menelaos is a man of feeling. He does not want to leave the body of Patroklos, and he returns as quickly as he can (706). Before he leaves, he encourages the others to remember the kindness of the dead man.

Menelaos has in fact done very well in the battle for a hero not quite in the first rank as a fighter (cf. 570 n.).

698–99. to a blameless companion: i.e., to his own charioteer, Laodokos. Antilochos chooses to run with the message rather than take his chariot.

The tense of the verb in 699 is continuous, not a completed action as translated (**had turned**). Laodokos was all the time maneuvering the chariot close to Antilochos.

705. Thrasymedes was already there (378) and naturally would take over single control on the departure of his brother.

722–61. The funeral cortege winds back across the plain, Menelaos and Meriones carrying the body of Patroklos, while the two Aiantes keep back the Trojans. For this memorable scene, Homer uses a cluster of five similes: the Trojans attack like dogs pursuing a wounded boar, the fight is like a fire-storm destroying a city, Menelaos and Meriones are like mules dragging a heavy tree down from the hills, the two Aiantes are like a rock opposing the force of mighty rivers in flood, and the rest of the Greeks fly before Aineias and Hektor like little birds before a hawk.

It has been pointed out (see introductory note to this book) that the scene bears a close resemblance to a more famous occasion, after the death of Achilleus himself, when Aias carried the body while Odysseus kept off the enemy. We may also compare the slow retreat of Aias at 11.543–73. It is in such situations that he is at his best; when the Greeks are attacking, we hear less of him.

BOOK EIGHTEEN

Book 18 is famous for the description of the designs on the Shield of Achilleus, made for him by the smith god, Hephaistos, to replace the shield lost with the rest of Achilleus' armor when Hektor killed Patroklos. There are, in all, five episodes in the book, the last three of which occur simultaneously during the night which follows this very long day of fighting:

1–147	Antilochos brings the news to Achilleus. Thetis comes from the sea to console him.
148–242	With Achilleus' help, the body of Patroklos is brought into the camp. Night falls.
243–314	Trojan assembly.
314–67	Mourning for Patroklos.
368–616	Thetis and Hephaistos. The making of the arms. The designs on the shield.

At the beginning here, as at the end of Book 17, there is clear evidence that the events and pictorial images in the narrative reflect that other situation, when it was Achilleus himself who was dead; in other words, the poet, whether consciously or not, is indebted to other poetry known to him, perhaps composed by him, about that far more significant occasion. The incidents of this sort here are (*a*) the position of Achilleus on the floor of his hut (26), (*b*) the coming of the Nereids from the sea to mourn (65–69), and (*c*) the gesture of his mother in line 71. For a discussion of all this, see Appendix D.

2. **Antilochos** set out in 17.698.

3. **steep-horned.** The ships had a raised section at each end; cf. 15.729 n. Achilleus characteristically watches the fighting; cf. 11.600.

9-11. For the warnings from his mother, see 17.408 n.

13. yet I told him. In 16.87–96.

26. he himself ... in the dust lay. This powerful line was used of Kebriones at 16.776, where it was pointed out that there is evidence in *Odyssey* 24.39–40 that it was associated with the dead body of Achilleus himself. Here it seems that the poet, because of the situation of mourning, puts Achilleus physically into the position his body will take soon after the end of the *Iliad*, and uses for him the description that will be used then. It is striking evidence of an *associative* method of composition by the poet.

36. Thetis' **aged father** is Nereus, god of the sea. Her situation in the **depths of the sea** may be thought to require explanation. She was, of course, married to Peleus—a marriage which the *Iliad* typically accounts for in a humanized way, saying that the gods for their own reasons compelled her to marry a human (85, 432). But behind this there is the common fairy tale of the young man who catches a mermaid down by the seashore; and in that tale it is a regular feature that when her human husband grows old (cf. 434), the mermaid leaves him and goes back to the sea. So Thetis is with her father now (although Homer seems to forget this in 59, 89, and 440).

39-48. The catalogue of Nereids. Thirty-three are named. There must be a connection, though not direct, with a catalogue of fifty Nereids in Hesiod's *Theogony* 243–62, where some nineteen of Homer's names recur, mostly in a different order, although lines 43 and 45 are reproduced almost exactly. (There is a similar situation with the list of rivers in 12.20–22.) Scholarly opinion, beginning in the ancient world, has been divided on the genuineness of these lines in the *Iliad*. Many have wished to cut them out, including Zenodotus and Aristarchus; and evidently it is just the sort of list which might be added at such an apparently suitable place. WILAMOWITZ (165) argues, on the contrary, that the beautiful names, which suggest peace, make an effective contrast between the harsh world of men and unchanging nature and thus have an aesthetic and poetic purpose.

Most of the Nereids' names are invented, but not by Homer and not for this passage. Many are known from elsewhere as sea goddesses, the most famous being Galateia (45). The largest group is etymologically connected with the sea—its color, its waves, shores, islands, grottoes. These are Glauke, Kymodoke, Nesaie, Speio, Thoë, Halia, Kymothoë, Aktaia, Limnoreia, Iaira, Amphithoë, Amphinome, Galateia, Ianeira, Ianassa, Maira, and Amatheia. Thaleia, "Plenty" (39) is elsewhere one of the Muses or Graces; Melite (42) means "Honeyed"; Agauë (42), Kallianeira (44), Kallianassa (46), and Klymene (47) are royal or divine attributes ("August," "Beautiful and Queenly," again "Beautiful and Queenly," and "Glorious"); so also is Panope, "All-Seeing" (45). Doto and Proto are almost like nicknames (popular Greek feminine names often ended in -o), the former meaning "The Giver," the latter "The First" (or perhaps "The Provider"). Dynamene, Pherousa, and Dexamene are not names at all but the participles of verbs, meaning "She Who Is Powerful," "She Who Carries," and "She Who Protects." Doris, "The Giver," was, according to Hesiod, also the name of the mother of the Nereids, the wife of Nereus. Nemertes and Apseudes are adjectives meaning "Infallible," used of oracles; we may compare Proteus, the prophetic old man of the sea, consulted by Menelaos in *Od.* 4.363–570. Oreithyia has come down from the mountains, for her name is that of a mountain nymph.

59–60 = 440–41 (cf. **89–90**). For the pathos of her situation (a mother who will not receive her son home again after the war), the poet disregards the fact, just assumed, that Thetis has now left Phthia and lives again in the sea.

68. The Nereids come out of the sea to the Greek camp. This will happen also at the death of Achilleus (*Od.* 24.47, 58; see also Proclus' summary of the *Aithiopis*). Seeing that the death of Achilleus himself is a more potent reason for their epiphany than the death of his friend, we may reasonably assume that Homer is reflecting the other situation. (See Appendix D; KAKRIDIS 65–75.)

71. took her son's head in her arms. The gesture is unexpected; and if, as we must assume, Achilleus is still lying on the floor (cf. 178, 203, 461), Thetis' position raises some difficulty. She would have to sit down and take his head in her lap, but line 70 explicitly says "stood by him." As KAKRIDIS 67–68 points out, the gesture of a mother taking her son's head "in her arms" is that of a mother whose dead son is lying on a bier (see especially Andromache with the corpse of Hektor in 24.724; also 23.136, 24.712). This is the third time in this book that the imagery of Achilleus' own death has been used.

84–85. In the humanized form of the legend (see 36 n.), Peleus was the most righteous of men, and the gods rewarded him by giving him a sea goddess, Thetis, for his wife. According to Aeschylus (*Prometheus Bound* 907–27) and Pindar (*Eighth Isthmian* 26–45), they had a further reason, namely, that Zeus and Poseidon were rivals for Thetis but were put off by a prophecy that she would bear a child stronger than his father. Whether this was known to Homer or not, he certainly knows of the famous wedding, when a human married a goddess and the gods themselves were present and gave gifts. The giving of the armor on that occasion has already been mentioned in 17.195–96.

98. I must die soon, then. Thetis' warning has no effect on Achilleus. He lives only for vengeance on Hektor. His quarrel with Agamemnon is of no importance now. This is a very powerful and psychologically motivated speech, comparable to Achilleus' great speech of 9.308–429.

110. the dripping of honey: probably from trees or rocks, the home of wild bees.

117–19. A typical mythological example. If even **Herakles** died, why should Achilleus expect not to? Hera was always the enemy of Herakles, as we see from numerous other allusions in the *Iliad* (8.362–69 n.).

137. Hephaistos was the divine smith. Armor made by him would be the greatest glory of a human warrior. Memnon in the *Aithiopis* also had armor made by Hephaistos.

148. The construction of the book at this point is very like that in Book 16, the return to the battle position after a scene with Achilleus mirroring 16.101. The situation portrayed here is that of the last lines of Book 17 (755–61). There has been some concern that the picture just before, in Book 17, of Meriones and Menelaos carrying the body, with the two Aiantes holding off the Trojans, seems to have been forgotten. This is perhaps to be answered by the assumption that we are at a later stage in the retreat. The Aiantes, at least, are still performing their former function (157).

177. to cut the head from the soft neck and set it on sharp stakes.

This alleged intention of Hektor would be as shocking to Greek taste as it is to us. C. Segal (*The Theme of the Mutilation of the Corpse in the Iliad* [1971], pp. 19–25) points out the steady deterioration in Hektor's attitudes. In 7.76–86 he proposed the chivalrous return of an opponent's dead body; in 16.836, he told the dying Patroklos that the vultures would eat him; in 17.126–27, the poet said that Hektor intended to cut off the head and give the body to the dogs to eat; and here Iris alleges that he intends to set the head up as a trophy on a palisade (probably meaning the Trojan city wall).

The allegation may, of course, not be true. It is just what is needed to arouse the fury of Achilleus. It is evidently not unconnected with Achilleus' future treatment of Hektor's own body.

219–20. The simile seems to continue the situation of 207–13, just as 16.384–92 follows on from 16.364–65. The whole picture is of the greatest vividness.

228–29. Three times ... three times. For this repeated theme, see 16.702–9; it has already been used in this book, at 155–58.

231. upon their own chariots and spears: i.e., in the confusion of trying to get away, while attempting to mount their chariots (normal procedure for retreat).

239. This is the end of the long day's fighting, which began in Book 11. Even so, the poet says that Hera miraculously brought the day to an end before its proper time (**unwilling**), so as to save the Greeks from further defeat. This is a stock theme (the hastened or delayed setting of the sun), more suitable to other occasions than this.

243–314. The Trojan assembly. This takes the form of a balanced pair of speeches by Poulydamas and Hektor, the one arguing for a prudent return to Troy, as Achilleus has now been roused, the other violently disagreeing. Poulydamas' speech is his fourth to Hektor in the *Iliad*. The sequence is as follows: 12.61–79 (Poulydamas: Let us leave the horses at the ditch; Hektor agrees); 12.211–29 (Poulydamas: Let us not push home our attack; Hektor disagrees); 13.726–47 (Poulydamas: Let us regroup and then discuss whether to attack or not; Hektor agrees, but in practice the proposed discussion does not take place, and they attack immediately); now, most importantly, Poulydamas proposes that they withdraw to Troy and return to the defense of the city; Hektor fatally (see 22.100–104) disagrees and persuades the Trojans to follow his lead. It is clear that this is not only a typical (thematic) situation but also the culmination of all the previous instances.

251. born on the same night. This is new. So Poulydamas is, as it were, Hektor's twin.

259–60. Poulydamas speaks as if they have been sleeping out on the plain for some time, whereas a close observation of the *Iliad* shows that there has only been one such night, that at the end of Book 8, yesterday evening from the present time. This is merely exaggeration on the part of the speaker, not a real inconsistency with the *Iliad* situation.

279. here. Rather, "there"; they are out on the plain near the Greek lines now.

290–91. lovely treasures . . . have vanished. The Trojans have had to use their wealth to pay for the maintenance of the allies who have come to help (cf. 17.225); there would also be the question of buying provisions for the city.

293–94. has given me the winning of glory. Hektor refers to Zeus's message in 11.192–94, transmitted by Iris in 207–9. But Zeus there limited his promise to the period until Hektor reached the ships and the day ended. This has now happened, and he has no right to expect further support. This is all part of Hektor's self-delusion, which adds to the tragedy of the second half of the *Iliad*.

300–302. if any Trojan. This is aimed at Poulydamas and those who think like him. It implies that their real motive for wanting to retire to the safety of the city is a concern for their personal possessions.

303, 306. Hektor bitterly mimics Poulydamas' words in 277, 278.

306–7. I . . . will not run from him. Very brave, but Hektor is deluded. When the time comes, he does run (22.137).

322. Homer rightly refers to **anger** in the simile; for Achilleus' anger, the dramatic subject of the *Iliad*, is in full force again, but directed now against Hektor, not Agamemnon.

325. in his halls. The translation entails an inconsistency; better, "in the palace" (i.e., of Peleus). The occasion is that of 11.764–88, when the two fathers and the two sons were assembled in Phthia. Patroklos had originally come from Opous (see 23.85), a town of Lokris (spelt Opoeis in 2.531).

336–37. Before your ... pyre I shall behead twelve glorious children of the Trojans. This is the only instance of human sacrifice in the *Iliad*, and Achilleus carries out the intention stated here in 21.27–33 and 23.175–76. There can be no question of Homer's approving such behavior (in fact, he condemns it as evil in 23.176), but it is not culpable in the "shame-culture" heroic code of the *Iliad*, provided the hero himself is of sufficient standing to get away with it. Nothing that Achilleus does—neither this nor his refusal to fight nor his treatment of Hektor's body—is blamed as immoral by the other Greeks.

behead is incorrect; Achilleus' intention is to cut their throats, to slaughter them like animals.

359. Zeus is sarcastic. He means that she is behaving as if the Greeks are her children.

371. the god of the dragging footsteps. Homer repeats the allusions to Hephaistos' lameness. He is strong-armed (383), and the top half of his body is massive (415); but his legs are shrunken (411), and he has mechanical servants (417) to support him as he walks.

373. tripods. The Homeric tripods are metal supports for mixing bowls, cauldrons, and other utensils. That they should have rotating wheels under their legs implies an advanced technological skill; no wonder the poet goes one stage further and says that they can move of their own accord, without being pushed (376). The "immortal gathering" would be in the house of Zeus.

382. Charis is Grace, the personification of art, fit wife for the divine smith. This is a charming bourgeois scene in heaven. A friend, not seen for some time, calls at the house; the wife invites her in, offers refreshment (387), and then calls her husband, "Hephaistos, come here." (Elsewhere—for example, in a famous story in *Od.* 8.266–366—Hephaistos' wife is Aphrodite.)

395–97. my great fall. It is not clear whether this is the same fall as that described at 1.590–94, nor is it clear whether Hephaistos' lameness was caused by his fall or whether he was lame from birth.

The natural interpretation is that the fall is the same as that in Book 1 and that it was after his fall that his mother, Hera, wished to hide him away. But in fact, of course, this is an invented story, to give Hephaistos an obligation to Thetis that will cause him to accede to her request. In this it is exactly parallel to the obligation of Zeus created in 1.396–406.

398–99. Sea goddesses protect; see 6.136, and the interpretation of Dexamene in 44, above. According to Hesiod, *Theogony* 358, Eurynome was a daughter of Okeanos and a sister of Doris, the wife of Nereus; she was thus Thetis' aunt.

The stream of **Ocean bends back in a circle,** because Ocean is thought of as running round the edge of the flat, disklike world (606–7).

410. took the huge blower off. The Greek is difficult to interpret, but a more likely meaning is, "the huge creature stood up from the block of the anvil."

417. The attendants are what are called in science fiction "androids"—essentially robots. They support the divine smith as he limps along.

434–35. he, broken by mournful old age. This is the misfortune of goddesses who marry humans, most acutely brought out in the legend of Dawn and Tithonos: that the humans grow old (*Hom. Hymn to Aphrodite* 218–38).

444–61. In these lines, Thetis summarizes the *Iliad* so far. They are not absolutely accurate, according to the information of the poem, but will pass as a mother's statement. She is not particularly concerned with the exact details of the fighting (450–56); and she assumes a love interest toward Briseis (446), which is not suggested elsewhere, except by Achilleus himself at 9.342.

470. The crucibles are melting pots, to hold the molten metals.

474–77. bronze, tin, gold, and silver. D. H. Gray has explained (*Journal of Hellenic Studies* 74 [1954]: 12–13) that the procedure followed by Hephaistos here is suitable only for ironworking. Other metals are melted for pouring into molds and for making alloys, but they are hammered cold and then by tapping with light tools for further shaping. "Hard and repeated hammering of red-hot metal (implied by the anvil, the ponderous hammer and the

pincers) is the peculiar characteristic of iron working." The poet
has made a technical mistake.

THE SHIELD OF ACHILLEUS (LINES 478–607)

The Shield of Achilleus is the most famous excursus in the *Iliad*
and is, of course, the reason for introducing, as a plot element, the
lending of Achilleus' armor to Patroklos, followed by its loss to
Hektor. It is obviously an original composition by Homer. By
describing a work of art, he creates a world; and it is his own
world, the world of the similes, the world of the eighth century B.C.,
not the Mycenaean Age. It is a world for the most part at peace,
and the occupations portrayed on the Shield are of life in the city
and life in the country—satisfying and social life, enjoyed by those
who take part or watch.

Homer lived in the period of later geometric and early orientalizing art, the end of the eighth century B.C. Some shields and some
silver and bronze bowls with ornamentation comparable to that
described here are known from this period (two are represented in
Plates 27 and 28 of SCHADEWALDT *VHWW*, and there are others in
Der Schild des Achilleus [= *Archaeologia Homerica*, vol. 2 N, pt.
1], by K. Fittschen [1973]). Both shields and bowls are round, with
pictorial designs appearing in concentric bands. There can be no
doubt that this is the sort of thing Homer had in mind, although his
description of the scenes on the Shield far surpasses anything those
human artists could achieve. The technique of metal inlay, however, which Hephaistos uses, adding *color* to the pictures on the
Shield, is not contemporary with Homer but must go back to the
Mycenaean Age; it should be compared with such things as the
inlaid daggers found in the shaft graves (so D. H. Gray, pp. 3–4 of
the article cited in the note above, on lines 474–77; see also
Fittschen, p. 17).

The **triple rim** of line 480 would be a raised rim formed by three
layers of metal at that point. The **five folds** making the Shield itself
(481) reflect the common Homeric shield made of a number of
layers of hide (that of Aias has seven layers, 7.220); but here
Homer unrealistically (but appropriately, in view of the fact that

Hephaistos is the maker) thinks of layers of metal (see 20.269–72, where he speaks of two layers of bronze and two of tin, separated by one of gold).

We must therefore imagine a round shield, with the designs symmetrically placed in concentric rings, the sun, moon, and stars evidently being on the boss at the center, and the river Ocean (606–7) forming the rim of the Shield, as the Ocean itself was thought to run round the perimeter of the world. A possible distribution of the figures is suggested below, in Chart 2.

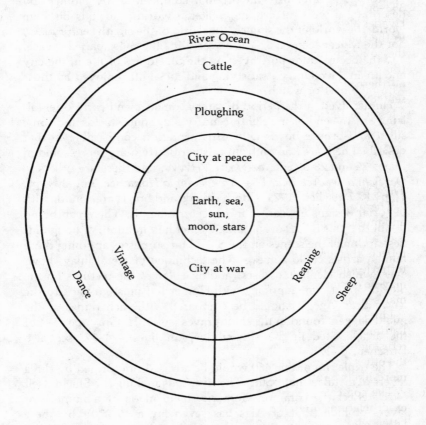

CHART 2. THE SHIELD OF ACHILLEUS

BOOK EIGHTEEN

THE EARTH AND THE SKY (LINES 483–89)

Lines 486–89 are almost the same as *Odyssey* 5.272–75, which describe Odysseus navigating his raft across the sea, except that Boötes is named there in place of the Hyades. The constellations named are among the most obvious of the night sky; although they may indeed have been used by sailors, their prime connection here is more probably with farming, for the rising of the Pleiades (i.e., when they first become visible before sunrise) was the beginning of summer, the time to start reaping, and their setting (before sunrise) was the time for the winter ploughing (Hesiod, *Works and Days* 383–84). What is said of the Pleiades applies more or less to the Hyades also, for the two star clusters are close together, above and to the right of Orion. Orion himself is the most striking object in the southern night sky throughout the winter, as the Great Bear (Big Dipper, Wagon, Plough) is the most striking object in the northern sky. Of the major constellations, the Great Bear does not set (489), because it revolves around the polestar (the North Star) at a lesser distance above the horizon than the elevation of the polestar itself.

THE TWO CITIES (LINES 490–540)

The City at Peace (Lines 491–508)

There are two scenes here. The first is of weddings, with dances and music and women watching from their doorsteps. The second is of a primitive legal process of considerable historical interest. It reflects the time when the old inescapable blood guilt for killing (often leading to exile, as in many of the biographies of the fighters), may be commuted to the payment of a sum of money to the dead man's relatives (cf. 9.632–36).

Lines 499–500 have been interpreted in two ways: either as Lattimore translates it—one man offering payment, and the other refusing to accept it—or one man stating that he has paid the sum, the other denying that he has received it. The latter is perhaps the more likely. Both alternatives relate to the same basic situation.

The contestants have taken the dispute to an **arbitrator**, whose exact relationship to the **elders** (503) is not clear. It seems to be the latter who propose solutions. The **two talents of gold** in 507 are most intriguing. They are not, it appears, the blood money; and indeed they would probably be too little for that, as two talents is only the fourth prize in the chariot race (23.269). Rather, they are for the elder (judge) whose opinion carries the day. No doubt they have been deposited, one by each of the contending parties. Such an arrangement seems strange to us; and it is not easy to see who would decide the winning judge, whether the arbitrator of line 501 or perhaps the contestants (by their acceptance of his judgment). (This scene has been much discussed, most recently by H. Hommel, *Palingenesia* 4 [1969]: 11–38.)

The City at War (*Lines 509–40*)

The picture in lines 509–13 is a little obscure. Even Homer seems to be confused by what he is imagining. In a two-dimensional picture, the simplest way to show a siege is to put the city in the middle, with enemy forces on either side of it (so, in fact, on the silver bowl illustrated in SCHADEWALDT *VHWW*, pl. 28, and in Fittschen, *Der Schild des Achilleus*, fig. 3). But Homer interprets this as *two* attacking armies, and this gives him the idea that they have differing intentions: to attack and sack the city, or to take half the citizens' possessions as a payment for stopping the war (an expedient which goes through Hektor's mind at 22.120). These alternatives then become, not so much the differing intentions of the two armies, as an ultimatum to the city—which the citizens refuse (513).

The citizens then send out an ambush, primarily, perhaps, to get food. This group is led by the gods of war, whom the metalworker has identified by making them larger than life-size. The ambush is successful, but it leads to a general engagement (533–40). The passage describing this is a little strange, for two quite natural lines stand at the beginning and end of it (533–34, 539–40), but, sandwiched in the middle, come four lines featuring the symbolic figures of **Hate, Confusion,** and **Death.** And these four lines appear (with one word different in the first line) in the pseudo-Hesiodic *Shield of Herakles* 156–59, a poem influenced by Homer's Shield of Achilleus but providing a more suitable home for these macabre figures. We cannot be sure at what time the lines came into the text of the *Iliad.*

BOOK EIGHTEEN

ACTIVITIES OF COUNTRY LIFE (LINES 541–72)

The three scenes, of ploughing, reaping, and gathering the vintage, represent three seasons: winter, summer, and autumn.

Ploughing (Lines 541–49)

W. Ridgeway ("The Homeric Land System," *Journal of Hellenic Studies* 6 [1885]: 336–37) argued that the description here is of the great common field of the community. Each member would have his own strip, and thus, at the season of ploughing, there would be many ploughs simultaneously moving up and down the field. In 548 Homer shows that he realizes that the artist in metalwork could reproduce the change of color of the earth behind the plough.

Reaping (Lines 550–60)

W. Ridgeway (see preceding note) pointed out that here we are dealing with the other type of property in primitive society, the land set aside for a king or a god, his **precinct**. This type of land has been referred to at 6.194–95 (Bellerophontes), 9.578–80 (Meleagros), and 12.313–14 (Sarpedon).

Lines 558–60 may describe the preparation of two distinct meals: for the king and his entourage, a sacrificed ox; for the laborers, a kind of broth or porridge of barley sprinkled in water. Alternatively, and this finds more favor with recent commentators, the barley was sprinkled on the roast pieces of meat, as happens at *Odyssey* 14.77. If so, this must be a special feast—one for the laborers to partake of, as well as the landowner.

The Vintage (Lines 561–71)

The gathering of the grapes is always a season of happiness. The **song for Linos** (570), however, was an ancient dirge or lament, with Eastern connections, parallel to laments for Adonis and others. (The great first chorus of the *Agamemnon* of Aeschylus refers to this lament in the refrain, "Sing woe for Linos, woe for Linos, but may the good prevail.")

FURTHER SCENES OF COUNTRY LIFE (LINES 573–605)

Further scenes of country life—of cattle, sheep, and the dance—are particularly suited to the outermost representational band in the design, since they provide the artist with lines of repeated figures.

Cattle (Lines 573–86)

We see a peaceful herd of oxen. The pastoral scene is then rudely disturbed when lions attack. We may be surprised, but lions attacking cattle are also a common feature in the world of the similes.

Sheep (Lines 587–89)

The sheep are in a meadow, and in the background are houses and sheepfolds, as in a peaceful mountain valley.

The Dance (Lines 590–605)

As if there were not enough of interest in the previous scenes, this last one, of dancing, adds a great deal more. In lines 590–92 the dance area portrayed on the Shield is said to be *like* one built by **Daidalos,** the famous craftsman, for princess **Ariadne,** daughter of King Minos, in Krete. Kretan connections with dancing have been alluded to in the incident between Aineias and Meriones at 16.617.

In lines 599–602 Homer describes the dance itself. It seems to be like a country dance, in two parts: first the dancers move round in circles (the poet shows this in the simile of a potter's wheel); then they form lines which run up to and through each other.

Ocean (Lines 606–7)

Ocean runs round the outside of the Shield, as it does around the disk-shaped Homeric world.

608–12. Having completed the detailed description of the Shield, Homer wastes little time over the rest of the armor.

BOOK NINETEEN

Book 19 presents an interlude before the battle: the situation is brought under control and loose ends in the story are tied up. The following outline shows how the action is divided:

1–39	Thetis brings the arms to Achilleus.
40–275	Greek assembly. Public reconciliation between Agamemnon and Achilleus.
276–348	Laments of Briseis and Achilleus.
349–91	Achilleus arms for battle.
392–424	Achilleus' conversation with the divine horses.

There has been considerable criticism of Book 19 on two connected grounds: first, that the reconciliation between Agamemnon and Achilleus is not necessary, and that it would be more heroic for Achilleus to rush straight into battle, without caring for anything else; and, second, that in the speeches in the assembly too much attention is paid to the mundane question whether the army should eat before fighting.

The answers to these objections are: first, as the quarrel broke out in a public assembly of the Achaian army, it is absolutely necessary that there should be a public reconciliation. It is even necessary that Achilleus should get, and be seen to get, the gifts of compensation offered by Agamemnon in Book 9; if this did not happen, his status (honor) would be less (compare what Phoinix says in 9.602–5 and what Achilleus himself says in 16.84–86 and 90). In fact, therefore, Book 19 is an important stage in the dramatic plot of the Anger of Achilleus; it is the moment when he renounces the quarrel initiated in Book 1. Second, as to the question whether the army should eat, it has been well pointed out by SCHADEWALDT 132–33 and by LOHMANN 69 that the poet has in mind a contrast between two uncompromising figures: Achilleus, the idealistic hero, impatient of practical considerations, and Odysseus, the man of common sense. Odysseus is of course right to insist on sustenance for the troops, as is proved by the fact that even Achilleus is artificially sustained through divine intervention (352–54).

38–39. that his flesh might not spoil. The procedure is like that of embalming. For the use of **ambrosia** as a preservative, cf. 16.670.

42–44. helmsmen, stewards, dispensers of rations. These non-combatant troops are not mentioned elsewhere. WILAMOWITZ 179 well points out that their presence would be more acceptable if this were a brief raid rather than the tenth year of a war of occupation. The poet has of course invented them to enhance the occasion. *Everyone* came to this assembly.

47–53. Tydeus' son (Diomedes), **Odysseus, Agamemnon.** The three wounded leaders were last seen in 14.379–81. They were wounded in Book 11, Koön's stabbing of Agamemnon being at 11.252.

59–60. Artemis is responsible for deaths of women, as Apollo for deaths of men. For **Lyrnessos,** see 2.690, and 291–96 n., below.

77. Homer seems at first sight to tell us that Agamemnon remained **sitting** while he spoke. His wound was in the arm, so it alone would not explain this. The Greek text, however, may alternatively mean that Agamemnon, instead of speaking from the center of the assembly (as would be normal), spoke from the seats reserved for the leaders (but, naturally, standing up). However this may be, the impression intended is that Agamemnon is nervous about his reception.

78–84. A nervous start. Agamemnon shows that he is afraid of interruptions. It is evident that he finds it particularly hard to make this public apology (cf. 139–44 n.).

85. This is the word. He refers to the army's criticisms of him as being to blame for the quarrel with Achilleus.

86–87. Agamemnon says that he is **not responsible** for his action in dishonoring Achilleus; it was **Zeus and Destiny and Erinys the mist-walking,** and they achieved it by sending Delusion (Ate) to affect his judgment. This attempt to exculpate himself is difficult for us to understand, especially as he had freely admitted he was wrong in 9.119. The explanation lies in the Homeric conception of Ate. If a man acts in an inexplicable and self-destructive way, he can hardly be acting normally; therefore, something external has taken over his decision-making faculties; this outside force is described as Ate, and it is sent by Zeus, because Zeus is ultimately responsible for everything. However, it is clear that ascribing the blame to Ate does not absolve the doer from responsibility for his actions; Agamemnon says so explicitly at 137–38. (On all this, see E. R. Dodds, *The Greeks and the Irrational*, pp. 2–8.)

Erinys is more usually concerned with the punishment of those who have transgressed against their closest relatives (9.454, 15.204). It seems, however, from here and from 418 at the end of this book, that the Furies (Erinyes) have wider responsibilities.

Erinys "walks in mist" because she belongs to the underworld (9.571).

91–133. A mythological example occupies the middle of Agamemnon's speech. Ate (**Delusion**) is allegorically described, as in 9.505–7 (in the "Parable of the Prayers"); then follows a long narrative of a particular action of hers, the "extreme case," in which even Zeus was deluded.

98–99. That **Herakles** was born in **Thebes** may have been a secondary stage in his legend, for originally it seems that he was the hero of Tiryns, which makes more intelligible his subservience to Eurystheus, king of Mykenai (133). Alternatively, as is suggested by NILSSON 207, Herakles was an all-Greek hero, and stories about him were told in various parts, so that his birth in Thebes may have been as old as his vassalage at Tiryns.

103. Eileithyia: goddess of childbirth.

110. fall between the feet of a woman. This old expression for birth indicates a crouching position for the mother.

115–16. Argos of Achaia is here the Argive plain, where not only the city of Argos is situated, but also Mykenai and Tiryns. A Perseid dynasty ruled at Mykenai before Atreus and his descendants. **Sthenelos** was son of Perseus and father of Eurystheus; he is, of course, different from Sthenelos, the son of Kapaneus, Diomedes' companion from Argos.

126–31. he slung her out of starry heaven. Cf. 1.591 n. This story explains why Ate now exclusively infests human activities.

133. the tasks Eurystheus set him. A clear reference to the labors of Herakles; the later canon of twelve seems not yet established for Homer (see 8.362–69 n.). The whole of the foregoing myth is probably an attempt to explain why such a great hero as Herakles should have had to obey such a poor figure as Eurystheus (cf. 15.638–52 n.).

139–44. This is the only time Agamemnon addresses Achilleus directly during the whole of the assembly; and even here he does not use his name or any honorific formula (as Achilleus does to him at 146 and 199) but merely addresses him as **you.** Twice he does use his name, but in the third person, talking to Odysseus (188, 195). LOHMANN 76, n. 133, has pointed this out, showing a subtlety in Homer which might easily be missed. Agamemnon does not find it easy to apologize; he is uncomfortable when speaking to the man he has wronged (compare the squinting apologies in the Parable, 9.503). Later in the *Iliad*, too, Agamemnon never speaks directly to Achilleus; he does not reply when Achilleus addresses him at 23.156–60 and 890–94.

140–41. all those gifts: the gifts offered in the Embassy in 9.122–34 (=264–76); see 243–48 n., below.

147–48. Achilleus is no longer interested in the gifts.

155–83. This speech of Odysseus, and his later one in 216–37, show him as the practical, experienced soldier in contrast to Achilleus' heroic idealism.

170. give over: cease from.

172–74. Odysseus realizes the importance of a public handing-over of the gifts.

176–77 = 9.275–76. The reference of **her** might raise a question, as Briseis has not been mentioned, but only alluded to, in 58–59; indeed, she is not named until 246. But as the whole quarrel relates to her, the reference is not very difficult.

181–83. Odysseus takes the opportunity to administer a rebuke to Agamemnon.

191. cut our oaths: see 2.124 n.

192. Agamemnon is none too pleased with Odysseus. He has to put up with the position he has made for himself—liable to being criticized by his inferiors and having to humble himself before the insubordinate Achilleus—but he cannot be expected to like it. His expression to Odysseus here is peevish.

196–97. Talthybios is Agamemnon's herald (1.320, 3.118). **Zeus** and **Helios** (the Sun) are to receive the sacrifice, as overseers of oaths. Compare 3.276–77, where an oath similar to the present one is administered.

212. turned against the forecourt: i.e., with his feet toward the door—a traditional position for the body awaiting burial. The reason, according to the B scholia, is symbolic, to prevent the ghost from returning (so also E. Rhode, *Psyche*, 4th ed., p. 23, n. 2).

222–23. For the metaphor from reaping, compare the simile of 11.67–69. The **straw** scattered on the ground is, of course, the bodies of the dead; the **harvest** being **thin** indicates no more than that the armies have great labor but little reward.

when Zeus has poised his balance. This translation indicates an even fight. More commonly the words are taken to mean "when Zeus has *inclined* his balance," i.e., when he has decided the battle, when one army is routed. That is the time when many are killed. (For the **balance** of Zeus, see 8.69–70 n.)

238–40. Odysseus takes seven assistants, all of them leaders of the second rank, and several of them the same as the young leaders of the guard in 9.81–84. The **sons of Nestor** are Antilochos and Thrasymedes. **Meges** and **Thoas** played a part particularly in Books 13 and 15; **Meriones** has been active throughout. These three are all leaders of contingents (2.627, 638, 651). For **Lykomedes,** see 17.345 n. **Melanippos** appears only here.

243–48. The gifts tally exactly with the offer made in 9.122–32 (= 9.264–74). Critics have wondered why there is no mention of the other, more extravagant, compensation offered by Agamemnon in Book 9: first choice of the spoils of Troy, twenty Trojan women, a daughter of Agamemnon's in marriage, seven cities. The most likely explanation is that those offers are more remote, contingent both on the Greeks' winning the war and on Achilleus' surviving it. Since Achilleus knows—and we know, too—that the second contingency is not going to be fulfilled, there would be considerable awkwardness in any repetition of them here.

249-68. The oath. With it may be compared the oath-taking in 3.267-313. **Zeus, Earth, and Helios** are appealed to there also; and the **Furies** (Erinyes), although not by name. Their function in these two passages seems to be particularly the punishment of perjury. The whole oath is directed to one point only: whether or not Agamemnon has gone to bed with Briseis.

The sacrificial victim here is neither burnt nor eaten but is thrown away—as accursed—into the sea. This symbolizes the punishment of Agamemnon, if he has sworn a false oath.

282-302. The lament of Briseis for Patroklos.

291-96. Briseis gives more information about her past than we have heard before. It appears for the first time that she has been married, and indeed perhaps to Mynes, the king of Lyrnessos (296), as has been traditionally assumed. This is in conflict with the description of her as "daughter of Briseus" in 1.392 and 9.132, for that suggests an unmarried girl. Strangely, too, her fate has been closely similar to that of Andromache, who lost father and brothers in the same expedition in which Briseis lost husband and brothers (see 1.184 n.).

297-99. formalize my marriage. This exemplifies the kindness of Patroklos, because such an outcome (lawful marriage) was hardly possible for a war captive. He had been trying to console her. The final words, "**You were kind always,**" have a parallel in the final epitaph on Hektor, spoken by Helen (24.767-72).

302. A psychological insight; cf. 338-39.

326-27. This is the only reference to **Neoptolemos** by name in the *Iliad*, although he is alluded to in 24.467.

That he was growing up on **Skyros** is a clear reference to the story that Deïdameia, daughter of Lykomedes, king of Skyros, had a child by Achilleus, during the time that his parents were attempting to hide him on that island to keep him out of the Trojan War. This popular later romance was already in the repertoire of the Cyclic poets, according to the BD scholia; and something of it appeared in the *Cypria*, if we may believe Proclus, whose summary speaks of Achilleus "marrying" Deïdameia. Elsewhere in the *Iliad* (9.668) there is a reference to Achilleus' having attacked and captured Skyros.

Toward the end of the war—after the end of the *Iliad* and the death of Achilleus—the Greeks sent for Neoptolemos to come from Skyros, and he helped them to capture and sack Troy, personally killing the old king, Priam, who had taken refuge at the altar in the courtyard of his palace. Thereafter, Neoptolemos sailed back to Greece, not to Achilleus' old home, but to Molossia on the western side, where later kings claimed to be descended from him (Pindar, *Sixth Paean* 98–120; *Seventh Nemean* 33–47).

369–91. The last of the four arming scenes in the *Iliad*. See 3.330–38. The basic description is here expanded by ornamental material, mostly similes describing the shield and helmet; by a general indication of how well the armor fitted him (384–86); and by the particular lines about the **Pelian ash spear** (388–91), which we have already seen at 16.141–44. This was the only piece of Achilleus' previous equipment which Patroklos had not taken.

There is a cumulative sequence in the brief similes that describe Achilleus here: his shield is like the moon (374), his helmet like a star (382), and he himself is like the sun (398).

392. Alkimos must be a shortened form of Alkimedon (16.197, 17.467).

400. See 16.149–51 n.

404. the . . . horse answered him. A particularly bold invention by Homer. What would verge on the comic in a stock situation becomes acceptable at such a high, heroic moment in the story as the invincible Achilleus' return to battle. Even so, Homer feels it necessary to justify the miraculous incident by having Hera permit it (407) and the Erinyes put a stop to it (418).

We have already seen these immortal horses showing human reactions in 17.426–28, when they wept for their charioteer.

413. child of . . Leto: Apollo.

417. there is destiny. Another reminder that the death of Achilleus is close. Hektor's dying words will further identify **god** and **mortal** (22.359).

418. the Furies. The Erinyes appear for the third time in this book (see 87 and 259), now preventing what is contrary to nature.

BOOK TWENTY

In Book 20 there is a slow buildup toward the *aristeia* of Achilleus. He obviously must not meet Hektor too soon—at least not decisively. The poet uses all his devices in this book and the next to postpone the climax. The beginnings are fairly low-keyed: Zeus formally invites the gods to take part (1–74), thus preparing for the fight between the gods themselves in Book 21; there is then a long scene between Achilleus and Aineias, mostly taken up by speeches and leading to nothing, for Aineias is rescued by Poseidon before he can be hurt (75–352); finally, the *aristeia* of Achilleus begins, and he kills fourteen Trojans in swift succession (353–503). During this last sequence Hektor comes up against him twice, but each time the inevitable is postponed; once Hektor withdraws on the advice of Apollo (379–80), once he is rescued by the same god (443–44).

Discussion of Book 20 has concentrated on the long central scene between Achilleus and Aineias, and especially on the unique prophecy of Poseidon in 302–8 that Aineias is destined to survive and that he and his descendants will rule over the Trojans. Since Aineias, though Hektor's equal in fighting ability, plays a relatively small part in the *Iliad*, and there is even a suggestion that he is disaffected toward the rule of Priam and Priam's sons (13.460; cf. 20.180), one receives the impression that there is more behind this character than is brought out explicitly in our poem. Scholars have speculated that the scene here, and particularly the prophecy of Poseidon, have been inserted into the epic to honor a royal family which claimed descent from Aineias in one of the small towns of the Troad in Homer's own day. There is some external evidence for the existence of such a dynasty in the late writer Strabo (13.607).

If this were so, we should have a unique piece of information about the poet's own circumstances, for such a compliment suggests a court poet. Consequently, the Aineias episode in this book has been exhaustively discussed by recent scholars as evidence for the identity of the poet and for the date of composition of the *Iliad*; it is sufficient to refer here to U. von Wilamowitz, F. Jacoby, W. Schadewaldt, P. Von der Mühll, K. Reinhardt, and E. Heitsch, all of whom have either subscribed to the hypothesis that Homer himself composed at the court of a local dynasty of Aineiadai or have ascribed this position to a later rhapsode who introduced these lines. As so often in Homeric studies, what started as a reasonable guess has become unshakable dogma, probably oversimplifying the question. The long centuries during which epic poetry was produced evidently led to much confusion about the past; and formulaic composition has its own pressures and rules. What if, over a period of time *before* Homer composed his *Iliad*, the character Aineias had built up a reputation as one who was destined to receive posthumous fame through his descendants? That may have been his individualizing characteristic, arising from his divine birth; for the future rule of Aineias' descendants is fore-told also in the post-Homeric *Hymn to Aphrodite* 196–97. If such a tradition existed, and even assuming that it originated with a local dynasty claiming descent from the hero, it would not involve any biographical information about the individual poet of these lines.

It is a strange coincidence, although doubtless more than a coincidence, that Aineias was taken over as the ancestor of the Julian family at Rome and appears as the hero of Virgil's *Aeneid*, the founder of the Roman race. Poseidon's prophecy in 302–8 might then be applied in a far wider way than our poet could ever have conceived.

5. For **Themis,** see 15.87 n. The purpose of the divine assembly is multiple: the poet is preparing for the Theomachy (the fight between the pro-Greek and the pro-Trojan gods) in 21.385–513; he also feels it desirable for Zeus to revoke the prohibition he imposed against the gods' taking part in the human battle in 8.7–16; and finally, an assembly of the gods enhances this occasion and thus the glory of Achilleus.

7. There was no river who was not there. The rivers (i.e., the divinities of the rivers) are expressly said to have come to the assembly because the river Skamandros is to play a large part in opposing Achilleus in Book 21 and then be attacked by the pro-Greek god of fire, Hephaistos (see 73–74). **Ocean** alone does not come, presumably because he could not leave his task of holding the world together.

13–14. the shaker of the earth. Poseidon speaks first, as being next to Zeus in the divine hierarchy.

26–27. Commentators have found Zeus's statement illogical, on the grounds that the pro-Greek gods are stronger than the pro-Trojans, and therefore the accession of the gods will not even up the fight. Simple mathematics, however, shows that, provided the difference between the strength of the gods is not greater than the difference between Achilleus and Hektor,

$$\frac{\text{Achilleus} + \text{pro-Greek gods}}{\text{Hektor} + \text{pro-Trojan gods}} \quad \text{is less than} \quad \frac{\text{Achilleus}}{\text{Hektor}}$$

30. against destiny: see 2.155 n.

32–40. the gods … with purposes opposed. The division among the gods is followed by their pairing-off in 67–74 and their fight in Book 21.

On the Greek side, **Hera** and **Athene** have been supporters throughout, and **Poseidon** especially in Book 13. The presence of **Hermes** is not explained, apart from his natural Greek connections; **Hephaistos** is closely sympathetic to his mother (1.572, 21.330).

On the Trojan side, **Ares, Apollo,** and **Aphrodite** have supported them throughout; **Xanthos** (Skamandros) is the local river; and **Artemis** and **Leto** fill up the numbers, as sister and mother of Apollo.

48. Hatred is bitter and competitive opposition, as in 11.4. She may be described as **defender of peoples** because the troops will try harder when Hatred enters the battle. The accession of the gods is thus leading to a more even struggle, as Zeus intended (26–27).

48–67. The poet attempts to describe vast elemental powers in conflict. The effect is by a long way more impressive than the petty and childish squabbling of the gods in human shape in 21.385–513.

Athene and Ares (48–53) are the prime gods of war; Ares' likeness to a stormcloud may remind us of his departure at the end of Book 5 (864–65).

From 56 to 67 we have the supernatural actions of the three brothers, **Zeus** (the sky), **Poseidon** (the sea and earthquakes), and **Aïdoneus** (= Hades, the underworld).

67–74. The pairing is the same as in Book 21. Aphrodite (not a warlike goddess) is not included; **Enyalios** (69) = Ares. For the epithets of Artemis in line 70, see 16.183 n. Hephaistos vs. Skamandros = fire vs. water.

74. For different names for the same things in the languages of gods and men, see 1.403–4 n. Perhaps in this case **Xanthos** and **Skamandros** result from separate attempts to put into Greek the same non-Greek name, a confusion which may also be discerned in the names of Alexandros and his sister Cassandra.

78. See 5.289 n.

79. We are perhaps a little surprised that **Aineias** should appear here and that his abortive confrontation with Achilleus should take up so much of the book. But Homer has a particular problem, explained in the introductory note to this book—namely, to postpone the meeting of Achilleus and Hektor—and no other Trojan warrior can take Hektor's place so well as Aineias. Prior to his appearance here, Aineias has been seen chiefly in 5.166 ff., where he was wounded by Diomedes and rescued by his mother, Aphrodite, and Apollo; in Book 13 (fighting against Idomeneus); in Book 16 (fighting against Meriones); and in Book 17 (in the fighting after Patroklos' death).

81. Lykaon. The mention of his name here foreshadows the meeting of Lykaon and Achilleus at the beginning of Book 21.

83–85. Where are those threats gone. This is a most obvious example of invention for the purpose of the present argument. Apollo wishes to persuade Aineias to stand against Achilleus, so he ascribes to him an improbable boast that he would do exactly that. Compare 17.24–27.

90–96. Achilleus also refers to this previous meeting between them (when he threatens Aineias in 187–94). For the attack on **Lyrnessos** (where Briseis was captured, 19.60), see 2.690. **Pedasos** was on the river Satnioeis (6.34–35), south of Troy, and near the other cities (Lyrnessos and Thebe) which, we are told, Achilleus stormed. The **Leleges** (96), previously mentioned only at 10.429, were the people of Pedasos (21.86).

101. pull out even the issue of war. The metaphor of a rope strained between the two armies is fairly common; cf. 13.358–60.

107. The sea's ancient is Nereus.

112–14. Hera addresses the other divine supporters of the Greeks. The poet seems for a time to forget the pairing-off of the gods to fight each other in 67–74.

125. all of us: all of us pro-Greek gods.

127–28. as Destiny wove with the strand of his birth. The Fates who preside at a human's birth include Klotho, the spinner, who spins the thread of his life.

145–48. When Poseidon was cheated by Laomedon of his reward for building the city walls of Troy (21.441–57), he sent a sea **monster,** which **Herakles** offered to get rid of, for a reward (see 5.640 n.). These lines refer to the preparations for Herakles' exploit.

180–83. Achilleus suggests a coolness between Aineias and Priam's branch of the family; cf. 13.459 n.

184–85. See 18.550 n. for the separate allocation of land to a god, king, or hero.

187–94. Another time before this . . . you ran from my spear. See 90–96.

196–98. Achilleus' words are not so much a friendly warning as an attempt to frighten; they are thematic in this sort of speech before a duel; cf. 17.13, 31–32.

200–258. Aineias' rambling speech has caused offense, both because of the long digression about his family tree in 215–40 and because of the repetition of statements indicating that they should not waste their time talking but get on with the fight (244–58, but also 200–202, 211–12). The impression given is that Aineias is nervous—only too willing to go on saying whatever comes into his head in order to postpone the moment when the action will have to begin. If this is right, there is a rich comedy in the scene, which the hearers would be expected to appreciate. It is closely similar to the speech of Glaukos to Diomedes in 6.145–211 (see note there on 150–211), where Glaukos also introduces a lengthy genealogy (after saying that such a digression is inappropriate). Compare also the apparently nervous conversation between Idomeneus and Meriones in 13.246–97.

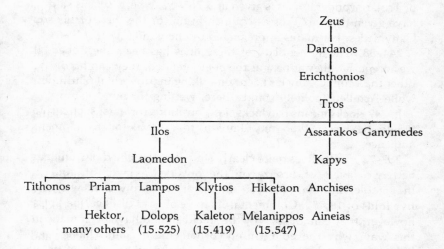

215–40. For the family tree of Aineias, showing his descent from Zeus, see the diagram above.

Dardanos, Tros, and **Ilos** are obviously the eponymous founders of Dardania, Troy, and Ilion. **Laomedon** was the king who fortified Pergamos, the citadel of Troy. **Erichthonios** has seemed suspicious because he appeared (as well as Erechtheus, 2.547) in the list of *Athenian* kings, and some scholars have seen his name here as due to Athenian colonizing pressures in the sixth century B.C. The name, however, means "Strength of the Land" and so might appear in any invented list of local ancestors.

Two figures here, on the outside of the tree—**Ganymedes** and **Tithonos**—connect the Trojan royal family with the gods, for Ganymedes was carried off to Olympos for his beauty, to be wine-pourer to Zeus, and Tithonos was carried off, to be her consort, by the goddess of the Dawn (cf. 11.1).

We may note that the junior branch of the family all have non-Greek names: **Assarakos, Kapys, Anchises, Aineias.**

The three younger brothers of **Priam**—**Lampos, Klytios,** and

Hiketaon—appeared among the counselors on the wall in 3.147. Each had a son killed in the fighting in Book 15.

221–29. The wonderful horses of Erichthonios. A different origin of Trojan wonder horses is given at 5.265–67, where Zeus is said to have given them to Tros as compensation for the theft of his son Ganymedes. For mares impregnated by the wind, cf. 16.149–51 n.

244–58. The authenticity of these lines has been questioned. If we accept that they appear as the poet intended, they can hardly be other than comic. Aineias keeps on talking in proverbial platitudes, while Achilleus politely stands there, waiting for him to stop.

In 247, **locks** means rowlocks, i.e., positions for oars; such a ship would be larger than any known to Aineias or to Homer's audience.

269–72. These lines quite clearly state that the shield of Achilleus had two layers of bronze on the outside, a layer of gold in the middle, and two of tin on the inside. It is consistent with the **five folds** of 18.481. Commentators have always disliked the lines, however; they cannot see why the shield should have been made in this way: why the gold (surely ornamental) should have been hidden away in the middle, and why there should be layers of tin at all, since it is a soft metal. The shield should have been made of layers of leather, with a bronze facing—but of course this is a divine shield, made by the metalworker, Hephaistos.

In 21.165, the gold seems to be on the *outside*.

275–76. Aineias' shield is made in the normal way, with a facing of bronze over layers of leather. As the shield is concave, the full thickness of the leather will be in the middle, and it will get progressively thinner toward the rim (cf. 11.32–35 n.). The "two circles" of 280 are therefore the edge of the bronze facing and the single thickness of leather at the rim. In 281, the epithet "man-covering" may have originated with the Mycenaean body shield; if so, however, that has been forgotten, because this is evidently a round shield (274).

286–87. A stock description of a huge stone (cf. 5.302–4, 12.445–50).

291. We should not be concerned that it is Poseidon, a pro-Greek god, who rescues Aineias, a Trojan. The gods are superior to humans, and (excepting the totally committed, like Hera and Athene) can take a wider view.

298–99. always he gives gifts ... to the gods. Virgil's stock epithet for Aineias is *pius*.

302–8. It is destined that he shall be the survivor. For a discussion of these extraordinary lines, see the introductory note to this book. The generally accepted view is that they form a compliment to a local dynasty of Homer's own day. It is possible, however, that this assumption is incorrect. The alternative is that a legend that Aineias was the one leading Trojan to survive the war had become part of the epic tradition before Homer; consequently, his survival is alluded to here and at *Hymn to Aphrodite* 196–97.

322–23. from the shield. It is difficult to reconcile this with 279–80, which certainly said that the spear tore right through the edge of the shield. Probably there is no other reason than momentary carelessness.

329. The **Kaukonians,** like the Leleges (96), are missing from the Trojan catalogue in Book 2 but appear in the list of the allies given by Dolon at 10.429.

353–80. Speeches by Achilleus and Hektor almost lead to a confrontation.

358. Ares, Athene. The two gods of war, as usual.

359. take the edge of. The metaphor involved in the Greek phrase is obscure, but the meaning is clear enough: not even a war god could make a frontal attack on such a force.

371–72. though his hands are like flame. The repetition of the second half of one line as the first half of the next (called *epanalepsis*) seems a verbal trick of Hektor's. He uses it again, with pathetic effect, at 22.127–28.

381–503. From this point on, Book 20 consists of a general *aristeia* of Achilleus. His heroic progress continues in Book 21, but in longer set scenes (the duels with Lykaon and Asteropaios, the fight with the river, the meeting with Agenor). Here his total domination of the battle has to be shown in a small compass, and the poet must try to demonstrate that Achilleus surpasses even

Diomedes and Agamemnon, whose *aristeiai* occupy the first parts
of Books 5 and 11, respectively.

There is a carefully structured sequence, as follows:

381–418	Achilleus kills four named individuals, ending with the gruesome death of Hektor's youngest brother.
419–54	This is enough to drive Hektor to face Achilleus, contrary to the express instructions of Apollo (376–78). Apollo saves him.
455–89	Achilleus kills ten named individuals—two, followed by a pair in a chariot, then four, followed by another pair in a chariot. The chariots indicate, as in the *aristeiai* of Diomedes and Agamemnon in Books 5 and 11, that the Trojans are now taking to flight.
490–503	General summary, with similes, of the effect of Achilleus' attack.

382–92. Iphition, by this description, is a leader of the
Maionians (see 2.864–66, where the Gygaian lake, and Mount
Tmolos are mentioned, although Iphition is not one of the two
leaders named there). **Hermos** (392) was a river of the later Lydia
(= Maionia).

396. The **son of Antenor** takes the second place in this first
group of four, balancing the son of Priam in the fourth place.

402. sprang from behind his horses. We are probably to assume
that Hippodamas despaired of getting away in his chariot and so
leaped to the ground to flee. (In 11.423, when this expression was
previously used, it referred to a man coming in to attack, and so
was more natural.)

REINHARDT 431 attractively suggests that Hippodamas was the
charioteer of Demoleon.

404. Poseidon, lord of Helike. Helike was a sanctuary of
Poseidon in Achaia (the north of the Peloponnese); see 8.203. But
there was a more famous sanctuary of Helikonian Poseidon near
Miletos, where the Ionians of Homer's day worshiped the god;
many scholars, and indeed some authorities in the ancient scholia,
assume a reference to the Ionian sanctuary.

407–18. The killing of **Polydoros** is a pathetic climax to these
first four killings. Achilleus hits Polydoros **in the middle of the
back,** where the fastening of the belt joined together the two halves

of his **corselet,** or breastplate. This is described in the same words as the spot where Menelaos was hit by Pandaros' arrow in 4.133, except that *his* belt joined in the front, and it was in the stomach that he was hit, not the back. That is a much more natural way to fasten a belt. We must assume that Homer is using formulaic lines a little carelessly. To achieve the gruesome effects described in 418 and 420, he wishes the spear to enter at the back and pass right through and out near the navel.

The **corselet** here is almost certainly of leather, not metal; see 4.133 n.

419. Polydoros, according to 21.91 and 22.48, was son of Priam and Laothoë, full brother of Lykaon, and half-brother of Hektor.

431–33 = 200–202, showing the similarity between the Achilleus/Aineias meeting and this, between Achilleus and Hektor.

438–42. This brief encounter between Achilleus and Hektor contains the seeds of the fight between them in Book 22. There, too, Athene interferes, but it is to return Achilleus' spear to him, not Hektor's. And there it is Hektor who desperately makes a furious charge; there is no Apollo to save him then.

445–47. Three times ... Three times. This repeated theme has been used several times before, typically with a Greek attacking and Apollo defending (5.436–39, 16.702–6, 784–87).

449–54 = 11.362–67, where it is Diomedes who says these words to Hektor. This too is a thematic situation.

457. Demouchos, like Deukalion in 478, is first of all incapacitated and then killed.

464. For supplication by the **knees,** see 1.407 n.

478–79. where the tendons come together: i.e., the elbow joint. Deukalion does not have the same reason for standing still and waiting for his death as Demouchos (457), who was hit on the knee. We may assume that he was unable to move, like Alkathoös in 13.435. The marrow gushing from the vertebrae in 482–83 is apparently an anatomical mistake (FRIEDRICH 46).

487. He dropped from the chariot. As mentioned in the note to 381–503, the reference to chariots here and at 461 implies that the Trojans are taking to flight.

496–97. The grain is removed from the husk by the trampling of the oxen.

498. Achilleus is now in his chariot, having mounted it to pursue the fleeing Trojans.

BOOK TWENTY-ONE

In contrast to the catalogue type of *aristeia* at the end of Book 20, Achilleus' heroic status is displayed in Book 21 by two individual duels and a desperate struggle with the river Skamandros. Then, following the disconcerting episode of the battle among the gods, the narrative returns to the human plane with Achilleus' encounter with Agenor, which forms a prelude to his meeting with Hektor in Book 22.

This tremendous book is carefully constructed, the poet preparing his way to each of his distinct main themes by a transitional passage. The structure is as follows:

1–33	*Transition: the Trojans take refuge in the river.*
34–210	Single combats beside the river; Achilleus with Lykaon and Asteropaios.
211–26	*Transition to the fight with the river.*
227–327	The fight with the river.
328–82	*Transition to the battle of the gods.*
383–513	The battle of the gods.
514–20	*Transition: Apollo goes to Troy.*
521–611	Achilleus pursues the Trojans to the city; Agenor provides a diversion.

Discussion of the book has concentrated on the fight with Lykaon (described by WILAMOWITZ 87 as "purest gold") and the battle of the gods ("poetically bad," according to LEAF 2:382). The objection to the battle of the gods is that, in contrast to the elemental struggle portended in 20.47–67 and, initially, here (387–88), the gods in the event behave like squabbling children, hitting one another and boasting of their success in a kind of caricature of the serious human fighting. There is certainly a striking drop in tone from the powerful scene between Achilleus and the river-in-flood, which just precedes; but unless we are going to adopt obscure analytical speculations about layers of composition in the *Iliad*, it is best for us to accept this episode, like others (particularly in Books 5 and 14) in which Homer uses the gods to provide lightness and relief from the human battle scenes. The gods are lacking in seriousness and dignity by the very feature that divides them from the humans: their immortality. Homer, if he could reply to his modern critics, might say, first, that their taste was not the same as his and his hearers', and, second, that he actually intended a lowering of tension before the dramatic climax of Achilleus's fight with Hektor in Book 22.

As in Book 20, no other Greek fighter but Achilleus is named; it is as if he is one man taking on the whole Trojan army.

1. the crossing place of ... the river. For the ford of the Skamandros, see 14.433–34 n. It is clear that the Trojans do not cross the river to get back to their city; when Lykaon emerges from the river at line 35, he comes out on Achilleus' side.

27–28. twelve young men ... to be vengeance for ... Patroklos. See 18.336–37 n.

35. Lykaon has been mentioned in passing at 3.333 and 20.81. He is, as Strasburger 85 says, the culmination of all the "minor figures" in the *Iliad*, those who serve as victims for the major characters and whose fates bring out the humanity and sympathy of Homer.

For the theme of the previously captured young man being met again in the battle, cf. Isos and Antiphos in 11.101–12. The poet tells us of the previous occasion in 36–44, and it is again referred to by Achilleus in 57–58 and by Lykaon in 75–79. This is similar to the repeated references in Book 20 to a previous meeting between Aineias and Achilleus (20.89–93, 187–94).

40–43. The **son of Jason** is Euneos, king of **Lemnos,** for whom see 7.467–69 n. He is the one point of contact with the Argonautic legends to be found in the *Iliad*.

Imbros is an island between Lemnos and Troy; **Eëtion of Imbros** is to be distinguished from Eëtion, king of Thebe, father of Andromache (6.395). **Arisbe** is on the Hellespont, not far from

Troy (2.836). Homer wishes to be exact about the stages of Lykaon's journey home.

65. to catch at his knees. Lykaon hopes to get into the position of a suppliant; cf. Tros in 20.463.

67. Achilleus now has his **spear** again. The poet does not need explicitly to tell us that he has recovered it from the tamarisks (18).

72. The word **edged** refers to the sharp tip of the spear.

76. The giving and receiving of hospitality has in many societies involved an obligation between host and guest. The **yield of Demeter** is, of course, corn; Lykaon and Achilleus have "broken bread" together.

84–87. Laothoë. Priam, an Eastern potentate, had other wives besides Hekabe. Laothoë, the mother of Lykaon and Polydoros (whose pathetic death was described in 20.407–18) was a princess, daughter of the king of the **Leleges** at **Pedasos** (cf. 20.92). Priam refers to these two of his children at 22.46–51.

89–90. You will have cut the throats of both. Lykaon has, in reality, no hope. He appeals for pity all the same.

106–13. So, friend, you die also . . . These are among the most sublime lines in the *Iliad*. Achilleus the killer shows a comradeship for the man he is about to kill, addressing him as "friend." He associates him with Patroklos and with himself, for he knows perfectly well that his own death will come soon (cf. 18.96). He has no particular hatred for the enemy; indeed he feels bound to him by the common bond of death.

115–16. sat back, spreading wide both hands. In a gesture of hopelessness, Lykaon offers his neck to the blow.

129–32. Achilleus is careless of the feelings of the god Skamandros, thus preparing us for the river's anger against him (which begins in 136–38).

As to the sacrifice of bulls and horses: we know that rivers were often imagined as in bull shape, an idea caused by the distant sound of roaring when a river was in spate (cf. 237); the sacrifice of a bull to the river Alpheios is mentioned in 11.727. The sacrifice of horses to a river is reported in other authors as either a non-Greek custom or from the distant past in Greece (Herodotus 7.113; Pausanias 8.7.2).

140–43. Asteropaios is the most commonly mentioned leader of the Paionians in the *Iliad,* appearing with Sarpedon and Glaukos as commander of the allied division in 12.102 and among the allied commanders in 17.217 and 351–55. He was not, however, the leader ascribed to the Paionians in the Trojan catalogue (2.848). The scholia inform us of an attempt by unknown scholars to correct the inconsistency by inserting, after 2.848, an additional line, "and also ambidextrous Asteropaios, son of Pelegon" (on "ambidextrous," cf. 163 n.).

149–60. The meeting between Achilleus and Asteropaios is like that between Diomedes and Glaukos in 6.119 ff. Achilleus here has more excuse than Diomedes there for not recognizing his opponent, for Asteropaios has been at Troy for only eleven days (156). Line 151 repeats line 127 of Book 6. Asteropaios, in his reply, gives his pedigree, although at considerably less length than Glaukos did in Book 6.

156. eleventh day ... in Ilion. The pathos of the death of those newly arrived at the front has been met with before. Rhesos had only just arrived in 10.434, as had the reinforcements from Askania in 13.793. And Lykaon had only recently returned (46).

163. being ambidextrous. Asteropaios' unusual facility distinguishes him from other warriors. He is rewarded by a qualified success, for he alone draws blood from Achilleus. The arm he hits is raised to throw the spear (161), so that it is natural that Asteropaios' weapon should then fly over Achilleus. The other spear is stopped by the gold of Achilleus' shield—here presumably on the *surface,* in contrast to its position in the middle in 20.268.

176–78. Three times ... and three times. Yet again we have the pattern of a threefold attempt, followed by **for the fourth time;** cf. 16.702–9 n. Commentators, blinded by their humdrum purpose of explaining difficulties, have failed to observe the bravery of Asteropaios; his last act, when he knew Achilleus was upon him, was to try at least to put the famous Pelian spear out of action by breaking it.

183. Achilleus uses Asteropaios' armor for prizes in the games of Book 23 (560, 808).

187–91. I am of the generation of great Zeus. Achilleus, instead of talking about his divine mother Thetis, who might seem more on a level with the river Axios, chooses to stress his more remote ancestor, Zeus. The family tree is

Zeus
|
Aiakos
|
Peleus = Thetis
|
Achilleus

194. Acheloios is the largest river in Greece, flowing through the northwest, on the border of Aitolia. Ocean (195) surrounds the world, and is not unreasonably considered the source of all other waters. In Hesiod's *Theogony*, Okeanos is father of the rivers (337) and grandfather of the Nereids (241–42).

203–4. the eels and the other fish were tearing him and nibbling. Asteropaios' body is already suffering the fate promised for Lykaon's in 122–27.

205–8. Achilleus causes havoc among the leaderless followers of Asteropaios, as Odysseus did among the Lykians (5.676) after Sarpedon was wounded.

209–10. Only **Thersilochos** has been mentioned before, at 17.216.

223. All this ... shall be as you order. Achilleus' reply has caused difficulty to commentators. He seems to agree to what the river asks but then to do the opposite (233). Probably his first words are a less precise statement than appears in translation; it is more like a vague "as you wish"; the main reply lies in 224–26.

229–32. who ordered you to stand by the Trojans. No such orders have been given by Zeus to Apollo. Either the river is illogically referring to the previous day (see 15.232–33) or to the implication of Zeus's general encouragement at 20.23–25; or else (most probably) this is ad hoc invention, comparable to that at 20.83–85.

234–327. The fight with the river is one of the most striking episodes in the *Iliad*, vividly describing the effect, even on a strong man, of being caught in a river in flood, unable to get firm ground to stand on.

278. by the flying shafts of Apollo. The prophecy of the manner of Achilleus' death is becoming more precise; cf. 19.417.

314. and the sound of timber and stones. For the river in flood, carrying debris with it, cf. 12.29.

335. whitening: probably means "bringing white clouds."

346–47. makes glad the man who is tending it. The scholiast explains that the gardener is pleased by the hardening of the surface by the drying wind because this means that the moisture stays down by the roots.

363. dancing on its whole circle: i.e., the whole round surface of the water is bubbling.

364. the fat of swine made tender: lard.

THE THEOMACHY, OR BATTLE OF THE GODS (LINES 385–513)

The Theomachy has been introduced by the conflict of Hephaistos and Skamandros, fire and water. For the lowered tone of this episode, see the introductory note to this book. The gods pair off to fight, as was arranged in 20.67–74. Aphrodite alone of those named in 20.33–40 was missing from the lineup there; she now becomes a second victim for Athene.

It is to be noticed that the more sensible gods (Apollo and Hermes) refuse to disport themselves for the amusement of Zeus (389), and this relieves Poseidon and Leto of any loss of dignity. Ares and Aphrodite are treated without respect; and even the great pro-Greek goddesses, Hera and Athene, behave in a childish and certainly unladylike way.

396–98. Ares knows what happened in Book 5, although Athene wore the "helm of Death" there (5.845). It is several times shown in the *Iliad* that Athene can handle Ares (5.766).

412–13. your mother's furies. Ares is Hera's son, but he supports the other side in the war. This unfilial behavior is enough in Athene's eyes to involve the Furies, who punish offenses against parents (9.454). Compare 5.894.

416. Aphrodite kindly helps her brother away. A love affair between these two is described in *Odyssey* 8.266 ff. and is perhaps alluded to here. In 5.355–63, however, Ares helps Aphrodite in similar circumstances without any romantic implications.

428–33. This speech of triumph, imitating the victory speeches of human warriors, does little credit to Athene.

441–60. Young fool. Poseidon tries his hand at a speech of aggravation—like a human.

443. to proud Laomedon we came down ... and were his servants. The service of Poseidon and Apollo to Laomedon has been referred to previously in the *Iliad*, at 7.452 and 20.145–48 (see notes). According to 7.452, both gods worked on the building of Laomedon's walls, and this was the usual tale in the ancient world.

462–67. Apollo is too sensible to respond to Poseidon's invitation. For 464–66, compare 6.146–47, the beginning of Glaukos' reply to Diomedes.

475–77. A most evident invention, to suit the present situation; cf. 20.83–85.

483–84. a lion among women. See 19.59–60.

497. Argeïphontes: Hermes (see 2.103 n.).

502–3. Leto is like a mother picking up her child's toys when the child has run away crying.

510 = 5.374, where the line is more pointed when applied to Aphrodite (see note there).

545. Agenor, son of Antenor, has played a larger part in the *Iliad* than one might notice. He was the first to kill a Greek opponent, in 4.467. He has appeared among the Trojan leaders in each of Books 11–16. In 20.474, a son of his (assuming that it is the same Agenor) was killed by Achilleus.

549. The **oak tree** was near the Skaian gate (9.354, etc.).

552–70. This speech of Agenor's is the third of four soliloquies in the *Iliad*, the others being by Odysseus in 11.403–10, Menelaos in 17.90–105, and Hektor in 22.98–130. They are closely similar; and, in particular, Agenor here is in many ways an advance echo of Hektor. For the purpose of delaying Achilleus, Agenor did not need to be present at all; Apollo could have taken his shape from the start, as he does in line 600. This speech, however, is in the character of the *human* fighter.

BOOK TWENTY-TWO

The death of Hektor at the hands of Achilleus is the climax of the *Iliad*, the culmination of the Wrath theme. To it the poet devotes the whole of Book 22, giving it all possible pathos by stressing the effect of the hero's death on his father and mother, his wife and child, and on the city of Troy. There is evidence, as so often, of careful composition. Three speeches, by Priam, Hekabe, and Hektor (25–130), balance three speeches at the end by Priam, Hekabe, and Andromache (405–515), the third speech in each case being the most affecting. The center of the book, with the action, falls into two parts: the chase (131–246) and the fight (247–404).

The fullest recent treatment of Book 22 is "Hektors Tod" in SCHADEWALDT *VHWW* 268–351.

4. sloping their shields across their shoulders. The phrase is the same as that appearing rather enigmatically at 11.592 and 13.488. Here at least it looks like a protective exercise against missiles from the walls (cf. 12.137–38).

6–7. Now Phoibos Apollo. This takes us back to the deception of Achilleus by Apollo in 21.599–605.

26–31. that star ... Orion's Dog. Sirius, the brightest star in the sky, rises in late summer, a time of oppressive heat in Mediterranean countries (cf. 5.5). The simile has two points of reference to the present situation: the shining of Achilleus' armor, and the destructive effects his coming portends.

45–55. The deaths of **Polydoros** and **Lykaon** were high points in Achilleus' *aristeia* in the preceding books (Polydoros in 20.407–18, Lykaon in 21.34–135). Lykaon himself referred to being "sold away to a far-lying island" in 21.78–79, and he referred to his mother

Laothoë and his grandfather Altes in 21.85. We may see how Homer keeps control of the main points of the narrative, providing cross-references and reminders for his audience.

60. The threshold of old age does not mean the *entrance to* old age but the *exit from* it (to death).

66–76. my dogs will rip me raw. A gruesome foreboding of his own end by Priam. Not only does he expect his body to be thrown to the dogs—a threat frequently made in these later books (see 42, 339, 348)—but he thinks of his *own* dogs, who feed around the table in his palace.

Lines 71–76 are striking, but they cause some surprise, not only because they are hardly appropriate to his present purpose of dissuading Hektor (although we can forgive Priam, an old man, for thinking primarily of himself), but also because they are so close to certain elegiac lines by Tyrtaios, the Spartan war poet of the seventh century. Tyrtaios is urging that young warriors should be prepared to risk their lives for the older men in the ranks:

For this is shameful, that falling in the front rank
An older man should lie before the young,
His head already white and his beard grey,
Breathing out his brave life in the dust,
Holding his bloody genitals in his hands—
Shame and disrespect that they should be seen by others,
His body uncovered; but all is seemly in the young,
While he has the glorious bloom of lovely youth,
He is fine for men to see, and lovely for women,
Alive, and beautiful when he has fallen among the first fighters.
(Frag. 10.21–30)

That there is a connection between Homer and Tyrtaios here is obvious; the striking and unnecessary reference to private parts makes that certain. The most sensitive recent commentators (SCHADEWALDT *VHWW* 300, n. 1, VON DER MÜHLL 333, LOHMANN 168) are convinced that Tyrtaios is the original and that these lines in Book 22 of the *Iliad* are a rhapsode's addition to Priam's speech—which in that case originally ended with line 68 (and we should read "dogs," not "my dogs" in line 66).

Even if this is so, the lines were of course added at a very early stage; and so for most of the history of the *Iliad* they have been part of Priam's speech.

92. gigantic refers to Achilleus, not Hektor.

97. The **jut of the bastion** is probably where the wall comes further out onto the plain, to protect the gate, as may be seen even now at Tiryns and Mykenai.

99-130. Hektor's speech follows the thoughts that pass through his mind. It is a soliloquy like those of Odysseus (11.403-10), Menelaos (17.90-105), and Agenor (21.552-70), all spoken in critical situations of personal danger. Hektor is closest to Agenor, who had indeed been in the same position at the end of Book 21 as Hektor is now. His first thought is of what people (especially Poulydamas) will say if he goes to safety in the city; then he wonders if there is any way of making a compact with Achilleus, perhaps offering massive compensation to the Greeks for the war. But he sees that this is hopeless, and he ends with the realization that there is nothing to do but fight. In the event, however, his nerve fails: when Achilleus comes near, he runs.

101. he tried to make me lead the Trojans inside the city. See Poulydamas' speech beginning in 18.254.

105. It is to be noticed that even Hektor is motivated by the heroic code of honor—the sense of **shame** about what people will say—rather than by a patriotic wish to fight for his country (6.441 n.).

114-16. It was not only the rape of Helen which brought on the Greek expedition, but all those **possessions** of Menelaos which were carried off with her. Compare 7.350, 363.

117-20. Taken with 18.511-12, these lines mean a division between the Greeks and the Trojans of all the Trojans' possessions; that is, the Greeks would take *half*.

124. naked. Like Lykaon (21.50).

125-28. In this beautiful sentence, Hektor's mind reverts to peacetime and the long private conversations of young lovers. In lines 127-28 he repeats with pathetic effect the phrase **a young man and a young girl** in the rare figure of speech called *epanalepsis*, which he has already used in 20.371-72.

The meaning of **from a tree or a rock** is much disputed. Other passages in ancient literature (beginning with *Odyssey* 19.163 and Hesiod *Theogony* 35) suggest that the words contain a proverb connected with old stories about the origins of man; and this is the explanation of the scholia, so that we may suppose Hektor to be saying, "One cannot start a long parley with him, going back to first beginnings." Others will see the tree and the rock as part of the pastoral background for the whispered conversation of the youth and maiden.

136–37. shivers took hold of Hektor . . . and he fled, frightened. Contrast line 96. This ambivalence about Hektor's real heroism appeared already in Book 16, where line 367 negated the impression of line 363. SCHADEWALDT writes very well of Homer's deep human sympathy here (*VHWW* 303–6).

145. The **fig tree** is presumably the same as that mentioned by Andromache at 6.433.

147–56. There have been attempts to identify these **springs,** one hot, one cold, and it has been found that there are indeed two springs of different temperature at the source of the Skamandros; however, they are not near Troy, being twenty miles to the south, high on Mount Ida (LEAF 2:441). It is possible that Homer's description therefore reflects some geographical knowledge; but Hektor did not run round those springs, nor did the women of Troy take their washing there **in the old days when there was peace.** The purpose of the poet's invention here is the same as that at line 127: to sharpen the contrast between peace and war, between the ordinary occupations of happier days and the brutal reality of the present chase. In *Odyssey* 6, the princess Nausikaa and her maids take the family's washing to the sea.

159–60. Compare the **prizes** in the funeral games of Book 23. The brief comparison here is expanded into a full simile in 162–64.

165. The important words *three times* have been accidentally omitted in the translation of this line; they should be added after **whirling.**

In view of the frequency of the pattern "three times . . ., but when for a fourth time" in recent books (most recently in 21.176–77; and cf. 16.702–9 n.), the triple circuit of this line will awaken the attention of the hearer for what is to happen when Achilleus and Hektor come round for the fourth time. Homer will keep him in suspense until line 208.

167–87. The idea of a *race* raises the suggestion of *spectators;*

and among them are the gods. Zeus now asks the same question about Hektor as he did about his son Sarpedon in 16.433–38 (whether he should rescue this mortal who is dear to him); Athene replies here as Hera did there (179–81 = 16.441–43); and Zeus offhandedly (as it seems to us) gives in to his favorite daughter, using the same words to her as he did when she pleaded with him at the beginning of Book 8 (183–84 = 8.39–40). This is a good example of the way formulaic composition works in repeated situations; and we may notice that the reply of Zeus in 184 is much less appropriate here than it was in Book 8. All the same, the exchange is not meaningless. Zeus, the supreme ruler of the world, *is* sorry for men; he is above the hatred felt by his wife and daughter. He does not, however, act against what is fated.

194. The **gates of Dardanos** seem to be the same as the Skaian gates; cf. 5.789 and 413, below.

199–200. As in a dream. The simile is taken from a common dream experience.

208. But when for the fourth time. We finally reach the responding line to the "three times" of line 165 (see note there).

209–13. For the **scales** of Zeus, see note at 8.69–70. For reasons of symbolism, the **heavier** fate is the loser; it moves in the direction of the underworld—**downward toward death.**

214–77. Athene now takes a hand in events, as she is encouraged to by her father, Zeus, in line 185. She deceives Hektor into standing and facing Achilleus, and she then interferes in the duel itself, to the great advantage of Achilleus, by returning his spear to him (276).

This is the most extreme case of divine assistance to a warrior in the *Iliad* (apart from the various ocassions when a human is rescued by being bodily removed from the scene); and it has caused much disapproval in modern times, as seeming unfair. It raises the whole question of what is meant by the "help" of the gods. We must try to see that Athene is not interfering to produce a result which would not otherwise have happened; it is wholly clear that Hektor is doomed and, indeed, that he is far weaker than Achilleus. Achilleus would win the duel easily without Athene's help; indeed, it is precisely (if we can understand this) because he does not need her help that he gets it. And it is no diminution of his honor to win with the help of Athene, as he expected to do (270–71); to an ancient reader or hearer, it would add to the glory of Achilleus that Athene is so demonstrably on his side.

A close parallel, but on a more trivial plane, is Athene's returning Diomedes' whip to him in the chariot race at 23.390; there, as here, she interferes to enable the natural winner to win. There was no way that Diomedes was going to come in second in that race; so he received the specific help of the goddess of victory. We may also compare Athene's stage-managing of the affair of Pandaros in Books 4 and 5 (see 4.93–103 n.); there again her intervention fulfilled what had to happen.

227. Deïphobos, Hektor's brother, was last seen in 13.527–39, where he was wounded by Meriones.

229–46. There is a strangely dreamlike effect in the conversation between Hektor and Athene/Deïphobos. As in a dream one may see someone in strange surroundings, or someone not seen for many years, and one's own mind offers the explanation why he is there, so, here, it is Hektor (236–37) who explains the appearance of his brother, and the apparition agrees. Notice also *"your* spear" in line 246. We are seeing this through the mind of Hektor.

267 = 5.289.

273–327. The duel. It is to be noticed that the fight is not a fight at all. Achilleus does not win simply by superior ability or strength but by divine intervention. Homer could have given us a heroic contest, like that between Hektor and Aias in 7.244–72 or that between Sarpedon and Patroklos in 16.462–91; but he chooses not to do so. For the really significant victories in the *Iliad*—the death of Hektor here and that of Patroklos at the end of Book 16—he prefers to use the gods.

276–77. Athene returns Achilleus' spear to him, so Hektor has no chance. For the implications, see 214–77 n.

294. of the pale shield. The adjective occurs only here. By normal Homeric practice, it must be straightforwardly descriptive, without other implications.

302. Zeus and Zeus's son. Hektor attributes his coming death to his two divine supporters, Zeus and Apollo. And indeed it is true that Zeus has used him to drive the Greeks back and so to fulfill his promise to Thetis; and it is a direct consequence of Hektor's successes that he now finds himself facing Achilleus alone.

In 304–5 Hektor comes to true heroism and nobility. He ran from Achilleus before; but now, before the watching armies—and knowing it to be hopeless—he attacks like an eagle (308).

312. charged. It is difficult to find the right word. *Hektor* is the one who is charging; as he comes close, Achilleus moves forward to meet him. The translation by Lang, Leaf, and Myers offers "made at him."

314. The four horns here are projections on the helmet (see 3.362 n.). The horn of 316, on the other hand, is the crest-holder.

318. Hesper, the planet Venus, is the brightest of the planets; cf. Sirius (the brightest star) in 26–32. Achilleus' new armor induced comparisons with the moon, a star, and the sun at the end of Book 19, with Sirius in 22.26, and with the sun again in 22.135.

330–67. The sequence and interchange of speeches are very close to those at the death of Patroklos—at Hektor's hands—in 16.829–62. There can be no doubt that the connection is intentional, the earlier occasion foreshadowing the present one.

Achilleus begins by boasting over his defeated opponent; then, after an appeal from Hektor for his body to be returned for burial—an appeal brutally refused by Achilleus—the dying man forecasts his victor's own death (as Patroklos did at 16.852–54); then three identical lines describe the death itself (361–63 = 16.855–57); after which each victor replies to the final words of his opponent. Achilleus is not deluded—as Hektor was—for he accepts the inevitability of his own death.

335–54. The concern for burial, and the enemy's threat that the body will be made the prey of **dogs** and **birds,** has been steadily increasing throughout the second half of the *Iliad,* and here we have its culmination. Hektor himself had wished to treat Patroklos' corpse as he now fears Achilleus will treat his (see 18.177 n.).

Entreating by the **knees** (338 and 345) is a metaphor taken from the position of a suppliant (see 1.407 n.).

359–60. when Paris and Phoibos Apollo destroy you. This too is the culmination of the various prophecies of Achilleus' death that have appeared since his mother foretold it to him at 18.96 (see 19.417, 21.278). Paris and Apollo will be jointly responsible, as

Hektor and Apollo were for the death of Patroklos.

378–94. The speech of Achilleus has caused surprise, because he changes his mind in the middle, using a line (385) which belongs to soliloquies (it occurs in each of the four soliloquies detailed in 99–130 n., above). Some scholars have thought that this marks a rough joint in the story—that in some other version Achilleus did proceed to attack the city now, after the death of Hektor, and that this led immediately to his death in the Skaian gates. We do not need to indulge in such extreme speculation. The idea of attacking the city is inherent in the situation (Poulydamas feared it at 18.265; Poseidon told Achilleus not to do it at 21.297). All that is happening in this speech is that Achilleus raises the thought of an immediate attack only to reject it. The closest parallel is in Aias' speech before his single combat with Hektor (see 7.195–99 n.).

393–94. These two lines *are* the "victory song" of 392.

395. Homer shows personal disapproval of Achilleus' action, as he does also at 23.176. The pathos of 401–4 increases the feeling of horror at Achilleus' behavior.

415–515. The three laments by Priam, Hekabe, and Andromache balance the three speeches at the beginning of the book. In addition, the speeches of Hekabe and Andromache look back to their talk with Hektor in Book 6 and forward to their final laments at the end of Book 24.

416–18. leave me to go out from the city . . . I must be suppliant to this man. Homer is preparing us for Book 24, when Priam does exactly this.

437–46. Andromache is a true wife to Hektor and is therefore associated with the home and household tasks.

440–41. inworking elaborate figures. For the weaving of patterns into the fabric, cf. 3.125–26.

458–59. Without realizing it, she speaks of Hektor already in the past tense.

468–70. threw from her head: i.e., her complicated headdress fell to the ground. She did not positively throw it from her, since she had fainted. The **circlet** of 470 is rather a veil or mantilla, hanging down from the head.

470–72. The meaning of the "gift of Aphrodite" here is wholly figurative. It was a love match, and the bride was beautiful; Aphrodite was therefore present at the wedding and gave the bride her veil. Compare the bow of Pandaros (2.827) and the good looks of Paris, also a "gift of Aphrodite" (3.64–65).

484–507. the boy is only a baby. She always mentions the child in her speeches to Hektor (cf. 6.432, 24.732–38); he is the strong bond between them. That she should be concerned at this moment with the sad life of an orphan, and the cruelty of other boys, has been thought strange, as also her later concern with Hektor's clothes, left in the house (510–14). As often, however, Homer understands more than his critics; these are considerations which might well occur to a wife and mother at such a time.

For explanation of the name **Astyanax** (506–7), see 6.403.

BOOK TWENTY-THREE

Book 23 falls into two separate but connected parts, the transition made in the simplest way possible, in the middle of a line:

1–257   The funeral rites of Patroklos.
257–897   The funeral games.

The funeral itself, which is described in considerable detail, continues the effect of all books since Book 18, with Achilleus as the central figure of interest. The games, on the other hand, return to the wide canvas of the earlier *Iliad*. Here we again see in action—but now in athletic competition instead of the deadly work of war—those characters whom we came to know well in the first half of the epic: people like Odysseus, Diomedes, Aias, Menelaos, Idomeneus, Meriones. Agamemnon makes a brief entry; Nestor speaks twice at some length. This is the last time we see the heroes, and Homer continues the process of character-drawing by portrayal of behavior which he has followed in the books of fighting. The vividness of the sports reporting, especially the very long description of the chariot race, which comes first, has always been much admired, and rightly so. Achilleus presides over the games, a model of politeness and propriety; the gentler side of his character is to the fore and prepares us for the civilized ending in Book 24, after the bloodthirsty violence of Books 20–22.

14. For Thetis' involvement, see the introductory note to Book 18 and Appendix D. There can be little argument that this line would be more appropriate at the funeral of Achilleus himself than at that of his friend.

20. **All that I promised you in time past:** in 18.334–37. "Behead"

(22) is a wrong translation here, as there; he will cut their throats (in 175–76, below).

24. This line is simply repeated, in the formulaic manner, from 22.395. It is not particularly appropriate here, because he does not proceed to do anything except detach Hektor's body from the chariot and leave it lying in the dust.

28. in their thousands. Two thousand five hundred, to be exact, according to 16.168–70.

34. The mention of cups suggests that part of the procedure was to offer the **blood** of the sacrificial victims **in cups** to the corpse of the dead. That the dead are thirsty for blood is seen in Odysseus' visit to the underworld in *Odyssey* 11, where it is only after a drink of blood that the ghosts can recognize him and speak.

61. Achilleus has lain down on the clear sand, by the shore of the sea.

68. stood over his head. This is the position always taken by dream figures. See 2.59, 10.496, 24.682.

69–92. The speech of the ghost of Patroklos, pathetically asking Achilleus to bury him as soon as possible. WILAMOWITZ 110 has perceptively argued that this is more of a dream than a ghost, for the speech reflects the feelings and thoughts of Achilleus more than any personal character of Patroklos; compare the words of the Deïphobos apparition in 22.229–46.

72–74. It was a common view in the ancient world that the ghost could not properly enter Hades until it had been buried or cremated. Elpenor, one of Odysseus' crew members, makes the same request to Odysseus in *Od.* 11.66–78 as Patroklos makes here. The **river** is the Styx (8.369).

85–88. by a baneful manslaying. Accidental homicide is a commonly used explanation for emigration. See the case of Epeigeus, who also took refuge with Peleus (16.570–76). Phoinix was a similar case, for he left home and took refuge with Peleus (9.478–82), although he differs in having refrained from the killing he had thought of (9.458). For **Opous**, see 18.325 n.

91–92. This **vessel** is mentioned, in the description of the funeral of Achilleus himself, at *Od.* 24.73–74 ("your mother gave a golden two-handled urn").

99–100. The situation is thematic. Odysseus had the same experience when he tried to embrace the ghost of his mother at *Od.* 11.204–8.

104. there is no real heart of life in it. Achilleus is not commenting on any particular deficiency in the ghost that he has just seen but is making a general statement about the dead. The word translated **heart of life** (*phrenes*) is used also in the *Odyssey* to distinguish the seer Teiresias from the other ghosts of the underworld. He is the only one who has been able to keep his *phrenes* (*Od.* 10.493); the rest are shadows.

113. Meriones is an efficient lieutenant, useful for minor commands; cf. 9.83.

126. a huge grave mound. There was in historical times a mound called the Tomb of Achilleus on the shore near the Sigean promontory; Homer seems to allude to this.

The Funeral Rites of Patroklos (Lines 128–77)

The funeral rites proper consist of:

1. A procession with chariots, the body carried on a bier, with Achilleus walking behind, holding the head.
2. The cutting-off of locks of hair in mourning for the dead.
3. The building of a huge pyre, with the body placed on top, wrapped in the fat of sacrificial animals.
4. The addition to the pyre of jars of oil and honey, dead horses and dogs, and the bodies of the twelve Trojan captives (human sacrifice).

132–33. sideman means the fighter in the chariot—superior, in fact, to the charioteer. The term **horsemen** means the chariot troops in general.

135. the locks of hair, which they cut off and dropped on him. Cutting-off of hair in honor of the dead has been common among many peoples. It is believed to be symbolic of the whole body and so a relic of early human sacrifice (E. Rhode, *Psyche,* 4th ed., p. 17, n. 1). It is frequently a theme in tragedy; e.g., Orestes at his father's tomb, in the tragedies by all three of the Attic dramatists.

142. For the **Spercheios,** see 16.174. It was not uncommon in ancient Greece for boys to dedicate a lock of hair to the god of the local river. The custom is referred to in Aeschylus, *Choephoroe* 6.

168. The **fat** would help the **corpse** to burn.

170–76. The offerings are to accompany the dead chief on his journey to the other world. Oil and **honey** are provisions for the journey; **horses** and **dogs** are companions; and the **twelve noble sons**—the Trojan captives—will be his servants. It is argued that all this provision for the future comfort of the dead, the details of which derive from ancient practices of the Mycenaean Age, would be more logical if we were dealing with inhumation (burial) rather than cremation; cremation, however, is (abnormally) used in the *Iliad* because the Greeks are in a hostile land (G. G. E. Mylonas in WACE/STUBBINGS 478–88).

The words **evil were the thoughts in his heart** (176) seem to show explicit disapproval by Homer of such inhumanity; cf. 22.395 (= 23.24).

179–83. These five lines are a repetition of 19–23, modified because he has now fulfilled half of what he promised.

185–91. **Aphrodite** and **Apollo**, the pro-Trojan gods, protect the corpse of Hektor, as Thetis did that of Patroklos in 19.38–39.

192–216. The episode of the **winds**. It shows the superhuman status of Achilleus that Iris herself, the messenger of the gods, takes his request to Boreas and Zephyros. The scene of the boisterous winds feasting in the house of Zephyros, totally unaffected by human grief, their reception of the attractive goddess, and their roaring progress over the sea, comes as a relief after the somber arrangements of the funeral.

195. **Boreas and Zephyros.** Why these two winds? Because they are the storm winds in the *Iliad*; they blow from Thrace (9.4–5), and they return there in line 230, below. This is evidence that Homer himself lived on the eastern side of the Aegean Sea.

201–7. There is comedy in the scene. The rough winds are at table; the goddess appears in the doorway; each of them gallantly asks her to come and sit beside him, but she demurely replies with an obviously invented excuse. The poet on his own account used the Aithiopians to motivate an absence of the gods in 1.423–24; Iris now does the same.

243–44. The **fat** will preserve the bones. **Until I myself enfold him** is an extension of thought beyond what is in Homer's Greek, which merely says "until I myself am hidden in Hades," i.e., "until I too am dead."

255. laid out the tomb and cast down the holding walls. The translation does not make the meaning clear. An alternative version would be, they "made round the place of the tomb, and put out a circle of stones at the base" (to mark the edge of the mound, which they now proceeded to pile up).

257. The words **But Achilleus** quietly introduce the second part of the book, the funeral games.

The Funeral Games of Patroklos (Lines 257–897)

Athletic contests were very popular in classical Greece. In particular, the four national games (Olympian, Pythian, Isthmian, Nemean) provided one of the few unifying factors in the normally divisive Greek political life, and, in addition to those four, there were local games of all sorts, evidence for which is contained in incidental references within the magnificent odes of Pindar for victors in the great games. The Olympian games (at Olympia in Elis) were recorded as having been founded (or refounded) in 776 B.C., not far from the time of the composition of the *Iliad*. The four-horse chariot race was the supreme contest. Admittedly, it is said not to have been added to the events at Olympia until 680, but these dates do not of course mean that there were no such contests before then; indeed, there is evidence for athletic competitions at Olympia right back into Mycenaean times.

All games known to Homer and mentioned in the *Iliad* are funeral games (for Amaryngkeus, 23.631; for Oidipous, 23.679; and cf. 22.164); and there are clear connections with Elis (a four-horse chariot is on its way there in 11.698–99, and Amaryngkeus was king in Elis). The four national games mentioned above also had legends which attributed their origin to funeral games held to honor a great hero.

There is also evidence that funeral games were a common topic of heroic poetry. This could be deduced in any case from some features of Homer's description, which are explicable only on the view that he is reflecting previous versions (see note on 850–83); but we hear also of others, especially some famous games for Pelias, king of Iolkos in Thessaly, information about which has come down to us in various sources. And of course, in a poem describing the death of Achilleus himself, there would be bound to be even more magnificent games than those Achilleus provides for his friend Patroklos here (see *Od.* 24.85–92).

There are eight events, of which the first, the two-horse chariot race, is by far the longest. It is followed by boxing, wrestling, and the foot race; then, in 798–883, come three events which have been criticized for unreality and obscurity compared with the others: the fight in armor, the discus, and archery; and, finally, the spear-throwing. In 621–23 and 634–38 a canon of five events seems to be given, which agrees with the five events considered to be certainly genuine in Homer's list. For the others, see 798–883 n.

Apart from the vividness of the sports reporting, there is strong character-drawing here, in Homer's usual style. It is reasonable to suppose that he has added human interest to the traditional theme of heroic games. This indeed is what makes the fight in armor so shocking; we are worried for the two contestants, Aias and Diomedes.

On funeral games in general, including their origin and their connections outside Homer, the best recent discussions have been L. Malten, "Leichenspiel und Totenkult," *Mitteilungen des deutschen archäoligischen Instituts (römische Abteilung)* 38–39 (1923–24): 300–40, and K. Meuli, "Der Ursprung der olympischen Spiele," *Die Antike* 17 (1941): 189–208.

The Chariot Race (Lines 261–653)

The five prizes (263–70) correspond in number to the five contestants. There is the same happy coincidence in the foot race (741–51).

264. ears: handles.

273. in the place of games: i.e., in the arena, here before you.

277–78. The **immortal horses** are described in 16.149–51; **Poseidon,** who had connections with horses, as well as with the sea and earthquakes, **gave them to Peleus,** presumably as a wedding present (see 18.84–85 n.). For their mourning (283–84), cf. 17.434–40.

The Five Contestants (Lines 288–351)

1. **Eumelos,** son of Admetos, from Thessaly. This man has played no part in the *Iliad* but was named in 2.714 as leader of one of the contingents from northern Greece, and in 2.763–67 it was said that his horses were the best in the army (an evident foreshadowing of his activity here). There is a connection in his case with the funeral games for Pelias, mentioned above, for Admetos' wife, Alkestis, was a daughter of Pelias (2.715), and Admetos himself competed in the chariot race in those games.

2. **Diomedes.** For his horses, see 5.265–72; Sthenelos took possession of them for Diomedes in 5.323–24. It is noticed that Diomedes does not use the wonderful white horses of Rhesos, which he obtained on the night expedition of Book 10.

3. **Menelaos.** Aithe and Podargos are typical horse names (cf. 8.185).

Lines 296–99 provide some evidence about the conditions of conscription of the army for Troy, evidence which may be added to that in 13.669 (Euchenor of Korinth) and 24.399–400 (a supposed Myrmidon). In this case, **Echepolos** (meaning "horse possessor"!), son of an improbably named **Anchises,** gave a horse to Agamemnon in lieu of service.

4. **Antilochos.** He was last seen sitting with Achilleus at the beginning of Book 18, after bringing him the news of Patroklos' death. He will play a large part in the present book. For the speech of his father, Nestor (306–48), see below.

5. **Meriones** (351). He merely makes up the number.

306–48. It is a long time since we had the pleasure of hearing from **Nestor.** He obviously could not let slip an opportunity like this for giving advice. Young Antilochos must have known it all already, but he stands silently, showing due respect for the old. In this way Homer not only adds to the characterization of Nestor but also gives us more factual information about the racecourse, describing the key moment when the driver turns his chariot round the turning post.

306. Poseidon was connected with horses (277–78), but he was also the great-grandfather of Antilochos (13.554–55 n.).

310. Nestor's horses were something of a joke; see 8.104.

315–17. These examples of the force of **skill** in other pursuits produce the figure of speech called a "priamel"; it is abnormal in Homer.

323–24. The Greek is difficult to understand. Most probably it refers to picking up speed again after turning at the turning post; translate, "ever watchful at what moment to urge his horses to a gallop by means of the oxhide whip."

336. It would be better to omit the words **of the course**. The driver should lean over to the left as he turns, to hold the chariot steady on its wheels.

346–48. Mythical horses. **Arion** comes from the Theban cycle of mythology, for he was the horse of Adrastos (Adrestos in the Ionic dialect used by Homer), king of Argos and leader of the Greek expedition of the Seven against Thebes. **Laomedon's horses** were those described in 5.265–67, sires of the pair used by Diomedes (291–92).

352. deposited the lots. In a helmet (see 861).

360. Phoinix is a reminder of the Embassy of Book 9; he also appeared as a divisional commander in 16.196.

373. the last of the race-course. It is rather sudden to find that they are already on the return leg. Homer has not chosen to describe the activity at the turning post, in spite (or because) of Nestor's detailed description of it.

376. the son of Pheres. Pheres was father of Admetos; **Eumelos** was therefore his grandson. The patronymic is sometimes used in this way; cf. Aiakides for Achilleus.

382–97. The race appears to be decided by the gods. **Apollo** causes Diomedes to drop his whip; **Athene** restores it to him, and then she makes Eumelos' chariot crash. What does all this mean? First, one must say that there are no accidents in the world of Homer's heroes. If Diomedes drops his whip, a god must have made him do it; if Eumelos crashes, a divinity must be angry. This way of looking at things is not difficult to understand. But the *return* of the whip to Diomedes is a physical interference beyond our understanding. To a believer, however, it would prove the real presence of the god. It is in fact exactly parallel to the return of the spear to Achilleus in his final fight with Hektor at 22.276–77; and in both cases (and this is important) divine interference fulfills the inevitable: the proper winner wins (cf. 357).

Athene's assistance to Diomedes is no surprise. She had helped him in Books 5 and 10, as she had previously stood by his father, Tydeus. Apollo supports Eumelos because he had bred those horses for Admetos (2.766).

420–24. The description is not clear, apart from the essential fact that they came to a place where the road was narrow and broken, a dangerous place to attempt to pass. It seems that the route led by or through a watercourse, dry in summer but a raging torrent in winter, as is commonly found in the Greek world. In 421, a closer translation would be, "and broken away part of the road."

Menelaos kept to what was left of the road, having to skirt the broken part and so, inevitably, slowing down. Antilochos, just behind him, turned off the road altogether (424), increased his speed (429), and took a short cut on the inside. In this way he drew up level with Menelaos; and when he moved back to join the still restricted road, there was imminent danger of a collision. Menelaos slowed down again to avoid it. (So CUILLANDRE 261–63, convincingly.)

441. The **oath** comes in 584–85.

448–98. A brittle exchange among the spectators enlivens the scene. Idomeneus speaks rather pompously, and this riles the lesser, meaner, Aias. Achilleus intervenes judiciously to calm them down. No doubt many of the Greeks are under strain after nine years of war.

476. Idomeneus is no longer young; see 13.361.
514. Neleian: as grandson of Neleus.

539–613. Young Antilochos is involved in two successive disputes, in both of which he is successful through personal charm. He has not been strongly characterized previously in the *Iliad*, but we shall find that his earlier appearances are relevant to the impression he makes here (see the next note and that on 566–613).

555–56. Achilleus is amused by the youthful eagerness of Antilochos. This must be the first time he has **smiled** since the death of Patroklos; in 786–92 the young man again speaks in a way that pleases Achilleus. We remember that it was Antilochos who was chosen to take the message to Achilleus at the beginning of Book 18 and realize that there is a sympathy between these two. This cannot be unconnected with the story in the *Aithiopis* (which followed the *Iliad* in the Cycle), that Memnon killed Antilochos and was himself then killed by Achilleus in revenge for his friend. Antilochos was thus in a relationship to Achilleus similar to that of Patroklos. (See Appendix D.)

560. that corselet I stripped from Asteropaios. This occurred in 21.183.

566–613. The outburst of Menelaos, accusing Antilochos of unfair tactics in the race. Here, even more than in the interchange with Achilleus, we should bear in mind previous events in the *Iliad* connecting these two. In 5.561–72, Menelaos was in serious danger from Aineias when Antilochos stepped next to him and thus saved his life; in 15.568–91, Menelaos encouraged Antilochos to an act of bravery; in 17.657, it was Menelaos who was sent by Aias to tell Antilochos to take the message to Achilleus that Patroklos was dead. Menelaos does indeed have obligations to Antilochos (607), which we should not forget.

567–68. The **herald** gave a **staff** to the man who wished to speak in an assembly; cf. 1.234.

584–85. swear by him who encircles the earth and shakes it. For Poseidon's connections with horses, cf. 277–78 n.

598–99. as with dew. An attractive, if difficult, simile. FRÄNKEL 42–43 suggests that the reason for obscurity here may lie in the simile's having been used more appropriately on some previous occasion for a different situation; its association is now little more than an image of pleasure to country people, of dew on the crops.

610. the mare, though she is mine. Compare Antilochos' words in 592, "the mare I won." Though willing to make concessions, each insists that by rights the mare is his.

616–50. The chariot race ends with yet another episode of human interest. We observe the politeness of Achilleus, his formal respect for the old, and see him standing quietly listening to Nestor's long speech, like Patroklos in Book 11 and Antilochos earlier in this book. When Nestor finishes in 650, Achilleus returns to his place.

621–23. These four types of contest—boxing, wrestling, spear-throwing, and the foot race—together with the chariot race just ended (and for which Nestor is now getting a consolation prize), seem to make a canon of five, the same five Nestor will mention in describing the games of Amaryngkeus in 634–38. It has seemed to many scholars that these five define the genuine events in Book 23 and that the other three (in 798–883) are later additions.

629–43. This is the fourth of the reminiscences of Nestor's youth with which he edifies us in the *Iliad*. The others are: 1.260–74 (Nestor helping the Lapiths against the centaurs); 7.132–57 (Nestor accepting a challenge to single combat); 11.669–761 (Nestor winning great glory in battle). Now we hear of his winning four out of five events in the games and failing to make a clean sweep only because of obscure gamesmanship on the part of his opponents in the chariot race. The introductory line (629) is clearly thematic for this kind of speech; it occurs also at 7.157 and 11.669.

630–31. Amaryngkeus was father of Diores, one of the leaders of the **Epeians** from Elis, one of whose towns was **Bouprasion** (2.615–24).

632–33. These are neighboring peoples. Men from Pylos might well go north to take part in games in Elis (cf. 11.697–99 for Neleus' loss of a chariot and four horses on just such an expedition); the **Aitolians** were across the sea to the north.

634–37. Neither the losing boxer nor the losing wrestler is otherwise known; the latter came from the second city of Aitolia, **Pleuron. Iphiklos** (called also Iphikles) was the father of Protesi-laos and Podarkes (2.705, 13.698); there is no reason why this should not be the same man. Of the spear-throwers, **Polydoros** is not known, but **Phyleus** was the father of Meges (2.628); he had once lived in Elis but had emigrated from there to the islands (2.629 n.).

638–42. For the twin Moliones, the **sons of Aktor**, see 11.708 n. They were local heroes of Elis. There are two difficulties with these lines: the meaning of the Greek words translated **crossing me in the**

crowd, and the physique of the twins. As to the first, three or four different explanations have been handed down in the scholia from the ancient world; the simplest is that the twins beat Nestor "by force of numbers," being two against one; this, however, is an awkward way of taking the Greek (two is not a crowd, as Eustathius says [1321.28]). For the second, a tradition explicitly attributed to Hesiod has it that the Moliones were what we call Siamese twins, their bodies being joined below the waist. This, in fact, is the only way to make sense of 641–42. If they were separate individuals, there could be no way they would be allowed to compete in the same chariot in the race; nor is it at all clear that it would be advantageous for them to do so. Homer is perhaps a little confused about this interesting tradition but thinks that the deployment of four arms instead of the usual two might give them an advantage in the management of the chariot. There is an illustration of an eighth-century jug which may represent the Moliones as Siamese twins in KIRK, plate 5c.

THE BOXING (LINES 653–99)

This lively event has been unreasonably depreciated by some modern commentators. Epeios' boastfulness is in character, and endearing rather than the reverse (see note on 667–75). If we compare the action with other ancient descriptions of a boxing bout (found in Theocritus, Apollonius, and Virgil), we discover that Homer is far the most civilized and in the spirit of amateur boxing (his victor even helps the defeated opponent to his feet).

655. A **jenny** is a female mule.

665. **Epeios** was later famous as the maker of the Wooden Horse, which led to the fall of Troy. He may have been a man of the people (cf. Thersites in Book 2), for we are told he served in the Greek army as a water carrier (Stesichorus, Frag. 23).

667–75. It is one of the most extraordinary indications that human nature remains the same that Epeios here, before his fight, speaks in terms similar to those that are notoriously used by modern professional boxers: "Who is going to be second?" (667); "I am the greatest" (669); "I'll murder him" (673).

677–78. **Euryalos** has played a minor part in the *Iliad*, as the third of the leaders from Argos (2.565). He, as well as Diomedes and Sthenelos, was one of the Epigonoi, the sons of the Seven against Thebes. **Talaos** was the father of Mekisteus and Adrastos (347).

679–80. The words "when he had fallen" (here translated **after his downfall**) strongly suggest in the Greek that he fell in battle. If this is so, the *Iliad* poet has a different story from the one familiar to us from Greek tragedy, in which Oidipous blinds himself and goes into exile. The reference to Oidipous in the *Odyssey* (11.275–76) is not inconsistent with the assumption here, for it states that he continued to rule in Thebes after his incest with his mother had become public knowledge.

The reference must be to funeral games for the dead king.

681–82. It is typical of the highly competitive Diomedes that, when he is not competing himself, he is acting as second to another competitor, and **much desired the victory for him.** He is Euryalos' cousin.

689–94. A good description of a clean knockout blow, with a simile of a fish arching its body out of the water.

THE WRESTLING (LINES 700–739)

The interest of this bout lies mainly in the contestants, the massive **Telamonian Aias** and the broad and stocky **Odysseus.** There is almost certainly a reflection here of their contest for the arms of Achilleus after the end of the *Iliad*, a contest that led to the suicide of Aias when the arms were awarded to Odysseus. If this is so, then it is not accidental that Odysseus has rather the better of the wrestling.

727–28. A successful fall to Odysseus. The bout will presumably be the best of three.

736. in equal division. It is not easy to see how they could share the prizes equally; cf. 809, 823.

THE FOOT RACE (LINES 740–97)

743–44. This is the only reference by name to the **Phoenicians** in the *Iliad*; they are commonly mentioned in the *Odyssey*, in the reminiscences of Odysseus and Eumaios. The city of Sidon was referred to in 6.289.

745–47. Thoas (14.230) was king of Lemnos. His daughter, Hypsipyle, was the mother of **Euneos** by Jason (7.467–69). For the selling of **Lykaon** to Euneos, who later allowed him to be ransomed and so to return to the fighting, see 21.40–41.

754. swift Aias: cf. 14.520–22.

758. The field was strung out gives a wrong impression. There are only three runners. Rather, "the runners set off at full speed from the start."

760–63. A vivid simile taken from weaving at a vertical loom. The threads of the **warp** are attached, alternatively, to two rods; the weaver pulls one **rod** to her, thus making an opening through which she draws the **spool,** or spindle, carrying the threads of the horizontal weft. The rod would be close to her breast.

764. A vivid description of runners immediately behind one another, as in a distance race.

774–77. Aias slipped . . . , for Athene unbalanced him. Aias has what we would call an accident, but to Homer and his audience it would be explained in terms of divine intervention (see 382–97 n.). Aias has been an unpleasant man in the *Iliad* (see 13.202–5 and also his bad-tempered quarrel with Idomeneus in 448–98, above); the Achaians are therefore not sorry to see him lose in this undignified way. We must assume that he gets to his feet quickly, for he still comes in second (779).

782–83. who has always stood over Odysseus like a mother. Odysseus is certainly the protégé of Athene, for he has exactly the qualities that she supports. For the maternal attitude of the goddess, cf. her protection of Menelaos in 4.130.

785–97. Antilochos adds to the occasion, pleasing and amusing Achilleus again (cf. 555–56 n.).

We come now (798–883) to three more doubtful events. They are exciting enough, but each has difficulties of interpretation. Seeing that a list or catalogue is obviously open to arbitrary accretion, it may be that these three were added to the games by a rhapsode after the time of Homer's first composition. The canon of five events in 621–23 and 634–38 would support this view. On the other hand, whoever composed these lines was in tune with the rest of the

Iliad, for at least in the first two events the contestants (Diomedes, Aias, Epeios, and Aias again) behave in a characteristic and recognizable way.

THE FIGHT IN ARMOR (LINES 798–825)

The fight in armor shocks us because it is far too dangerous, and we have grown to like and respect Aias and Diomedes. But the practice of single combat at the funeral of a chief is of great antiquity and may even have been the origin of funeral games; it was indeed to perform at funerals that gladiators were first introduced at Rome. We thus have a strange situation: that the least acceptable of the games, least authentic in the *Iliad*, has roots which go furthest back in time.

800. that Patroklos stripped: in 16.663–65.

806. A horrific line under the circumstances; it is in part taken from a description of the battlefield (10.298).

808. For Asteropaios' armor, cf. 560; for a Thracian **sword**, see 13.577.

809. It is not clear how they could hold the armor **in common** (cf. 736).

810. a brave dinner before them both. Assuming they survive!

819. This can only mean that the spear of Aias actually got through Diomedes' shield and reached his breastplate, or **corselet**.

824–25. Achilleus, as presiding judge at the games, decides that **Diomedes** has won on points, no doubt because of the greater menace of his style in 820–22, which had also impressed the onlookers.

THE DISCUS (LINES 826–49)

The weight that is used in the discus throw seems to be a round **lump** of metal, not a flat disk. But it is thrown with a whirling motion (840), and so the contest is closer to the discus than to putting the weight.

For this event only a first prize is offered, which distinguishes it from the previous multiple competitions, in which all competitors won a prize.

827–29. Eëtion, Andromache's father, had been king in Thebe (cf. the lyre Achilleus was playing in 9.186–88, and the horse Pedasos in 16.152–53, both won by Achilleus on that expedition).

834–35. Iron was still a rare and valued metal.

836–38. Polypoites and **Leonteus.** The poet wishes to remind us of the two Lapiths who held the gate against Asios in the Trojan attack of 12.127–94. They are there described as standing like mighty oak trees. As competitors with them he has added the huge **Aias** and **Epeios,** the victor in the boxing.

840. Homer does not explain why the **Achaians laughed.** We must assume that there was something funny in what they saw— a poor throw or an awkward style.

845–47. The herdsman used a **throwing stick** to drive a straying cow back into the herd.

We may notice that Aias has now entered for three events and has come in second in each. In both the wrestling and the fight in armor the bout was inconclusive, but in both cases the words of Homer show that Aias was behind "on points"; here he is a clear second. This is an aspect of Homer's method of characterization; Aias is *essentially* one who comes in second (cf. 17.279–80); he does not get the help of a god.

THE ARCHERY (LINES 850–83)

The account of the archery event makes a vivid, if improbable, tale. The odd fact about the preliminaries is that in the prize arrangements Achilleus provides for an unforeseeable accident which then occurs. The reason for this is evidently, as many commentators have remarked, that this story is not being told for the first time. What was originally an accident has become an expected part of the event.

859–60. Teukros is particularly famous as an archer. His *aristeia* was in Book 8.266–334. He tends, however, to be "unlucky": he was hit on the shoulder by a stone in 8.327, making him drop his bow; and his new bowstring broke in 15.463. **Meriones** normally fights with the spear, but he used a bow at 13.650; he is also a Kretan, and Kretan archers were famous.

In the contest the two men share one bow.

875–81. A truly extraordinary shot!

BOOK TWENTY-THREE

The Spear-Throwing (Lines 884–97)

An awkwardness in the account of the spear-throwing event is that the prizes seem to be mentioned in reverse order in 885 and that what turns out to be the second prize is in fact the weapon for the contest (but so was the first prize in the discus).

888. Meriones keeps on trying. This is his third event. He is young and competitive, like Antilochos, and for that matter Diomedes, but is a less engaging personality than either of them, though brave and loyal to his superior Idomeneus (17.605–25 n.).

890–94. Son of Atreus. Achilleus brings the games to an end with a compliment to Agamemnon, thus completing the public reconciliation which occurred under tension in Book 19. It may be noticed, however, that Agamemnon can still find no words to reply to Achilleus (see 19.139–44 n.).

BOOK TWENTY-FOUR

Book 24 is a worthy conclusion to the *Iliad*. It closely corresponds with Book 1, for here the Wrath theme, initiated in Book 1, modified in Books 18 and 19, and culminating in Book 22, is finally resolved when Achilleus speaks politely and gently to the old king, Priam, and agrees to the ransom of the body of his enemy, Hektor. Like Book 1 also, Book 24 is a unity in itself; it has the single theme of the return of Hektor's body to Troy. We may divide it as follows:

1–467   Priam's expedition to ransom the body.
468–676   Priam with Achilleus.
677–804   Priam's return to Troy; the burial of Hektor.

So the *Iliad* ends with its secondary hero, Hektor; but Achilleus is still in the center, especially since we realize—having been told so often—that his own death is now not far away. The shadow of it lies over his conversations with Priam.

WHITMAN 259–60 sees an even closer correspondence between Books 24 and 1, with five themes appearing in Book 1 and the same five, in reverse order, in Book 24, as follows (the descriptions of the themes are a little changed from those used by Whitman):

BOOK 1

a) The rejection of the father (Chryses) who wishes to ransom his daughter.
b) Quarrel between Achilleus and Agamemnon.
c) Thetis speaks to Achilleus and agrees to take a message to Zeus.
d) Thetis and Zeus.
e) Dispute among the gods.

Book 24

e) Dispute among the gods.

d) Zeus and Thetis.

c) Thetis speaks to Achilleus, having brought a message from Zeus.

b) Friendly converse between Achilleus and Priam.

a) Agreement that the father (Priam) may ransom the body of his son.

Thus expressed, the correspondence between the two books may appear closer than it really is. But there is no doubt that Book 24 does tie up the loose ends, material and psychological, of the whole epic; and even the passage of time (see note on line 31) serves to round off the action of the *Iliad*, so that, at the end of Book 24, the Greeks and the Trojans are back in much the same position they were in at the beginning of Book 1.

14–18. A continuation of what Achilleus was doing at the beginning of Book 23 (in lines 13 and 25). Apollo's protection of the body in the following lines continues from 23.185–91.

24. Hermes, referred to simply by the title **Argeïphontes** (see 2.103 n.) a number of times in this book, was the god of thieves (5.390) and so an appropriate choice for this action.

26. the girl of the grey eyes: Athene.

28–30. Paris, who insulted the goddesses and favoured her who supplied the lust. This is the only explicit allusion in the *Iliad* to the Judgment of Paris (that occasion when he was asked to decide who was the most beautiful, Hera, Athene, or Aphrodite; after which, having given his verdict in favor of the last-named, he received Helen as his reward). It may be assumed, however, that Hera's and Athene's extreme animosity toward Paris and the Trojans in the *Iliad* reflects their resentment at Paris' decision. See 4.31–36, 5.422, 20.313–17.

31. the twelfth dawn after the death of Hektor. The twelve days include three days for the funeral of Patroklos (the two new dawns came in 23.109 and 226) and nine days of dispute among the gods, mentioned again in 107 (the total "twelve" is repeated at 413). This period of time is echoed again at the end, when Achilleus agrees with Priam to a truce of eleven days to enable the Trojans to bury

Hektor—the fighting to begin again on the twelfth (664–67, 783–803). The length of these two periods balance two in Book 1: the duration of the plague (nine days) in 1.53–54, and the absence of the gods, feasting among the Aithiopians and due to return on the twelfth day, in 1.423–25. The effect of all this is to isolate the action of the *Iliad* from what went before and what came after in the Trojan War tradition.

60–63. gave her as a bride. For the wedding of Peleus and Thetis, see 18.84–85 n.

78. Samos is the island later called Samothrace (13.12).

80–82. A simile from fishing. It appears that a piece of **horn** protected the line just above the hook and also contained a small **lead weight** to make the line sink.

110. but I still put upon Achilleus the honour that he has. In other words, Zeus is giving Achilleus the chance to do the right thing of his own accord; cf. 1.207 n.

130. It is a good thing to lie with a woman. See 676.

142. at long length: i.e., they continued to talk together.

153. One of Hermes' titles is "The Guide" (21.497).

163–65. for he had been rolling in it. Cf. 22.414.

167. all those men. They weep particularly for their own lost ones; cf. 19.302.

175–87 = 146–58, with only the necessary changes from the third person to the second.

212–13. I wish I could set teeth in the middle of his liver and eat it. The bitterness of Hekabe, the mother, is far greater than that of Priam, or Hektor, or Achilleus. See note on 756–57. VON DER MÜHLL 377 points out her similarity to the title character of Euripides' *Hecuba*.

219. a bird of bad omen: cf. 12.243.

235. with a message. In other words, on an embassy.

249–51. Of these nine sons, only **Helenos, Paris, Polites,** and **Deïphobos** have appeared in the *Iliad*. The rest are unknown.

257. Mestor is almost unknown. Apollodorus (*Epitome* 3.32) says that he was killed by Achilleus on the expedition from which Aineias only just escaped (20.90–92, 188–90); if this is a real tradition, it must derive from the *Cypria*.

Troilos seems to have been primarily a figure in popular romances about Troy, which led eventually to the medieval story of Troilus and Cressida (the latter name is a corruption of "Chryseis" in *Iliad* 1). In the epic version, at least as reflected by Virgil (*Aeneid* 1.474–78), he was a young son of Priam, an unequal opponent for Achilleus, killed as he tried to get away on his chariot (cf. **whose delight was in horses** here).

268–74. Obviously a technical description of the yoking of a mule wagon. It is not easy for us to reconstruct the operation because of uncertainty about the exact meaning of some of the features named. The **knob** (269) is on the center of the yoke, which is simply the crosspiece fitted on top of the wagon pole, near its front end, and firmly tied there by the **yoke lashing** (270). **It** in 271 is the yoke itself, not the lashing. The **guiding rings** of 269 are at each end of the yoke, and would take the reins. Lines 272–74 describe the fixing of the yoke in place, so that it will be anchored to the pole while nevertheless allowing play of the sides, back and forward, as the wagon is being pulled.

278. The **Mysians** lived in central Asia Minor, not far from the Enetoi, whose country is described in 2.852 as the home of mules.

279–80. So Priam is to travel separately from the herald, the one in a horse-drawn chariot, the other in a mule wagon.

292–93. which to his own mind is dearest of all birds. She means an eagle, which is the bird of Zeus because it inhabits the mountaintops.

294. The **right** is the lucky side; cf. 12.239.

303. unstained: clean.

315–16. This is the great golden **eagle** (the Greek words translated "dark" and "black" are of very uncertain meaning). Its wingspan is about seven feet, which fits the description of 317–19, that the wing on each side was as wide as a doorway.

324. Idaios is Priam's herald.

342. land of the main: i.e., the mainland, as opposed to the sea.

349. For **the tomb of Ilos,** see 10.415 n.

Because they reach this tomb and allow the mules and horses to drink from the river, WHITMAN 217 argues that the symbolism of Priam's visit to Achilleus suggests a visit to Hades, the realm of the dead. There, too, there is a river that must be passed, and the way is dark; Hermes, in addition to his other functions, acts as guide for the souls of the dead, a role which he plays at the beginning of the corresponding book of the *Odyssey* (*Od.* 24.10). Even the heavily barred gates of the Greek camp (447) and of Achilleus' courtyard (452–56) have their counterpart in the gate of hell (8.367).

350. This is the place called the "crossing place" (i.e., ford) of the Skamandros in 14.433 (where see note) and in 21.1 and 692, below. They do not *cross* the river but merely pause to allow the mules and horses to drink.

356. let us run away with our horses: i.e., abandoning the mule wagon.

371. Rather, "You seem to me like *my* father" (cf. 398).

398. The name **Polyktor** suggests "of many possessions."

400. it was my lot to come. Even in a false story, this is evidence of the method of conscription of the army. It appears that each family had to provide one soldier.

401. I have come to the plain. Presumably as a scout or spy, like Dolon in Book 10.

421. since many drove the bronze in his body. This occurred in 22.371.

426. if ever I had one. This phrase appeared also at 3.180, 11.761. It is the expression of one looking back to happier days—"unless it was all a dream."

429. This **cup** is the one described in 233–35.

The poet is, as usual, accurate in his portrayal of behavior. The old man would naturally rely on a material inducement; the young man is idealistic.

438. Argos in this context simply means Greece.

444. sentries. These are the guards sent out to the space between the ditch and the rampart in 9.80–88.

467. The **child** is Neoptolemos (19.326–27). Priam does not in practice mention either him or Thetis to Achilleus.

474. Automedon and **Alkimos** (=Alkimedon, 19.392) are now numbers two and three in the immediate entourage of Achilleus (cf. 574–75), as Patroklos and Automedon were before (9.201–11).

480–82. This is an extraordinary simile. It is taken from the commonly mentioned situation of a killer leaving home and coming as a suppliant to the king of another land (see 16.570–76, with the references in the note there); the simile is of the shocked astonishment among those present at the sudden appearance of the wild figure. But there is a reversal of roles here; for the man who has come is innocent of any deed of violence, while the killer is the man sitting among his followers.

487. For the **door-sill of old age,** see 22.60 n.

495–97. Fifty were my sons. We have seen before (e.g., 21.84–87) that Priam had children by other mothers than Hekabe; he is a polygamous Eastern potentate. Twenty-two sons of Priam are named in the *Iliad*, of whom eleven are killed in the course of the poem, and two (Mestor and Troilos, 257) died at an earlier stage of the war. The nine who are left are those named in 249–51.

527–33. The **two urns,** of good and bad things, derive from folktale. It is to be noticed that humans either get a mixture or receive only from the urn of bad things; no human receives unmixed blessings.

534. Not **Such were the shining gifts,** but "So the gods gave shining gifts"; the antithesis—of the evil which was bound to be added to them—comes in 538.

544–45. There is rather much of **the north** in the translation here. The words so translated (literally, "up") mean "out to sea" and "inland." Achilleus is making a reasonable geographical definition of Priam's realm, bounded by the island of **Lesbos,** to the south; **Phrygia,** inland to the east; and the **Hellespont,** to the north.

Makar was a legendary king of Lesbos.

557–58. since you have permitted me to go on living. By his actions Achilleus has accepted Priam as a suppliant.

559–70. Achilleus' sudden outburst of annoyance has worried commentators since the ancient world. Even Aristotle commented on it as inconsistent. LOHMANN 171 sees it as intended to produce a parallel with Agamemnon's rough treatment of Chryses in 1.25–32. But surely the explanation is much more natural. Achilleus is not yet completely calm; Priam's refusal of the offered seat annoys him, and he fears (as Homer tells us clearly) that he may lose his temper and kill the old man against his own wish and promise. To this touch of insight into the violence of Achilleus' character are to be added the simile "like a lion" in 572 and the attempt to avoid an accidental flare-up in 583–86.

588. The other cloak (580) was probably to be laid *over* the body, as in 18.353.

592–95. Be not angry with me, Patroklos. Achilleus says this because he had promised Patroklos in 23.182–83 that he would not do the very thing he is doing here. Patroklos will be compensated for the loss of the ultimate vengeance by the dedication to him (by burning) of part of the ransom: **your share of the spoils.**

THE STORY OF NIOBE (LINES 599–620)

The story of Niobe is the clearest example in the *Iliad* of the peculiarly Homeric use of the mythological *paradeigma*. Here, more obviously even than in earlier "examples," Homer has blatantly invented essential details in order to fit the mythological story to the situation for which it is being adduced as a parallel.

Achilleus says, "Eat, for even Niobe ate, and she was mourning for more children than you are." In the ensuing story, everything is inconsistent with the Niobe legend as we know it from elsewhere except for the offense caused to Apollo and Artemis and their vengeance (604–9) and the four disputed lines 614–17 (on which, see below). All the other details arise from Homer's initial decision to use Niobe as an example of a mourner who took food.

The children lay unburied for nine days (610), evidently to parallel the situation of Hektor. To avert any possible buriers, the poet invents the detail that the people of that place were petrified— turned into stone—by Zeus; in this, he has transferred the motif of petrifaction from Niobe to the people (see below), no reason being given. Eventually the children were buried (as Hektor was); but because he has so rashly got rid of the people, the poet has to say that the gods themselves performed that office (an unparalleled act, for normally gods keep away from corpses). All this shows the poet's invention at work. But more imaginative still is the central point, that Niobe ate food. For the one thing that we all know about Niobe is that she was inconsolable, so that Zeus, eventually taking pity on her tears, turned her to stone, and she can still be seen as a rock face with water perennially running down it. There is no place in the usual story of Niobe for her to dry her eyes and eat food.

Thus Homer has invented the central theme, the very purpose of quoting the myth. As KAKRIDIS 99 says, "Niobe eats for the simple reason that Priam must eat."

As in other mythological examples (e.g., 1.259–74), the *paradeigma* is presented in a careful ring composition:

a	599–601	In the morning you may take your son back.
b	601	Now let us eat.
c	602–3	For even Niobe ate.
d	603–6	Her twelve children had been killed.
e	607–8	Niobe's offense.
d'	609–12	Her children were eventually buried.
c'	613	She ate food.
b'	618–19	Let us also eat.
a'	619–20	Afterwards you may take your son back.

The story of Niobe, originating in part from an imagined human likeness in a rock face, is the extreme case of the mourning mother. In mythology she was the daughter of Tantalos. Her offense (607–8) is of a pattern with other stories of humans who came to an evil end because, forgetting the limitations of their state, they entered into competition with the gods (cf. Thamyris in 2.595).

Lines 614–17 describe the situation at the end of the usual story. **Sipylos** is a mountain in Lydia ("Maionia" for Homer); **Acheloios** is a river *there*; i.e., it is not the great river of Greece (21.194). The rock that was thought to be Niobe has not been certainly identified (see J. G. Frazer, *Pausanias*, 3:552–56).

Even the ancient critics considered the four lines 614–17 to be a post-Homeric addition. The scholia object to them as inconsistent with the rest of the *paradeigma*; and modern scholars have (with some distinguished exceptions) agreed. It is now to be seen that formally they break the ring composition, for they come in after c' and before b' in the scheme presented above, interrupting the otherwise exact correspondence. Moreover, if it is true, as was suggested above, that the motif of petrifaction was transferred by Homer himself from Niobe to her neighbors, it is disconcerting to find it eventually used of her as well.

Beautiful and impressive though these lines are, the arguments against their genuineness here seem very strong; the situation is in fact similar to the one encountered in the lines that tell of the ultimate fate of Bellerophontes in 6.200–202, where (as here) a reference to the well-known end of the story interrupts an ordered narrative.

649. sarcastic. Better, "ironical." Achilleus says one thing but has a different reason in his mind. He knows that Priam must and will find his own way out of the Greek camp, helped by one of the gods (cf. 563–64). He therefore puts him in a situation that will facilitate this. For a superficial excuse, however, he invents the reason that some Greek may come for a strategic discussion.

664–67. For the time elements involved, see the note on 31. It is interesting that Achilleus should be able to promise to hold back the Greek army for as long as Priam needs for the funeral.

676. at his side lay Briseis. Compare Thetis' words in 130. Achilleus is now at peace. The story that began with the forcible removal of Briseis by Agamemnon is finished.

692. the crossing-place. See 350.

696–97. they drove their horses ... while the mules drew the body. Rather awkward expression. The position is the same as on the outward journey: Priam drives the horse chariot, Idaios the mules.

699–700. Kassandra has not appeared in the *Iliad* before this, except that a suitor for her was killed in 13.363. Her function as a prophetess, known from later sources than the *Iliad*, makes her behavior here quite appropriate. **Pergamos** is the acropolis of Troy.

719–76. The final scene of the *Iliad* is the mourning for Hektor, and here we have three short laments from the three women of Troy: Andromache, Hekabe, and Helen, the same three to whom he spoke in his visit to Troy in Book 6. Andromache speaks first, having that right as his wife; she is concerned, as always for the child (compare her speeches in Books 6 and 22). Second is Hektor's mother, Hekabe. There is not much she can say; the death of her son leaves her with nothing (compare her speech in 22.431–36). Third, and, in a way, most moving, is Helen, the sister-in-law; her last tribute is to the kindness and humanity of Hektor.

At the end of each lament is a formal line, like a refrain (746, 760, 776).

720. the singers. Professional mourners were an Eastern custom.

732–34. among them I shall also go. Her own fate was foreshadowed also in 6.456–58.

734–36. some Achaian will ... hurl you from the tower. The child, Astyanax, was thrown over the battlements at the sack of

Troy by Neoptolemos, son of Achilleus, as the story was told in the *Little Iliad* (cf. Euripides' *Trojan Women*). It is difficult to decide whether Homer is alluding to a legend already known to him or whether the later version arose from these lines.

752–53. sell them as slaves. Lykaon, for example, had been sold to the king of Lemnos (21.40). **Samos** is Samothrace (as in 78).

756–57. even so did not bring him back to life. For the depth of hatred and bitterness in the mother, cf. 212–13 n. As C. Segal says, there can be no reconciliation for the bereaved mother (Segal, *The Theme of the Mutilation of the Corpse in the "Iliad"* [1971], p. 69).

758–59. gentle arrows. This implies a gentle death, like sleep; Apollo kills men, as his sister Artemis kills women (19.59–60).

765. the twentieth year. Here is the final difficulty of the *Iliad*. How can Helen say this, when the war is just beginning its tenth year? Three explanations have been given:

1. The scholia simply say that it took the Greeks ten years to assemble their forces.

2. Some modern commentators (VON DER MÜHLL 389, KULL-MANN 192) think that there is a reference to the abortive expedition which the Greeks were said to have mounted before they eventually got to Troy; on that former occasion they reached Mysia, where their chief adversary was Telephos.

3. It has been suggested that the phrase is formulaic, echoing *Odyssey* 19.222–23, where the statement that appears here as 765–66 is used of Odysseus—whom, of course, it suits, because of his ten years of wandering after the Fall of Troy.

The third explanation is in line with the modern theory that the pressure of formulaic composition leads to carelessness about details, although it is an extremely violent example. The other two are unconvincing, for it is difficult to see why either of the actions cited should have taken as long as ten years.

All the same, there are complicated questions of chronology raised by the Trojan War. For example, how old is Neoptolemos supposed to be? His presence in Troy in the last year of the war implies that at least seven or eight years elapsed between the time Achilleus was hidden on Skyros (19.326–27) and the beginning of the war. Telemachos in the *Odyssey*, on the other hand, must not be more than twenty years old when his father returns.

770. but his father. There is something universal about the relations described, the mother-in-law sometimes critical, the father-in-law indulgent. For the kindness of Priam to Helen, cf. 3.162–65.

775. It shows the essential humanity of the poet of the *Iliad* that the final epitaph of "manslaughtering Hektor" is that he was kind, even to Helen.

782–803. The funeral arrangements. They follow (more briefly) the practice of the Greeks at the funeral of Patroklos in the first part of Book 23.

Appendix A

TRANSMISSION OF THE TEXT OF THE *ILIAD* AND COMMENTARIES ON IT

We can only guess how accurately the *Iliad* was transmitted during the first two hundred years or so of its existence (from about 750 to about 550 B.C.). Much depends on the unknown date when it was first committed to writing. During this early period, it seems to have been in the hands of *rhapsodes*—reciters of epic verse who performed on public occasions—who may have introduced corruptions and interpolations into the text, difficult now to detect.

It is commonly believed that this uncertain stage ended with the establishment of an official text in Athens in the sixth century B.C. (LATTIMORE 13, n. 2). Our modern text, however, does not go back with detailed certainty to that edition of the early classical period; it derives, rather, from postclassical Alexandria in Egypt, where there was much scholarly activity, the major names being those of Zenodotus and his great successor, Aristarchus (third to second century B.C.). A modern editor has, as evidence, (1) great numbers of medieval manuscripts, the most famous of which is Venetus A, of the tenth century; (2) papyrus fragments from the ancient world, dating from 300 B.C. to 700 A.D., hundreds of which are now known, covering almost every line of the *Iliad*; (3) the scholia (on which, see below); and (4) quotations from the *Iliad* found in ancient authors, grammarians, and dictionaries. From all this it is clear that the "vulgate" text has hardly changed from what was commonly read in the Alexandrian period.

With the single exception of the Bible, the *Iliad* has been more continuously and voluminously commented on than any other work of Western literature. In this long tradition of elucidation and discussion we are indebted to countless scholars and teachers from the earliest times to the present day. Ancient comments have reached us in the form of scholia—marginal notes in certain manuscripts (especially Venetus A, mentioned above) and papyri. These derive from books and monographs now lost, and they include three classes of information: (a) textual discussion by scholars of the late ancient world, particularly Aristarchus; (b) general elucidation of difficulties and interpretation on many levels; and (c) explanations of difficult words.

The scholia are voluminous, many times the length of the *Iliad* itself, and they themselves divide into classes which correspond in general to the three classes of information just mentioned, namely, the A scholia (found in Venetus A), the bT scholia (in a group of other manuscripts), and the D scholia (called also the scholia minora—the commonest and least important). Scholia material is also the main source behind the largest commentary known to us, that of Archbishop Eustathius of Thessalonica, composed about 1170 A.D.

All modern commentators are indebted, directly or indirectly, to the scholia and Eustathius. Editions which have been particularly consulted in the preparation of this book are those of Ameis, Hentze, and Cauer (1868–1932), Pierron (1869), Faesi and Franke (1871–77), Monro (1884–88), Leaf (1900–1902), and van Leeuwen (1912–13). There are also many general works on Homer, as well as works treating particular aspects, the most frequently quoted of which are listed in the Bibliography on pp. 288–90.

Appendix B

METHODS OF FIGHTING IN THE *ILIAD*

The *Iliad* is full of descriptions of fighting. Eleven books are largely devoted to it (Books 5, 8, 11–17, and 20–21), and there are fighting sections in other books as well. It will help the modern reader avert a feeling of monotony to remember that Homer and his audience understood fighting and liked to hear about it and that—despite what may at times seem diffuse and indecisive action (particularly in the long, central Books 13–15)—Homer had a very clear idea of what he was describing.

The descriptions of armor are not historically consistent, and the archeological background of what is worn and used is chaotic. Yet a general picture emerges. The heroes wear greaves on their legs, a breastplate, and a helmet, and they carry a large shield and a sword, both slung by straps over their shoulders; in their hands they take either one thrusting spear, for hand-to-hand fighting, or two smaller, throwing spears—more like javelins. All that is metal is bronze. They travel to, around, and away from the battlefield in chariots, but they do not engage in fighting from chariots; that art has been forgotten, and some major warriors—notably, Odysseus and Aias—do not seem to have chariots at all.

Action at the front is repetitive. There is a background of massed troops, to be thought of as lighter-armed. From it the leading figures step forward as champions, to hurl a spear or to engage in individual combat with a figure from the opposing side. The effect is much like that of the knights of the Middle Ages, and it leads to the cult of personality, individual heroes being able to win great fame by their accumulation of battle successes.

APPENDIX B

There are two kinds of fighting situations: the melee and the rout. In the former, the armies are locked together, and this situation leads to many expressive similes from the poet; the best qualities of a fighter here are courage, strength, and self-defense. This is when Aias son of Telamon comes into his own. But, sooner or later, one side exerts the greater pressure, and the other turns to run. This turning point in the battle is often signaled by the mention of chariots: we hear of someone being hit *as he mounts his chariot*; or a leader (usually a Greek) kills his opponents *in pairs*— (5.37–83, 144–65; ALBRACHT 1:13–27). In this situation—the rout— the chief attacking quality is speed. Achilleus is outstanding in *all* respects; but it is in these circumstances that he is most dangerous, and that is why his stock epithet is "swift-footed." If the fighting books are read with this distinction in mind, the action becomes clearer.

Descriptions of wounds combine realism with fantasy. There is great variety in the descriptions, and they betray a knowledge of human anatomy that is impressive and in most cases accurate, although there are some improbable wounds (13.546, 617). The similes paint a more realistic picture than the casual reader may notice. For example, those who fall "like a tree" have regularly been hit in the head and are therefore knocked out; and the frequent picture of an attacker leaping in "like a lion" often relates not so much to his first attack as to his subsequent attempt to remove the armor, when he crouches over his victim like a beast of prey (STRASBURGER 38–42; see 17.63–64). After a man has been hit, the poet has the choice of several stock lines which mean "he died." There is no long-drawn-out pain, and no maimed and wounded clutter up the field.

Homer seems to realize the danger of monotony, for he constantly varies the action. Major encounters relieve lists of minor figures slain; numerous similes add color and change the context; intervention by the gods produces an extra dimension, or we are actually taken to Olympos to see the reactions of the gods among themselves; and always there is Homer's interest in people, not only the great heroes, whose every action is used to support their individual characterization, but also the little men who are named only to be killed and whose very unimportance adds a balancing pathos to the victor's triumph.

Appendix C

MYTHOLOGY AND THE GODS

"Greek mythology" was a vast collection of tales about the past, consisting of semihistorical legends mixed with folktale themes and enlivened by poetic invention; the stories that it contained were sung by bards like Homer, no doubt normally in short lays very different from the *Iliad*, but in the same style and language. Judging by the allusiveness with which a non-Trojan myth is introduced tangentially in the *Iliad*, we may deduce that the Homeric audience had a wide familiarity with mythology.

There were four main cycles of myth: the Trojan cycle, the Theban cycle, the story of the Argonauts, and the tales of Herakles. Generally speaking, the characters in them were kept separate.

The Trojan cycle included the preliminaries of the war, with the abduction of Helen by Paris, the events of the war itself and the sack of Troy, and the misfortunes that befell the individual heroes on their journeys home to Greece. The *Iliad* describes a few days in the last year of the war, and its sparing allusions to such earlier events as the assembly at Aulis (2.303), the death of Protesilaos (2.698–702), and expeditions against local towns (1.125) may leave the reader a little skeptical about the passage of nine years.

The epics of the Theban cycle, had they been preserved, would have been very relevant to Homer, and we can only regret the loss of the *Thebaid*, which would have provided the best of all possible parallels to the *Iliad*. The comparison would lie in the fact that at Thebes, as at Troy, the myth told of an attack on a walled city by a large Greek force, against the desperate defense of the inhabitants. To be precise, there were two attacks, for the earlier and more famous expedition of the Seven against Thebes was unsuccessful. It was left to the Sons of the Seven (the Epigonoi) to destroy Thebes—to succeed where their fathers had failed (4.405–6). This is a case where there is an overlap of personnel between the cycles, for three of the Epigonoi play a part in the *Iliad* (4.405–10 n.), in particular the magnificent Diomedes, who is a leading figure in Books 4–11 and 23. As a result, there are several allusions to the earlier attack on Thebes, which included the exploits of Diomedes' father, Tydeus (see 4.365–400).

As to the Argonauts, there are precisely three references in the *Iliad*, all to a son of Jason and Hypsipyle called Euneos, now king of Lemnos (see 7.467–69 n.). Herakles, on the other hand, is frequently mentioned. He was the hero *par excellence* of the generations before the Trojan War. Piecemeal allusions are made to his exploits throughout the *Iliad*, and they add up to a fairly consistent picture (8.362–69 n.).

Apart from the four main cycles, there were countless local legends, which were more or less familiar outside their own parochial circle, depending on chance or the fame of the heroes involved. There are, for example, detailed allusions in the *Iliad* to the war of the Lapiths against the centaurs (1.261–68) and to the hunt for the Caledonian boar (9.529–49).

It is evident that a major effort of systematization has been made on all this material. It would have been only too easy for the poets to fall into impossible time relationships, such as that discussed in the note on 7.148. Overall, there is chronological consistency among the different cycles. In the *Iliad*, for example, the destruction of Thebes by the Epigonoi is assumed in 2.505, and Euneos, son of Jason, might indeed be king of Lemnos now. This *ordering* of the myths is probably to be attributed to Ionian poets, Homer's immediate predecessors.

The myths are almost exclusively located in the Mycenaean Age. This is shown by internal evidence, and particularly by the geographical location of the myths and their heroes, which fits the distribution of the Mycenaean citadels as shown by the findings of archeology (NILSSON *passim*). By the passage of time and the growth of myth, the age of the Mycenaeans had been turned into a heroic age, a time of action and danger. Such heroic ages have been part of the retrospective vision of other peoples also; their distinguishing features have been a concentration on the military virtues of personal honor and loyalty to one's immediate superior, accompanied by political instability and eventual disaster (cf. H. M. Chadwick, *The Heroic Age* [1912]).

Another essential feature of the world of Greek mythology is the closeness of men to the gods. The greater gods are represented in the *Iliad* as a family living on Mount Olympos, most of whom take sides in the struggles going on down on earth, some (particularly Athene and Hera) favoring the Greeks, others (particularly Apollo and Aphrodite) the Trojans. Zeus, king of the gods, is impartial but knows that Troy is doomed. He is far more powerful than all the rest of the gods put together (8.18–27), but he has as much difficulty exerting his authority over them as a human father of a large family may have.

The influence of the gods on men is subtle and various, ranging from psychological encouragement to physical assistance. This is an area where it is most difficult for modern unbelievers to see their way. The gods are not mere manipulators of the plot, divine machinery used by the poet. Each acts for the most part within the scope of his or her proper function, as a kind of explanation of events. Since Homer had no concept of chance or luck, everything that is not spontaneous is thought to be the work of a god. If the Trojans push the Greeks back—a thing which Homer and his audience could not conceive as happening through superior Trojan fighting ability—then the god of war (Ares) must be on the Trojan side (5.590–95, 703–4); if a Greek hero does something really exceptional, Athene is there to assist (5.793, 22.214); if Helen goes to her husband, Paris, it is because Aphrodite persuades her (3.383–420). A good archer has received his bow from Apollo (2.827); a good hunter has been taught by Artemis (5.51). We would tend to regard this as a kind of allegory, but that is not the way it appeared to Homer or to his characters and his audience. To them the gods were just as real as the humans and were capable of physical interference which allowed no allegorical explanation. For they really believed in these gods; and we can recognize true religious feeling in the *Iliad*; for example, in the prayer of the priest in 1.36–42; in the hush that comes over the assembly when Odysseus rises to speak in 2.279 (an indication that Athene was present); and in the moral teaching in the Parable of the Prayers in 9.502–12.

A much-noted and unexpected result of the divine-human interplay in the *Iliad* is that, by comparison, the gods often appear frivolous. Life for the humans is real and earnest; the gods "live at their ease" (6.138) because they do not know disease or death. They are quite often used by the poet as light relief from the somber actions down below, as, for example, at the end of Book 1, where the bickering between Zeus and Hera on Olympos reflects the quarrel between Achilleus and Agamemnon on earth, and the book, which began with the plague and with bitter recriminations in the camp of the Achaians, ends with laughter and festivity in heaven.

Appendix D

THE "*AITHIOPIS* THEORY"

A new approach to the interpretation of Homer has come into some popularity since 1945. Certain scholars, commonly called neo-analysts, using the evidence in the *Iliad* which shows influence from other poetry, have tried to deduce the external conditions within which Homer's creative imagination was operating. The most significant names in this discussion are KAKRIDIS, SCHADEWALDT (*VHWW* 155–202), and KULLMANN. Such scholars are naturally Unitarians in their view of the composition of the *Iliad*; on the other hand, they do not suppose that it was created straight out of the poet's head. The most fruitful field for their discussion has been that part of the Trojan War story covered by the *Aithiopis*, the poem which followed the *Iliad* in the epic Cycle (see LATTIMORE 24–27). Neoanalytical scholars have pointed out that there are incidents in the *Iliad*, often showing clear signs of Homer's inventive mind, which are most easily explained as echoes of incidents known to have occurred in the *Aithiopis*. The debt could be the other way, with the *Aithiopis* imitating the *Iliad*; but in many cases it can be argued that the primary situation (such as the death of Achilleus himself) is the one outside the *Iliad*, while the situation we read in the *Iliad* is secondary.

Only the most extreme neoanalyst claims that the *Iliad* is indebted to the *Aithiopis* itself, the epic ascribed to Arktinos of Miletos (LATTIMORE 26), for it is generally accepted that the poems of the epic Cycle were put together to complete the story of the *Iliad* and the *Odyssey* and so were necessarily later; but Arktinos certainly used preexisting material for his work, and it is the preexisting legend which neoanalysts see as the immediate model of Homer.

It will be best first to tell the story of the *Aithiopis* insofar as it relates to incidents in the *Iliad* and then to detail the parallels. The chief defense of Troy after the death of Hektor was Memnon, son of the Dawn. In an incident in the battle, Memnon was about to kill the old King Nestor, whose chariot was in confusion because a horse had been shot by an arrow from Paris, when Antilochos, Nestor's son, intervened and saved his father's life at the cost of his own. There had been a close friendship between Achilleus and Antilochos, and Achilleus now took revenge for the death of his friend by killing Memnon. Immediately thereafter, Achilleus attacked the city of Troy and was killed in the Skaian gate by Paris, with the help of Apollo. There was a memorable fight for his body, which was eventually rescued by Aias and Odysseus, the former carrying it, the latter keeping off the Trojans. When the body of Achilleus was back at the ships, Thetis and the Nereids came up out of the sea to mourn, while the Muses sang the dirge. Achilleus was cremated, a funeral mound was piled, and funeral games were held. (The source for all this is primarily Proclus' summary of the contents of the Cyclic epics, but Nestor's rescue by his son Antilochos is told by Pindar in the *Sixth Pythian* 28–42, and the events at the death of Achilleus are described by Agamemnon in *Odyssey* 24.36–92.)

We may now list the main parallels in the *Iliad*:

1. The scene in Book 8, where Nestor is cut off by the shooting of one of his horses by Paris and is rescued by Diomedes (8.78–100).
2. The relationship between Achilleus and Patroklos, which, together with the revenge killing of Hektor, parallels the Achilleus/Antilochos relationship and the revenge killing of Memnon.
3. The mutual attraction between Achilleus and Antilochos, shown in incidents in the funeral games (23.555–56 n.).
4. The rescue of the body of Patroklos (see introductory note to Book 17).
5. The description of Achilleus' posture at the beginning of Book 18, the coming of his mother and the Nereids to lament, and her gesture in holding his head (see introductory note to

Book 18); also her involvement in the Greek mourning at 23.14.

6. The funeral, funeral mound, and funeral games of Patroklos in Book 23.

In addition to these main themes, there are many details which appeared in both stories, but they are exactly the kind of thing that might be due to repeated thematic composition; and this may be true of some of the above as well. Items 1, 3, and 5, however, strongly suggest that Homer had the other story in his mind when he was composing those parts of the *Iliad*. Nor is this surprising. The whole *Iliad* foreshadows the death of Achilleus; it is not strange that the circumstances of that death should be in the poet's mind. The neoanalytical argument for a connection with the *Aithiopis*, however, is deceptive. It is at least as likely that Homer himself had, on other occasions, sung the tale of Achilleus' death, and the parallels that we see in the *Iliad* are rather the result of interaction between parts of the poet's own repertoire.

Speculative though these considerations are, they are also important, for they bring us close to Homer himself, the poet of the *Iliad*; and they also show something of the method of the oral poet: composing by thematic association, in the way that his "Muse" directed him (1.1 n.).

Bibliography

The following books are referred to in the commentary by name of author only. There are brief supplementary bibliographies on the Catalogue of Ships (2.494–759 n.) and on Book 10 (see introductory note to that book).

Albracht, F. *Kampf und Kampfschilderung bei Homer.* Vol. 1, 1886. Vol. 2, 1895.

Bowra, C. M. *Tradition and Design in the Iliad.* 1930.

Cuillandre, J. *La Droite et la gauche dans les poèmes homériques.* 1943.

Delebecque, E. *Le Cheval dans l'Iliade.* 1951.

Fenik, B. *Typical Battle Scenes in the Iliad.* 1968.

Fränkel, H. *Die homerischen Gleichnisse.* 1921.

Friedrich, W.-H. *Verwundung und Tod in der Ilias.* 1956.

Hope Simpson, R., and Lazenby, J. F. *The Catalogue of the Ships in Homer's "Iliad."* 1970.

Jachmann, G. *Der homerische Schiffskatalog und die Ilias.* 1958.

Kakridis, J. T. *Homeric Researches.* 1949.

Kirk, G. S. *The Songs of Homer.* 1962.

Kullmann, W. *Die Quellen der Ilias.* 1960.

Lattimore, Richmond. *The Iliad of Homer.* 1951.

Leaf, W. *The Iliad.* Text and commentary. 2d ed. 1900–1902.

Lohmann, D. *Die Komposition der Reden in der Ilias.* 1970.

Lorimer, H. L. *Homer and the Monuments.* 1950.

Mazon, P. *Introduction à l'Iliade.* 1948.

Nilsson, M. P. *Homer and Mycenae.* 1933. Identified in text as NILSSON *HM*.

———. *The Mycenaean Origin of Greek Mythology.* 1932. Identified in text as NILSSON.

BIBLIOGRAPHY

Page, D. L. *History and the Homeric Iliad.* 1959.

Reinhardt, K. *Die Ilias und ihr Dichter.* 1961.

Schadewaldt, W. *Iliasstudien.* 2d ed., reprinted 1966. Identified in text as SCHADEWALDT.

———. *Von Homers Welt und Werk.* 3d ed. 1959. Identified in text as SCHADEWALDT *VHWW.*

Strasburger, G. *Die kleinen Kämpfer der Ilias.* 1954.

Van der Valk, M. *Researches on the Text and Scholia of the Iliad.* Vol. 1, 1963. Vol. 2, 1964.

Von der Mühll, P. *Kritisches Hypomnema zur Ilias.* 1952.

Wace, A. J. B., and Stubbings, F. H. *A Companion to Homer.* 1962.

Whitman, C. H. *Homer and the Heroic Tradition.* 1958.

Wilamowitz-Moellendorff, U. von. *Die Ilias und Homer.* 1916.

For discussion of the techniques of *oral composition*, in particular the repetition of stock formulas and stock themes, the essential works are:

Parry, Milman. *The Making of Homeric Verse.* 1971. (This book contains the collected papers of Milman Parry, originally published between 1928 and 1937, together with an important fifty-page Introduction by his son, Adam Parry.)

Lord, A. B. *The Singer of Tales.* 1960.

Index

Achaians, Argives, Danaans, 1.2
Achilleus, 1.149–71, 9.308–429,
16.60–61
Aegis, 1.202, 2.447–49, 5.738–42,
17.593–94
Agamemnon, 1.31, 1.118, 2.73–74,
4.153–54, 6.37–65, 10.69–71, Book
11, introd.
Agenor, 21.545
Aiantes, 4.273, 13.701–22
Aias, son of Oïleus, 2.527–35,
13.202–5, 14.520–22, 23.774–77
Aias, son of Telamon, 13.325,
17.722–61, 23.845–47
Aineias, 5.166, 13.459, Book 20,
introd., 20.79
Aithiopis, Appendix D
Alexandros. *See* Paris
Ambrosia, 5.777
Antenor, 2.819–23, 3.204–24, 12.93
Antilochos, 4.457, 5.565, 17.653,
23.555–56, 23.566–613
Aphrodite, 3.389–420
Apollo, 1.9, 24.758–59; Lykegenes,
4.101
Ares, 5.702, 5.831–34, 13.298–303
Argeïphontes. *See* Hermes
Argos, 1.30
Aristarchus, Appendix A
Aristeia, Book 5, introd.
Arming, 3.330–38
Artemis, 6.205
Ate, 8.236–37, 9.502–12, 19.86–87
Athene, 1.194, 4.390, 6.88, 10.245,

10.507, 22.214–77, 23.782–83,
24.28–30; Alalkomeneïs, 4.8; Atry-
tone, 2.157; Grey-eyed, 1.551;
Spoiler, 4.128; Tritogeneia, 4.515
Atreides, 1.224
Atreus, 1.7
Automedon, 9.209

Body shield, 7.219
Briseis, 1.184
Bronze, 1.371

Characterization, 8.78–100, 9.223
Chariots, 4.301–9

Danaans, 1.42
Diomedes, 4.401, Book 5, introd.,
9.693–96, 10.137–79

Epigonoi, 4.405–10, Appendix C
Erinyes (Furies), 9.454–57, 19.86–87

Fate, 2.155, 16.431–61
Folktale (or fairy-tale) motifs, 5.385–
91, 5.845, 6.160–66, 6.179–95,
9.550–99
Foreshadowing, 1.242, 5.480, 8.119,
12.110, 15.416, 16.570–76, 16.830–
54
Formulaic composition, 8.555–59,
13.389–93, 22.167–87, 23.24

Gods, 1.194, 2.279, 2.791, 4.93–103,
5.702, 14.188, 22.214–77, 22.273–

327, 23.382–97, Appendix C; gifts of the, 2.827, 4.106–11, 5.51, 7.146, 11.353, 15.441, 22.470–72
Gorgon, the, 5.738–42
Greaves, 1.17
Guest friendship, 6.215, 10.266–70

Hades, 1.3
Hecatomb, 1.65
Hektor, 8.299, 8.538–40, 12.237–38, 13.823, 15.604, 16.838–42, 18.293–94, 24.775
Helen of Argos, 2.160–61
Helle (passage of), 7.86
Hera, 1.55, 24.28–30; Ox-eyed, 1.551
Herakles, 8.362–69
Hermes, 5.385–91, 24.349; Argeï-phontes, 2.103
Honor, 1.408, 6.441, 9.308–429, 22.105
Horns (on helmet), 3.362
Horseman (as title), 9.432. *See also* Rider
Human sacrifice, 18.336–37
Humor, 4.395, 5.778, 8.80, 11.561, 11.635–36, 13.246–97, 14.1–8, 14.153–351, 14.317–28, 20.200–258, 23.201–7

Idomeneus, 13.210
Invention by the poet, 1.259–74, 1.396–406, 4.395, 6.435, 7.113–14, 7.123–60, 8.192–95, 9.254–58, 9.410–16, 9.550–99, 12.87–104, 17.24–27, 18.395–97, 20.83–85, 21.475–77, 24.599–620

Kebriones, 8.119, 8.318, 12.91, 16.727, 16.775–76
Kronos, 8.478–81; Devious-devising, 2.205

Left (of the battle), 11.498, 13.308–9
Libation, 1.471
Lykians, 2.824–27, 4.197, 5.105
Lykomedes, 17.345

Menelaos, 5.565, 7.94, 11.463, 17.570, 17.666
Meriones, 5.65–67, 17.605–25, 23.888
Milton, 1.1, 1.591–94, 2.599
Mixing bowl, 1.470
Moliones, the, 2.621, 11.708, 23.638–42
Muse, 1.1, 2.484–93, 14.508
Mythological example (*paradeigma*), 1.259–74, 4.370–400, 5.382–415, 5.800–813, 6.127–43, 9.529–99, 19.91–133, 24.599–620

Nectar, 1.598
Neoptolemos, 19.326–27, 24.765
Nestor, 1.247–48, 2.80–83, 7.325, 11.655–802, 23.629–43; Gerenian, 2.336

Ocean, 1.423–24, 5.5
Odysseus, 1.311, 2.169, 2.260, 3.193–94, 4.330, 4.349, 8.97, 10.137–79, 10.245, 11.404–10, 23.782–83; Sacker of cities, 2.278
Olympos, 1.18

Pandaros, 4.93–103, 5.192
Papyri, Appendix A
Paris, 3.59, 6.503–29; the Judgment of, 24.28–30
Patroklos, 1.307, 11.840
Patronymics, 1.7; -iades, 16.686; -ides, 1.224; -ion, 1.405
Pelasgian, 16.233–35
Peleus, 18.36, 18.84–85
Pergamos, 4.508
Poseidon, 13.10–38, 23.277–78
Poulydamas, 11.57–60, 18.243–314
Prayer form, 1.39
Priam, 22.66–76, 24.495–97
Pylos, 11.681

Repetition, 1.371–79, 2.60–70, 9.264–99, 9.693–96, 12.77
Rhapsodes, Appendix A

Rider (as title), 16.20. *See also* Horseman

Ring composition, 1.259–74, 4.370–400, 5.800–813, 6.127–43, 7.129–60, 9.529–49, 24.599–620

Sacrifice, 1.40, 1.458–66

Sarpedon, 5.480, 12.310–28, 16.419–683

Scepter, 1.234

Scholia, Appendix A

Second-person address by the poet, 16.20

Seven against Thebes, the, 4.365–400

Shakespeare, 2.478–79

Shield. *See* Body shield

Similes: clustered, 2.455–83, 11.543–73, 15.615–37, 17.722–61; details in, added for pathos, 12.433–35; double point of contact in, 11.474–81, 12.151, 13.137–42, 13.795–99; lions in, 17.63–64; trees in, 4.482, 13.651–52, 16.482–86

"Single-foot," of horses, 5.236

Stock epithets, 1.17, 1.84, 5.375

Suppliant's position, 1.407

Teukros, 4.273, 13.91, 23.859–60

Thematic composition, 9.693–96, 11.377, 16.702–9

Themis, 15.87

Thetis, 1.351, 18.36, 18.84–85

Thigh pieces, 1.40

"Three times . . . but when for a fourth," 16.702–9

Titans, 5.898, 8.478–81

Tripods, 18.373

Tydeus, 4.365–400

Uranian, of gods, 1.570, 5.898

Virgil, 1.1, 3.146–48, 5.150, 12.433–35, 16.259–65, Book 20, introd., 20.298–99, 24.257

Winged words, 1.201

Xanthos, 6.4

Zeus, 1.518–19, 2.319, 16.431–61, 22.167–87

CONCERT SOUND AND LIGHTING SYSTEMS
Second Edition
Second Edition

CONCERT SOUND AND LIGHTING SYSTEMS

Second Edition

John Vasey

Focal Press
Boston   London

Focal Press is an imprint of Butterworth–Heinemann
ℛ a member of the Reed-Elsevier group.

Library of Congress Cataloging-in-Publication Data
Vasey, John.
  Concert sound and lighting systems / John Vasey.—2nd ed.
    p. cm.
  Includes index.
  ISBN 0-240-80192-X
  1. Theaters—Electronic sound control. 2. Stage lighting.
3. Rock music. I. Title.
  TK7881.9.V37 1993
  621.389'2—dc20   93-38270
                                                       CIP

British Library Cataloguing in Publication Data
A catalogue record for this book is available from the British Library.

Butterworth–Heinemann
313 Washington Street
Newton, MA 02158–1626

10 9 8 7 6 5 4

Printed in the United States of America

CONTENTS

Preface   xi
Acknowledgments   xiii

PART I
INTRODUCTION TO CONCERT SYSTEMS   1

CHAPTER 1
Introduction to the Touring Concert   3

The Touring Party: Who's Who   3
Local Crew   4
Local Personnel   5
Your Career Path   5

CHAPTER 2
Power   7

Metering Three-Phase Power   8
Transformers   8
Laying Power Cables   10
Chain Motor Power   10
Sound-Power Distribution System   10
Ground Loops   10
Lighting-Power Distribution System   11
Generators   13

CHAPTER 3 ————————————————————
Rigging   15

Rigging of Points   15
Chain Motors   16

PART II ————————————————————
SOUND SYSTEMS   21

CHAPTER 4 ————————————————————
Speaker Systems   23

Types of Speakers   23
Stacking Speakers   24
Flying Speakers   24
Delay Systems   24
Center Clusters   25
Distributed Systems   26
Analyzing Speaker Systems   26

CHAPTER 5 ————————————————————
Power Amplifiers   33

Patching Amplifier Racks   33
Fault Finding   35
Turn On/Off Procedure   36

CHAPTER 6 ————————————————————
Multicore System   37

Signal Distribution   37
Splitter Systems   40

CHAPTER 7 ————————————————————
Drive System   41

Graphic Equalizer   41
Crossovers   41
Limiters   44
Drive Multicore Cables   44

CHAPTER 8 ————————————————————
House Mixing Consoles   47

Input Channel   47
Output   51
Talkback Module   51
Power Supply   52
Gain Structure   52

Console Care   52
Mixing   53

CHAPTER 9
Effects Units   57

Digital Delays   57
Reverberation Units   57
Musical Instrument Digital Interface System   58
Use of Effects   58

CHAPTER 10
Inserts   59

Limiters   59
Noise Gates   60

CHAPTER 11
Monitor Systems   63

Monitor Consoles   63
Monitor Speakers   65
Mix Contents   65

CHAPTER 12
Microphones and Direct Boxes   69

Types of Microphones   69
Direct Boxes   73
Microphone Placement   74

CHAPTER 13
Sound System Setup Procedure   75

Preparation   75
Setup   77
Show Time   85
Load Out   85
System Check   86

PART III
LIGHTING SYSTEMS   87

CHAPTER 14
Trusses and Grids   89

Rigging Trusses and Grids   89
Ground Supports   89
Lifting Grids   91

CHAPTER 15 ────────────────────────────────
Lamps   93

Types of Instruments   93
Hanging Lamps   96

CHAPTER 16 ────────────────────────────────
Dimmers   97

How a Dimmer Works   97
Ramps   98
Types of Dimmers   98
Dimmer Patching   99

CHAPTER 17 ────────────────────────────────
Control Cables   101

Care of Multicore Cables   102

CHAPTER 18 ────────────────────────────────
Control Consoles   105

Manual Consoles   105
Computer Consoles   105

CHAPTER 19 ────────────────────────────────
Intercom Systems   109

CHAPTER 20 ────────────────────────────────
Smoke Machines   111

Foggers   111
Dry Ice Machines   111
Pyrotechnics   112

CHAPTER 21 ────────────────────────────────
Drapes   113

Black Dressing   113
Cycloramas   113
Scrims and Gauzes   113
Screens   114
Curtain Tracks   114
Kabuki Drops   114

CHAPTER 22 ────────────────────────────────
Follow Spots   115

Operating Follow Spots   115

CHAPTER 23
Color   119

CHAPTER 24
Lighting Plots   121

Reading a Lighting Plot   121
Circuit Coding   123
Putting Together a System   123

CHAPTER 25
Lighting System Setup Procedure   129

Setup   129
Show Time   135
Load Out   135
Maintenance   135
Safety   135

APPENDIX A
Color Media Guide   137

APPENDIX B
Circuit Laws and Cable Wiring   153

APPENDIX C
Production Checklists   157

APPENDIX D
Safety Awareness   165

Further Reading   167
Glossary   169
Index   179

PREFACE

Good sound and lighting are the foundation of any concert; poor sound ruins the audience's enjoyment of the concert and poor lighting destroys the performance's dramatic impact. Good sound and lighting systems enhance a concert, create interest, and command attention. Production excellence, however, is not easy to achieve.

I wrote this book to establish a foundation for sound and lighting equipment personnel and to offer necessary information on the exceedingly diverse subjects associated with concert production. This book is intended to provide clear, practical guidance for people interested in working with today's sophisticated production technologies. It is not, however, intended to in any way replace or reduce the need for practical training.

For those of you already working in sound and lighting fields, the information in *Concert Sound and Lighting Systems* may serve as a source of reference; equipment operation is explained in detail. Because there are no fixed rules for operating sound or lighting consoles, it is not possible to include the artistic elements of operation beyond the most basic concepts. Once you learn how the equipment works, your imagination is free to realize its full potential.

If you are just beginning your career in sound and lighting, you will soon realize that the more prepared you are for a job, the easier and more enjoyable that job will be. After each show one always asks, "Could I have done better?" The answer always is, "Of course." There is always more to learn, and each show provides you with the chance to grow as you are confronted by different problems. Dedicated professionals are needed to maintain and operate today's concert equipment. In addition to the technical knowledge required to set up, operate, and maintain the equipment, you are responsible for the well-being of everyone present. The concert production environment is potentially dangerous, and any mistakes could harm the crew, the performers, or the audience. There is no room for mistakes with heavy loads suspended overhead and complex electrical equipment all around.

The larger a crew, the more complex a setup becomes. It is therefore important to work as part of a team. Many people are involved in concert production, and everyone must work together. Each person is as important to the success of the show as the next. The technical success of a show is as important as the performance. Without sound or lighting equipment, performers would be seen in a very different light and would not be heard at all. The technology has created the need for logical and artistic people to complement musical performances, thus bridging the gap between art and science to give the audience the best possible performance.

This book is divided into two main categories: sound and lighting. Before I tackle these subjects, however, I will discuss power and rigging, both of which are common to sound and lighting systems. A good understanding of power and rigging is crucial, because your life, and the lives of the crew, performers, and audience may depend on it. The sections on sound and lighting explain each component of these systems and provide an overview.

The appendixes provide electrical formulas and cable wiring information as well as a sample production checklist to illustrate the arrangements and checks for each performance. For this new edition, I have added an appendix on safety. The book concludes with a glossary of commonly used terms and a bibliography for further reading.

Setting up and maintaining touring concert systems is not simple. I hope that this book will help those workers who are starting out on the road.

ACKNOWLEDGMENTS

I wish to acknowledge all the people I have worked with over the past 16 years who have helped to prepare this book. I also wish to acknowledge all the people who keep the show on the road.

Most line drawings, photographs, and sketches were prepared by George Gorga with contributions from Phoebus Manufacturing, Shure Microphones, Yamaha Corporation, Avolites, JBL, Rosco, Vari-Lite Inc., and Jands Production Services. Additional photos were supplied by Mark Hammer and Heidi Duckworth. Lighting plot courtesy of Steve Cohen. Cover photograph by Mark Hammer courtesy of Midnight Oil.

PART I

INTRODUCTION TO CONCERT SYSTEMS

CHAPTER 1

INTRODUCTION TO THE TOURING CONCERT

The need for touring concert sound and lighting systems has increased with the demand for concert tickets. Every year there is a bigger tour than the year before, with more equipment and technology, and a larger touring staff. The venues needed to accommodate elaborate productions are usually larger, and so is the audience. Touring sound and lighting systems have developed to provide the equipment necessary for performances in large arenas. At first concert tours used available equipment designed and manufactured for theater use, but as the industry grew, specific products were developed for touring concert systems. Advancements in technology from valves to transistors to silicon chips have been part of the evolution of touring systems. This evolution will continue as performers strive to present shows that surpass previous efforts.

Most touring concert equipment for major concert tours is provided by service companies that provide both sound and lighting equipment or specialize in one or the other. Selection of a particular company depends on location, performers' artistic requirements, venue size, and, most important, budget. The budget usually dictates all decisions, so that all too often artistic requirements are trimmed to fit financial necessities. The budget is usually determined by the performers' popularity and their ability to attract an audience.

Various people are involved with concert production, each with his or her part to play on the team. A production or stage manager coordinates the crew, which is broken down into sound, lighting, and performers' crew divisions.

THE TOURING PARTY: WHO'S WHO

Performers. The performers do the show, talk to the media, and encourage people to buy their records and concert tickets.

3

Tour Manager.   The tour manager oversees travel arrangements, collects money, pays bills, and addresses problems as they arise.

Production Manager.   The production manager oversees and arranges the technical requirements and staff for the show. These requirements are documented in the contract rider that the performers' booking agent or management company sends to the show's promotor. The production manager, who has an overview of the entire production, may have a background in sound, lighting, or stage management and can coordinate the touring and local staff.

Sound Engineer.   The sound engineer operates the control console and mixes the sound the audience hears. He or she also helps set up and pack the equipment.

Monitor Engineer.   The monitor engineer operates the monitor console, which controls the sound that the performers hear on stage. He or she also helps set up and pack the equipment.

Sound Crew.   The sound crew gets the sound equipment unloaded, set up, packed, and reloaded. The crew also repairs equipment damaged in transit, but usually does not perform technical repairs.

Lighting Operator.   The lighting operator operates the control console for the lighting system artistically. He or she is usually also the lighting designer, who formulates the show's overall look and selects the type, position, and color of the lighting instruments. The lighting operator also helps set up and pack the equipment.

Lighting Crew.   The lighting crew gets the lighting equipment unloaded, set up, packed, and reloaded. This includes repairing equipment damaged in transit and changing burned-out gels and lamps.

Stage Manager.   The stage manager is usually responsible for the performers' equipment, such as drums, guitars, and keyboards. The stage manager may have assistants such as a drum roadie, a keyboard roadie, and a guitar roadie. The stage manager may also have a specific performer's equipment to deal with, for example, guitars.

Set Crew.   The size of the production may call for a crew to be responsible for risers, set pieces, flooring, and props.

Truck and Bus Drivers.   The drivers usually must drive through the night after the show has been reloaded to get to the next venue in time to start all over again.

LOCAL CREW

In addition to the touring crew, whose size depends on the amount of equipment, a local crew is required at each venue to set up and pack. The local crew is divided into the following categories:

Venue Technical Manager.   The venue technical manager arranges the necessary local staff hired by the touring production manager and specified in the contract rider.

Loaders.   The loaders unload and reload the trucks.

Stagehands.   The stagehands move the equipment into position and assist the touring crew with the setup. The stagehands may be further designated into specific areas of the production, for example, sound or lighting.

Riggers.   The riggers attach the chain motors used to lift the speakers and lights to the roof of the venue. The riggers may be divided into climbing and ground work.

Electrician.   The electrician connects the power cables for the sound and lighting equipment to the venue electricity supply. This usually involves a three-phase connection for the lighting equipment and one connection for the sound equipment. Other services depend on the production, for example, video equipment and computerized lighting system.

Runners.   The runners work under the production manager's direction as required, for example, fetching parts from the music store, collecting towels from the hotel, and buying batteries.

Forklift Driver.   The forklift driver works as directed.

Spotlight Operators.   Spotlight operators are only required at showtime to operate the follow spots. Some of the follow spots may be positioned in the lighting grid above the stage, and a good head for heights is required.

House Light Operators.   The house light operator switches the venue lighting on and off under the production manager's direction.

LOCAL PERSONNEL

Additional local people employed for a concert are as follows:

Local Promotor.   The local promotor buys the show from the booking agent representing the performers and sells the tickets to the show. The local promotor also ensures that the requirements set out in the contract rider are met. This includes local staff, dressing rooms, and catering.

Caterers.   The caterers meet the requirements of the contract rider and ensure that crew members are well fed.

Venue Staff.   The venue staff required depends on the size of venue but usually consists of ticket collectors, security, ushers, parking attendants, refreshment stall operators, and program and merchandise sellers.

YOUR CAREER PATH

Being part of the touring team requires more than technical knowledge of the equipment. You must be able to work with different local people each day and to live and travel with the touring crew. Usually a bond develops among crew members as a tour progresses, and those members who do not fit in will usually find themselves replaced by people who do.

Working and traveling with a new challenge every day can be an enjoyable way of life. The rate of pay depends on experience, competence, and track record in the industry. A traveling allowance, called a per diem, is supplied as well. The only way to get experience and climb the ladder to a better job is to start on the road once you know how to set up the equipment.

The show must run on a schedule, and the crew must be ready for work at call time. The schedule is usually worked out so that the setup can be a coordinated procedure. If people are late for their call times, the whole schedule is disrupted.

There is a career path through the ranks of a crew, from sound crew to console operator, from console operator to production manager. There is also a saying that "you are only as good as your last gig," which means that if you cannot handle the heat, get out of the kitchen.

CHAPTER 2

POWER

Power must be treated with care to avoid accidents and blown fuses. A licensed electrician should connect the power to the supply.

Available power varies among countries, but it is generally a three-phase, four-wire, 50/60 cycles per second (Hz) alternating current (AC) system. Three cables—the phases—carry 240/120 V, and one neutral cable has no voltage. The supply voltage is 120 V/ 60 Hz in the United States, 220 V/ 50 Hz in Europe, and 240 V/ 50 Hz in the United Kingdom, Australia, and New Zealand.

AC means that the voltage varies between + 240/120 and − 240/120 V at 50/60 times per second (50/60 Hz) (Figure 2–1).

The power source must be checked for fuse value and location. The amount of power the sound system requires depends on the number of power amplifiers being used. Allow 4 A per power amplifier. All the amplifiers will not draw 4 A, but if the system must reproduce transient peaks, which will draw maximum power, then the fuses should be capable of handling the demand. The current draw is proportional to the program being amplified.

The amount of power for the lighting system depends on the number of lamps and their wattage in use at any one time. Sometimes a lighting system may have more lamps than power available, so all the lamps cannot be on at once. The number of lamps on at any given moment must be within the capacity of the available power or, instead of a dramatic burst of light, there will be a blown fuse and a blackout.

Ohm's law states that current (amperes) = watts divided by volts, or power (watts) = volts multiplied by amperes.

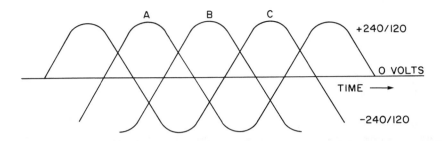

Figure 2–1.   Three-phase power. The voltage varies between + 240 V/120 V and − 240 V/120 V at 50/60 cycles per second (Hz).

METERING THREE-PHASE POWER

A three-phase power cable has five cores: three phases that carry the voltage, one neutral that has no voltage, and one earth.

Phase to neutral should read 240 V in the United Kingdom and 120 V in the United States. This could vary from 250/130 to 230/100 V depending on the distance from the supply transformer and the load on the supply.

Phase to phase should read 415 V in the United Kingdom and 208 V in the United States. Again, this will vary with the supply.

Neutral to earth should read zero. There may be a trickle voltage of 10 V maximum. The neutral and earth cores are connected at the supply; this is called a multiple earth neutral (MEN).

Phase to earth should read 240 V in the United Kingdom and 120 V in the United States. This reading will determine if there is an earth core. If there is no earth, the reading will be zero.

TRANSFORMERS

A *transformer* is an AC device for changing AC to a higher or lower value. It consists of two separated and insulated copper wire coils wound around a common soft-iron core and arranged so that electrical lines of force around one winding will pass through to the other through the iron core. There is no electrical connection in the usual sense between the two coils (Figure 2–2). One winding, called the primary, is connected to the power source. The other winding, the secondary, gives out the voltage, which depends on the number of coils. If there are 240 turns on the primary and 120 on the secondary, this would reduce 240 V to 120 V. A separate coil is necessary for each phase. It is common to have several taps on the secondary to give a selection of voltages (Figure 2–3). Transformers get very hot when they are under load and should be situated in a well-ventilated area.

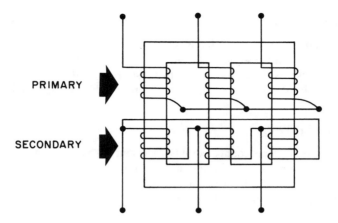

Figure 2–2. Three-phase transformer. No electrical connection exists between the primary and secondary transformer windings.

Figure 2–3. Three-phase transformer. These are the various taps available for a suitable secondary voltage.

LAYING POWER CABLES

Because power cables carry large currents, there is a magnetic field around them that can cause hum in audio cables. Power cables should never be left in coils while under load as this causes inductance that results in a buildup of heat and possibly a melted cable. Power cables should cross audio cables at right angles.

CHAIN MOTOR POWER

When motor power is connected, it is important to check that the phasing is correct and the motor goes up when the up button is pressed and down when the down button is pressed. The limit switches in the motor, which stop the motor a few links from the hook, depend on the phases' being in the right order.

SOUND-POWER DISTRIBUTION SYSTEM

A power distribution system is needed to distribute the power from the main building supply or generator. The system must be protected by fuses or breakers at each connection. If a supply fuse blows, switch off all the amplifier racks before restoring the fuse as the surge of power may blow fuses or breakers in the distribution system. Most of the electricity goes to the power amplifiers (Figure 2–4).

Loading a Three-Phase Distribution System

All three phases must be loaded as evenly as possible. The front of house (FOH) control, monitor system, and musicians' equipment must be on the same phase because a fault between an instrument and sound equipment on different phases could cause a potential difference of 415/208 V, death to anyone in its path.

Power amplifiers are loaded on phases one and two, and the monitor system, instruments, and FOH control are loaded on the third phase. If a separate power source is used for the musicians' equipment, it must be checked to ensure that it is on the same phase as the monitors and FOH. A meter reading of 415/208 V measured between active on instrument power and active on monitor power shows that they do not share the same phase. When they are on the same phase, the reading is zero. It may be necessary to load the third phase with amplifier racks to balance the load between the phases on larger systems.

GROUND LOOPS

Ground loops are caused when the ground wiring of two or more components loop from one to another, either through signal cables or when the chassis of a piece of equipment finds a second ground, such as a scaffold pipe. The induced radio frequency (RF) and power line hum cause a hum that is amplified with the signal. Instead of going directly to earth and disappearing, the noise currents travel along paths not intended for signal and which then modulate it (Figure 2–5).

The likelihood of ground loops is greatly reduced by using balanced lines. The

Figure 2–4. Sound-power distribution board. The distribution board is used to route the supplied electricity to wherever it is required on the stage. Most of the electricity is needed for the power amplifiers.

balanced signal line does not use the shield of the cable for any signal, and the shield is not connected to mains ground when it passes through the balancing transformer.

Under no circumstances should the mains ground be removed from any piece of equipment because it is there to prevent potential shocks. Although removing it may appear to solve the hum, it is a potentially dangerous solution. Removing the mains ground relies on the signal cable to provide a ground, a very dangerous practice.

LIGHTING-POWER DISTRIBUTION SYSTEM

A distribution system is required to distribute the power from the main building power supply or generator. The distribution system should isolate each dimmer rack and also provide outlets for chain motor power, smoke machines, console,

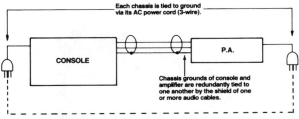

The ground path between the two AC plugs provides a redundant ground (ground loop) since the audio cable shield(s) already does the job.

A typical sound system ground loop caused by redundant audio shield and AC mains ground paths.

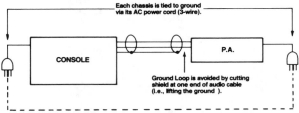

Dual ground path provided by AC cords does not create ground loop since the two chassis are not grounded redundantly via cable shield.

Elimination of the typical ground loop by cutting the shield of the audio cable retains AC safety.

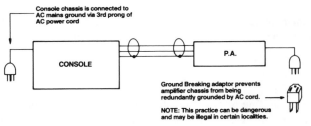

One way to eliminate ground loops is to break the AC ground on one or more pieces of sound equipment, although the practice is not recommended.

Figure 2–5.   Typical ground loops in a sound system. (Courtesy Yamaha Music.)

fans, and so on. Each point of distribution should be protected by a fuse or circuit breaker. When any connections are made, turn off the supply to the outlet being connected to avoid any arcing between plug and socket. Such arcing would burn the connectors and is extremely dangerous.

GENERATORS

A *generator* is a diesel engine that produces electricity. Generators used for powering sound and lighting systems should be in excellent working order and capable of constantly varying loads. A generator may stall if suddenly asked to deliver maximum power at an instant if it is not running properly, the last thing anyone wants during a performance.

CHAPTER 3

RIGGING

Rigging is a specialized field that requires a great deal of practical and theoretical knowledge. A qualified rigger is legally required in most parts of the world to rig the points for attachment of the chain motors.

RIGGING OF POINTS

To rig the points in suitable positions, the rigger must first know how to make up bridles on the ground. For example, in a venue with rigging beams 15 feet apart and 60 feet above the floor and a stage 6 feet high, at least 30 feet of clearance is required between the stage and the motor hook. Under these conditions, the point must be at least 36 feet above the ground, which is 24 feet below the beams and at least 5 feet away from the nearest beam. The bridle must be made up with one 20 foot wire attached to a spanset, chain, or wire, to wrap around the roof beam, and a 15 foot wire, again with a spanset, chain, or wire, to wrap the beam. At the point where the 20 foot wire and the 15 foot wire meet, the chain motor hook attaches. At the end of each wire there should be a bow shackle. A third bow shackle joins the motor hook onto the wires (Figure 3–1).

It is vital to check all rigging equipment thoroughly before it is used. As the wires are hoisted into the roof, they must be checked to ensure that they are sitting correctly in the shackles. Wire ropes should be checked for any broken strands, since once one goes the rest could easily follow. Do not use kinked wires. In fact, do not use any piece of rigging equipment that does not look up to par. Hessian sacks can be used to protect slings from the rough edges of roof beams.

The desired position of the point should be chalked on the floor as a circle with an X in it about a foot wide, making it easy for the riggers to see it from the roof.

Figure 3–1.   A bridled point. Bridling is often necessary to place the points in optimum position.

Obviously, if points are available with a straight drop, that is far easier than rigging bridled points. It is not generally known that reeving (choking) a sling around an object with one eye through the other will halve the safe working load of the sling (Figure 3–2).

CHAIN MOTORS

The chains on the motors must be inspected each time they are rigged. Two ton motors must be checked for any twisted links by running the block the whole length of the chain. The chain can easily become twisted in transit, and when the motor is taken to its maximum height a twisted link could jam or shear, obviously with disastrous results. A twisted chain causes a lot of additional friction as it passes through the block.

The most fragile part of the chain motor is the contactor, which switches the motor on and off. The terminals of the contactor can become burnt by continuous clicking on and off, so it is advisable to keep the motor going once it is under load. The power supply for the chain motors must be phased correctly so that the motor moves up when the up button is depressed. If the phasing is incorrect, the safety limit switches in the motor will not work. The limit switches are set to make sure that the motor does not run into the hook but stops a few links from it.

The person operating the motors must ensure that no one is standing under a load being raised or lowered. Common sense must be of paramount concern, since taking chances with rigging is taking chances with lives. Also, learn how to tie knots correctly (Figure 3–3).

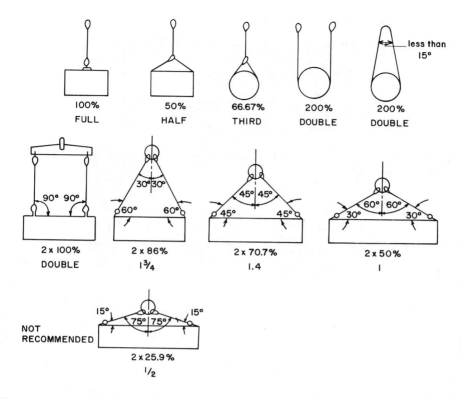

100%	50%	66.67%	200%	200%
FULL	HALF	THIRD	DOUBLE	DOUBLE

less than 15°

90° 90°	30° 30° 60° 60°	45° 45° 45° 45°	60° 60° 30° 30°
2 x 100% DOUBLE	2 x 86% 1¾	2 x 70.7% 1.4	2 x 50% 1

NOT RECOMMENDED

15° 75° 75° 15°

2 x 25.9% ½

Figure 3–2. Methods of slinging. These are variations in the loads imposed on the slings. (Courtesy Department of Industrial Relations of New South Wales.)

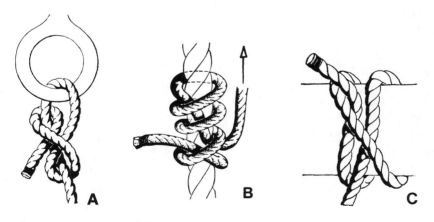

A   B   C

Figure 3–3. Useful knots. Learn how to tie knots correctly, or have someone experienced tie them. Do not take chances. (A) To secure ends of tackles to beckets, the *buntline* or *becket hitch* is foolproof; it cannot come undone like half hitches. (B) To secure stopper, or two ropes pulling in opposite directions, the *rolling hitch* is safe and very useful. It is preferable to a clove or blackwall hitch, provided rolling turns are put on in proper direction of pull. (C) The *clove hitch* is used to commence rope lashings. It is not safe for other purposes unless ends are secured with additional half hitches. (Courtesy Department of Industrial Relations of New South Wales.)

17

RED	=	5 FEET
WHITE	=	IO FEET
BLUE	=	20 FEET

Figure 3–4. Wire-rope color code. Wires are color coded so that their length can be easily identified for quick and efficient setup.

SAFE LOADS OF STEEL WIRE ROPE SLINGS
WIRE ROPE OF G1570 GRADE

Rope Diameter	mm	SINGLE SLING OR SNOTTER	NIP OR REEVABLE SLING SQUARED LOADS	ROUND LOADS	2 LEG SLINGS AND UNEQUALLY LOADED 3 OR 4 LEG SLINGS 30°	60°	90°	4 LEG SLING - Flexible Loads Only
				Safe Working Load—Kilograms or Tonnes				
6 x 24 (15/9/F) FIBRE CORE	5	220	110	160	420	380	310	620
	6	320	160	240	620	550	450	900
	7	440	220	330	850	760	620	1.2
	8	580	290	430	1.1	1.0	820	1.6
	9	730	360	540	1.4	1.2	1.0	2.0
	10	900	450	670	1.7	1.5	1.2	2.5
	11	1.1	540	810	2.1	1.9	1.5	3.0
	12	1.3	650	970	2.5	2.2	1.8	3.6
	13	1.5	750	1.1	2.9	2.6	2.1	4.2
	14	1.8	880	1.3	3.4	3.0	2.5	5.0
	16	2.3	1.1	1.7	4.4	4.0	3.2	6.5
	18	2.9	1.4	2.2	5.6	5.0	4.1	8.2
	20	3.6	1.8	2.7	6.9	6.2	5.0	10.1
	22	4.3	2.2	3.2	8.3	7.5	6.1	12.2
	24	5.2	2.6	3.9	10.0	8.9	7.3	14.5
	26	6.0	3.0	4.5	11.7	10.4	8.5	17.0
	28	7.0	3.5	5.3	13.6	12.1	9.9	19.8
	32	9.2	4.6	6.9	17.7	15.9	12.9	25.8
6 x 37 (18/12/6/1) FIBRE CORE	36	12.2	6.1	9.1	23.5	21.1	17.2	34.4
	40	15.1	7.5	11.3	29.1	26.1	21.2	42.5
	44	18.2	9.1	13.6	35.1	31.4	25.6	51.2
	48	21.8	10.9	16.3	42.0	37.7	30.7	61.5
	52	25.4	12.7	19.0	49.0	43.9	35.8	71.5
	56	29.5	14.7	22.1	57.0	51.0	41.5	83.0
	60	34.6	17.3	25.9	66.8	60.0	48.8	97.5
Load factor		1.0	0.5	0.75	1.93	1.73	1.41	2.82

Note: Safe Loads for *Heavy Duty or Rough Usage* shall be reduced to 4/5ths of the above values.
A handy rule to remember—To find the Safe Load of a Wire Rope (in kilograms)—Used as a Single Sling: Square the rope diameter and multiply by 8.
Example—20 mm diameter rope. Safe Load is 20 x 20 x 8 = 3200 kg =.3.2 tonne.
This table is based on Regulation 144 (2) of the Construction Safety Act and Australian Standard AS 1666-1976.

Figure 3–5. Safe loads of steel wire–rope slings. Reductions in capacity depend on application. (Courtesy Department of Industrial Relations of New South Wales.)

VIOLET	=	I TON
GREEN	=	2 TON
LIME	=	3 TON

Figure 3–6.   Spanset color code. Spansets are color coded for their load capacity. This capacity is reduced depending on the method of slinging.

Wire ropes should be color coded for length so that each sling can be readily identified (Figure 3–4). It is important to understand how much the safe working load of wire rope slings is derated in various applications (Figure 3–5).

Spansets, made from loops of nylon, are color coded for their safe working load (Figure 3–6). Their lightweight properties give them many advantages over chains or wire ropes, but unlike chains and wire ropes they are not fire resistant, necessitating additional care.

PART II

SOUND SYSTEMS

CHAPTER 4

SPEAKER SYSTEMS

Several different types of speaker systems are in use, each with its own characteristics that must be taken into consideration during flying and stacking.

Environment dictates how the speakers should be used to obtain the best results. Sometimes it may be necessary to get as much power from the speakers as possible by taking advantage of acoustic coupling. Other situations may require maximum dispersion of the cabinets. A cabinet's dispersion characteristics are normally governed by the dispersion characteristics of the mid- and high-frequency bands because the lower frequencies are omnidirectional.

TYPES OF SPEAKERS

A multitude of speaker cabinets designed for all types of sound reenforcement are available. The most common types of cabinets used for concert sound reenforcement are three-way active cabinets. Each cabinet is divided into three distinct parts that are driven by different signals.

1. *Low band.* The low band of the cabinet is for the lower frequencies, typically from 0 to 250 Hz. The designs of the low chambers vary a great deal and use either 18- or 15-inch speakers, loaded in either a folded horn or reflex ported design.

2. *Mid band.* The range of the mid band varies among cabinets. Some designs use a front-loaded horn design or infinite baffle; others use a front-loaded horn with phase plugs. Mid speakers are either 10 or 12 inches, and they cover frequency ranges from 250 to 1200 Hz. Cabinets that use phase plugs have a wider frequency response, anywhere up to 4000 Hz.

3. *High band.* The components that cover the higher frequencies are horns with compression drivers. The compression drivers use an alloy or titanium diaphragm to provide fidelity and extended high-frequency response. The frequency range of the high-band section depends on the crossover point of the mid band. The high band generally runs from mid-band crossover frequency all the way up. Exceptions to this use tweeters for the ultrahigh frequencies.

In addition to three-way active cabinets, sub-low cabinets are sometimes used. Their frequency range is generally 0 to 63 Hz.

STACKING SPEAKERS

Speakers should be situated to provide good, even coverage to the audience with minimum obstruction. When stacking a speaker system, make sure the deck is solid and level. Often a scaffold that appears to be solid and level sinks or bends with the concentrated weight of a speaker system, causing the speaker stack to lean. The scaffolding should be inspected before, during, and after stacking to ensure its safety. The speaker stacks for outdoor concerts must be secured so that they cannot blow over. Sub-low cabinets should be stacked directly on the floor so that the cabinet can couple with the ground. Other speaker cabinets should be above head height so that the sound from the cabinets can disperse.

FLYING SPEAKERS

Speakers are flown to provide wide coverage with no sight line obstructions of the stage in arena-style venues. They are also flown to provide front row sound for people seated in the balconies. Most modern speaker cabinet designs incorporate flying hardware. Positioning cabinets in a flown array depends on where people are seated (Figure 4–1).

DELAY SYSTEMS

Use

Delay systems are used to maintain clarity and level over a large area. Although a large number of cabinets can be used for power, after a certain distance clarity is lost. In some indoor venues where there is a great deal of reverberation, the reverberant signal may make the amplified signal unintelligable in the higher frequencies, necessitating additional horns to maintain clarity. The delay system must blend in with the sound from the main system, and not sound like a separate system. The audience should only hear a loud and clear sound that appears to come from the stage area.

Figure 4–1.   Flown speakers. Speakers are flown to provide wide coverage with no sight line obstruction.

Setting Delay Time

The equation for setting the amount of delay time to a delay system is the distance in meters divided by 340 and multiplied by 1000, which equals the time in milliseconds. Measure the response of the main system at the delay system position first, then tune the delay system to bring up the overall response to equal that of the main system. Often this means that minimal or low frequencies are not required. The average speed of sound is 340 meters per second, which increases with heat and humidity. The actual speed depends on atmospheric pressure and air density, so that the equation provides only a rough estimate. Once the rough time is set it can be tuned exactly by using a pulse, that is, a single click, and setting the time so that the click appears to come from the main speaker stacks.

CENTER CLUSTERS

Center clusters are sometimes flown between stereo clusters to achieve powerful, even coverage of a venue. A center cluster can be used exclusively for vocals so that the audience hears the voices as coming from between the stereo clusters.

DISTRIBUTED SYSTEMS

A distributed system is used for low-level amplification to a large number of people. The distributed sources of sound should be placed at specified distances and on the same arc so that they can share a common signal, which is delayed for each arc of cabinets. Every source of sound requires individual level control so that it can be adjusted to suit the surrounding area. This can be done by adjusting either the amplifiers or the relevant crossovers.

ANALYZING SPEAKER SYSTEMS

A spectrum analyzer measures the whole spectrum of sound as a person hears it, and displays it on a series of light-emitting diodes (LEDs) that match the layout of a graphic equalizer. Analyzer response must be set to suit each application. For reading a musical program, a fast attack and slow decay is suitable; for acoustic measurements with pink noise, a slow attack and slow decay is best. Divisions of the audio spectrum are shown in Figure 4–2.

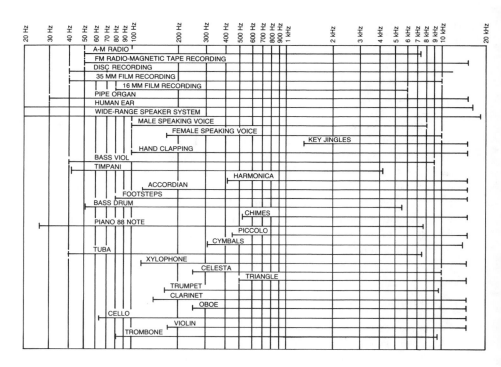

Figure 4–2. Divisions of the audio spectrum.

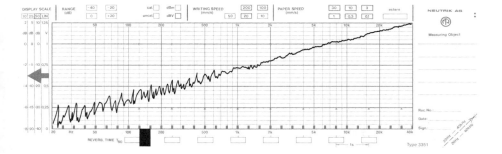

Figure 4–3. White noise. White noise has equal energy in each frequency band according to a linear scale and therefore has a rising response on a logarithmic scale.

Pink Noise

To measure a speaker system's performance with an analyzer, a source of sound, pink noise, is required. Pink noise is noise with equal amounts of energy in all frequencies that has been passed through a filter to bring the energy to the level heard by the human ear (Figures 4–3 to 4–8).

Using the Analyzer

Sound varies among the thousands of seats in an auditorium. The speakers should be positioned to give as uniform a response as possible, and the crossovers should be set before the equalizer is touched. To analyze the speaker system without room interference, the measurement microphone should be positioned one and one-half times the height of the speaker stack, although sometimes this is not practical. Most clubs and concert halls have a very live sound because their large number of reflective surfaces improves room gain. In large halls this gain can be as much as 30 dB but is not uniform. The high frequencies are attenuated more than the low

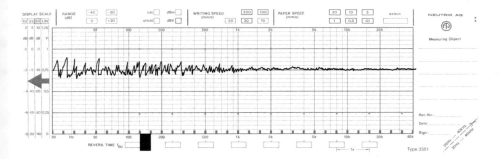

Figure 4–4. Pink noise. Pink noise has a flat response when the spectrum is divided according to the way the ear hears (logarithmically) and is therefore used in acoustic measurements.

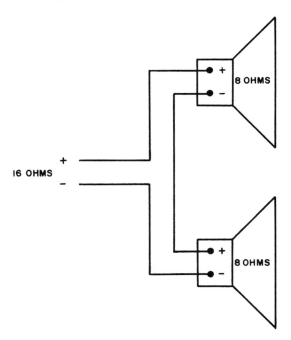

Figure 4–5. Speakers wired in series. Speakers and drivers are wired in series to match imped-ance to the type of amplifier being used.

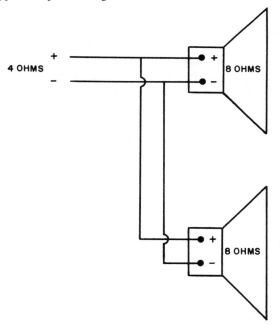

Figure 4–6. Speakers wired in parallel. Speakers and drivers are wired in parallel to match impedance to the type of amplifier being used. In some cases, two pairs of speakers are wired in series and each pair is wired in parallel to match the impedance for optimum use of available amplifier power.

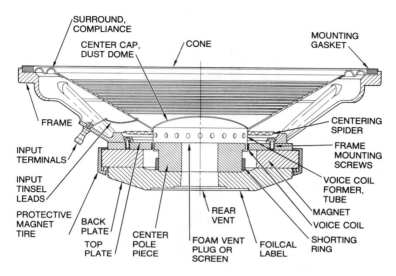

Figure 4–7.   Cross section of a speaker, showing arrangement of speaker parts. (Courtesy JBL Professional.)

frequencies by molecular air absorption. Analyzing at the back wall will naturally show a loss of high frequencies, and trying to equalize them back in would make the sound painful everywhere else in the room. The initial measurement should be near to and in front of the speaker stack and then at various positions in the room to give an overall view of the necessary adjustments that must be made (Figure 4–9).

Some hints for using the analyzer are as follows:

1.   Try to maintain the average curve of equalization around the zero mark and generally cut obtrusive peaks rather than boost all others to preserve headroom in the system.

2.   In stereo systems, no matter how much equalization is required, avoid boosting a particular frequency or band of frequencies on one channel and cutting the same frequencies on the other channel. No matter how much the frequency response has improved, a considerable phase shift has been introduced that will also create a noticeable image shift.

3.   Try to avoid sharp response changes. Compromise by setting one frequency at 0 and the adjacent frequencies at −2 rather than at +2 and −4. Carry a tape of a piece of music you know well and use this as the final judge of the system's response to the music.

If you are equalizing a room and the analyzer shows a marked deviation from flat, that is, more than 5 dB, moving the speakers or the listening position may be the answer rather than destroying the overall equipment response. The measure-

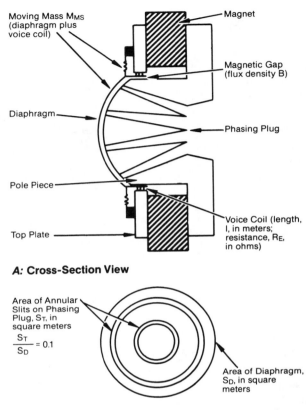

Figure 4–8.   Cross section of a compression driver showing arrangement of high-frequency horn driver parts. (Courtesy JBL Professional.)

ment microphone may have ended up at a node or antinode, that is, at a point of minimum or maximum pressure at a low frequency. The measurement microphone sums the acoustic energy from the speakers and the reflected sound from the room surfaces. That summation can cause a peak or a dip by cancellation, and the resultant curve is a disaster. Fortunately the ear is not as clinical as the analyzer and generally misses the aberrations in sound that it does not want to hear, so set the analyzer to an intelligent compromise between what the analyzer says and what the ear wants to hear.

At one-night gigs, where time is limited, place the measuring microphone in a central position and put the pink noise through each stack and through a check at the mixing position. The farther back you get, the more reverberation and the less direct sound you receive. A drop in high frequencies due to absorption, and a huge

Figure 4–9.   Spectrum analyzer. This unit measures the entire spectrum of sound as one hears it and displays it on a series of light-emitting diodes (LEDs).

rise in lower frequencies from the back wall also occur. Take all these variables into account when selecting a mixing position. Finally, after equalizing for a flat response, make subtle changes to make it sound right, since music is highly subjective and spectrum analyzers do not always share your taste.

CHAPTER 5

POWER AMPLIFIERS

The input for power amplifiers comes from the mixing console, usually through graphic equalizers, crossovers, and limiters. This signal is then amplified to drive the speakers. All power amplifiers perform the same function but have different power capacities and features such as visual output displays and ampere status warnings for shorts or direct current (DC) voltage on the output. The input voltage of an amplifier varies between 1 and 1.75 V root mean square (RMS). The maximum input voltage must be applied to the input to get maximum amplifier power. Amplifier output requires a heavy-duty cable to deliver the signal to the speakers. The cable must be capable of taking high currents to ensure a minimum of voltage drop and full power to the speakers. The harder an amplifier works, the hotter it gets, and cooling is thus critical. Dust buildup in an amplifier will restrict airflow and cause the amplifier to overheat. Amplifiers with thermal protection will switch off, but those without protection will develop faults. Figure 5–1 shows an amplifier with its lid removed.

PATCHING AMPLIFIER RACKS

Most power amplifiers have two channels, a left and a right. To drive three-way active speaker systems, the amplifiers should be installed in racks to minimize the wiring needed to connect them to the input signals, the power supply, and the speakers. The input signal assigned to an amplifier determines the speaker component connected to the output. Signal and speaker cables are coded with numbers: 1, low; 2, mid; 3, high. The number of speaker components connected to an amplifier channel depends on the ohmage of the speaker components and the way they are wired. Speakers can be wired in series or parallel (see Chapter 4). The total

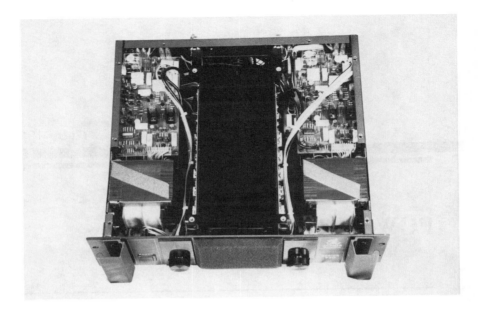

Figure 5–1.   An amplifier with lid removed. Many different power amplifiers are available.

resistance of speakers wired in series is calculated by adding the value of each speaker. The resistance of speakers wired in parallel is a little more difficult to calculate. For instance, for two speakers wired in parallel, the value of each speaker is multiplied and then divided by the sum of the two values added together. A speaker cabinet with two 8 ohm speakers wired in series would put a load of 16 ohms on an amplifier. A cabinet with two 8 ohm speakers wired in parallel would put a load of 4 ohms on an amplifier. The amount of power that an amplifier delivers depends on output load. The lower the speakers' resistance (ohms), the higher the output power (watts), and the greater the amplifier's power, the cleaner the sound.

A rack of four two-channel amplifiers used to drive four speaker cabinets assigns four channels to low frequencies, with each channel driving a 4 ohm load (two 8 ohm speakers wired in parallel). Two channels are assigned to drive the mid-range speaker components (a 4 ohm load). Each amplifier channel assigned to mid-range components drives two cabinets, each containing two 16 ohm speakers wired in parallel (8 ohms). The two cabinets connected in parallel reduces the load to 4 ohms. The high frequencies are reproduced by compression drivers, typically 16 ohms, with two in parallel for an 8 ohm load. Compression drivers designed to reproduce only the higher frequencies, and low-frequency signals will quickly destroy a compression driver's diaphragm. High-frequency drivers do not require as much power as speakers for the lower frequencies. Two

Figure 5–2. Racks of amplifiers. Amplifiers are installed in racks to minimize the wiring necessary to connect them.

drivers on each amplifier channel with a load of 8 ohms will reduce amplifier output power (Figure 5–2).

Power amplifiers are usually set with the volume full up, with most level adjustments being made by the electronics controlling the system. Sometimes certain cabinets may need to be turned down by the volume controls on the amplifiers. The amplifiers are the last components to be switched on in the signal path and the first to be switched off because any electronics in the chain that are powered up while connected in line will cause a loud, possibly damaging, click through the speakers (Figure 5–3).

FAULT FINDING

Following is a checking procedure to isolate a problem in a system and determine whether a speaker component or an amplifier is faulty:

First, disconnect the speaker cable. Test the speaker cable with the known working amplifier channel, making sure the amplifier channel is turned down when you are connecting and disconnecting speakers. If the speaker is faulty, the amplifier may have gone DC. Check amplifier fuses and replace if blown. Do not reconnect the speaker cable yet. If the fuse has blown with no load attached to the output, the amplifier has probably blown power transistors and may therefore

Figure 5–3.   Rear panel of an amplifier.

produce a DC output. If an amplifier goes DC, it means that the rail voltage of approximately 90 V DC goes straight to the output. This voltage destroys speakers. A reading of more than 0.5 V DC on the output of an amplifier indicates it has gone DC. Some amplifiers have a DC protection circuit that disconnects the output if a DC voltage appears at the output. Finally, if the amplifier requires repair by a technician, the rack may be repatched to accommodate all the components by connecting all four high-frequency drivers into one channel. The now available channel can be repatched with the input and output from the faulty channel.

TURN ON/OFF PROCEDURE

The correct turn on/off procedure is as follows: First, check that volume controls are down and amplifiers are switched off. Turn on power to the rack. Check if rack fans are on. Some amplifiers are built with fans, and others need fans installed in the racks to keep them cool. Turn on the amplifier power switch and check if amplifier fans are working. Finally, turn volume controls up. Check each signal and amplifier channel to isolate any problems.

CHAPTER 6

MULTICORE SYSTEM

The multicore cables are used to distribute the microphone input lines and the crossover outputs to desired points in the sound system. These cables are referred to as *snakes, trunks,* or, more commonly, *multicores.*

SIGNAL DISTRIBUTION

The microphone inputs are plugged into an input box that connects to a splitter, in which each line is split to two different outputs. One output connects to the front of house (FOH) console, the other to the monitor console (Figure 6–1). The cables used to connect the microphone inputs to the FOH console are tinned copper pairs, each pair individually shielded with aluminum-polyester and stranded tinned copper drain wire. The most common cable used is Belden 8769 with 19 pairs or 8773 with 27 pairs. Various connectors are available to connect the multiway cables to the input box, splitter box, and consoles. All multipin connectors are delicate and must be handled with extreme care. Each connector has a locating arrangement that permits it to mate in one way only. Forcing the connection could damage the connectors and pins. The most suitable type of pins are gold coated and do not tarnish (see Figure 6–1 and 6–2).

When a microphone is connected to the FOH console and the monitor console through the multicore system, it lowers the input gain. If the line is disconnected from one of the consoles, gain increases to the console that remains connected. Condensor microphones and direct boxes, which require phantom power, should not be disconnected when their control channels are on, since this will cause a loud click that can damage the speaker system. Before any microphones or direct boxes are connected, both consoles should have the relevant channels muted. Separate

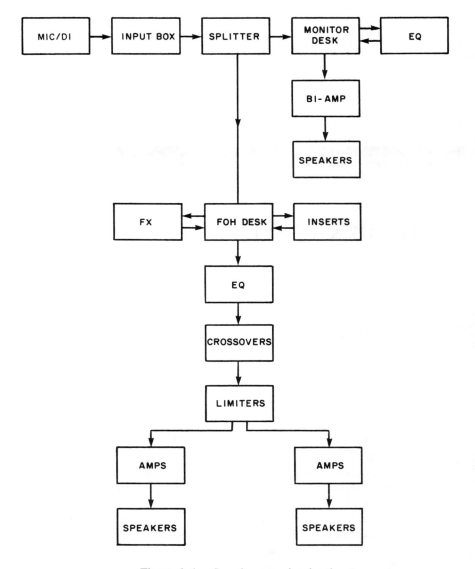

Figure 6–1. Sound system signal path.

multicore cables should be used to distribute the crossover outputs to the amplifiers to reduce the possibility of crosstalk between the low-level microphone
inputs and the high-level crossover outputs. The cable most commonly used is
Belden 8778, which has six pairs individually shielded.

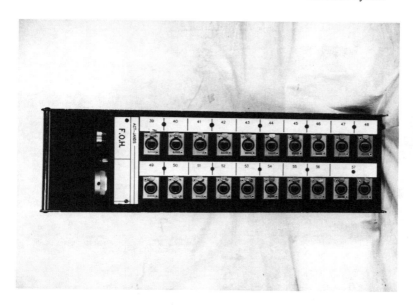

Figure 6–2. Multiway input box. This box terminates the multiway cable to a series of connectors that accept the signal inputs, e.g., microphones and direct boxes.

Figure 6–3. Multiway splitter box. These boxes are sometimes fitted with transformers to isolate the front of house and monitor consoles and provide an isolated split for a mobile recording.

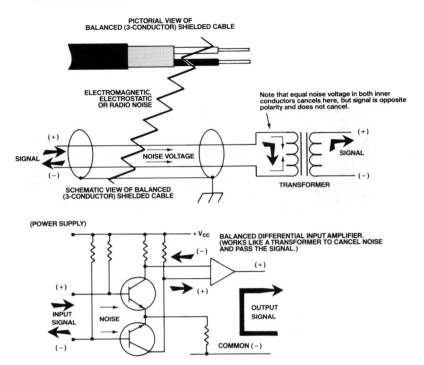

Figure 6–4. Noise rejection in a balanced line. The radio frequency interference (RFI) cuts across both conductors, inducing equal voltages in the same direction. These voltages "meet" in the differential amplifier (or transformer) and cancel out, while the signals generated by the microphone flow in opposite directions in each conductor, and hence do not cancel out. Theoretically, in a perfectly balanced system, only the desired signal gets through the differential amplifier or transformer. (Courtesy Yamaha Music.)

SPLITTER SYSTEMS

Splitter boxes can be fitted with transformers to isolate the FOH and monitor consoles and provide an isolated split for a mobile recording facility. Phantom power will not pass through an audio transformer. Some splitter systems use transformers to isolate the FOH and monitor consoles so that there will be no interference between consoles, and gain reduction will be minimal. These systems will not pass phantom power and require an external source of phantom power for condensor microphones and direct boxes. Transformer splitter systems designed for use with mobile recording facilities use the transformers to isolate the signal sent to the recording facility, which allows the FOH and monitor consoles to be unaffected by the console in the recording facility (Figures 6–3 and 6–4).

CHAPTER 7

DRIVE SYSTEM

The drive system consists of the audio components in the audio chain, which drive the amplifiers once the signal has left the mixing console (Figure 7–1).

GRAPHIC EQUALIZER

This unit consists of 27 potentiometers (pots) or faders that are on third-octave centers from 40 to 16,000 Hz (16 kHz). These controls enable the sound system to be tuned to suit a given environment. Tuning is a subjective operation that requires considerable experience and skill. Listen closely to any equalizing with an analyzer and let your ears be the final judge. Each side of a stereo sound system requires a graphic equalizer, and it is the first component in the drive chain (Figure 7–2).

The digital graphic equalizer offers the facility to store and recall settings. The use of digital equalizers makes the whole process of system equalization more efficient by allowing quick comparisons between settings.

CROSSOVERS

The crossover, or frequency dividing system, divides the signal into two, three, or four separate bandwidths. The crossover allows control of the level fed to the amplifiers which drive the low frequencies, mid frequencies, and high frequencies respectively. A fourth bandwidth may be acquired for sub-low octaves. The crossover frequencies depend on the type of speaker system. The slope between each frequency band at the crossover point is generally 24 dB per octave.

Figure 7–1.   Drive rack.

The crossover points on a three-way active speaker system using additional sub-low cabinets would have the following bandwidths:

1. Sub-low cabinets, 20 to 63 Hz. The sub-low cabinets can be used as part of the entire speaker system and tuned with the other frequency bands or used independently with signal fed from an auxillary send from the mixing console. When the sub-low cabinets are used as part of the entire speaker system, some crossover units feed a mono sum of the left and right stereo inputs.
2. Low-frequency bandwidth, 20 to 250 Hz.
3. Mid-frequency bandwidth, 250 to 1200 Hz. The mid-frequency band varies depending on the type of mid-range cabinets. The range of the mid band may vary between 250 and 1000 Hz to 250 and 4000 Hz.
4. High-frequency bandwidth, 1200 Hz and up. The crossover point of the mid range determines the high-frequency crossover point.

Some crossover units have phase correction and can correct phase errors that occur in the loudspeakers and cabinets. Phase alignment should commence at the

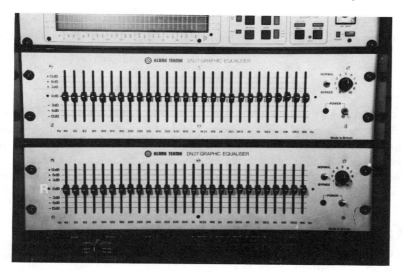

Figure 7–2. Graphic equalizer. This enables the sound system to be tuned to suit the environment.

highest frequency band; all other frequency bands should be adjusted in sequence from highest to lowest. If after an initial adjustment further adjustments are needed on any frequency band, all lower bands then require adjustment to compensate. To set phase alignment accurately, use an analyzer to provide a pictorial view of the crossover regions and set phase controls for the flattest response. A sine wave from

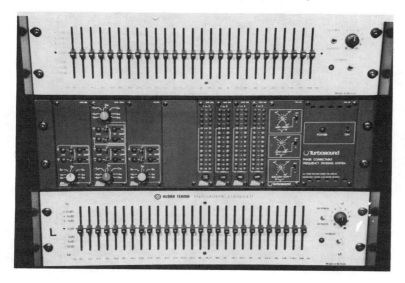

Figure 7–3. Crossovers. These divide the signal into two, three, or four separate bandwidths.

a signal generator at each crossover point can be used. Alter the phase control for minimum volume, then switch the polarity switch to invert one of the outputs to achieve a true summation (Figure 7–3).

LIMITERS

After the signal leaves the crossover it passes through a limiter, a device that limits the amount of signal reaching the amplifiers to avoid distortion or damage. The limiter's threshold is set to the input voltage of the amplifiers being driven, and the ratio should be infinite for maximum protection. Some crossovers are equipped with limiters inserted halfway through the filter network to avoid frequency shifting problems associated with the more normal end of line limiting.

DRIVE MULTICORE CABLES

Drive multicore cables distribute the outputs of the drive system to the amplifiers. Figure 7–4 illustrates the rear of a drive rack. Generally there is a multicore cable

Figure 7–4.   Rear of a drive rack. Drive cables connect to the rack with multipin connectors.

for each side of a stereo system. Because all the multiway cables are strapped together, the drive cables end up on one side of the system, usually based on where the monitor console is situated. A cross-stage drive cable distributes the signal to the amplifiers on the opposite side. The common standard of drive-cable color coding is white for the left side and red for the right side.

CHAPTER 8

HOUSE MIXING CONSOLES

The several different types of front of house (FOH) mixing consoles all perform the same basic function—to control the level, tone, and output designation of all console inputs (microphones, effects, tapes)—and follow similar signal paths. The more sophisticated a console, the more functions it can perform and the more facilities it has available for complex applications (Figure 8–1).

INPUT CHANNEL

Below is a step-by-step explanation of all functions found on an input channel in the order the signal follows.

Input

The input is connected through an XLR female socket on the rear panel of most consoles. This can be a microphone or direct box connected to a multicore line, a tape machine, or effect return.

Microphone/Line Switch

This switch selects between a low impedance input such as a microphone or direct box or a high-level, line-level input such as a tape machine or effects return.

Input Gain

Input gain controls the amount of level the channel accepts. These controls can be a fully variable pot or a switch with several fixed values.

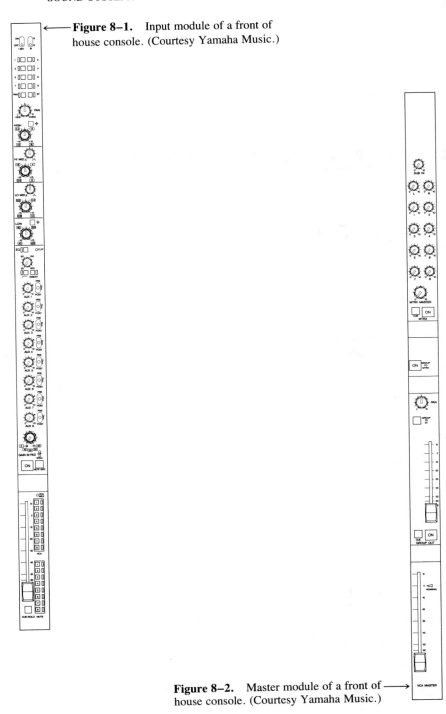

Figure 8–1. Input module of a front of house console. (Courtesy Yamaha Music.)

Figure 8–2. Master module of a front of house console. (Courtesy Yamaha Music.)

Pad

The pad also alters input gain, but only by specific amounts. It is used in conjunction with the input gain control for precise adjustments.

Phase Reverse Switch

The phase reverse switch reverses input polarity, a feature useful for correcting the phase cancellation caused when two microphones are very close.

Group Select Switches

The group select switches assign channel output to the group-mixing buses or directly to the main stereo output.

Equalizer Section

The equalizer section controls channel tone. The two types of equalization are *peaking* and *shelving*.

Peaking.   Select the center frequency and cut or boost the Q (bandwidth), which is either fixed or variable, around the selected frequency. A frequency of 1600 Hz will allow gain control of higher and lower frequencies. The bandwidth between the lowest and highest frequency can be adjusted on some consoles from a broad band to a narrow band. Parametric equalizers provide control of the bandwidth.

Shelving.   The frequency selected determines the point at which everything above or below it will be cut or boosted. A low shelf (160 Hz) will allow all frequencies below 160 Hz to be cut or boosted. A high shelf (5 kHz) will allow all the frequencies above 5 kHz to be cut or boosted.

High-Pass Filter

The high-pass filter allows all frequencies above the filter frequency to pass and attenuates all frequencies below it. The amount of attenuation is usually between 12 to 18 dB per octave. Use high-pass filters to reduce the rumble picked up on stage that discolors the desired sound.

Equalizer On/Off

Some consoles have a switch to bypass the equalizer for comparison before and after equalization.

Insert Point

The insert point in the channel, normally after the equalizer and before the fader, is where limiters, noise gates, and de-essers are inserted into the channel through insert jack sockets mounted on the rear panel above the input or on jack fields on the console front.

Auxiliary Sends

Auxiliary sends are often labeled echo send or foldback send and provide discrete outputs from the channel. Some consoles have a switch to designate the send either prefader, where the control operates independently of the fader, or postfader, where the output depends on the fader. The auxiliary sends can be used for effects sends, sub-low cabinet sends, and monitor sends back to the stage, among other things.

Pan Pot

Pan controls select channel position in the left and right dimension for stereo application. The pan pot is also used to assign mono groups on some consoles.

Prefade Listen Switch

Prefade listen (PFL), also called *cue* or *solo,* selects the channel to the headphone output and cue meter. This allows you to listen to that particular channel independently of the fader.

Phantom Power

The phantom power switch supplies 48 V to power condensor microphones and direct boxes. The 48 V flows down both balanced audio lines, that is, pins one and two; zero reference is at the shield of the cable (pin one). Phantom power will not pass through a transformer. A reading of 48 V between pins one and two and between pins one and three is needed if phantom power is to power microphones and direct boxes.

Mute Switch

The mute switch turns the channel on. The PFL function will still operate with the channel off on most consoles.

Fader

The fader sets the level sent to the channel's output to assigned groups and also the auxiliary sends switched to the postfade position.

Voltage-Controlled Amplifier Controls

The voltage-controlled amplifier (VCA) allows the gain to be adjusted by an external DC voltage. They are more useful than faders because the audio signal can go directly to the main outputs, thereby shortening the path of the signal through the mixer and reducing the chance of signal degradation. The VCA controls look the same as faders except that the DC control voltage, not the signal, passes through the control. Grouping channels with the VCA master controls allows the level of the assigned channels to be adjusted without any accumulated noise. Because the VCA master only controls signal level, not signal destination, the channel must be assigned through the group select switches.

Mute Assign

A mute assign switch allows a master switch to mute groups of channels assigned to a mute master.

OUTPUT

The output section provides master level control for groups, auxiliary sends, and VCA masters (Figure 8–2).

The matrix allows the different console outputs to be grouped as required to provide the desired balance. Several matrix outputs are available for different combinations for different destinations, that is, main stereo speaker systems, delay systems, center fills, and tape machines.

Auxiliary returns accept the signal from line-level units, effects, and tape players.

TALKBACK MODULE

The talkback module, which differs on all consoles and may have some or all features, can contain an oscillator for calibrating the console and the entire sound system. It may also have a switch and microphone input that can be assigned to all

Figure 8–3.   Front of house console. The many different types of front of house consoles all perform the same basic functions. (Courtesy Yamaha Music.)

Figure 8–4.   Rear panel of a front of house console. All connections to the console are made in the rear panel. (Courtesy Yamaha Music.)

the groups and also to the talkback output, which can be connected to the monitor console to feed through the monitors for on-stage instruction for equipment and sound checks. Some modules have a feature for intercom, headphones, and microphone systems for communicating with the stage (Figures 8–3 and 8–4).

POWER SUPPLY

The power supply for the mixing console is usually a separate unit. This keeps the transformers, which convert AC input into DC voltages to drive the electronics, away from the console. The normal voltage supplied to the console from the power supply are + and −18 to 20 V to drive the electronics, plus 48 V for the phantom power and additional voltage for meter lamps, console lamps, and VCA control (Figure 8–5).

GAIN STRUCTURE

The gain structure (Figure 8–6) is the relationship between all the components in the signal chain. It should be set so that the console output, graphic equalizers, and crossovers correspond. Do this by using a tone to set channel input level, crossover levels, and amplifier levels to zero. What the output meters show on the console is exactly what amplifier output will be. The best way to run the console is to have adequate headroom available for transient peaks without residual noise. If an input signal is too high, it will distort both channel and console output, affecting all input. The input must be set to a reasonable level by the input attenuator. It is pointless to turn down the crossovers or amplifiers if the console is overloading. Instead, have some headroom on the system and keep the console input gains down. Leave enough headroom for live music, since transient peaks need room to move to avoid distortion, blown components, and a generally bad sound.

Figure 8–5. Mixer power supply. This is usually a separate unit from the mixer. (Courtesy Yamaha Music.)

CONSOLE CARE

Consoles must be kept clean with regular dusting, since an accumulation of dust will destroy console components. Never use spray cleaners. Pots and faders can become noisy if they get dusty or dirty, and spray cleaners will only exacerbate the problem by removing their lubricating film along with the dust. Cover a console when it is not in use to reduce its exposure to dust.

MIXING

Mixing is not something to learn from a book. Although you must understand the equipment being used, the room acoustics, and the material being performed, mixing is an art that builds on knowledge and experience. There are a number of steps to take to keep the sound system under control and sounding good.

Most important is gain structure. Ease your way into a mix; do not start with everything running flat out. Be careful to retain enough headroom for soloists and vocalists. Always start the sound check with the rhythm section, then the melody instruments, and then the vocalists and soloists. Build the mix on the foundation of the rhythm. It is pointless to have the drums and bass so loud that they drown everything else out.

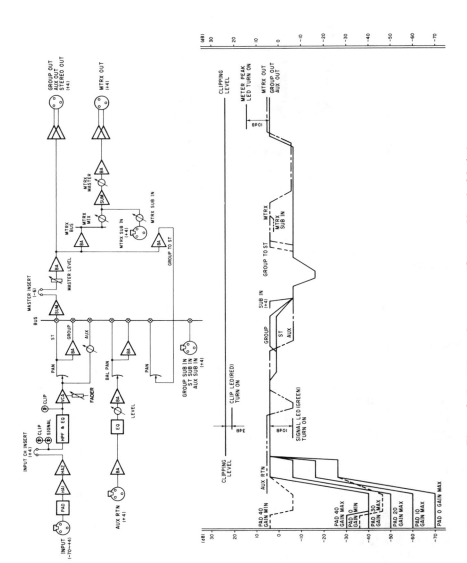

Figure 8–6. Mixer gain structure. (Courtesy Yamaha Music.)

Try to keep the sound dynamic so that it has some life and is not just a wall of noise. It should be possible to pick out each instrument and distinguish it from others being played. Beware of overequalizing or you will end up trying to tune each instrument to fit in with others rather than letting them fit in naturally. If a drum keeps ringing, no matter what you do with the equalizer, the answer may be to get the drum tuned properly or move the microphone. The drum tone may have the same frequency as a resonant frequency in the room.

Check all microphone positions before starting a sound check to correct, if necessary, microphone position, proximity to other microphones, source of the sound being miked, and fittings and stands.

Make effects complement the music, not confuse it. Subtle reverberations can enhance the sound, and loud repeats can be used for dramatic effects.

The level of the sound depends on the type of music, the environment, and the available power. A very reverberant room, where all the low frequencies are subject to large amounts of room gain and the higher frequencies are absorbed, requires a different approach than an open field or a room with minimal reverberation.

CHAPTER 9

EFFECTS UNITS

A multitude of different effects units are available. Most of them are digital delays or reverberation units. Effects for live performances either reproduce the sound of the performer's recording or complement the performance creatively. Echoes, or separately identifiable repeats, should blend in with the music and not sound like an electronic malfunction. Figure 9-1 shows an effects rack.

DIGITAL DELAYS

The digital delay is a device that uses digital technology to store an audio signal and play it back. The digital delay has evolved from the tape echo, which had difficulty maintaining signal quality. Digital delays store the signal by digital sampling, a technique that samples the sound several thousand times a second and converts it into a binary code that is stored in the unit's memory. The more memory available in a unit, the better the frequency response and the longer a delay. The advantage of digital storage is that it turns the sound into numbers; it maintains excellent frequency response and provides options to modify the stored sound, including flanging, phasing, pitch change, echo, and chorus effects.

REVERBERATION UNITS

Reverberation units store information the same way digital delays do but build several different delays to create reverberation. The more sophisticated a reverberation unit, the more intricate the reflections can be to simulate acoustic environments that probably could not be found in reality. Reverberation units have a standard set of programmed room sizes, but these can be altered to create a particular effect.

Figure 9–1. Effects rack. Live effects are used to reproduce the sound of the performer's recordings or to complement it.

MUSICAL INSTRUMENT DIGITAL INTERFACE (MIDI)

The MIDI system is a language that sends and receives information between digital instruments and effects units. There are 16 channels to send and receive information in each MIDI cable. MIDI is a hexadecimal message sent as a series of bytes. There are two types of messages sent, status and data bytes. Status bytes represent the type of message and the data bytes represent the action to be carried out. A MIDI controller connected to several effects units can be programmed to change programs at the touch of a button. The most practical way to operate effects for live performances is to give each song, or if necessary each part of a song, a program number.

USE OF EFFECTS

Study the instruction manual for the digital effects. The first step to understanding a unit is to know how to store and recall programs. With that knowledge, you can then explore the vast capacity of these units to mix in stereo.

CHAPTER 10

INSERTS

Units inserted in the audio chain to modify or control the signal are called inserts. Most consoles have insert points available for each channel, subgroup master, auxiliary outputs, and main outputs. Inserts can be equalizers, if more equalization is required than available on the console; noise gates, for reducing the spill from other instruments or residual noise from direct sources; or limiters, for controlling the level or creating compression effects. The two most common inserts are limiters and noise gates (Figure 10–1).

LIMITERS

Limiters fix a ceiling of maximum level without changing the dynamic range below the threshold. The amount of gain reduction depends on the ratio control setting, which can vary from no compression to infinite compression at the threshold. The level at which compression begins is set by the threshold control. An output level control can adjust the overall gain. Compression is the process of reducing dynamic range, so that a compressed signal will have a higher average level.

To smooth out variations in microphone level, use a low compression of 2 : 1. To smooth out variations in instrument level, use a 4 : 1 ratio. Smooth a bass sound by lessening the variations between the strings and increasing the sustain. To raise a signal out of a mix, apply compression and raise the level. The compressed signal will have a reduced dynamic range and a higher average level. To protect the speakers, the limiter ratio should be infinite and the threshold set at the amplifiers' input voltage.

Figure 10–1.   Insert rack. The two most common units inserted are limiters/compressors and noise gates.

NOISE GATES

Noise gates are used to control the point at which a channel is on, when the gate is open, to keep residual unwanted background noise from being amplified. The channel remains off until a certain input level is achieved. The amount of signal gated is a function of both the ratio and threshold. The attenuation limit sets the desired amount of noise suppression. Attack and release controls the speed of attenuation. Attack applies to the signal heard as it comes out of the noise gating mode. Release governs the time for the signal to die away once the gate is shut. Noise gates can be operated by an external source that switches the gate on when an external signal is applied through the key connector. Some gates will switch on once a signal has reached a certain level and then remain on, even if the signal falls below the threshold.

A quick setup procedure for noise gates is as follows: Set ratio and attenuation limit to the maximum. Set attack and release controls to their fastest. Listen to the signal. Set the threshold for the desired cut-off point. Adjust the ratio to achieve the desired rate of signal decay. Use the attack and release controls to set the smoothness of attenuation. Finally, set the attenuation limit control for the desired amount of noise to be suppressed.

CHAPTER 11

MONITOR SYSTEMS

The monitor system enables each musician to hear what the other musicians are doing. The difference between a front of house (FOH) mix and a monitor mix is that the FOH mix is usually a stereo output to the left and right speaker stacks and the monitor mix is customized for each musician. The monitor mix provides information that allows each musician to stay in time and in tune. Sometimes, however, musicians get carried away with their monitor requirements and end up wanting a full mixed version of the group, with their own contribution the loudest. Monitor mixing is much more complex than FOH mixing, since each mix output must be individually mixed and listened to on its own at the side of the stage. This can be confusing because it may sound dreadful alone but be just what is needed on stage. Because of this, it is important to listen continually to the mixes and watch the musicians closely. The monitor operator is the person the group depends on to combine all the individual efforts on stage into a complementary whole. The monitor operator must walk around the stage at sound checks and listen to how each mix contributes to overall sound.

MONITOR CONSOLES

These consoles (Figure 11–1) differ from house mixing consoles by the number of outputs. A monitor console may have up to 16 outputs, with each channel having a level control for each output. A 32 into 12 console has 32 input channels and 12 outputs. Graphic equalizers (Figure 11–2) are inserted across the outputs to equalize each cabinet driven by each mix. The graphics are inserted rather than patched in the chain so that the monitor operator will hear what is coming from the speaker after it has been equalized. It is important to know exactly which outputs are close

Figure 11–1.   Monitor console. These consoles differ from house mixing consoles in their number of outputs. (Courtesy Yamaha Music.)

to feedback, and which channels in particular, so they can be quickly adjusted if any feedback starts. There is nothing more annoying when listening to or performing music to hear feedback screeching through the speakers.

Figure 11–2.   Equalizer rack. Graphic equalizers are inserted across each output to equalize each cabinet driven by each mix.

Tuning the monitor system depends on the monitor speaker's position and musical content. A wedge monitor with only vocals can have the lower frequencies rolled off to reduce the amount of rumble. A monitor cabinet for a drummer will require a fatter sound with a different sort of tuning. Do not overequalize and end up hacking the sound to pieces. Of course you will hear feedback if you cover the end of the microphone or point it into the cabinet, but that does not happen during a performance. Always discuss a monitor mix with the musicians before ploughing into it. No matter what level you start at, musicians invariably want more, not less, which will leave you no headroom and on the brink of feedback. In addition, the musicians must sometimes compromise (for example, the singers need more vocal so the guitar player must make do with less), so the monitor operator must use tact in suggesting necessary changes.

MONITOR SPEAKERS

The main type of monitor cabinet is the *wedge monitor,* so called because it is wedge shaped. Wedges may contain a number of different components such as two 12-inch speakers and a compression driver and one 15-inch speaker and a compression driver, or vice versa. These cabinets can be run with passive crossovers or biamplified and run two-way. The crossover point is related to the type of component. Side-fill cabinets placed on either side of the stage are more substantial than wedges. Drum and keyboard monitor cabinets usually must handle more power and lower frequencies than wedges can handle.

The use of in-ear monitor systems is becoming more common. They allow for consistent monitoring night after night, no matter what the situation. Ear-worn monitors are not a cure-all for monitoring woes. They present a new series of challenges for the monitor engineer. Ear monitors can reduce ear fatigue by reducing the exposure to excessive levels, but they can also be dangerous if not properly protected. Brick wall limiting should be used to provide protection from any unexpected feedback from on-stage wedges or electronic failures.

MIX CONTENTS

Each monitor mix depends, of course, on the musicians, their music, and the size of the stage. A monitor system schematic is shown in Figure 11–3. An eight-send monitor system for a group of musicians consisting of drummer, keyboard player, saxophone player, guitarist, bass player, and lead vocalist would typically consist of the following:

Mix 1: Side-Fill Stage Right. This mix would have a general balance of drums, vocals, and possibly some instruments.

Mix 2: Side-Fill Stage Left. This mix is similar to mix 1.

Mix 3: Lead Vocalist. A pair of wedges for the lead vocalist would contain the lead vocal, snare drum, and melody instrument.

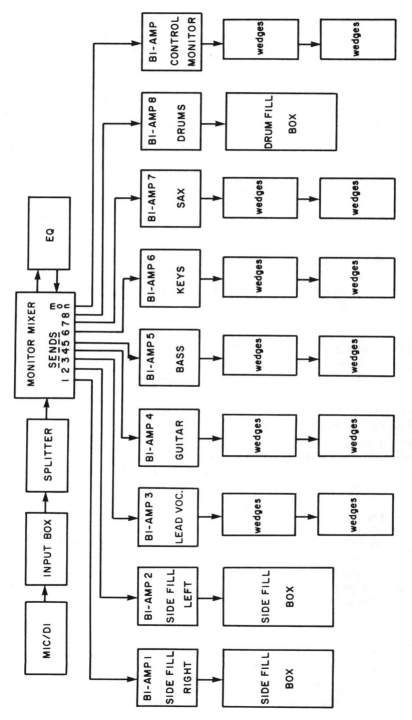

Figure 11–3. Monitor system schematic.

Mix 4: Guitar Player.   This mix would contain only the guitar player's vocal, and most of the information required would come through the side fill.

Mix 5: Bass Player.   This mix would contain only the bass player's vocal, and most of the information would come through the side fill.

Mix 6: Keyboard Player.   The keyboard player would need snare, vocals, and other instruments.

Mix 7: Saxaphone Player.   The saxaphone player would need the saxaphone and other instruments depending on his position on stage.

Mix 8: Drums.   The drum monitor would contain the drums, bass guitar, and vocals.

CHAPTER 12

MICROPHONES AND DIRECT BOXES

Microphones convert acoustical energy into electrical energy.

TYPES OF MICROPHONES

The *dynamic microphone* employs a diaphragm in a strong magnetic field. Sound waves striking the surface of the microphone cause the coil to move in a magnetic field, which generates a voltage corresponding to the sound pressure on the diaphragm's surface.

The *condensor microphone* (Figure 12–1) uses electrostatic principles rather than the electromagnetic principles used by the dynamic microphone. The condensor microphone has a diaphragm placed adjacent to a backplate, and capacitance varies with sound pressure. Condensor microphones sometimes require a pad inserted between the diaphragm and the microphone preamplifier.

The *C-ducer microphone* is a sensing tape with preamplifier and power supply. Because the C-ducer is flexible, it can be affixed to the curved surfaces of instruments such as the harp and guitar (Figure 12–2).

The *ribbon microphone* uses a thin metal ribbon suspended between the poles of a magnet to sense the sound pressure.

The *pressure zone microphone* (PZM) uses the pressure zone at an acoustical boundary to eliminate distortion problems common with other microphones. The active element in a PZM is the pressure-calibrated electret capsule, mounted so that it faces the boundary and lies with the pressure zone. All incoming sound is received indirectly, free of distortion caused by phase interference (Figure 12–3).

A hypercardioid lavaliere microphone, the *isomax microphone* is extremely small and can be positioned in otherwise inaccessible areas.

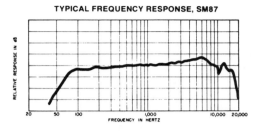

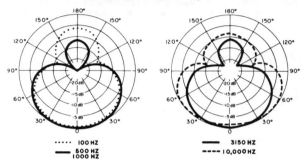

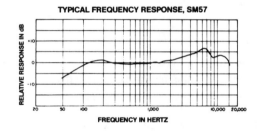

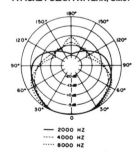

Figure 12–1.   Microphone patterns. (Courtesy Shure Bros.)

Figure 12–2.   Microphones on a drum kit.

Figure 12–3.   Microphone on an amplifier. (Courtesy Shure Bros.)

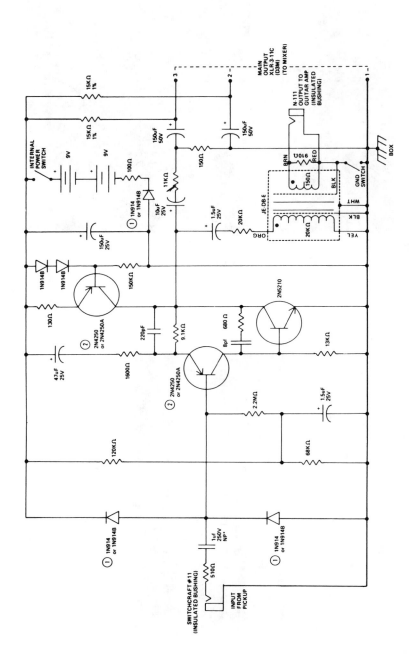

Figure 12–4. Active direct box schematic. (Courtesy Yamaha Music.)

The *radio microphone,* which incorporates a standard microphone into a radio transmitter, has limiters between the microphone and the transmitter to keep the signal from overloading the transmitter.

DIRECT BOXES

The *direct box,* also known as a DI (direct injection), matches the impedance of an instrument to the input impedance of a mixing console. An active direct box has a transformer and a circuit powered by batteries or the phantom power supply. A passive direct box has only a transformer and provides no boosting for low-level

Microphone Plot

Lne #	Channel Name	FOH Chnl	Mon. Chnl	Mic.Type	Stand
CONCERT: ALLSTARS			VENUE/DATE: APOLLO		
1	KICK	1	1	RE-20	S/B
2	SNARE TOP	2	2	SM 57	S/B
3	SNARE BOTTOM	3	3	SM 57	S/B
4	HI HAT	4	4	C-451-CK1	S/B
5	RACK TOM 1	5	5	MD 421	M/B
6	RACK TOM 2	6	6	MD 421	M/B
7	RACK TOM 3	7	7	MD 421	M/B
8	FLOOR TOM 1	8	8	MD 421	S/B
9	FLOOR TOM 2	9	9	MD 421	S/B
10	O/H - LEFT	10	10	C-414	L/B
11	O/H - RIGHT	11	11	C-414	L/B
12	SIMMONS - LEFT	12	12	DIRECT	—
13	SIMMONS - RIGHT	13	13	DIRECT	—
14	BASS DIRECT	14	14	DI	—
15	BASS MIC	15	15	RE-20	S/B
16	GTR - LEFT	16	16	SM 57	S/B
17	GTR - RIGHT	17	17	SM 57	S/B
18	CP-70 PIANO	18	18	DIRECT	—
19	DX-7 LEFT	19	19	DI	—
20	DX-7 RIGHT	20	20	DI	—
21	KURTZWEILL - A	21	21	DIRECT	—
22	KURTZWEILL - B	22	22	DIRECT	—
23	CONGAS - LEFT	23	23	MD 441	M/B
24	CONGAS - RIGHT	24	24	MD 441	M/B
25	BACKING VOCAL 1	25	25	SM 58	L/B
26	BACKING VOCAL 2	26	26	SM 58	L/B
27	BASS VOCAL	27	27	SM 58	L/B
28	GTR VOCAL	28	28	SM 58	L/B
29	¢ VOCAL	29	29	SM 58	STRAIGHT
30	SPARE VOCAL	30	30	SM 58	STRAIGHT
	KEY				
	S/B - SMALL BOOM				
	M/B - MEDIUM BOOM				
	L/B - LARGE BOOM				

Figure 12–5. Microphone patching list. The patching list identifies input location and designation, type of microphone, microphone stand, and any additional electronics to be patched into the channels of the front of house and monitor consoles.

signals. The direct box can be connected to any high-impedance instrument such as an electrical bass or synthesizer. Some instruments provide a balance-line output for direct connection to mixing consoles (Figure 12–4).

MICROPHONE PLACEMENT

Most microphones are positioned as close to the source as possible for live concerts. The closer the microphone is, the stronger the signal, the less spill from other instruments, and the less chance of feedback. Microphone stands should be as rigid as possible so that they do not stray from their set position. Condensor microphones are more delicate than dynamic microphones, but all must be treated with care to maintain their quality (Figure 12–5).

CHAPTER 13

SOUND SYSTEM SETUP PROCEDURE

PREPARATION

The difference between various pieces of sound equipment assembled in the same room and a sound *system* is the operator's speed of assembly, ability to set up and operate a series of shows on schedule, and ability to rectify faults. Touring sound systems do require constant maintenance to give optimum performance.

It is essential to be prepared so that equipment can be set up quickly and efficiently on site. A sound system list is a good idea (Figure 13–1). The setup must be coordinated with lighting and other production staff so that people are not tripping over each other and making the whole task of setting up a show a nightmare. Call times are necessary for setup, sound check, and show so that all crew members arrive on time and keep to a schedule.

First, establish the type and number of speaker cabinets and their stacking or hanging configuration. Knowing the number of speaker cabinets allows you to identify the number of amplifiers, speaker cables, and rigging hardware required. The equipment should be color coded as follows to identify its desired location at the venue:

Red: stage left (PA right)

Yellow: stage right (PA left)

Green: front of house

Orange: on stage

CONCERT PRODUCTIONS

ENGINEER	DATE OUT	DATE IN	ARTIST:	SUB HIRES	NO.OF CASES	CUBIC METRE
F.O.H.MIXER(S)						
F.O.H.DRIVE						
F.O.H.EFFECTS						
F.O.H.ACC.CASE						
MONITOR MIXER						
MONITOR E.Q.						
MON.ACC.CASE						
MON.SPEAKERS						
MON.POWER AMPS						
MON.SPKR.CABLES						
PWR.DIST.BOARD						
3 PHASE CABLES						
240 VOLT CABLES						
MICROPHONES						
MIC.STANDS						
MIC.CABLES						
MULTICORE						
SYSTEM SPARES						
SPKR.SPARES						
FOH.SPEAKERS						
FOH.PWR.AMPS						
FOH.SPKR CABLES						
CHAIN MOTORS						
RIGGING						
FLYBELTS						
EXTRAS						

Figure 13.1 Sound system list. Adequate preparation ensures a smoother set up.

Colored tape or stickers will facilitate locating the equipment. If the same equipment is used for a series of shows at different venues, the color code will send the same cabinets, amplifiers, and speaker cables to the same side each time, therefore making it easier to identify any faults.

The number of wedge cabinets, side fills, and drum monitors determines the number of amplifiers and the number and type of speaker cables and crossovers. Check the console, graphic equalizers, and crossovers to ensure that all components function correctly.

The front of house (FOH) control equipment can be lined up and marked with the channel assignment, and the gain structure can be set between console and drive electronics.

The power distribution system must be capable of handling the amount of amplifier racks being used. Have spare fuses handy in case you must replace a blown fuse quickly, without interrupting a scheduled sound check or performance.

Microphone lists can be drawn up with the multicore and monitor console numbers. Often the FOH and monitor consoles will not have the same channels patched in the same order. Mark the multicore numbers above the inputs of the monitor console so that the inputs can be patched automatically.

The more careful the preparation, the smoother the setup. Because unforeseen problems often occur, it is important to have spare time in which to address them. The sound equipment should be assembled as quickly as possible so that any running repairs do not delay scheduled sound checks or rehearsals. A delayed sound check can disrupt many schedules.

For outdoor concerts, carry enough weatherproofing to cover the equipment. Tie down any speakers stacked outdoors with ropes or cargo straps.

Before attempting to load the truck, work out how many cases are the same size so that you may stack them in blocks. Pack all the larger, heavier cases on the bottom and the light ones on top. Load in logical order so that power cases, rigging cases, and chain motors end up at the rear of the truck and can come off the truck first to enable setting up. Mark the weight of each case on the top and bottom to avoid accidents. Because most transit damage to equipment occurs from vibration in the truck, pack in the cases as tightly as possible and tie them with ropes or straps. Other transit damage occurs during loading and unloading, so everyone must be careful.

SETUP

Do the following to get the sound system out of the truck, set up, packed, and reloaded. The more equipment and the more crew on a show, the more complex a setup becomes. It is necessary to define crew members' areas of responsibility, as many of the setup steps can be done simultaneously.

Unloading the Truck

One member of the sound crew should stay in the truck to ensure that each case is leaving the truck with enough people (Figure 13–2). The other members of the

Figure 13–2.   Unloading the truck. One member of the sound crew should stay in the truck to ensure that the stagehands are handling cases properly.

sound crew should direct the cases to their destination in the venue and commence the setup. Color coding allows for a minimum of direction.

Rigging

Chalk the position of the points on the floor clearly and correctly so that the riggers can see them clearly from the roof. This eliminates the need for shouting.

Motors should be positioned and all necessary rigging attached to the hook (wire rope bridles and spansets to wrap around the roof beams). Check two-ton motors for any twisted links by running the block the length of the chain. The block can easily become twisted in transit, and a twisted link can jam in the motor or the block. If a motor is rigged with a twisted link, this can be remedied by passing the motor between the two chains before attaching any load to the hoist.

Check the motor power to ensure that the phasing is correct and that the motor moves up when the up button is pressed and down on down. Only one member of the crew should operate the motors (Figure 13–3). If the phasing is incorrect, the safety switches in the motor do not function. The motor control cables can be attached to the bar that holds the speakers (the bumper) and loomed together. The best position from which to operate the hoists is in the center between the left and right clusters. As each motor is connected to the motor control box, label it so that

Figure 13–3.   Rigging. Only one member of the crew should operate the motors.

when it is disconnected and reconnected you do not have to move the motors to identify them. Motor 1 should be the motor closest to the center of the stage, motor 2 the next one, and so on. Each side of the speaker system will have the same motor numbers starting in the center and moving outward all the way around to the cable pick.

Power Connection

The venue electrician normally makes the three-phase power connection (Figure 13–4). You must check this service before turning on the power. Have the connection double-checked by the FOH and monitor engineers. If any trouble occurs during the show, the FOH engineer will be too far away to deal with a power failure; the monitor engineer therefore must know what to do if the power fails.

Establish the location and rating of the fuses (or breakers). Access to the fuses or breakers is crucial in the event of faults. The power distribution cables can be

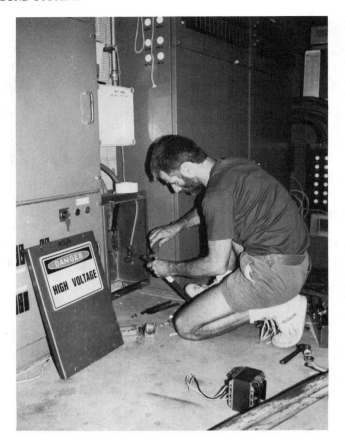

Figure 13–4.   Power connection. The venue electrician normally makes the three-phase power connection.

run out to where the power amplifiers will be situated. At outdoor concerts all power connections must be weatherproofed. Connections should never be directly on the ground but must be strung up on the scaffolding or placed inside a case. It is not good enough to wrap plastic around the connection. Also, heavy dew could cause a short in power cables left exposed overnight.

Hanging the Speakers

As soon as the bumper is lifted, it is time to attach the speaker cabinets. While the points are being rigged, which often takes longer than you want, the speaker cables can be attached to the bumper and all the cabinets lined up in the right order ready to be attached.

The speaker cables must be coded and a plot drawn up so that each cabinet can be easily identified by its cable number (Figure 13–5). The cables should be

Figure 13-5. Hanging the speakers. Speaker cables must be coded and a plot drawn up so that each cabinet can be easily identified by its cable number.

patched into the amplifier racks so that they are in series horizontally to enable lower cabinets to be turned down, if necessary, without affecting the higher rows. Of course there are exceptions to this. When the cabinets are attached to the bumper, their angles must be checked to ensure that they will be covering the proper venue areas. The speaker cables should be pulled out of sight lines so that they do not block the view of people sitting at the sides of the stage. It is often impossible, however, to keep the view totally clear for everyone.

Stacking Speakers

Before attempting to stack speaker cabinets, make sure that the scaffold or deck that will support them is flat and capable of taking the weight. Check the scaffold during and after stacking, since the weight of the speakers may force the foundations down into soft ground and scaffold pipes may bend if not strengthened properly.

The higher and heavier a stack, the harder it can fall. If the deck is uneven to start with, then the higher the stack goes the more it will lean, which can be very dangerous. At outdoor concerts the speakers must be tied down during stacking, because a gust of wind may blow over a column of cabinets. The enemies of outdoor concerts are wind and rain, and often they come together. The best form of defense is to be prepared. Tarpaulins tied to the top of speaker stacks must be able to drain any water immediately, because a tarp full of water could easily pull down the whole stack. Keep the cabinets tied down until it is time to unstack them.

Flying Speakers

Once all speakers and speaker cables are attached, all cabinets are at the correct angles, and all rigging is firmly attached, the bumpers can be raised. The person operating the chain motors must make sure that no one is standing under them when they are moving. The bumpers should be as level as possible before being moved up to their trim height. Although all the motors should move at the same speed, they do not, so when the bumpers are at trim height they should be leveled, with only one person instructing the operator. Use the motor code to identify the motors for clear instructions. The motors must be watched continuously while they are moving. If one motor stops, for whatever reason, the other motors will become overloaded, obviously with disastrous results. Motors can stop because a contactor breaks in the motor or a control cable snags. A motor can become overloaded if the bumper is not level and too much weight is transferred to the other motor, although the motors are protected by an overload clutch. In short, raising and lowering the chain motors is a task requiring complete concentration.

Amplifiers

Amplifiers must be positioned in well-ventilated, accessible areas. Amplifier racks with fans that blow air front to back should be placed in rows back to back so that the fans are not blowing hot air out the back of one rack and straight into the front of another one (Figure 13–6). Racks that draw the air in the back and also out the back should be placed in a U shape if they do not fit in a row. At outdoor concerts the amplifiers must be protected from the sun and rain but still need room to breathe. At outdoor concerts the amplifiers usually must work hard as engineers battle with the wind trying to get the sound to the audience. Signal assignment must be checked to be sure that the correct signal is being sent to the speaker cabinets; for instance, horns do not last long with low frequencies. The power for the amplifier racks supplied from the power distribution system should be evenly allocated over the three phases. The FOH control equipment, monitor system, and stage instruments must all share the same phase.

FOH Control Equipment

The multicore cables must be run out to where the mixer will be positioned. Before running them, check the route so that the cables do not pass through heavy traffic areas or across fire exits. Cables running through public areas must be covered and secured to the floor. Multicore connectors should never be dragged along the ground. Before setting the mixer, check that the position does not violate any local bylaws, does not obstruct the view of the stage from seats behind the console, and is suitable for controlling the sound system (Figure 13–7). Often specific seats are held for the mixing positions, and these can sometimes be reshuffled to accommodate sound requirements.

Figure 13–6. Amplifiers. Amplifiers must be positioned in well-ventilated, accessible areas.

Figure 13–7. Front of house control position. Before setting the mixer, check that the position does not violate any local bylaws or obstruct the view of the stage from seats behind.

Connect the mixer, drive rack, and effects rack and then the multicore cables and power. Then turn on the system. Set the gain so that the console and crossovers are running evenly. Set a substantial show level signal to check each amplifier channel. When the amplifier channels are being turned up, the person in control of the FOH equipment must listen for any distortion. When all amplifier channels have been checked and all cabinets are functioning, the system can be tuned. After tuning from the control position, walk around the venue to check for even coverage. Any offensive area can be trimmed by turning down specific amplifiers.

After tuning and trimming, check the effects units and then the microphone set and microphone inputs and inserts. Coordinate the microphone line check with the monitor engineer, and use a talk-to-stage microphone to direct the person in charge of input source. This person should carry a spare microphone and spare microphone cables so that any faults can be quickly determined and rectified.

Monitor System

The monitor system can be set as soon as the lighting rig is raised and the stage is clear. Often it is possible to set the monitor control area before the lights are raised. When tuning the monitors, establish the threshold of feedback so that it can be quickly controlled during the show. All cables running around the stage should be laid flat and taped down so people cannot trip over them during the show.

Miking Up

Before the microphones are set, place them on their stands, as per the microphone list, and position the input boxes. Once the instruments are set, the microphones can be positioned and connected to the input boxes. Miking up should be a joint sound crew effort. Patching microphone cables on your own is very time consuming because the input boxes are usually tucked out of sight. When all the microphones are set, it is time for the line check. Microphones are delicate and must be treated with care, especially the highly sensitive condensor microphones.

Sound Check

Once everything is working, a sound check can begin. When a suitable balance has been established at the FOH control position, check the coverage around the venue for any anomalies. The sound check should start with the rhythm section, then the melody section, and then the vocalists. Sometimes it is better to have the band start with the monitor system and settle with the sound on the stage before turning on the main speaker system. The sound check should conclude with the first song to be performed that night so that all the settings on the console are ready for that particular piece of music.

After Sound Check

After the sound check for the main artist, reset the consoles for the opening acts. The settings on the consoles should be recorded or marked before they are tampered with. Keep the amount of resetting to a minimum. By the time the consoles are marked for the opening act, the stage should be ready to be remiked. A team effort will make this a straightforward process. Often an opening act will not be as prepared as you would like, so sound checks can turn into debugging sessions or even rehearsals. These kind of opening acts need assistance and direction. Finally, all interval tapes and disks should be cued up and ready for show time.

SHOW TIME

The sound check will have set the balance to suit the room while it is empty. The sound will change when the audience is seated, as will the temperature. Monitor the gain structure of the system regularly so that it maintains its optimum performance. If the system has been lined up properly, the engineer will be able to see, at a glance, the headroom available or if there is excessive level. Do a line check between any microphone repatches for opening acts. Microphone cables that must be repatched during changeovers between acts should be clearly marked so that they can be patched correctly in the difficult environment of a show.

The pressure is on to be ready for show time, and with people rushing around the stage, moving equipment, and a screaming audience, mistakes can be easily made. To avoid these mistakes, which usually take far too long to rectify, make sure there is enough light to see the markings on the cables and carry a flashlight to be sure. Mark microphone stands for their assigned position and their input number. Because a mispatched microphone is an engineer's nightmare, keep a spare microphone, stand, and cable by the monitor console for speedy replacement if needed. If a singer handles the microphone roughly, place a spare microphone on stage so that he or she can switch to the spare immediately.

LOAD OUT

Basically the *load out* is the reverse of the setup, only much quicker. First pack the microphones, then the mixing consoles and electronics. Loom the cables together to make packing up easier. Make sure that multicore connectors are protected and not dragged along the ground. Once everything is loaded, an "idiot check" of the venue will ensure that nothing has been left behind.

Division of Duties

The division of duties will change depending on each show's requirements, number of cabinets, number of acts, and performance schedule. To maintain some teamwork, duties are divided between the two main sound crew members—the FOH engineer and the monitor engineer.

The typical duties assigned to a FOH engineer are the FOH control equipment, multicore system, rigging and motors, speaker system, and amplifiers. The duties usually assigned to the monitor engineer include the monitor system, power system, microphones, microphone stands and cables, speaker system, and amplifiers.

The speaker system is the FOH engineer's prime responsibility. Additional crew members will assist with it and with the amplifiers, microphones, stands, and cables where necessary. The duties remain the same whatever the crew's size, and the sound crew must always load and unload the sound equipment.

On a concert tour with a vast amount of equipment, the sound crew must give clear instructions to the stage hands and loaders and supervise loading and unloading. If the equipment has been marked with a location code, it will automatically be sent to the desired point. Work out truck-loading plans *before* it is time to load the truck and tape them to the wall of the truck.

SYSTEM CHECK

The system check procedure includes attention to the power connection, power supply, mixing console, drive system, each amplifier channel, each speaker cabinet, monitor system, and all microphone lines. Also, the power supply must be checked before any equipment is connected.

Carry out on-site maintenance whenever possible to keep abreast of minor problems. Faulty cables and microphones should be clearly marked and their ends taped over. Spare cables, diaphragms, speakers, and castors should be part of the system. Keep a record of repairs so that recurring faults can be identified. If a compression driver blows a diaphragm every second or third show, for example, the driver may be cracked and out of alignment, which becomes very costly. The date the diaphragm is changed should be noted for this reason.

PART III

LIGHTING SYSTEMS

CHAPTER 14

TRUSSES AND GRIDS

RIGGING TRUSSES AND GRIDS

A variety of methods are used to join truss sections, nuts and bolts, pins, and camlocs. No matter what method is used, however, check each connection before the truss is lifted (Figure 14–1). The correct position to sling the chain motor is about one-fifth the length of the truss from the end. The length of the truss should be capable of supporting the load suspended without any deflection. Different types of trussing have different load capacities. The longer a truss is, the more support it requires. A truss cannot get longer and the distance between the motors greater without reducing the truss's load capacity.

A series of trusses connected together and lifted on several motors is called a *grid*. The number of motors used on a grid depends on the load. As a general rule, have all cross-stage trusses supported by a pair of motors. Trusses longer than 40 feet may require an additional motor in the center depending on the load. Trusses supported by three motors must have motor tension checked so that the center motor does not end up taking most of the load. The center motor's function is to provide additional support and reduce the amount of bounce in a truss.

GROUND SUPPORTS

When no suitable flying facilities are available, ground supports on a solid level surface must be used. It is dangerous to lift a grid on ground supports because the grid may twist if the supports are not raised together. If the supports are not raised together, one of the supports will end up taking more of the load, which could be disastrous. Remember that the heaviest part of a grid is the corner where the cables

89

Figure 14–1.   Rigging a truss. Various methods are used to join truss sections such as nuts, bolts, pins, and camlocs.

Figure 14–2.   Raising the grid. Before lifting a grid, check all lamps for tightness and check anything attached to the grid for safety.

90

drop, and this corner gets heavier the higher it is raised. Trusses supported on ground supports should not be climbed on but focused from a ladder.

LIFTING GRIDS

Before lifting a grid, check all the lamps for tightness and anything attached to the grid for safety (Figure 14–2). The motor controller should clearly identify where the motors are connected. A grid with a large number of looms requires a cable pick to relieve some of its load. When the grid is being raised, the cable pick should also be raised.

Once the grid is at its desired height, it must be leveled. Do not rely on line of sight but use trim chains or a tape measure for accurate trimming. Trim chains can be easily made with lightweight chain and tagged with their length, usually between 18 and 25 feet. Each motor can be adjusted so that the grid ends up perfectly level. If the grid is not leveled correctly, unnecessary strain is placed on the trussing, which could fracture the welding and cause an accident.

CHAPTER 15

LAMPS

Lamp is the general term for an incandescent light source. A number of lamps are available to provide a wide range of wattages at different voltages (Figure 15–1).

The intensity of a light is determined by the throw, the distance from the light source to the object it is lighting. The intensity is governed by the inverse square law. Once a beam leaves a light, the area illuminated by the beam increases the farther it throws, and the same quantity of light must illuminate a larger area. If the distance between a light and the stage is doubled, then the intensity will be reduced to one quarter of the original.

TYPES OF INSTRUMENTS

Par cans hold par 64 bulbs and raylight kits. The *64* refers to the diameter of the bulb in eighths of an inch. The par lamp is a tungsten-halogen (quartz) lamp with a parabolic aluminized reflector forming part of the bulb. Par cans can be bolted onto bars, typically with six lamps, which are wired to a multiway connector. Lamp 1 on a multiway bar is the lamp closest to the connector. Par bulbs can also be used as floor lamps in shortnose cans. The only adjustment available on a par can is left/right and up/down. The bulb can be turned in the can to change the direction of the beam. When the filament is vertical, the beam is wider than when the filament is horizontal (Figure 15–2).

Profile spots can adjust the round size with the iris, shaped size with the shutters, and beam edge with the lens (Figure 15–3). Adjusting the lens allows for a hard or soft edge. A smooth even beam is the most suitable for most applications. The lenses should be mounted with the curved (convex) sides facing each other while the flat sides face the outside and bulb. Gobos (metal stencils) can be placed

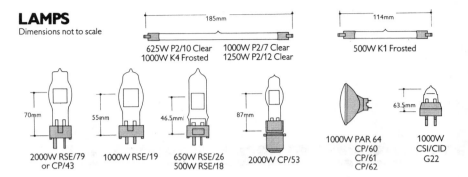

Figure 15–1. Lamp types. A selection of lamp types used for concert lighting. (Courtesy Rank Strand.)

in profile spots so that the image of the gobo is projected onto a screen or cyclorama.

Fresnel spots let you adjust between a flood or a spot by moving the bulb behind the lens. Closer to the lens is a flood, and away from it is a spot.

The *ground row* provides four cells for four separate control channels and colors. Each cells supplies an even spread of light for lighting cycloramas or scenery.

Molefay lamps are internal reflector lamps that radiate a beam of both intense light and heat. They are used in banks of eight for audience lighting and general flood.

High-intensity arc-type lights are used in follow spots and in some computerized lamps. These lamps require a ballast to operate. To maintain optimum

Figure 15–2. Par cans. These hold par 64 bulbs and raylight kits.

Figure 15–3. Profile spots. Their round size can be adjusted with an iris and shaped with the shutters.

results, the quartz arc tube should not be handled. To operate the lamp for periods of less than 3 minutes will seriously shorten the lamp's life.

Most lamps work on the similar principle of heating a piece of wire, the filament, to the point at which it gives off light. Filaments are weakened when they are heated and are in their most delicate state while on or still warm. To avoid any rough treatment of the lamp while it is on, an approximate focus of the lamps

Figure 15–4. VARI*LITE Series 200 automated lighting system. VARI*LITE VL2 spot luminaire and VL3 wash luminaire. (Courtesy of Vari-Lite, Inc.)

should be done while at ground level so that only slight adjustment is required in the air when the lamp is on.

With the development of microchip technology has come the computerized light (Figure 15–4). Varying degrees of technology are built around a light source. The most sophisticated models can alter pan, tilt, beam size, color, and beam shape and change with split-second timing through every degree of color in the spectrum. The most unsophisticated have limited color change and limited movement and beam controls. Lamps used in conjunction with a sophisticated control console enable a designer to have an infinite number of possibilities. Then the only limit is one's imagination.

Color changers can be fitted to the front of most lamps to provide a scroll of color that is moved on rollers. The color changer is controlled by either a manual or memory console.

HANGING LAMPS

Lamps are generally hung on the rails of trusses with hook clamps. Bars of lamps also have hook clamps. The lamps hung on the grid must have safety wires attached, gel-frame properly seated, and have undergone testing and a rough focus before the grid is raised. Anything that falls from the truss can cause serious injury. Tape any cables running along the trusses firmly in place so they do not hinder the crew.

Often lamps are situated on the floor as well as on the grid. These lights are prone to be moved, usually out of people's ignorance of lighting and the precise nature of focusing. Any cables run out to floor lamps should cross audio cables at right angles to avoid mains-induced hum in the audio cables.

CHAPTER 16

DIMMERS

HOW A DIMMER WORKS

A *dimmer* is an electronic device that controls the amount of power a load uses by turning off parts of the mains waveform, thereby reducing the amount of time the lamp receives mains voltage. By switching on a variable portion of the mains waveform, the amount of power sent to the lamp can be controlled. This is known as *phase control*. The actual devices that switch the mains waveform are collectively known as *thyristors*. These are divided into two groups: *triacs* and *silicon-controlled rectifiers* (SCRs).

The thyristor is like a switch controlled by a trigger pulse. To provide control for SCR triggering, a voltage that falls at a set rate during the mains half cycle is generated and resets to a maximum level when the mains waveform passes through the zero volt point. The generated voltage is called a *ramp* because of its shape.

The ramp voltage is compared with the DC control voltage from the console (between 0 and 10 V), and an *oscillator enable pulse* is generated whenever the control voltage is greater than the ramp voltage. The oscillator then produces a stream of very narrow pulses for the duration of the oscillator enable pulse and so triggers the gate of the SCR, turning it on. The ramp voltage waveform generated in the dimmers is reset and repeated every mains half cycle. The control voltage input is internally compared with the ramp voltage, and the thyristors triggered, when the voltage exceeds the ramp voltage. A low control voltage triggers the thyristors late in the half cycle, giving low output power. A higher control voltage triggers the thyristors earlier, giving higher output power. The shape of the ramp voltage therefore governs the dimmer's control law.

RAMPS

The *square law ramp*, established as a standard by the United States Illuminating Engineering Society, takes into account the human eye's nonlinear response to changes in light intensity. For a control level of 50%, you would see a light level 50% of maximum.

The *true power ramp* will give an output of 50% for a setting of 50%. A 1000 watt bulb will only be using 500 watts at a 50% setting. With the *exponential ramp*, the light output varies the most in the control range of 70 to 100%. The *linear ramp* is not a curve but a straight line with the greatest variation in light output in settings between 30 and 70%. The *luminance ramp* is similar to the square law ramp for settings above 40%. Below this level the light output increases rapidly compared with the square law ramp. Finally, a *switching ramp* allows an on-off control; below 50% the channel is off and above 50% it is on full.

TYPES OF DIMMERS

Dimmers are packaged in several different ways. Those packaged for touring should be able to remain patched for transportation (Figure 16–1). A dimmer's

Figure 16–1.   Dimmer rack. Dimmers packaged for touring should be able to remain packed for transportation. (Courtesy Avolites.)

size is stated by the amount of power it can handle. The most common sizes of dimmers used for touring are 2.5 and 5 kw. A 2.5 kw dimmer can supply power to two 1250-watt bulbs or five 500-watt bulbs. A 5 kw dimmer can supply 5000 watts of power. If the dimmer has more than it can handle, it will blow the fuse. The type of connectors on dimmer packs and the voltage also varies. Some dimmers are mounted in the lamp bars, which assign a control channel on the bar.

DIMMER PATCHING

Patching refers to plugging the lamps into the dimmers with the correct control channel. The looms from the lamps terminate in different ways, but the principles are the same. Each lamp terminates at the rack as a single circuit. Take care that no 120 V lamps are patched into 240 V dimmers unless they are on a series splitter (twofer). A 120 V lamp cannot be paired with a 240 V lamp. If two lamps are paired in series, supposedly with 120 V bulbs, and one is bright and one is dull, then the bulbs are mismatched. The dull one is the 240 V lamp and should be changed for a 120 V lamp. Aircraft lamps are 28 V, and four lamps in series is one 120 V circuit.

CHAPTER 17

CONTROL CABLES

The control cable carries the control voltage from the console to the dimmers. The console sends a voltage between 0 and 10 V DC depending on the console setting. Each console channel connects to the dimmer racks, where it is patched to the appropriate dimmers. Along with the console control cables are intercom lines and a power feed for the console.

Muliplex systems use digital information to control the dimmers. The console sends out a string of digital data to each dimmer, which receives the information

Figure 17–1. Multiway connectors on a lighting board.

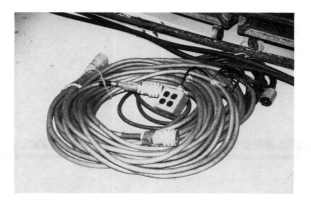

Figure 17–2.   Multiway cable. Before running the multiway cable to the console, make sure there are no restrictions on the way.

allocated to it. The digital multiplex code uses a paired shielded cable instead of a multicore cable with a pair of wires for each control channel (Figure 17–1).

CARE OF MULTICORE CABLES

Before running the multiway cables to the console, check that there are no restrictions on the route you select (Figure 17–2). Cables usually must be strung up

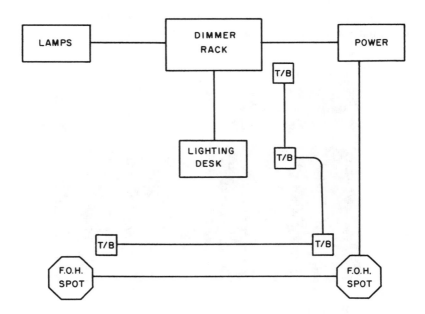

Figure 17–3.   Lighting system schematic. Connections between console, dimmers, and lamps.

above any fire exit doorways or run through a duct. The connectors should be protected by a padded sock and never be dragged along the ground. If the connector snags, a great deal of soldering will be needed.

A fault with the multicore cable can be easily determined. Console output should be 10 V DC. Read the output connector on the console, then on the end of the cable that connects to the dimmer racks. If there is no reading on the console connector, then a console fault exists. A lighting system schematic is shown in Figure 17–3.

CHAPTER 18

CONTROL CONSOLES

The control console controls the level of each channel and groups channels together into scenes.

MANUAL CONSOLES

Manual consoles take the operator's physical movements of the faders and send a control voltage to the dimmers directly related to the fader's position on the console (Figure 18–1). A fader position of five will send a 5 V DC signal to the dimmer it is connected to. The more channels on a console, the more complex scenes can become. Most consoles have two presets, which allow the scenes to be preset and then faded in by the scene master.

Scene control masters control the level of the scene patched into the pin matrix, which has a series of sockets that receive a pin (Figure 18–2). Each channel has a socket, and the number of scenes determines the number of times each channel is repeated. When the pins are inserted, each scene master will bring up the channels that are pinned. Each channel has a flash button for instant full power, and the matrix masters also have flash buttons. Some consoles have chasers that are pinned on the matrix and have step control.

COMPUTER CONSOLES

Computer consoles have the same functions as manual consoles, but they have a large memory and can store several complex scenes (Figures 18–3 and 18–4). The computer can record different levels for channels, unlike the matrix system, which

Figure 18–1. Manual console. The operator must move the faders to control the dimmers.

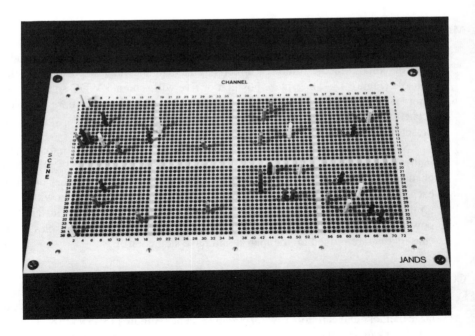

Figure 18–2. Pin matrix. Scenes are patched into the pin matrix with special pins.

Figure 18–3. Computer console. These consoles have a large memory and can remember several complex scenes.

Figure 18–4. VARI*LITE Artisan control console. The console is the heart of the VARI*LITE Series 200 automated lighting system. (Courtesy Vari-Lite, Inc.)

is a fixed level. The chase sequences in a computer console are much more sophisticated than on manual consoles.

Before attempting to operate a computer console, study the console manual. After you understand the book completely, begin to get hands-on experience.

The most important thing about operating any console is the timing. All the computers in the world cannot make you a terrific lighting operator. Sensitive, accurate timing used to create a mood and give a song more dramatic impact is the key to good operating.

CHAPTER 19

INTERCOM SYSTEMS

The intercom system allows the lighting crew to communicate during a show. The lighting director can cue follow spot operators, and the stage manager can call start and finish cues for the house light operator. Good communication is necessary for a smooth performance (Figure 19–1).

Each headset is fitted with a microphone. The belt pack, which connects the headphones to the system, has a call button that lights up when any station is

Figure 19–1. Intercom headphones and beltpack. The intercom system allows the lighting crew to communicate during a show.

calling, an on/off switch for the microphone, and a volume control for station level.

Keep the stations off such metal objects as spot stands. If the station finds a second earth reference, the system may hum, which will make it even more difficult to hear. The microphone should be switched off at all stations unless it is being used. Any microphones left on will amplify any spill, which competes with the person speaking and makes it difficult to hear.

Stations must be distributed to all the follow spot, dimmer, house light control, and console operators. A station is required for the stage manager at the stage entrance for cueing the house light operators. Other stations may be required for curtain cues, pyrotechnics, and so on.

CHAPTER 20

SMOKE MACHINES

Smoke is used to create many effects. The smoke provides a medium for the beams of light so that they can be seen instead of just illuminating the stage floor. All smoke machines get hot as part of the process of making the smoke and must therefore be handled very carefully.

FOGGERS

Fog machines use water- or oil-based fluids to produce a puffy smoke that needs fans to spread it across the stage. Because fluid vaporization is never complete, a residue eventually builds up and must be cleaned regularly to maintain optimum machine performance. Place the fog machine so that the area in front of it is clear, allowing the smoke to dissipate.

DRY ICE MACHINES

The difference between dry ice and fog is that dry ice falls to the floor while fog rises. Dry ice machines are like big kettles that heat water. The ice is lowered into the boiling water, resulting in smoke. Fans and flexible tubing are required to get the smoke to where it is needed.

Dry ice burns the skin; wear gloves when handling it. The ice comes in blocks or pellets, and the blocks must be broken up so that the ice is evenly distributed in the machine. Do not let the machine boil dry. Turn the machine off when it is not in use, and remember to allow time for the water to boil before the smoke is needed.

PYROTECHNICS

The term *pyrotechnics* refers to any flash or bang. Many stage fireworks are available. Because they are potentially dangerous, the operator must be licensed.

CRACKED OIL

Cracked oil smoke is made from compressed air cracking a fine oil. An air compressor is connected to outlet tanks containing the oil. The compressed air is fed into the oil through a collection of spray jets. A fine mist is the result.

CHAPTER 21

DRAPES

All drapes must be fireproofed and are required, by law, to be labeled with the date and method of fire retardation. The drapes should have their size marked on them and also on the center position. Be careful when handling drapes because they are very delicate. The drapes should be the last thing added to the grid before it is hoisted to its operating height. Keep the drapes tied up and out of the way until it is necessary to lower them for focusing once the stage has been set.

BLACK DRESSING

Black drapes are used to mask off the hardware of the stage and form a boundary for the performing area. The drape at the rear of the stage is called a *backdrop*. The narrow strips of drape that are hung on either side of the stage to mask the wings are called *legs*. The drapes used to mask the trusses are abbreviated drops called *borders*.

CYCLORAMAS

Cycloramas (cycs), plain cloths that close off the back of the stage, are hung down to stage level, extending up and out to create an impression of great space. Lay out a roll of plastic or cloth on the stage to keep the cyc clean while it is being attached (you cannot have a great space with a handprint in the middle).

SCRIMS AND GAUZES

Scrim and *gauze* are synonyms for a finely woven, delicate fabric used to create a translucent effect.

SCREENS

Rear projection screens are used to display images projected from behind the screen. These screens are fire retardant because of the plastic material used in their manufacture.

The screen provides a wide viewing angle of the images projected. A white screen provides bright and even images of rear projections. A gray screen, the most widely used, is good for medium-level ambient light conditions where a bright projected image is desired. A black screen is excellent for high ambient light conditions, giving the image a greater contrast, and deep colors more intensity and richness.

CURTAIN TRACKS

Curtain tracks are used for curtains that open or close during a performance. Tracks are used for front of stage curtains. In a theatre this curtain is called the house curtain, and these curtains obscure the stage from the audience until they are removed. Drapes part in the center when they open; opening drapes requires a smooth, consistent motion. Tracks may be used to display a range of backdrops, from black to white to painted. When sections of track are joined together, check them to make sure there will be no snags along the length of the track. It is a disaster when a curtain does not open when it should.

KABUKI DROPS

A Kabuki drop is a method of removing the drape. The Kabuki pipe that the drape is suspended from has a series of spikes that the drape is hooked onto. The pipe is fixed to a swivel mechanism, and, when rotated so that the spikes face downward, the drape falls to the floor with an even motion.

CHAPTER 22

FOLLOW SPOTS

Follow spots are used to light the stage's focal points (Figure 22–1). The follow spots are operated manually; the operator controls the intensity, color, and movement of the spot. Follow spots are positioned in front of the stage in the venue or on the grid above the stage (Figure 22–2). The position of follow spots should be high so that the beam does not wash the whole stage and does not shine in the performers' eyes (Figure 22–3).

OPERATING FOLLOW SPOTS

A follow spot operator receives cues from the lighting director on the headphone intercom system. The follow spot operator should not switch off the microphone on the intercom station and should not speak to the director unless absolutely necessary. Spot cues are usually given as standby spot number, gel-frame number, and then position. The command to change to the cue is always given with ''go'' as the last word. Cues may be given to follow certain action on the stage. It is important to give spot light operators clear and distinct cues. Because the follow spots highlight the subject being spotted, any mistake will be immediately obvious to the entire audience, the performers, and the crew.

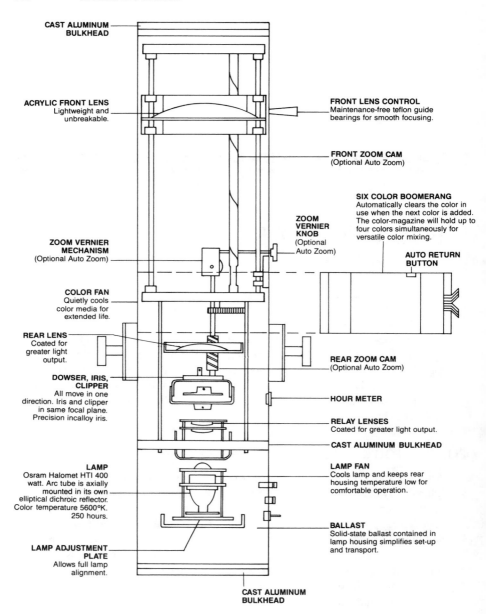

Figure 22–1. Ultra-arc follow spot. Follow spots are used to light the focal points of the stage. (Courtesy Phoebus Manufacturing.)

Figure 22–2. Short-throw follow spot. These spots are usually positioned in the grid above the stage.

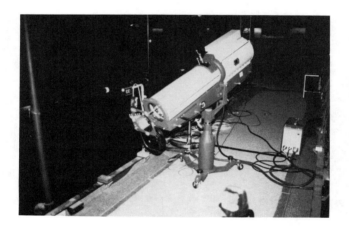

Figure 22–3. Front of house follow spot. The position of follow spots should be high so the beam does not wash the stage or get into the performer's eyes.

CHAPTER 23

COLOR

Color gives the lighting designer a palette to work from to create the moods and scenes that enhance a performance. The color media guide (Appendix A) outlines some recommendations of the use of the complete range of colors available. The recommendations are not hard and fast rules, however. Stage lighting is an art, not a science.

Some countries have stringent fire regulations prohibiting the use of certain gels. The self-extinguishing polycarbonate filters, such as Supergel by Rosco, comply with the most stringent requirements. All gels will melt if there is any dust on the surface. The dust particles become like red-hot rocks with the heat from the lamp.

Blue filters always fade more quickly than other colors. All filters change the color of the lamp by allowing part of the spectrum to pass through while absorbing all other colors. The blue absorbs green and red; red is in the hot part of the spectrum, and the heat makes the color evaporate, resulting in a faded filter.

Whenever any gel is cut, mark the color number on each piece with a Chinagraph pencil. The mark should be in the center of the filter so that it can be easily identified from the ground.

Patterns or gobos are metal stencils placed in profile spots to project the stencil's image. A number of composite patterns can be used to create animated effects (Figure 23–1). Mesh is used to shade certain patterns. A wide range of gobos are available to give special effects without any special equipment, and they can be used boldly or subtly to good effect.

Figure 23–1. Composite pattern. A number of composite patterns can be used to create animated patterns. (Courtesy Rosco Laboratories.)

CHAPTER 24

LIGHTING PLOTS

Most of the information that relates to a lighting system is contained on the plot. Lamp types, position, control channel, gel color, and cable numbers are all marked on the plot. Because the plot is the point of reference for any lighting system, it is necessary to know how to read the plot and put together the equipment to turn the plot into a working system (Figure 24–1).

READING A LIGHTING PLOT

Draw the lighting plot to scale to allow for calculation of the number of truss sections, corners, truss rigging, chain motors, lamp positioning, and length of cables required. The legend, or means of notation, can be presented in different ways, so always check the legend of each plot. The legend allows you to calculate the number and type of lamps, number of cables, number of dimmers, power requirements, and number of control channels. The position and size of drapes, whether truss borders, legs, cycloramas, or backdrops, should be marked on the plot.

Several lists can be drawn up from the plot to order the correct equipment. Many plots will supply additional information to clarify trim heights, follow spot requirements, smoke or pyrotechnic effects, number of talkback stations, dimmer position, and control console position. A system list itemizes types of lamps, number and lengths of cables, accessories and dressing, rigging, and trussing (Figure 24–2). A gel-color-filter cutting list can be drawn up so that the right amount of gel is cut to fit the lamps being used.

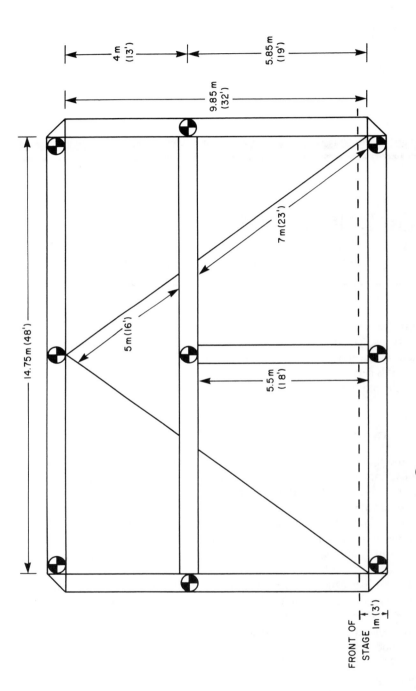

Figure 24–1.   Rigging plot. Draw it to scale to allow calculation of trusses and motor positions.

CIRCUIT CODING

The dimmer patch must be worked out to identify the control channel and lamps connected to each of the dimmers. The lamps are identified by the code of the cable connecting the lamp to the dimmers. The circuit code identifies the position of the lamps on the grid. In some circumstances a lamp's position will not lend itself to standard coding, necessitating special circuit codes. A standard code for identifying a lighting system's circuits can be used, however.

All cross-stage trusses are coded starting at the front downstage rail at the bar of lamps nearest to the dimmers, beginning with A1. Subsequent bars or circuits are coded A2, A3, and so on. Once the downstage rail is coded, the upstage rail of the front truss is coded B1, B2, and so on. The letters I and O are not used to avoid confusion with 1 and 0. At all times the lowest number is on the dimmer side of the stage.

All trusses running up and downstage use DSL for downstage left, USL for upstage left, DSR for downstage right, and USR for upstage right. Lamps hung in a vertical array use L1, L2, and so on for stage left and R1, R2, and so on for stage right. Lamps positioned diagonally are marked XL for cross-stage left and XR for cross-stage right.

Any lamps positioned on the stage and not on the grid are identified with the code FL followed by a number. Ground rows and cyclorama lights are coded with GR followed by a number, with the lowest number being closest to the dimmers.

PUTTING TOGETHER A SYSTEM

Once all the lists have been drawn up from the information on the plot, the system can be assembled. Use copies of the plot as a checklist to mark off the items prepared, checked, coded, and packed. A system that has been well prepared and coded can be assembled quickly at the venue (Figure 24–3).

All the lamp bars can be gelled and the correct bulb type fitted and marked with the circuit code. The bars must be checked for loose or stripped screws or loose or frayed cables, and repaired as needed. It is far easier to repair items on the ground than to try to fix them while they are 20 feet in the air.

The cables that carry the power to the lamps can be strapped together and coded. All the cables distributing the circuits to a truss can be loomed, but the number of cables strapped together should remain manageable. It is pointless having an unmanageable loom that becomes a tangled mess. Any adaptors necessary to convert the end of the multiway cable to individual circuits can be attached and marked. Individual circuits are required for lamps not on bars.

Ellipsoidal spots must have the lenses and reflectors cleaned and the lamp's mechanical parts checked for smooth operation. Any gobos being used can be fitted. These lamps can accept a variety of bulbs with different voltage and wattage as long as they are clearly marked: a 120 V bulb lasts a fraction of a second in a 240 V dimmer.

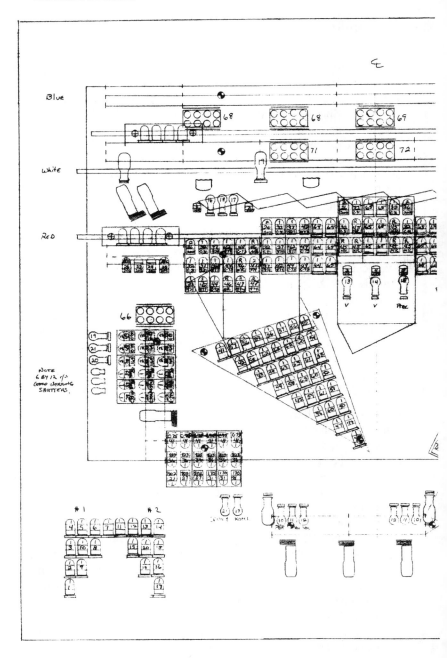

Figure 24–2.   Lighting plot. Lamp types, position, control channel, gel color, and cable numbers are all marked on the plot. (Courtesy of Steve Cohen.)

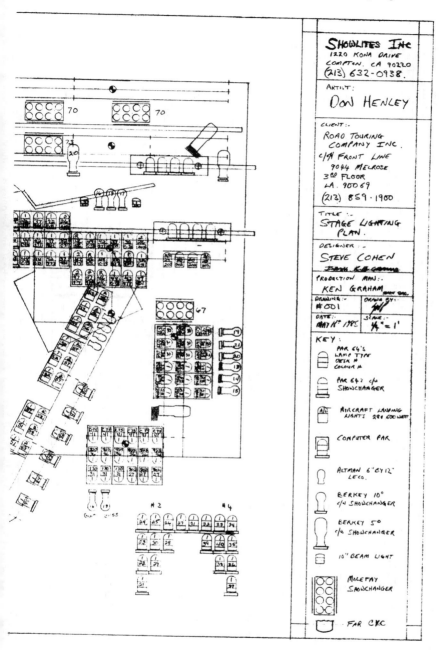

CONCERT PRODUCTIONS — LIGHTING SYSTEM LIST

ARTIST: _____ ENGINEER: _____

P/U DATE: —/—/— D/O DATE: —/—/— 1st SHOW: —/—/— LAST SHOW: —/—/—

ITEM	SYSTEM	ADDITIONAL ITEMS						SUB-HIRES/COMMENTS	No. CASES	CUBIC (M³)
CONSOLE										
MULTICORE										
DIMMERS		FEED/S					OTHER			
3-PHASE POWER/DISTRIBUTION				DISTRIBUTION						
CONTROL/DIMMER ACCESSORIES		CONTROL LINKS		POWER LINKS			OTHER ACCESSORIES			
INSTRUMENTS PAR 64		VNSP	NSP	MFL	WFL	ACL	RAY			
PROFILE		6 x 9	6 x 12	6 x 16	6 x 22	CCT 30°	CCT 10°			
MOLEFAY		2 W	6-W	OTHER/S						
CYC		PALS 4	IRIS 4							
FRESNEL		1K	2K							
OTHER										
SPOTS(F.O.H.)										
SPOTS(TRUSS)		SPOT SEATS		SPOT ADAPTOR			OTHER			
SPOT RIGGING										
SPARE LAMPS										
INTERCOM		MASTER		HEADSET		BELTPACK	MIC CABLES			
WETLAND LOOMS							SPLITTER BOX			
CABLES/A-C's HEADERS				LEGS						
DRESSING		TABS		CLAMPS		BORDERS	SCRIM/CYC			
TAB TRACK		SECTIONS				JOINS	BOBBINS			
FX/MISCELLANEOUS										
CHAIN MOTORS//GROUND SUPPORT										
MOTOR CONTROL										
MOTOR-TRUSS RIGGING WIRE ROPES										
SPANSETS										
SHACKLES										
TRUSSING SECTIONS										
ACCESSORIES										
TRUSS RIGGING PIPES										
CLAMPS										
OUTRIGGERS										
OTHER										
EXTRAS/COMMENTS										

NOTES

Check dimmers for any loose screws or electrical faults. Dimmers should be patched and marked clearly with the circuit code so that all the cables can be automatically plugged into the right socket. Patching the dimmers requires a great deal of concentration, so the best time to patch them is when there is peace and quiet, not during a setup. The dimmers not only provide the circuitry to control the amount of power sent to each lamp, but they also distribute power to all the lamps. The power distribution system must therefore be cbecked for any burnt connectors and loose wires. Dealing with a large number of instruments requires a great deal of power. Any mistakes or faults can be extremely dangerous and costly.

Check whatever is being used to fasten the truss sections together. The right number of snap-out pipes, 90° scaffold clamps, swivel clamps, and pipes must be packed. Clamps should be checked for any stripped or jammed threads.

Drapes should be checked for ties and runners and to ensure that they have no tears and are clean. Mark the size of the drape on each corner and also make a center mark. All drapes used for shows must be fireproof and be marked with the fireproofing method and date. Also, all curtain tracks must be checked for bends and snags.

Cut and install the gels for the follow spots. All follow spots must be checked for mechanical and electrical functions and have clean lenses. Spots to be positioned on the truss need the correct hardware for mounting and seats with seat belts for the operators.

Smoke machines will deteriorate quickly if not maintained. They must be cleaned regularly to remove any blockages that inhibit the flow of smoke. The amount of fog fluid depends on the number of performances.

Label the control console and check the functions and multicore cables. It is often not possible to assemble an entire lighting system before it is set up at a venue because of the amount of space and power necessary, which makes checking the console functions difficult. Do any programming or matrix patching that you can before setup.

The power feeder cable that gets the power from the supply to the distribution board for the dimmer racks must be able to connect to the supply. The connection is either through screw terminals or bolted on to a bar with lugs. If in doubt, make sure you have the right lugs for the cable.

The intercom system used for cueing spotlight operators must be in perfect condition, since coordination of the show relies on it. Spare headsets and belt packs should always be available.

Chain motors and rigging equipment have stringent safety laws. Do not use any piece of rigging equipment you suspect is faulty. The motor control and motors must be electrically and physically checked. Enough slings and shackles should be packed to enable the motors to be rigged where required, allowing for height and bridles.

Work lights, tools, ladders, gaffer tape, insulating tape, and spare lamps, clamps, bolts, and fuses are needed. All cases that have been packed should have their estimated weights marked on them.

Now that various pieces of lighting equipment have been packed as a lighting system, gelled up, and coded for a particular show, the boxes can be loaded into the truck and taken to the venue. Remember that heavy boxes go on the bottom and light ones on the top. Keep same-sized cases in blocks as much as possible. Work out a truck pack before the truck is loaded; rigging cases and motors should be the first cases unloaded, so load them last. Pack the cases in tightly and strap them to reduce damaging vibration.

CHAPTER 25

LIGHTING SYSTEM SETUP PROCEDURE

SETUP

The setup procedure outlines the series of events that result in the lighting system's being ready for a show. Each design requires its own specialized approach because the number of lamps will always differ, as will their positions and the amount of time available to set up. The order of events are the same whatever the size of the rig and the number of crew setting up. The larger a system is, the more things will be done, by more crew, simultaneously. Keep copies of the lighting plot on hand so that everyone can refer to them. The pressure is usually on the lighting crew to get the lighting grid in the air as quickly as possible so that the stage can be set with sound and band equipment. It is important to communicate with the other members of the production crew so that the setups can be a coordinated procedure.

Unloading the Truck

One member of the lighting crew should stay in the truck as it is being unloaded to ensure that the equipment is handled properly and nothing gets dropped or damaged (Figure 25–1). Other crew members should stay in the venue and direct and assist the equipment to its desired location as it is brought in. All cases should be clearly marked for desired location so that minimum direction is required. The color code to use is as follows:

Red: stage left
Yellow: stage right
Green: front of house (FOH)
Orange: on stage

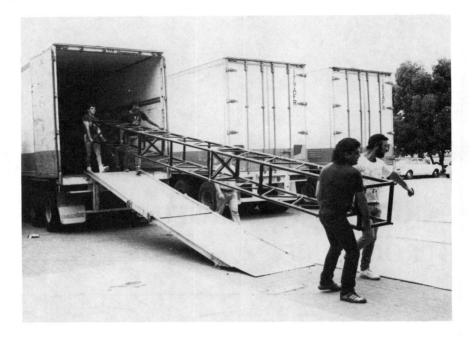

Figure 25–1.   Unloading the truck. One lighting crew member should stay in the truck to ensure stagehands unload everything properly.

Rigging

Chalk the position of the points required on the stage so the riggers can see them from the roof. The chain motors must be positioned and any rigging necessary attached to the motor hook.

The chain motor power must be connected and the phasing checked so that the motor moves in the right direction (Figure 25–2). Motor control cables can be run along the trusses to the motor controller, so as soon as each motor is rigged, it can be lifted and attached to the truss. As soon as the last motor is rigged, the grid should be ready to be lifted. When the trusses are supported on ground supports the ground should be solid and level. If a ground support is not leveled, it will lean, the truss will be hoisted higher, and the chance of an accident will increase.

Power Connection

The three-phase connection is usually made by the venue electrician or a qualified outside electrician. Establish the location and rating of the fuses or breakers in the event of a power failure. The power connection should commence as soon as the cable is unloaded; it should be one of the first things off the truck because the venue electrician may not be used to working at the same pace as a touring crew.

Figure 25–2.   Rigging a chain motor. Chain motor power must be checked for correct phasing so that the motor moves in the right direction.

Assembling the Trusses

As the truss sections arrive on stage, they must be positioned and connected. Each connection must be checked at each setup (Figure 25–3). As the grid is being assembled, all additional pipes and outriggers can be fitted, borders attached, and truss spots mounted.

Looming

While the points are being rigged, which can sometimes take longer than desired, the looms can be run out and attached to the trusses.

Hanging the Lamps

As soon as the grid is lifted, it is time to hang the lamps. The bars of lamps should be marked with their coded number, the same number on the cable that connects the bar to the dimmers. Mark the position of each bar on the trusses, or, if this is not possible, check the position of the lamps. Once the cables are connected the looms can be tested to reveal any faults. Check the lamps to make sure the gel frame is seated safely, all bolts are secure, and the gel is in good condition. Do a rough focus now so that minimal adjustment is necessary later. Lamps sometimes get

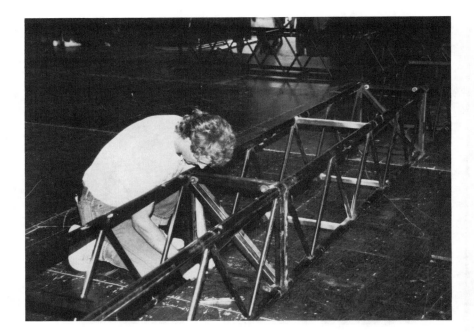

Figure 25–3.   Assembling the trusses. Each connection must be checked at each setup.

damaged in transit or just burn out, so make sure they all work before the grid is raised to its operating height. It is much easier to change lamps with your feet firmly on the ground (Figure 25–4).

Drapes

While the lamps are being checked, all the drapes can be attached to the grid. Check legs and borders for neatness and symmetry and tab tracks for any snags. The legs and backdrop may have to be tied until later in the setup so that they do not restrict access onto the stage.

Raising the Grid

When the lamps, looms, and drapes are ready, attach the ladder, drop bag, and trim chains. When the grid is being raised, the person operating the chain hoists must ensure that nobody is standing under it (Figure 25–5). Once the grid is at its operating height, each point must be trimmed to its exact height as measured by the trim chains. Raise cable picks with the grid to reduce the looms' weight on the grid. When trusses are being lifted on ground supports, raise them evenly so that one support does not become overloaded.

Figure 25–4.   Hanging lamps. Do a rough focus so that minimal adjustment is necessary when focusing.

Dimmers

Now that the grid is up at trim and the stage is clear, the dimmers can be patched. By this time the electrician should have connected the power, which can be checked before it is connected to the power distribution for the dimmers. Set the console and run out the multicore control cable. Do a circuit check to determine any dimmer faults (Figure 25–6).

Follow Spots

If follow spots must be hoisted onto catwalks or cradles, the riggers should sling the spots so that they do not get dropped. Once the spots are in position, they can be set up and focused. While the spots are being set, the intercom can be run out and checked. The intercom must run to all spots, dimmers, console, house light control, and stage entrance.

Floor Lamps

After the stage has been set with sound and band equipment, position the floor lamps, smoke machines, and fans. Cables that run across the stage should be kept

Figure 25–5.   Raising the grid. When the grid is being raised, the person operating the chain hoists must ensure that nobody is standing under it.

Figure 25–6.   Dimmers. The dimmer racks assign the correct control channel to each lamp.

as far away as possible from any audio cables. Lighting cables should cross audio cables at right angles if necessary and not run parallel to them.

Focus

The easiest way to focus is while it is quiet. If the focus can be coordinated with a piano tuner or sound crew break, this is the best time. The more lamps to focus, the more organized you must be. The lighting director should know exactly where each lamp on the plot will be focused. The stage can be marked with the spacing for lamps so that symmetrical beams will be focused accurately. A list of channels for the focus can be given to the board operator so that the lighting director can stay on stage and direct the focus. A hand signal or a whistle tells the board operator to move to the next channel. An intercom station on stage during the focus can obviate the need for screaming. It is dangerous to climb on trusses in the dark, so concentration is necessary.

SHOW TIME

During the show the lighting crew may be involved with operating the console, operating a follow spot, operating smoke machines, opening and closing curtains, or being on dimmer watch. The show's start and finish should be coordinated with the stage manager so that the house lights go out and come on when they are supposed to.

LOAD OUT

First, get the floor lamps off the stage, and the console, multicore cables, and dimmers packed while the stage is being cleared. Once the stage is cleared the grid can be lowered and the rig dismantled, cased, and loaded into the truck.

MAINTENANCE

Some daily maintenance is usually required because the electrical equipment and lamps are fragile. Wheels do get smashed, cables do get damaged, and lamps do get broken, so regular maintenance is a good idea.

SAFETY

Safety in rigging, both mechanical and electrical, cannot be overemphasized. Time is always short because show time is always looming, and it may seem tempting to cut corners, thereby missing a loose nut or frayed cable. The only way to avoid accidents is to check, check again, and keep checking. For example, do not block fire exits, fire extinguishers, or hoses with empty cases. Do not leave cables under load coiled up, because they may melt and possibly cause a fire. Have an electrical fire extinguisher available adjacent to the dimmers. Some cities have

Figure 25–7.   Safety wire on lamps. Safety chains or wires are necessary for all lamps suspended above stage.

very strict regulations about dimmer positions and require the dimmers to be set in mesh cages. Safety chains or wires are necessary for all lamps suspended above the stage (Figure 25–7). Finally, before climbing the ladder onto the grid or trusses, empty your pockets of coins and tools!

COLOR MEDIA GUIDE: SUGGESTIONS ON HOW TO USE SUPERGEL AND ROSCOLENE COLOR FILTERS

ACTING AREAS/WARM

The color range here includes amber, pink, straw, and salmon, with several choices in each color category. These colors are often cross lit with those recommended for cool acting areas. The warm colors suggest daylight and brightness. They are generally used for scenes set in the morning or noon.

Supergel	Roscolene	Applications
01 Light Bastard Amber	802 Bastard Amber	Enhances fair skin tones. Suggests strong sunlight.
	803 Pale Gold	Good where a tint of color is needed. Excellent for natural skin tones.
03 Dark Bastard Amber		Most saturated Bastard Amber.
04 Medium Bastard Amber		Especially useful when cross lit with a cool color. Excellent for natural sunlight.
05 Rose Tint		Excellent area light and warm cosmetic color.
06 No Color Straw	804 No Color Straw	Slightly off-white. Good for interiors.
07 Pale Yellow		Double saturation of 06.
	805 Light Straw	Less green than 07. Excellent realistic sunlight in a light-colored show.
	808 Medium Straw	Warmer straw. Flattering to skin tones. Useful for dance.
09 Pale Amber Gold		Deep straw. Late afternoon sunsets.
30 Light Salmon Pink		Excellent for general area washes. Gives overall warming effect to skin tones.
31 Salmon Pink	834 Salmon Pink	General wash. Good for follow spots. Useful in a warm and cool combination.
	835 Medium Salmon Pink	Similar uses as 31 and 834. Provides deeper tones.
33 No Color Pink	825 No Color Pink	A pale, almost colorless pink. A popular color among dance lighting designers.
	826 Flesh Pink	Useful for bright musicals.
35A Light Pink		Close to 33.
36A Medium Pink		Good for general washes and crosslighting.
38 Light Rose		Greater saturation with similar uses as 36.

ACTING AREAS/COOL

Blue and violet are the colors on the cool side of the spectrum. There are probably more shades of blue represented in Supergel and Roscolene than any other color because virtually every stage production requires some blue in the palette.

Supergel	Roscolene	Applications
61 Mist Blue (greener)		Excellent for general area washes. Very light cool tint of blue.
63 Pale Blue (greener)		Helps maintain white light when dimmer is at low intensity.
64 Light Steel Blue		
65 Daylight Blue		Useful beams of realistic moonlight.
66	848 Water Blue	Useful for achieving depressed moods and dull skies.
	849 Pale Blue (greener)	Good cold light. Pale greenish blue, useful moonlight source.
67 Light Sky Blue	851 Daylight Blue	Excellent sky color. Useful for cyc and border lights.
	852 Smoky Blue (redder)	
70 Nile Blue	850 No Color Blue	Useful for very light midday skies.
71 Sea Blue	853 Middle Blue (greener)	Occasionally used for general cool tint.
72 Azure Blue		

ACTING AREAS/NEUTRAL

These colors, in the lavender, gray, and blue ranges, work as complementary colors for both the warm and cool area colors or where just a touch of color is desirable. The Supergel diffusers offer the designer extra flexibility.

Supergel	Roscolene	Applications
52 Light Lavender	840 Surprise Lavender	Touch of color when white light is not desirable.
53 Pale Lavender		Good on costumes or when instruments are down on dimmer.
54 Special Lavender		Excellent for general area or border light washes. It is a basic follow spot color.
55 Lilac (bluer)		Use when a touch of color is needed. Use when white light is not desirable.
57A Lavender	841 Surprise pink (redder)	Same as 53.
58A Deep Lavender	842 Special Lavender	Same as 53.
	844 Violet	Gives good visibility without destroying night illusions.
		Excellent backlight. Enhances dimensionality.
78 Trudy Blue	880 Light Gray	Rich medium blue.
	883 Medium Gray (very dark)	Usually used in combination with light tints of color. Reduces the brightness of color but does not affect hue on saturation. Useful where dimmer control or lower wattage lamp is not practical.
	882 Light Chocolate	Warms light and reduces intensity.
100 Frost	801 Frost	
101 Light Frost		
104 Tough Silk		
113 Matte Silk		
114 Hamburg Frost		
120 Red Diffusion		
121 Blue Diffusion		
122 Green Diffusion		
123 Amber Diffusion		

ACCENTS/WARM

These colors, which embrace a wide range of yellow, amber, pink, orange, and magenta, are frequently used in sidelights, downlights, and backlights. They add a warm cast while sculpting actors, scenery, or props with light.

Supergel	Roscolene	Applications
10 Medium Yellow		Yellow with green. Good for special effects. Accent unflattering in acting areas.
11 Light Straw		Pale yellow with slight red content. Useful for candle effects.
		Can be used for area lighting. For bright day feeling.
	806 Medium Lemon	Less green than 10. Unflattering in acting areas. Useful for contrast lighting, accents, hot day sunlight.
	807 Dark Lemon	Darker than 806 with a higher red content.
14 Medium Straw		Pale amber—higher red content than 12.
		Sunlight, accents, area lighting with caution to skin tones.
15 Deep Straw	809 Straw	Warm golden amber with some green. Useful for special effects such as candlelight and firelight. Tends to depress color pigment values. Use with care.
	810 No Color Amber	Good warm glow color for fire effect.
	811 Flame	Warm pinkish amber. Afternoon sunset. Good sidelight.
	813 Light Amber	Dark pink amber. Sunlight. Deep sunsets.

Continued

ACCENTS/WARM (Continued)

Supergel	Roscolene	Applications
20 Medium Amber	815 Golden Amber	Afternoon sunlight, lamplight, and candlelight. Tends to depress color pigment values.
	817 Dark Amber	Greater red content than 20. Useful for torchlight and light from wood fires. Use with great care. Destroys most pigment color values.
21 Golden Amber		Useful as amber cyc light and late sunsets.
23 Orange		Provides a romantic sunlight through windows for evening effects.
32 Medium Salmon Pink		Deepest of the salmon pinks.
40 Light Salmon	827 Bright Pink	Similar to 23 with a higher red content.
		Basic follow spot color. Useful in live entertainment situation and as strong accent.
	829 Bright Rose	Less saturation than 827.
	830 Medium Pink	Use in romantic settings. Often used in dance.
	828 Follies Pink	Musical pinks. Lush accents. Very versatile color.
48 Rose Purple		Pale evening color. Excellent for backlight.
	838 Dark Magenta	Greater intensity than 48.
	839 Rose Purple	Greater intensity than 838.
49 Medium Purple		Darkest of the magenta purple range.
50A Mauve	836 Plush Pink	Subdued sunlight effect. Useful in backlights.

ACCENTS/COOL

These shades of blue and green are widely used in evening or moonlight scenes where additional color accents are needed. Like the warm accent colors, they are most frequently used in sidelights, downlights, and backlights.

Supergel	Roscolene	Applications
68 Sky Blue		Excellent for early morning sky tones. Popular among designers for cyc and borders.
69 Brilliant Blue	856 Light Blue	Used for dramatic moonlight effects.
73 Peacock Blue	854 Steel Blue	Good for fantasy, moonlight, and water effects.
	855 Azure Blue	Moonlight. Natural sky on cyc. Slightly greenish.
76 Light Green Blue	858 Light Green Blue	Distinctive greenish blues.
77 Green Blue	859 Green Blue (Moonlight) (redder)	Useful for romantic moonlight.
	860 Bright Blue	
	862 True Blue	
	861 Surprise Blue	Primary blue. For use with three-color light primary system in cyc lighting.
	857 Light Medium Blue	
81 Urban Blue		Very cold brittle feeling.
82 Surprise Blue		Deep rich blue with slight amount of red.
86 Pea Green	878 Yellow Green	Good for dense foliage and woodland effects.
89 Moss Green	871 Light Green	Useful for mood, mystery, and toning.

CYC/SKY

The colors chosen for this group are often used for other purposes, but the shades of amber, red, blue, and green work particularly well on cycloramas. Cycs are generally used to set the horizon of the scene. Some stages use blue-colored material for their cycs, and these should be lit only with blue or green filters.

Supergel	Roscolene	Applications
21 Golden Amber	815 Golden Amber	Useful for torchlight and light from wood fires.
22 Deep Amber	817 Dark Amber	Use with great care. Destroys most pigment color values. Useful as amber cyc light and late sunsets.
26 Light Red	821 Light Red	Very useful as a backlight. Dramatic specials. Vibrant red. Good alternative primary.
27 Medium Red	823 Medium Red	Bright red. Alternate to primary red when higher light transmission is required. Good red primary for use with three-color light primary systems in cyclorama lighting, footlights and border lights.
	846 Medium Purple	Midnight and moonlight illusions. Enforces mysterious mood. Useful for evening cyc wash.
	843 Medium Lavender	Excellent for nighttime scenes. Rich, vivid accents, good in backgrounds. Unrealistic.

65	Daylight Blue	Useful for achieving depressed moods and dull skies.
67	Light Sky Blue	851 Daylight Blue — Excellent sky color. Useful for cyc and border.
68	Sky Blue	852 Smoky Blue (redder) — Excellent for early morning sky tones. Popular among designers for cyc and borders.
69	Brilliant Blue	856 Light Blue — Used for dramatic moonlight effects.
73	Peacock Blue	854 Steel Blue — Good for fantasy, moonlight, and water effects.
		855 Azure Blue — Moonlight. Natural sky on cyc. Slightly greenish.
76	Light Green Blue	858 Light Green Blue
		859 Green Blue (Moonlight) — Distinctive greenish blues. Useful for romantic moonlight.
		860 Bright Blue (greener)
		862 True Blue (bluer)
		857 Light Medium Blue — Primary blue.
81	Urban Blue	861 Surprise Blue — For use with three-color light primary system in cyc lighting.
82	Surprise Blue	Very cold, hard, brittle feeling.
		863 Dark Medium Blue (greener) — Deep rich blue with slight amount of red.
90	Dark Yellow Green	Good for nonrealistic night skies.
95	Medium Blue	874 Medium Green — Alternate primary where higher transmission is desired.
	Green	877 Medium Blue Green — Used on foliage in moonlight areas or for creating a mood of mystery. Good for toning scenery painted in blues, blue-greens, and greens.

SUNLIGHT

Some of these colors are repetitions of those listed under Acting Areas/Warm, but this group is limited to those colors that most nearly approximate sunlight. Real sunlight changes color slightly as the day wears on, so colors should be chosen and color changes specified to coincide with the time of day.

Supergel	Roscolene	Applications
01 Light Bastard Amber	802 Bastard Amber	Enhances fair skin tones. Suggests strong sunlight.
04 Medium Bastard Amber		Especially useful when cross lit with a cool color. Excellent for natural sunlight.
09 Pale Amber Gold	805 Light Straw	Less green than 07. Excellent realistic sunlight in a light-colored show. Deep straw. Late afternoon sunsets.
10 Medium Yellow		Yellow with green. Good for special effects. Unflattering in acting areas.
11 Light Straw		Pale yellow with slight red content. Useful for candle effects. Can be used for area lighting. For bright day feeling.
	806 Medium Lemon	Less green than 10. Unflattering in acting areas. Useful for contrast lighting accents and hot day sunlight.
	807 Dark Lemon	Darker than 806 with a higher red content.
14 Medium Straw		Pale amber—higher red content than 12. Sunlight, accents area lighting with caution to skin tones.
15 Deep Straw	809 Straw	Warm golden amber with some green. Useful for special effects. Candlelight and fire-light tend to depress color pigment values. Use with care. Good warm glow color for fire effect.
	810 No Color Amber	Dark pink amber. Sunlight. Deep sunsets.
	813 Light Amber	Afternoon sunlight, lamplight, and candlelight. Tends to depress color pigment values.
20 Medium Amber		
	815 Golden Amber	Greater red content than 20. Useful for torchlight and light from wood fires. Use with great care. Destroys most pigment color values.
	819 Orange Amber	Provides excellent effect in Par fixtures.
25 Orange Red	818 Orange	Same as 819. Less red.
23 Orange		Provides a romantic sunlight through windows for evening effects.
	869 Pale Yellow Green	Excellent accent tint. Soft tone frontlight at low dimmer readings.

MOONLIGHT

Moonlight is represented by lavender or blue, but there is a wide range of mood among the choices available here. The shade of moonlight chosen usually reflects the mood of the play's action.

Supergel	Roscolene	Applications
57 Lavender	841 Surprise Pink (redder)	Excellent backlight. Gives good visibility without destroying night illusions.
58 Deep Lavender	842 Special Lavender	Enhances dimensionality.
	844 Violet	
65 Daylight Blue	851 Daylight Blue	Useful for achieving depressed moods and dull skies.
67 Light Sky Blue	852 Smokey Blue (redder)	Excellent sky color. Useful for cyc and border.
68 Sky Blue	856 Light Blue	Excellent for early morning sky tones. Popular among designers for cyc and borders.
69 Brilliant Blue	848 Water Blue	Used for dramatic moonlight effects.
	849 Pale Blue (greener)	Pale greenish blue.
70 Nile Blue	850 No Color Blue	Useful for very light midday skies. Occasionally used for general cool tint.
71 Sea Blue	853 Middle Blue (greener)	
72 Azure Blue		
73 Peacock Blue	854 Steel Blue	Good for fantasy, moonlight, and water effects.
	855 Azure Blue	Natural sky on cyc. Slightly greenish.
81 Urban Blue		Very cold brittle feeling.
82 Surprise Blue		Deep rich blue with slight amount of red.

NIGHT/EVENING

These shades of blue are used for night where moonlight may or may not be the basic form of illumination. Night is black, which is the absence of color. These colors allow the audience to see the action while maintaining the "feel" of night.

Supergel	Roscolene	Applications
76 Light Green Blue	858 Light Green Blue	
	860 Bright Blue (greener)	Useful for romantic moonlight.
	862 True Blue (bluer)	
	861 Surprise Blue	Primary blue. For use with three-color light primary system in cyc lighting.
	857 Light Medium Blue	
85 Deep Blue		

SPECIAL EFFECTS

This large group of colors may be used for such special effects as fire and ghosts, but special effects include special color accents that add just the right note to a stage picture. The descriptions should help locate the exact color needed. This group is, above all others, subject to your imagination and style.

Supergel	Roscolene	Applications
10 Medium Yellow		Yellow with green. Good for special effects. Accent unflattering in acting areas.
11 Light Straw		Pale yellow with slight red content. Useful for candle effects. Can be used for area lighting. For bright day feeling.
	806 Medium Yellow	Less green than 10. Unflattering in acting areas. Useful for contrast lighting, accents, and hot day sunlight.
	807 Dark Lemon	Dark than 806 with a higher red content.
	813 Light Amber	Dark pink amber. Sunlight. Deep sunsets.
19 Fire	815 Golden Amber	Strong red amber. Excellent for fire effects. Useful for torchlight and light from wood fires.
	817 Dark Amber	Use with great care. Destroys most pigment color values.
22 Deep Amber		Useful as amber cyc light and late sunsets.
24 Scarlet		Very useful as a backlight. Dramatic specials.
	819 Orange Amber	Very deep amber. Red with a touch of blue.
25 Orange Red	818 Orange	Provides excellent effect in Par fixtures.
26 Light Red		Same as 819. Less red.
	821 Light Red	Vibrant red. Good alternate primary.
27 Medium Red	823 Medium	Bright red. Alternate to primary red when higher light transmission is required.
45 Rose	832 Rose Pink	Cycs. Good red primary for use with three-color light primary systems in cyc lighting, footlights, and border lights. Use on scenery and background effects. Adds tone and modeling to scenery.

(Continued)

SPECIAL EFFECTS (*Continued*)

Supergel		Roscolene		Applications
46	Magenta	837	Medium Magenta	Similar uses as 45 where more saturation is needed.
48	Rose Purple			Pale evening color. Excellent for backlight.
		838	Dark Magenta	Greater intensity than 48.
		839	Rose Purple	Greater intensity than 838.
49	Medium Purple			Darkest of the magenta purple range.
		843	Medium Lavender	Excellent for nighttime scenes. Rich, vivid accents, good in backgrounds. Unrealistic.
		846	Medium Purple	Midnight and moonlight illusions. Enforces mysterious mood. Useful for evening cyc wash.
76	Light Green Blue	858	Light Green Blue	Distinctive greenish blues. Useful for romantic moonlight.
		859	Green Blue (Moonlight)	
		860	Bright Blue (greener)	
		862	True Blue (bluer)	
79	Bright Blue	857	Medium Blue	Cool, clear, bright blue.
		861	Surprise Blue	Primary blue. For use with three-color light primary system in cyc lighting.
		863	Dark Medium Blue (greener)	Good for nonrealistic night skies.
		866	Dark Urban Blue	Extremely dark blue. Highly saturated. Useful for crossover lights.

86A	Pea Green		Good for dense foliage and woodland effects.
89	Moss Green		Useful for mood, mystery, and toning.
90	Dark Yellow Green		Alternate primary where higher transmission is desired.
94	Kelly Green		Fantasy and unrealistic effects. Unflattering on skin tones.
95	Medium Blue Green		Used on foliage in moonlight areas or for creating a mood of mystery.
		878 Yellow Green	Good for toning scenery painted in blues, blue-greens, and greens.
		871 Light Green	Usually used in combination with light tints of color. Reduces the brightness of color but does not affect hue or saturation. Useful where dimmer control or lower wattage lamp is not practical.
		874 Medium Green	
		877 Medium Blue Green	
		880 Light Gray	
		882 Light Chocolate	Warms light and reduces intensity.
		801 Frost	
		883 Medium Gray	
100	Frost		
101	Light Frost		
104	Tough Silk		
113	Matte Silk		
114	Hamburg Frost		
120	Red Diffusion		
121	Blue Diffusion		
122	Green Diffusion		
123	Amber Diffusion		

Compiled by Thom Daly, Mitchell Gottlieb, and Jon C. Oleinick, Rosco Laboratories, Port Chester, N.Y., 10573.

CIRCUIT LAWS AND CABLE WIRING

Ohm's Law

The relationship between voltage, current, and resistance in a circuit is defined by Ohm's law, which is simply stated by the formula

$$E = I \times R$$

where E is in volts, I is in amps, and R is in ohms. This can also be stated

$$I = E \text{ divided by } R \text{ or}$$

$$R = E \text{ divided by } I$$

Resistors in Series

To find the total resistance in a series circuit, simply add together all resistors. In other words, a 10 ohm, 150 ohm, and 1000 ohm resistor connected in series would equal a single 1160 ohm resistor. The formula is shown in Figure B–1.

Resistors in Parallel

Resistors in a parallel circuit are a little more difficult. The formula for two resistors in parallel is

$$\text{Total resistance} = \frac{R1 \times R2}{R1 + R2}$$

$$R_T = R_1 + R_2 + R_3 + R_4 + \cdots$$

Figure B–1. Formula to define resistance in a series circuit.

$$R_T = \cfrac{1}{\cfrac{1}{R_1} + \cfrac{1}{R_2} + \cfrac{1}{R_3} +}$$

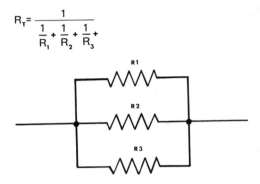

Figure B–2. Formula to define total resistance.

$$C_T = \cfrac{1}{\cfrac{1}{C_1} + \cfrac{1}{C_2} + \cfrac{1}{C_3} +}$$

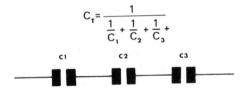

Figure B–3. Formula for more than two capacitors in series.

$$C_T = C_1 + C_2 + C_3 + \cdots$$

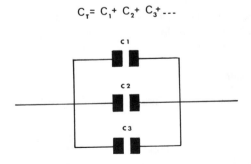

Figure B–4. Formula for capacitors in parallel.

For more than two resistors in parallel, the formula is given in Figure B–2.

CAPACITORS IN SERIES

Capacitors in series are similar to resistors in parallel in that one adds the reciprocals. The formula for two capacitors in series is

$$\text{Total capacitance} = \frac{C1 \times C2}{C1 + C2}$$

The formula for more than two capacitors in series is shown in Figure B–3.

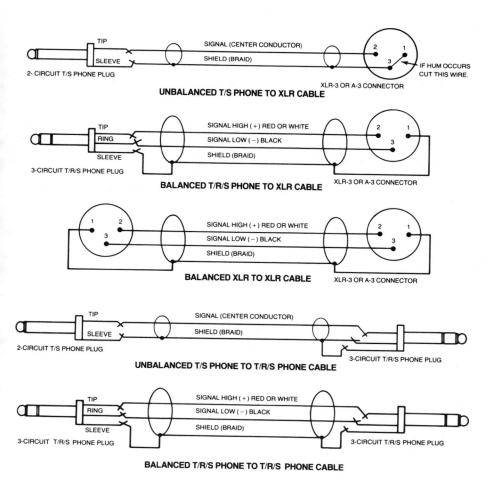

Figure B–5.   Audio cable connector wiring. Standard wiring method for audio signal cables. (Courtesy Yamaha Music.)

Capacitors in Parallel

Capacitors behave in direct contrast to resistors. When capacitors are in parallel, use the formula shown in Figure B–4.

Power in a Circuit

When current passes through a component, energy is given off in the form of heat. Normally, one associates resistors with this action as that is part of their job. When it is necessary to know how much power a resistor is giving off, use the formula

$$W = E \times I$$

where W is in watts, E is in volts, and I is in amps.

Cable Wiring

Unfortunately there is no common standard of wiring for concert equipment. It is important to check the wiring standard and color coding of any connecting cables being used, whether they carry signal level, speaker level, or power (Figure B–5). An incorrectly wired cable can destroy the performance of an entire sound or lighting system. A faulty cable is potentially dangerous; take special care when handling main power cables and connectors. Most consoles have phase-reverse switches so that they can accommodate any standard of wiring for inputs. Phasing must be consistant throughout the system so that no phase cancellation occurs. The wiring standards for all equipment in use must be established and a record kept with the equipment for reference.

PRODUCTION CHECKLISTS

The production checklists will help avoid any problems associated with presenting a show. With the checklist, one can identify most problems and arrange for suitable alternatives before the show. Always call ahead and check each detail to ensure a coordinated and smooth procedure.

Here is a hypothetical checklist for a tour with an indoor performance requiring two semitrailors and nine touring crew members. Each show's requirements will differ.

Day: Wednesday

Date: 10-6-88

City: Anytown

Venue: Apollo

Address: 879 Desert Hwy

Phone number: 418-267-3521

Show Times

Sound check: 4:30 PM

Doors open: 7:00 PM

Opening act: 8:00 PM

Changeover: 8:40 PM

Showtime: 9:10 PM

Call Times

Rigging: 8:00 AM

Lighting: 9:00 AM

Sound: 10:00 AM

Set: 11:00 AM

Band equipment: Noon

Contacts

Venue technical manager: Bert Smith

Promotor's representative: Harry Jones

Opening act contact: Steve Normal

Security: Peter Muscle

Catering: Sharon Lunch

Venue Description

Capacity: 4720

Shape: proscenium hall

Construction material: concrete/steel

Age of building: 18 years

Highest seat: 32 feet above stage

Fire law restrictions: control cables must be placed in duct

Proscenium width: 54 feet

Air conditioning: exhaust system

Pyrotechnics restrictions: fire marshall must be in attendance

Load In

Access: loading dock rear of stage

Clearance: 9 feet 6 inches

Distance to stage: 25 feet

Difficulties: none

Loading lights: yes

Parking

Trucks: 2 trucks on dock

Cars: 20 spaces

Busses: near loading dock

Limousines: at stage door

Forklifts

Height capacity: 15 feet

Weight capacity: 2000 pounds

Fuel: propane

Tires: pneumatic

Stage

Size available: fixed—60 feet wide, 54 feet deep

Size of modules: N/A

Type: wood

Stairs: N/A—level with dock and dressing rooms

Masking: black front

Soundwings

Size available: 16 feet wide, 8 feet deep

Type: side of stage

Barricade

Type: fixed

Height: 4 feet

Distance from stage: 4 feet

Width: full width of stage

Mixing Positions

Sound console: house center

Lighting console: house center

Other: N/A

Cable route to console: through duct

Power

Service 1:	600 A, three phase	Distance to stage:	on stage lef
Service 2:	200 A, three phase	Distance to stage:	on stage lef
Service 3:	100 A, three phase	Distance to stage:	on stage ri

Rigging

Beam to floor: 47 feet

Beam to ceiling: 6 feet

Beam to beam, up and downstage: 12 feet

Beam to beam, cross stage: 8 feet (no central beam)

Weight limits: 20,000 pounds

Catwalks: adjacent to beams

Sportlights

Number available: four

Type: zenon troupers

Intercom: not suitable

Houselight Control

Type: quartz

Control location: stage left

Dimmable: yes

Catering

Facilities available: kitchen/dining room

Meal times:
breakfast—7:30 AM
lunch—1:00 PM
dinner—6:00 PM

Dressing Rooms

Performers: two very large rooms with bathrooms

Opening act: 1 large room, no bathroom

Tuning room: adjacent to stage

Production office with telephone: yes—off stage left

Other Facilities Available

Laundry: no

Photocopier: yes—in booking office

Work lights: yes

Drapes for acoustic treatment: N/A

Drapes for masking: yes

Ladders: 16 foot "A" frame/tallescope

Video: no

Local Staff Required

Stage hands

Minimum call: 3 hours

Breaks required: after 4 hours

Call times and numbers: 8:00 AM, 8 × hands

Loaders

Minimum call: 3 hours

Call times and numbers: 8:00 AM, 4 × loaders

Breaks required: after 4 hours

Follow spot operators

Minimum call: 3 hours

Call times and numbers: 7:30 PM, 4 × operators

Piano tuner

Time required: 2:00 PM

Piano type: electrical/acoustical CP70

Electrician

Time required to connect: 8:00 AM

Time required to disconnect: 11:00 PM

Riggers

Time required: 8:00 AM

Climbing: two

Ground work: one

Forklift driver

Time required: N/A

RUNNER

Time required: 8:00 AM with vehicle

OVERNIGHT SECURITY

Time required: N/A

Number of guards: N/A

Additional Outdoor Checklist

Generators
Power capacity
Generator fuel
Scaffolding
Mixing tower
Roof
Tarpaulins
Plastic
Raincoats
Work lights
Power feed cable
Access to mix tower

Budget Items

Stage
Sound wings
Mixing platform
Barrier
Roof
Sound system
Lighting system
Equipment transport
Personnel transport
Follow spots
Follow spot operators
Stage hands
Loaders

Riggers

Forklifts

Forklift driver

Piano tuner

Electrician

Runner

Telephones

Risers

Weatherproofing

Fuel

Drapes for masking

Drapes for acoustic treatment

Dressing rooms

Generators

Generator fuel

Accommodation

Catering

Security

Crew

SAFETY AWARENESS

Working in the live music industry the exposure to hazards and risks is great. To ensure safety and reduce the risks to the vanishing point a safety assessment has to be done as a matter of routine before embarking on any task. Most safety regulations ask for reasonable and practical precautions. The safety of yourself, your artists, and the paying public has to be considered all the time. Ultimately safety is a matter of using caution with common sense. Learn first aid!

Electrical Safety

Always meter supply before connection.

Always isolate the supply before connection.

Never replace a fuse with one of greater value.

Never disconnect grounds.

Any excess cable must be laid in a figure eight, never coiled in a circle.

Rigging Safety

Never stand under a moving load.

Wear a harness when working at heights.

Learn how to tie knots efficiently.

Never stand directly under riggers working overhead.

Never use frayed or damaged slings.

Always double check all rigging procedures.

Always secure tools to your harness when working at heights.

Fire Safety

Never block fire exits or fire equipment.

Always check smoke detectors before using smoke machines.

Know the position of the nearest electrical extinguishers.

Sound Level Safety

Prolonged exposure to high sound levels can cause hearing loss. The recommended maximum audience exposure in the UK is 104dbA over the duration of the event. Hearing protection should be worn when exposed to high levels for long periods.

Public Safety

Never leave electrical connections in public areas unsupervised.

Never expose an audience to any danger.

Make sure that equipment is kept secure from the public.

FURTHER READING

Ballou, Glen M. *Handbook for Sound Engineers: The New Audio Cyclopedia,* 2d ed. New York: Macmillan Publishing Co., Inc., 1991.

Baskerville, David. *Music Business Handbook and Career Guide,* 5th ed. Peru, IL: Sherwood Publishing Company, 1990.

Borwick, John. *Loudspeaker and Headphone Handbook.* Boston: Butterworth–Heinemann, 1988.

Capel, Vivian. *Public Address Systems.* Boston: Butterworth–Heinemann, 1992.

Davis, Don and Davis, Carolyn. *Sound System Engineering,* 2d ed. Englewood Cliffs, NJ: Sams, 1987.

Davis, Gary and Jones, Ralph. *The Sound Reinforcement Handbook,* 2d ed. Milwaukee, WI: Hal Leonard Publishing Corporation, 1988.

Eargle, John. *Handbook of Sound System Design.* Elar Publishing Company, Inc., 1989.

Giddings, Philip. *Audio Systems Design and Installation.* New York: Macmillan Publishing Company, Inc., 1990.

Harris, Cyril M. *Handbook of Acoustical Measurements and Noise Control.* New York: McGraw-Hill, Inc., 1991.

Huntington, John. *Control Systems for Live Entertainment.* Boston: Focal Press, 1994.

Moody, James L. *Concert Lighting: Techniques, Art and Business.* Boston: Focal Press, 1989.

Strong, William J. and Plitnick, George R. *Music Speech Audio.* Norwalk, CT: Soundprints, 1992.

Thompson, George, editor. *The Focal Guide to Safety in Live Performance*. Boston: Focal Press, 1993.

Trubitt, David, editor. *Concert Sound*. Milwaukee, WI: Hal Leonard Publishing Corporation, 1993.

GLOSSARY

absorbtion   Damping of a sound wave passing through a medium or striking a surface. The property materials, objects, or media possess of absorbing sound energy.

AC   Abbreviation for alternating current.

acoustics   The science of sound. The factors that determine the quality of received sound in a room or auditorium.

ad lib   To cover an unexpected situation in a show or hide a lapse of memory.

alignment   The process of setting controls and functions for optimum system performance.

ambience   The combination of reverberation and background noise that characterizes the sound of a given room.

ampere   The common unit of current; the rate of flow of electricity.

amplifier   An electronic device for magnifying electrical signals to a level that speakers respond to.

amplitude   The peak of a sound waveform.

analog   Electronic signal whose waveform resembles that of the original signal, as opposed to digital.

anechoic   Without echo. In an anechoic chamber the walls are lined with a material that completely absorbs any sound.

arc light   A lamp using a carbon-arc discharge as the source of illumination.

arena   A venue where the audience is seated to the sides of the stage as well as the front.

attack time   The time taken for the onset of gain reduction in a compressor.

attenuator   The reduction of level at the source.

auto transformer   An iron-cored coil across an AC supply that allows various voltages to be selected.

azimuth   The angle between the gap of a tape head and the tape.

baffle   General term for a wall, board, or enclosure carrying a speaker. The baffle separates the front and back radiations from the speaker, because they would otherwise cancel out each other.

balanced line   Program cable in which twin signal wires are both isolated from the earth.

bandwidth   The interval between cut-off frequencies.

barndoors   A metal fitting attached to the front of a flood light, allowing the light to be cut off by two or four hinged flaps.

base   The part of a lamp to which the electrical connection is made. Also the mechanical support of the lamp.

bass   Low frequency end of the audio spectrum.

bass reflex   Type of speaker cabinet with an outlet (port) permitting enclosed air to improve the efficiency at low frequencies. This is due to the inversion of phase within the enclosure so that the radiations from the port aid the radiations from the cone.

batten   A length of rigid material hung on spot lines in a theater.

beam   The cone of light from a lighting instrument.

beam light   A light with no lens that gives a parallel beam.

black light   Ultraviolet light.

boom   Vertical pipe for hanging lamps. An extendable arm on a microphone stand for supporting microphones.

border   An abbreviated drop. Used for masking trusses and fly bars.

break jack   A jack arranged to break the normal circuit when a plug is inserted.

bridle   The wire ropes that attach to chain motors to achieve the correct rigging position using available rigging points.

bulb   The glass or quartz part of a lamp that encloses the filament or electrodes.

bus bar   Common earth or other contact wire.

cans   Term for headphones.

carbon arc   Light is created by the gaseous discharge between two cerium-cored carbon rods. These rods burn for a limited time; an operator must maintain the intensity and sharpness of the light.

cardiod microphone   A microphone with a heart-shaped directivity pattern.

channel   Sequence of circuits or components handling one specific signal.

circuit breaker   A device used to open a circuit automatically, when it is over-loaded, instead of a fuse.

clamp   C and G clamps, so called because of their shape, are used to attach lamps to pipes or trusses.

clipping   Distortion in a mixer or amplifier due to severe overloading.

compression   The process of reducing dynamic range. A compressed signal has a higher dynamic range.

compressor   A variable-gain amplifier in which the gain is controlled by the input signal, used to reduce dynamic range.

concert pitch   System of tuning music based on a frequency of A = 440 Hz.

condensor microphone   Type of microphone in which the signal is generated by the variation of capacitance between the diaphragm and a fixed plate.

counterweight system   A mechanical system for flying lamps, drapes, and scenery with a counterweight that runs up and down a track at the side of the stage.

crossfade   To fade in one channel while fading out another.

crossover   A unit for dividing the signal into separate frequency bands.

crossover frequency   The transition frequency at which the crossover splits the signal.

crosstalk   Unwanted breakthrough from adjacent channels.

cue   A point at which certain adjustments are required during a performance.

cue sheet   A record of the scenes and changes for each segment of the show.

curtain   A drape that hides the stage from the audience.

cyc light   A light fitting with a specially shaped reflector producing a broad elongated light beam, enabling a cyclorama to be lit evenly overall from a relatively close distance.

cyclorama   A stretch of taut vertical cloth used as a general-purpose scenic background. Also called cyc.

damping   Process of reducing unwanted resonant effects by applying absorbant material to a speaker cabinet. Poor damping allows the motion of the speaker to continue once the signal has been removed, creating a booming sound that masks the clarity.

DC   Abbreviation for direct current. It flows in one direction only, unlike AC.

decay time   The recovery time of a compressor, or other processing device, for the circuit to return to normal once the signal has been removed.

decibel   One dB is the smallest change in loudness that the average human ear can detect. 0 dB is the threshold of human hearing. The threshold of pain is between 120 and 130 dB. The decibel is a ratio, not an absolute number, and is used to identify the relationship between true power, voltage, and sound pressure levels. Decibels alone have no specific meaning. For example, dBV is a voltage ratio; 0 dB = 0.775 V root mean square (RMS). dB SPL is the sound–pressure level ratio. It measures acoustic pressure. dBM is a power ratio. dBA takes into account the unequal sensitivity of the ear, and sound-pressure level is measured through a circuit that compensates for this equal loudness. These measurements are termed *A weighted*.

diffraction   The manner in which sound can bend around obstacles.

diffuser   Translucent material used in front of lamps to soften and disperse the light quality and reduce the intensity.

digital sound   The process of converting a normal analog signal into a series of numerical measurements that can be transmitted as a digital code.

dimmer   An electrical circuit regulating the current flowing through the lamps it is connected to, thus adjusting lighting intensity.

direct injection   The process of feeding an electronic musical instrument directly to control console instead of through a microphone.

dispersion   The extent to which light rays or sound waves are scattered or diffused.

downstage   A position at the front of the stage closest to the audience.

drop   A cloth suspended from fly bars or grid to mask the stage, e.g., a backdrop.

dynamic range   The range of signal levels from lowest to highest. A program with wide dynamic range has a large variation between the loudest and quietest parts.

echo   Sound that has been reflected and arrives with such a magnitude and time interval after the direct sound as to be a distinguishable repeat of the original.

ellipsoidal spotlight   A spotlight in which the light collected from an ellipsoidal reflector (mirror) is focused on a lens. The shape of the light beam is adjustable by an internal variable iris, silhouette stencil (gobo), or independent framing shutters. Most of these lamps are designed to project perforated metal gobos.

EPROM   Erasable programmable read only memory.

equalization   The process of modifying the amplitude and frequency response to produce flat overall response, minimize noise, or create an artistic effect.

expander   An amplifier that increases gain as the input level increases, a characteristic that stretches dynamic range.

feedback   Signal from the output of system returns to the input, creating unwanted oscillation that can quickly become out of control and cause severe damage to speaker components.

flash through   A check of the lighting system one channel at a time.

flat   A unit section of scenery. A tall screen.

flies   The space above the stage occupied by sets of lines, hanging drapes, and lamps.

flood   A type of light fitting that illuminates a wide area.

fluorescent lamp   A tubular lamp in which a mecury vapor discharge energizes a fluorescent powder coating on the inside of the tube.

fly   To lift equipment above the stage with electrical chain hoists or on a counterweight system.

focus   To position the lamps so that the beams light the desired areas.

FOH   Front of house; the front of an auditorium, the opposite end to the stage.

foldback   The term given to signals returning from the house console to the stage. Foldback becomes a monitor system when a separate console is used to control the on-stage monitors.

follow spot   High-intensity lamp that requires an operator to follow the subject being lit and control the intensity and color.

frammel   A strip of wood placed between speaker cabinets to separate and angle them vertically to reduce phase interference between cabinets.

frequency   The rate of repetition of signal, measured in hertz (Hz).

Fresnel lens   A lens with a surface composed of a series of concentric ribs of stepped cross-sections, making it thinner, lighter, and more efficient than a solid lens.

fuse   Protective device for an electrical circuit to prevent overloading.

gaffer tape   A wide plasticized cloth tape with many uses in concert production.

gain   The increase in signal power from one point to another.

gel   Color filter. Originally made of gelatine, color filters are now made of plastic.

gobo   A metal stencil placed in the gate of a profile spot to shape the beam of light.

graphic equalizer   An equalizer that has slider-level controls; once set, the sliders represent the response curve.

grid   The framework of trusses from which the lamps are hung.

ground row   Series of lamps in the form of troughs laid on the ground to illuminate a cyclorama or other background.

harmonic distortion   A form of distortion in which unwanted harmonics are added to the original signal.

harmonics   Overtones that are multiples of the fundamental tone that shape the waveform and make it possible to distinguish different instruments even when they are playing the same note.

headroom   The space, usually expressed in decibels (dB), between the operating level and the maximum available level. Inadequate headroom will distort transient peaks.

hertz (Hz)   The unit of frequency. One hertz equals one cycle per second.

hiss   Noise that sounds like prolonged sibilant sounds.

house lights   Auditorium lighting.

hue   The predominant sensation of color.

hum   Electrical interference caused at mains frequency, 50/60 Hz.

impedance   The degree to which a circuit impedes the flow of an alternating current. Measured in ohms.

induction   Production of current across a space due to electrical or magnetic fields.

infinite baffle   Speaker mounting that allows no air paths between front and rear of speaker.

instrument   The general name used for lighting fixtures.

intensity   Of light: the power of a light source, its brightness. Of sound: the objective strength of sound, loudness.

inverse square law   An equation relating the intensity of the light to the distance from the object.

iris   An adjustable circular shutter used in a profile spot to vary the size of the beam.

jack   Term for terminating point of a circuit. A common term for phone plug connector.

lamp   A general term for an incandescent light source (bulb, bubble). Also used as a general term for any lighting instrument.

LED   Light-emitting diode.

leg   A narrow strip of drape used to mask the sides of the stage.

Leko   A brand of ellipsoidal profile spot.

lighting plot   A scale plan diagram indicating the positions and types of lamps used. Details of color, cabling, accessories, patching, and trim height may be included.

limiter   A type of compressor that fixes a ceiling of maximum level without changing the dynamic range below the threshold.

line level   Preamplified signal, in contrast to microphone level. The actual signal levels vary, with nominal microphone level being -50 dBM and nominal line level being $+4$ dBM.

loudness   The subjective impression of the strength of sound.

luminaire   A complete lighting unit consisting of a lamp with parts designed to distribute the light, position and protect the lamp, and connect the lamp to the power supply.

luminary   A light source.

mask   To conceal the equipment from the audience.

matrix   Electronics for accepting several signals and giving one output.

microphone   A transducer for converting acoustic energy to electrical energy.

MIDI   Musical instrument digital interface.

mirror ball   A spherical ball with a surface covered in small plane mirrors. Multiple moving spots of light shine from the ball when it is lit and rotated.

mixer   The electronics that allow the combination of several signals in desired proportions.

modulation   The control of one waveform by another.

monitor   A speaker cabinet fed with signal to provide information a performer requires.

multiplexor   Unit for encoding and decoding multiplex signals.

noise   Any unwanted sound.

noise gate   An amplifier that has a zero output until the input level exceeds a chosen threshold level.

nook light   Small, open-fronted trough fitting with a short strip light and curved reflector.

notch filter   An equalizer with a very narrow bandwidth.

octave   The interval between a given tone and its repetition eight tones above or below on the musical scale. A note that is an octave higher than another note is twice the frequency of the first note.

off stage   A position outside the performing area.

omnidirectional microphone   Equally sensitive in all directions.

on stage   In the performing area.

open circuit   A circuit that is not continuous and cannot pass any current.

oscillator   A device for producing continuous oscillation or a pure tone at any desired frequency.

oscilloscope   A device for visual display of electronic waveforms.

PA   Abbreviation for public address system; an alternate term for sound system.

pad   A series of resistors to introduce a fixed amount of gain reduction for impedance-matching purposes.

pan   In lighting: to move the beam of a lamp from side to side of the stage. In sound: to alter the position of a signal laterally.

par light   A tungsten-halogen (quartz) lamp in which a parabolic aluminized reflector forms part of the bulb. The internally silvered reflector, together with the molded lens front glass, provide a fixed beam. Par bulbs are available in various beam sizes.

parametric equalizer   An equalizer that can vary frequency, level, and bandwidth.

patching   The term used for connecting cables in the right circuits.

phantom power   Method of sending DC supply to a condensor microphone or direct box by connecting the positive side to both signal wires of a balanced line and the negative to the screen.

phase   The position that a waveform has reached at any given instant in the cycle. Waves are in phase when their cycle positions coincide.

pink noise   Pink noise is white noise that has passed through a filter to bring the response to an equal energy level (per octave) as heard by the human ear.

pitch   Subjective effect of sound related mainly to frequency but also affected by intensity and harmonic structure.

potentiometer   A variable resistor used for volume and tone controls. Commonly called a pot.

prefade listen   Facility available on mixing consoles for listening to a signal before it is fed to the main program outputs.

presence   Quality of immediacy. Boosting the upper middle frequencies will achieve presence.

profile spot   A lamp with a beam that can be either soft or hard.

proscenium   The wall dividing the stage from the auditorium. The opening through which the audience views the stage is called the proscenium opening.

pyrotechnics   Any bangs, flashes, or explosions.

RAM   Random access memory. Memory (information) that can be memory written in or read out in any order.

recovery time   The time taken for a compressor/limiter to restore the gain to normal when the signal is reduced.

resonance   The tendency of any physical body to vibrate most freely at a particular frequency due to excitation by a sound with that particular frequency.

reverberation   The sustaining effect of multiple sound reflections in an enclosed area.

ribbon microphone   Microphone that uses a thin metal ribbon suspended in a magnetic field.

rig   To install and set up equipment in required position. The finished assembly of lamps positioned, patched, and focused for a performance.

rostrum   A scenic platform, a riser.

rumble   Low-frequency vibration.

scrim   Thin netting (gauze) used to provide translucent cycs or create scenic diffusion.

set   A group of risers arranged to give a decorative effect.

sightlines   Theoretical lines indicating what the audience can see.

signal to noise   The ratio of the desired signal to residual system noise.

silhouette   A pictorial style that concentrates on subject outline for its effect. Surface detail, tone, texture, and color are suppressed.

silicon chip   A method of fabricating resistors and transistors into miniaturized circuits on a wafer of silicon, which is cased in a plastic or ceramic body with leads bonded onto the silicon.

spanset   An endless loop of nylon strands used for rigging purposes. As the spanset is a soft sling, it can be used for a variety of rigging applications. Spansets are color coded for weight loading.

special   A light performing a particular function.

spiking   Marking a position on the stage.

strike   To remove a piece of set or equipment from the performing area.

tab   Any curtain.

talkback   Headphone intercom system.

teaser   A border used to mask trusses or fly bars.

threshold   The point above which level changes take place.

throw   The distance from the light to the object being lit.

tilt   The vertical movement of a light.

transformer   Component having two coils of wire, the primary and secondary, whose lengths are in a fixed ratio to permit voltages to be stepped up or down and circuit impedances to be matched for maximum power transfer.

translucent   Allowing light to pass through without being transparent.

tree   A high stand or tower with horizontal arms for mounting lamps.

trim   The grid: to level a grid or truss. The dimmers: to adjust dimmer response to control voltage. Dimmers out of trim do not give the subtle control required for stage lighting.

Unidirectional microphone   A microphone that is sensitive to sound from one direction only.

upstage   The stage area toward the back, away from the audience.

VCA   Voltage-controlled amplifier, used instead of faders to control channel gain in a sound control console.

volt   The unit of electrical force.

VU meter   A meter for indicating program volume that gives signal power, in decibels, on a steady tone and volume units (percentage utilization of the channel) on program.

wavelength   The distance between corresponding parts of a waveform.

white noise   A full audio spectrum signal with the same energy level at all frequencies.

windshield (popshield)   A foam sock placed over a microphone to reduce the amount of wind amplified.

wings   The areas on either side of the stage.

zero level   The level used for lining up audio equipment. 0 dB equals 1 mW. This corresponds to 0.775 V rms across a resistance of 600 ohms.

zoom lens   A variable-focus lens.

INDEX

Accent areas, color gels for, 141–143
Acting areas, color gels for, 138–140
Amplifiers, 82
  and cables, 33, 44
  checking, 84
  and compression drivers, 34–35
  cooling, 33, 36, 82
  input voltage, 33
  on/off procedure, 36
  patching, 33–35
  power, 7, 10, 82
  and setup, 77, 82, 84
Arc-type lights, 94–95
Australia,voltage in, 7
Auxiliary sends, 49–50

Backdrops, 113, 132
Bass player and monitor mix, 65
Becket hitch, 17
Belden 8769, 37
Belden 8778, 38
Borders, 112, 132
Bridles, making up, 15–16
Budget, 3
Buntline, 17

Cables
  and amplifiers, 33, 34

  control, 101–103, 133
  crossover, 96, 133–135
  and fire safety, 135
  and front of house console, 82
  lighting, 101–103, 127
  looming, 123
  microphones, 37–38
  power, 10, 11
  and setup, 79–80
  and speakers, 33, 37–38, 80–81
  see also Multicore cables
Capacitors
  in parallel, 156
  in series, 155
Cases for packing, 127
Caterers, 5
C-ducer microphone, 69
Chain motors, 5, 121
  contactors, 16
  hooks, 15
  inspection of, 16
  power source, 11
  safety laws, 127
  and setup, 77, 78–80, 82, 89, 127,
    130
Checklist for production, 157–164
Circuit coding, 123, 127
Clove hitch, 17

Color and lighting design, 119–120, 137–151
Color changers, 96
Color codes
    and cables, 33, 37–38, 80–81
    and setup, 75–77, 78, 82, 129–130
    and spansets, 19
    and wire ropes, 18
Compression, 59
Compression drivers, 34–35, 86
Condensor microphone, 69, 84
Connectors, 37, 82, 85, 103
    checking, 127
Control cables, 101–103, 133
Crossovers, 41–44, 77
    and monitor speakers, 65
    and multicore cables, 38
    and phase alignment, 42–44
Curtain tracks, 114, 127
Cyclorama, 113
    color guide, 144–145
    projections on, 94, 123

De-essers, 49
Delay time, setting, 25
Digital control of dimmers, 101–102
Digital delays, 57
Dimmers, 97–99, 105
    checking, 127
    control of, 101–102
    and intercom, 110
    patching, 99, 123, 127
    power, 11
    safety regulations, 135–136
    and setup, 133
    types, 98–99
Direct boxes, 37, 72–74
    and phantom power, 50
Direct injection (DI). See Direct boxes
Drapes, 113–114, 127
    and lighting plot, 121
    and setup, 132
Drive system, 41–45
Drums and monitor mix, 65, 67, 77
Dynamic microphone, 69

Echo send, 49–50, 57
Effects, 55, 57–58, 149–150
Equalizers, 26–31, 33, 59
    and front of house console, 49, 52

graphic, 41, 63–64
and monitor console, 63–64
on/off switch, 49
peaking, 49
shelving, 49
Europe, voltage in, 7
Exponential ramp, 98

Fader, 50
Feedback, 63–64
Fire safety
    and cables, 135
    and drapes, 127
    and gels, 119
    and spansets, 19
Fireworks, 112
Floorlamps, 133–134
Foggers, 111
Foldback send, 49–50
Follow spot, 110, 115–117, 133, 135
    checking, 127
    operator, 5
Forklift driver, 4
Fresnel spots, 94
Front of house console
    cables, 82
    care and cleaning, 52–53
    engineer and load out, 85
    equalizers, 49, 52
    gain structure, 52, 53
    headroom allowance, 52, 53
    input channel controls, 47–51, 52
    microphone connections, 37, 51
    output controls, 51, 52
    positioning, 82
    and power distribution system, 10
    power supply, 52, 82–84
    and setup, 77, 79, 82–84
    and speaker systems, 40
    talkback module, 51
    and tape players, 47, 51
    and transformer, 52
Fuses, 7, 79
    and power distribution system, 10, 12
    spare, 77

Gauges, 113
Gels, 119, 121, 127, 131, 137–151
    and fire safety, 119
Generator, 13

Gobos, 93–94, 119, 123
Grids
    lifting, 91, 130, 132
    lighting system, 130, 131, 132
    rigging, 89
    sound system, 89, 91
Ground loops, 10–11
Ground row lights, 94, 123
Ground supports, 89–90
Group select switch, 49
Guitar player and monitor mix, 65

Hall, sound characteristics of, 27–31, 85
Headroom allowance, 52, 53
Hessian sacks, 15
High band cabinet, 24, 33, 36
    crossover bandwidth, 42
High-pass filter, 49
House lights, 5

Induced radio frequency (RF), 10
Input gain control, 47–48
Inserts, 59–61
Intercom, 51, 101
    and lighting system, 109–110, 127,
    135
Isomax microphone, 69

Kabuki drops, 114
Keyboard and monitor mix, 65
Knots, 16–17

Lamps, 93–96
    focusing, 131, 135
    hanging, 96, 131–132
    and lighting plot, 122, 123
    pairing, 99
    positioning, 121, 122, 123
    safety chains, 136
    types, 93–96
Legs, 112, 132
Lighting
    cables, 101–103, 127
    computerized, 5, 96, 105–108
    and intercom, 109–110, 127, 135
    and load out, 135
    maintenance and repair, 4, 123, 127–
    128, 135
    power needs, 5, 7, 11–12

rigging, 89, 121, 130–133
and setup, 84, 128–135
see also Lamps; Gels
Lighting control consoles, 105–108, 127,
    133
    cable connections, 101–103
    manual, 105
Lighting designer, 4
Lighting operator, 4
Lighting plots, 121–128
Limiters, 44, 49, 59, 72
Linear ramp, 98
Loaders, 5
Load out
    and lighting system, 135
    and sound system, 85–86
Local crew, 4–5
Looming, 123, 131, 132
Low band cabinet, 23, 33, 36
    crossover bandwidth, 41
Luminance ramp, 98

Maintenance and repairs
    and front of house console, 52–53
    and lighting system, 4, 123, 127–128, 135
    and smoke machines, 111
    and sound system, 86
Microphones, 69–74
    cables, 37–38
    and front of house console, 47, 50, 84
    hums, 110
    levels, smoothing out, 59
    and lighting system, 109–110
    measurement, 27, 29–30
    and phantom power, 50
    positioning, 55, 74, 84, 85
    and set-up, 77, 84, 85
    spares, 84, 85
    types, 69–72
Mid band cabinet, 23, 33, 36
    crossover bandwidth, 42
MIDI, 58
Mixing console. See Front of house con-
    sole; Monitor system
Monitor system, 63–67
    consoles, 63–65
    engineer, 4
    mix contents, 65–66
    power distribution system, 11

and setup, 77, 79, 84
and speakers, 65
splitter system, 40
tuning, 65
Moonlight, color guide for, 147
Multicore cables, 37–40
care of, 102–103
and drive system, 44–45
and lighting, 127
and setup, 82
see also Cables
Multiple earth neutral (MEN), 8
Multiplex systems, 101–102
Musical instrument digital interface system (MIDI), 58
Musicians' equipment, power source, 10
Mute assign switch, 51
Mute switch, 50

Neutral-to-earth meter reading, 8
Night/evening, color guide for, 148
Noise gates, 49, 59, 60–61
and setup, 61

Ohm's law, 7, 153
Oscillator enable pulse, 97
Oscillators, 51
Outdoor concerts, 77, 80, 81–82

Pad, 48
Pan pot, 50
Par cans, 93
Par lamps, 93
Pay for crew, 6
Per diem, 6
Performers, 3, 10
Phantom power, 37, 40
and front of house console, 50
Phase alignment, 42–44
Phase-to-earth meter reading, 8
Phase-to-neutral meter reading, 8
Phase reverse switch, 49
Pin matrixes, 105
Pink noise, 26, 27, 30
Points, rigging of, 15–16
Potentiometers (Pots), 41
Power cables, 10, 11
and setup, 79–80
see also Cables; Multicore cables

Power distribution system, 77, 79–80, 127
and safety, 11
Prefade listen switch, 50
Pressure zone microphone (PZM), 69
Production manager, 3, 4
Profile spots, 93–94
Promoter, 5
Pyrotechnics, 112

Radio microphone, 72
Ramp, 97, 98
Rear projection, 114
Resistors
in parallel, 153–155
in series, 153
Reverberation units, 57
Ribbon microphone, 69
Riggers, 5
Rigging, 78–79
and lights, 89, 121, 130–133
points, 15–16
and sound, 78–79
trusses and grids, 89
Rolling hitch, 17
Runners, 5

Safety
and chain motors, 127
and dimmers, 135–136
and lighting, 135–136
and power, 11
see also Fire safety
Saxophone player and monitor mix, 67
Scaffolding, 24
Screens, 114
Scrims, 113
Service companies, 3
Set crews, 4
Setup
and amplifiers, 77, 82, 84
and chain motors, 77, 78–80, 82, 89, 127, 130
and color codes, 75–77, 78, 82, 129–130
and dimmers, 133
and front of house console, 77, 79, 82–84
and lighting system, 84, 128–135

Setup (*continued*)
    and monitor console, 77, 79, 84
    and noise gates, 61
    and outdoor concerts, 77, 80, 81–82
    and sound system, 75–85
Silicon-controlled rectifiers (SCRs), 97
Smoke machines, 111–112, 135
    cleaning, 127
    power source, 11
    and setup, 133
Snakes. *See* Multicore cables
Sound checks, 53–55, 77, 84–85
Sound crew, 4
Sound engineer, 4
Sound system
    and grids, 89, 91
    and load out, 85–86
    maintenance and repair, 86
    and power system, 7, 10
    rigging, 78–79
    and setup, 75–85
    see also Amplifiers; Front of house
        console; Monitor system; Speakers
Spansets, 19
Speakers
    analyzing, 26–31
    cabinets, 23–24
    and cables, 33, 37–38, 80–81
    center cluster, 25
    delay system, 24–25
    distribution system, 26
    fault finding, 35–36
    flying, 24, 82
    hanging, 80–81
    and load out, 86
    and monitor, 65
    resistance, calculation of, 33–34
    stacking, 24, 81–82
    types, 23–24
    wiring, 33–34
Special effects, 149–150
    see also Effects
Spectrum analyzer, 26–31
Splitters, 37, 40
Spotlight. *See* Follow spot
Square law ramp, 98
Stage manager, 3, 4, 109
Sub-low cabinets, 24
    crossover bandwidth, 42

Sunlight, color guide for, 146
Supergel, 119
Switching ramp, 98

Tape players, 47, 51
Three-phase connection, 5, 79–80, 82,
    130
    and distribution system, 10
    metering, 8, 10
Thyristors, 97
Tour manager, 4
Transformer, 8
    and front of house console, 52
    and splitter system, 40
    ventilation, 8
Triacs, 97
Truck and bus drivers, 4
Trucks
    loading, 127–128
    unloading, 77–78, 129
True power ramp, 98
Trunk. *See* Multicore cables
Trusses
    assembly, 131
    clamps, 127
    and lighting plot, 91, 123
    rigging, 89
Tweeters, 24

United Kingdom, voltage in, 7, 8
United States Illuminating Engineering
    Society, 98

Venue electrician, 130
Venue staff, 5, 79
Venue technical manager, 5
Vibration damage, 128
Vocalists and monitor mix, 65
Voltage-controlled amplifier (VCA) con-
    trols, 50, 52
Voltage supply, 7, 33

Weatherproofing, 77, 80, 81–82
Wedge monitor, 65
Wire ropes, 15
    and color coding, 18–19
    safety loads, 18